D1738173

THE ACCESSION STORY

The Accession Story

The EU from Fifteen to Twenty-Five Countries

Edited by
GEORGE VASSILIOU

OXFORD
UNIVERSITY PRESS

Great Clarendon Street, Oxford OX2 6DP

Oxford University Press is a department of the University of Oxford.
It furthers the University's objective of excellence in research, scholarship,
and education by publishing worldwide in

Oxford New York

Auckland Cape Town Dar es Salaam Hong Kong Karachi
Kuala Lumpur Madrid Melbourne Mexico City Nairobi
New Delhi Shanghai Taipei Toronto

With offices in

Argentina Austria Brazil Chile Czech Republic France Greece
Guatemala Hungary Italy Japan Poland Portugal Singapore
South Korea Switzerland Thailand Turkey Ukraine Vietnam

Oxford is a registered trade mark of Oxford University Press
in the UK and in certain other countries

Published in the United States
by Oxford University Press Inc., New York

First published 2007

British Library Cataloguing in Publication Data
Data available

Library of Congress Cataloging in Publication Data
Data available

Typeset by SPI Publisher Services, Pondicherry, India
Printed in Great Britain
on acid-free paper by
Biddles Ltd., King's Lynn, Norfolk.

978–0–19–921587–4 (Hbk)

1 3 5 7 9 10 8 6 4 2

Preface

The enlargement of the European Union from fifteen to twenty-five nations is undoubtedly one of the most important, if not *the* most important development, since the establishment of the Union. The dream of many European generations has, at last, come true. A persistent 400-year-old cycle of violent integration followed by a violent break-up, which has caused endless suffering in Europe, has finally been broken through the peaceful integration of the EU. Europe has at last become a single entity and, thus united, can now face the many challenges of the twenty-first century.

It was therefore an absolute necessity, even an obligation, to try to record this historic process. The book is limited to presenting the 'Accession Story' and does not deal at all with possible effects of the enlargement, either on the Union as a whole or on any of the candidate countries. In all the candidate countries joining the Union, the accession was seen as the only option, dictated by the new realities of the international system, and by the common histories of the peoples of Europe. This is why practically everybody in the political spectrum, from left to right, supported the accession, probably each one for different reasons, but still enthusiastically. There were only a few isolated exceptions which in essence confirmed the image that practically the totality of the society supported this objective. At the same time, between the fifteen 'old' members there may have been some individuals or political sections that were sceptical or even opposed to it. However, the overall appeal of the concept of a united Europe was so strong that it was impossible to take a stand against it. Obviously, the EU enlargement would influence, in many ways, practically all countries. There would be both positive and negative repercussions. All contributors to the book, however, are convinced that the benefits of the accession far outweigh any possible short-term negative effects that it would entail.

The book consists of two parts. The first part deals with enlargement from the point of view of Brussels and the second from the point of view of the candidate countries.

On the new members' side, by far the most suitable persons to write the relevant chapters were the chief negotiators/coordinators. This is not intended in any way to diminish the importance of the governments, politicians, and the thousands of civil servants who worked hard for several years in order to prepare their countries and adopt the *acquis communautaire*. However, it was the chief negotiators/coordinators who had the responsibility to act as the link between Brussels and their countries, to help in the coordination at home, prepare the ground, and negotiate with the Community.

Under different circumstances, it might have been practically impossible to ensure the cooperation of all these individuals. Fortunately, however, with the start of the negotiations, a very close relationship developed between, at first the six, and subsequently the ten candidates. We met at least twice a year in turn in each of the countries, exchanged views and experiences, and agreed on any common action without, however, thinking of creating a block of candidates versus the 'old' members. Accordingly, we all agreed that it would be both of general interest and beneficial to each one of us if we each were to write down his country's story and experiences in a short and concise way.

On the Brussels side, we ensured the cooperation of the protagonists during the final decisive years. The efforts from Brussels, during these years, were guided by:

- the Enlargement Commissioner, Mr Günter Verheugen;
- the Director General of the DG Enlargement, Mr Eneko Landaburu; and
- Mr Poul Christoffersen, permanent representative of Denmark to the EU and President of COREPER, both in 1998 when the Copenhagen criteria were formulated and during the second semester of 2002, when the final negotiations were conducted and agreement reached in Copenhagen.

Finally, we should express our gratitude to all those in the Commission who were involved with the accession negotiations. In particular we would like to thank:

- the Presidents of the Commission, Jacques Santer and Romano Prodi;
- Commissioner Hans van der Broek;
- Director General Nikolaus van der Pas;
- Deputy Director General Michael Leigh, and all country directors, i.e.
    - Leopold Maurer for Cyprus;
    - Michael Leigh for the Czech Republic;
    - Nikiforos Sivenas and Dirk Lange for Estonia;
    - Giorgio Bonacci for Hungary;
    - Camos Grau for Latvia;
    - Dirk Lange for Lithuania;
    - Arhi Palosuo for Malta;
    - Françoise Gaudenzi Aubier for Poland;
    - Dirk Meganck for Slovakia;
    - Jaime Garcia-Lombardero for Slovenia.

Last, but not least, we would like to express our gratitude to the thousands of political personalities, civil servants, organizations, Chambers of Commerce and Industry, trade unions, agricultural unions, etc., who in one or another way contributed to the success of this colossal and unprecedented effort.

G. V.

Contents

List of Tables

List of Figures

List of Contributors

Günter Verheugen—German foreign Minister 1998–1999; European Union Commissioner for Enlargement 1999–2004; Vice President of the European Commission, Commissioner for Enterprise and Industry since November 2004.

Eneko Landaburu—European Commission: Director-General for Regional Policy and Cohesion 1986–2000; Director General, DG Enlargement 2000–2003, Commission Chief Negotiator with Candidate Countries; Director—General, DG External Relations 2003 to date.

Poul Skytte Christoffersen—Head of Cabinet to the Secretary General of the Council of the European Union 1980–1994; Ministry of foreign Affairs in Copenhagen 1994; Ambassador, Permanent Representative of Denmark to the European Union 1995–2003. As such, President of the Permanent Representatives Committee in 2nd semester 2002 and EU Chief Negotiator at the level of officials in the final phase of enlargement negotiations in 2002; Ambassador Royal Danish Embassy in Rome 2002–2003; Permanent Representative to FAO, WFP and IFAD 2003–2005; Professor, Copenhagen Business School 2004 to date.

Editor—Cyprus

Dr. George Vassiliou—President of the Republic of Cyprus 1988–1993, Head of the Negotiating Team for the accession of Cyprus to the European Union and responsible for co-ordinating the harmonization process within the country 1998–2003.

Czech Republic

Pavel Telicka—Deputy Minister of Foreign Affairs and Chief Negotiator for the accession of the Czech Republic to the EU 1998–2002; Ministry of Foreign Affairs, Director General of Integration Section Dec. 1996–Jan. 1998; Designated ambassador, Head of the Mission of the Czech Republic to the EU 2004; Co-Founder and President of BXL Consultants 2004 to date.

Karel Bartak—Journalist, reporter and correspondent with the Czech News Agency (CTK) since 1978; worked in several countries including France, Russia, Ukraine, Georgia, Slovakia. Head of CTK Brussels office from 1995, focusing on NATO and EU enlargement as well as other developments in EU and Benelux. Official in the European Commission since summer 2006.

Estonia

Mr. Alar Streimann—Estonia's Chief Negotiator with the European Union and Foreign Ministry deputy chancellor 1998–2003; Permanent Representative of Estonia to the Council of Europe since September 2003.

Hungary

Peter Gottfried—1995–1996, President of the Office for European Affairs of the Ministry of Industry and Trade; 1996–1998, Deputy of the State Secretary for Integration; 1998–2002, State Secretary for European Affairs; 2002–2004, Deputy then Head of the State Secretariat for EU Affairs; 2004–2006, President of the Office for EU Affairs in the Prime Minister's Office.

Peter Györkös—1998–2003, Director General for the EU-coordination in the Ministry for Foreign Affairs, Secretary of the Negotiating Team and the Inter-Ministerial Committee for European Integration; 2004–2006, Vice-President of the Office for European Affairs in the Prime Minister's Office.

Latvia

Mr. Andris Ķesteris—Chief negotiator of Latvia; Under Secretary of State for European Affairs at the Ministry of Foreign Affairs of Latvia since 1999; Permanent Representative of Latvia to the EU 2003–2004; Head of Cabinet of Commissioner for Energy, Mr. Andris Piebalgs, December 2004 to date.

Ms. Kristīne Plamše—Former correspondent of the Latvian daily newspaper 'Diena' in Brussels (from 1997–2003); Second Secretary at the Permanent Representation of Latvia to the EU 2003–2005; Assistant at the Cabinet of Commissioner for Energy, Mr. Andris Piebalgs, 2005–2006. Currently Member of Cabinet at Cabinet of Commissioner of Energy.

Lithuania

Mr. Petras Auštrevičius—Chief Negotiator of Lithuania, Director General of the European Committee under the Government of Lithuania. Member of National Parliament (Seimas) since November 2004.

Malta

Mr. Richard Cachia Caruana—Personal Assistant to the Prime Minister 1987–1991; Head of the Prime Minister's Secretariat 1991–1996; Senior Consultant, KPMG 1997–1998; Head of the Prime Minister's Secretariat 1998–2003; Member of the Cabinet Committee on EU Affairs 1998 to date; Chief Negotiator for Malta's EU accession negotiations 1999–2003; Chairman, Inter-Ministerial Committee for European Union Affairs 2003 to date; Ambassador, Permanent Representative of Malta to the European Union 2003 to date.

Poland

Jan Kułakowski—Secretary of State in the Chancellery of the Prime Minister and Government Plenipotentiary for Poland's Accession Negotiations to the European Union 1998–2001; General Secretary of the World Confederation of Labour 1976–1985; Ambassador and Head of the Representation of the Republic of Poland to the European Communities in Brussels 1990–1996; Adviser to the Government of Poland for European Integration and Foreign Assistance and a

Member of the Committee for European Integration 1996; Member of the European Parliament 2004 to date.

Dr. Leszek Jesień—advisor to Poland's Chief Negotiator Mr. Jan Kułakowski, as well as to the Prime Minister Jerzy Buzek. Currently, Secretary of State for international and EU affairs in the Prime Minister's Office. Also, the EU advisor to the Prime Minister Kazimierz Marcinkiewicz. The Head of the Konrad Adenauer Chair of European Integration at the Tischner European University in Kraków, Poland.

Slovakia

Ján Figel'—Chief Negotiator of the Slovak Republic to the European Union and State Secretary of the Ministry of Foreign Affairs 1998–2002; Chairman of the Foreign Parliamentary Committee in the Slovak National Council 2002–2004; Commissioner for Education, Training, Culture and Multilingualism since 2004.

Miroslav Adamiš—Director General of the European Integration Section in the Ministry of Foreign Affairs 2000–2003; Ambassador and the Permanent Representative to the European Union 2003–2004; Head of the Cabinet of Commissioner Ján Figel' since 2004.

Slovenia

Dr. Janez Potočnik—Head of the negotiating team for accession of the Republic of Slovenia to the EU 1998–2003; Commissioner for Science and Research since 2004.

Dr. Fedor Černe—Member of the negotiating team for accession of the Republic of Slovenia to the EU responsible for environmental issues. Currently official of the Government for European Affairs.

Dr. Emil Erjavec—Member of the negotiating team for accession of the Republic of Slovenia to the EU responsible for agriculture. Currently, Professor at the University of Ljubljana.

Dr. Mojmir Mrak—Special advisor to dr. Janez Potočnik responsible for the financial package issues during the accession negotiations. Currently, Professor at the University of Ljubljana.

Introduction

Challenges and Opportunities of the Enlargement of the European Union

Günter Verheugen

Politically enlargement became a reality on 1 May 2004, when eight new Member States of Central and southern Europe—Poland, the three Baltic states, the Czech Republic, Slovakia, Slovenia, Hungary—as well as Malta and Cyprus joined the EU. It would be premature to make a final judgement. However, the most important effects of the strategic decision on enlargement have already taken place: today's Europe is a safer and better place to live in and to do business in than fifteen years ago.

Over almost half a century, the European integration has helped put an end to the conflicts of the past and to strengthen peace, security, justice, and well-being throughout the western part of Europe. The breakdown of the Iron Curtain offered the opportunity to overcome the European divisions, to heal historical injustice, and to project peace, stability, and prosperity to a much larger part of the European continent. The enlargement of the EU was driven by the historical experience that Europe is only a safe and prosperous place where it is uniting. It was not only in the European interest but in the interest of more peace, more stability, more prosperity, more cooperation, and more justice in this world that enlargement took place.

Europe has already gained from enlargement. Since the invitation to some Central and East European countries to become part of the European Union in 1993, the enlargement preparation process has already contributed decisively to achieving political stability, economic progress, and social progress. Democratic institutions, changes of government on the basis of free elections, reinforced protection of human rights, and market economy principles are now common features in a large part of Central and Eastern Europe. Today's enlarged Union, encompassing more than 450 million people, is better equipped to master globalization and to confront global challenges. The enlarged Union adds weight to the European Union's external relations and further boosts the need to develop a common European foreign and security policy, enabling the Union to better respond to the new challenges and risks of the twenty-first century and to play its full role as a partner in the transatlantic relationship, which remains crucial.

The credit for the impressive developments at the European continent during the last fifteen years mainly belongs to the peoples of the new Member States themselves. Their fight for democracy and freedom has put an end to the Cold War and led to the breakdown of the Soviet Empire. This fight has proven that dictatorship is finally unable to suppress the free will of the people and demonstrated the attractiveness and strength of the universal values of freedom, democracy, and the respect for human rights.

In the last fifteen years the citizens of the new Member States have successfully undertaken a complete system transformation, mostly on their own. To that end they have undergone deep reforms and shouldered social burdens over years without losing their path towards the EU. Causes of conflict, such as minority issues and border problems, have been removed. These impressive reform efforts and achievements are still underestimated and should be more appreciated than is the case at the moment.

The perspective of enlargement has supported the successful system transformation in a large part of Central and Eastern Europe and has helped to create intense political and economic ties between the two parts of Europe that were formerly divided by the Iron Curtain. The political, economic, and legislative conditions for accession were clearly defined from the outset, in 1993. This provided clear guidance for the transformation process in Member States belonging to the EU since 2004. The prospect of EU membership has no doubt accelerated the reform process. The new Member States meet all membership conditions, transformation from centrally planned into functioning market economies and from communist regimes into democratic societies; both are now complete. The combination of political and economic reforms, the full implementation of the EU legislation in the new Member States, and substantial EU assistance after their accession has already created a stable and attractive investment climate not only for European business but also for our partners in the world.

As a result of the hard and successful work and after sometimes difficult negotiations the accession negotiations were concluded at the end of 2002 and the treaty signed in April 2003. This treaty, ratified by all Member States and acceding countries, is the legal instrument setting the conditions of accession. Nine of the ten countries decided to legitimize their accession to the EU through referendum. As a result more than 25 million voters expressed their clear support for the EU membership of their home country thus giving this enlargement a high level of democratic legitimacy.

As a result of the accession negotiations the new Member States will fully implement all EU policies, including the Schengen system and the common currency. In addition, summarizing the results of continued monitoring of the preparation for accession in the ten countries it is clear that the new members adhered to the EU at a very high level of preparation. The fact that no safeguard measures had to be taken underlines the win–win situation that enlargement has created. Therefore this enlargement did not weaken but strengthen the European integration.

1. ECONOMIC BENEFITS OF ENLARGEMENT ARE ALSO OBVIOUS

The historical and political arguments in favour of enlargement are compelling. In addition it will produce substantial economic and social benefits. Enlargement has been proven to be a very efficient and low-cost policy, if measured in financial terms. The budgetary cost of enlargement for the period 2004–6 will amount to nearly €41 billion. In this context it is worth noting that the EU has still to provide more financial assistance per capita to stabilize the Balkan region compared to the per capita spending for enlargement until 2006, not to speak of the potential costs of non-enlargement.

Enlargement of the EU represents a significant growth potential. Once the accession of Bulgaria and Romania has taken place the EU will have gained another 30 million EU citizens. The further extension of the EU single market to all twelve countries will foster competition, which is likely to lead to price decreases. This will generate higher efficiencies and therefore support the potential for growth and employment.

Although their income level is still well below EU average, the new Member States have a strong economic potential. Called the 'New Eastern tigers', the annual growth rate in these countries is much higher than the EU average until the end of this decade. As a result the EU is integrating fast-growing markets. Per capita income will converge to the EU level over time, even if it might take more than a couple of years. The high catch-up potential stems from an interaction of abundant, highly qualified labour, modernization of infrastructure, and high productivity growth.

The economic integration between the eastern and the western part of Europe had already started in 1989. Due to the perspective of EU membership this process speeded up in the mid-1990s, when the so-called Europe agreements came into force, thus providing substantial market opening. Trade and foreign direct investment (FDI) have been the two main channels of integration. As a result, the immediate impact of enlargement should not be exaggerated, given the already close economic ties and the relatively low economic weight of the newcomers. The enlargement perspective has encouraged trade integration. As a group, these countries have become the second most important trading partner of the EU and the EU itself represents the most important trading partner for them. The membership perspective has also been an important factor for attracting foreign direct investment in today's new EU Member States. Indeed, FDI played a major role for the successful transformation towards market economies. In the context of transition and real economic convergence, FDI has and will continue to contribute to replace the outdated capital stock and to introduce new technology and management skills. When conducting the enlargement negotiations, the European Commission has therefore put high emphasis on the need to courageously fight against corruption and to create and preserve a very good investment climate.

Enlargement has created a larger level playing field in Europe. It implies the full dismantling of remaining restrictions giving room to a larger single market with nearly 500 million consumers finally, where all business will compete under a common regulatory framework. The full implementation of single market rules and an improved market access are expected to lead to higher efficiencies resulting from higher competition, a better allocation of resources, and higher specialization.

Accession has also entailed the coordination of the new Member States' economic policies with those of the other Member States and progress with regard to economic and monetary convergence. The implementation of such economic policy requirements will improve economic and monetary stability in the new Member States. A wider economic area enjoying rising incomes, low inflation, fiscal discipline, and sustained growth provides an excellent incentive. High macroeconomic stability in an enlarged single market will generate a favourable climate and will encourage investment from entrepreneurs. On the other side, the present EU will profit from the reform experiences in the new Member States, in particular as regards tackling the challenges of an ageing population. Moreover, as a result of economic reforms, the new Member States have privatized industries and banks, liberalized markets and prices. They also have set up new administrations to ensure fair competition and oversee market rules, in order to ensure the implementation of competition rules or for example the financial markets' supervision. Today, the degree of privatization and market liberalization in certain sectors is sometimes higher in the new than in the old Member States. The commitment of the newcomers to undergo deep reforms and the highly motivated and qualified people in the future Member States represent another asset of the enlarged EU.

2. ENLARGEMENT AND BEYOND

The historical enlargement of the EU had not been yet completed on 1 May 2004. Two other countries, Bulgaria and Romania, are still under way since their accession preparations are not yet completed. The two countries will join in 2007 (or in 2008 by the latest) and thus complete the biggest round of enlargement in the history of the European integration.

Turkey is also a candidate country. Accession negotiations have started after a successful pre-accession period in which Turkey managed to meet the Copenhagen criteria. At present, Turkey is undergoing an impressive reform process and the European Union is committed to help it in its efforts to successfully reform towards a full democracy, the respect of the rule of law, of human rights, and the protection of minority rights. It is obvious that the Turkey that will eventually join the EU will be a different country. It will demonstrate that a large country with a Muslim population can share and implement our values.

The countries of the western Balkan region also have a perspective of EU membership. However, most countries, with the exception of Croatia, are still very far from complying with the EU accession criteria. Only Croatia has already started accession negotiations.

These political decisions foreshadow the developments of the EU within the foreseeable future. Further enlargement rounds are at present not on the agenda. However, given the fundamental need to avoid new dividing lines in Europe the EU has developed a European neighbourhood policy towards its eastern and southern neighbours aiming at fostering cooperation, the respect of universal values, and good governance. While leaving aside the question of EU membership, the European neighbourhood policy will spread democracy and prosperity beyond the borders of the enlarged EU.

The enlargement process with twelve European countries is a success story. Not everybody knows that and not everybody wants to know it. But it is a fundamental truth that all the promised benefits came true. Political and economic stability is achieved, human rights and the rule of law are guaranteed, and more security is provided. Europe is in a much better shape than fifteen years ago.

During the enlargement process it was possible to solve a lot of sometimes centuries-old conflicts between neighbours and in European regions. Only one part of the heritage of the past remained unsolved: the Cyprus problem. It was a very risky strategy to open the way for the membership of the Republic of Cyprus even without the solution of the political conflict. The EU side always considered Turkey as the risk factor. It was not anticipated that the majority of Greek Cypriots would reject a UN-sponsored settlement of the conflict. But the story is not yet finished. Inevitably, the ongoing negotiations with Turkey will eventually create a momentum for a new initiative to settle the Cyprus problem. In the meantime, we should do everything to help the Turkish Cypriot community to catch up. We should not tolerate that the Turkish Cypriots will be the only victims of the enlargement.

The full story of the great enlargement is not yet told. Many people contributed but it happened as it happens very often: those who took the credit for the hard work and the final success are not always those who did the job in practice. There is one group of personalities which was really crucial and is nevertheless widely unknown: the chief negotiators of the twelve negotiating countries. They were the main interlocutors of the European Commission and they were responsible for the smooth functioning of the whole process. I highly welcome the fact that one of them, de facto their dean, my friend George Vassiliou, former President of Cyprus and chief negotiator of his country, was able to convince his colleagues that they should tell the enlargement story from their own perspective. George Vassiliou in his normal modesty will certainly not disclose that his role was much bigger than the role of chief negotiator of a small country. His good services were always required when internal conflicts between candidate countries threatened to delay the whole process. Vassiliou was a real partner for me. His advice was always clear and wise.

Are there lessons to be learnt? Yes, there are many. The most important lesson is that Europe has the capacity to manage almost impossible tasks if the political will and the moral commitment are strong enough. I strongly believe that we can do everything if we only want it and if we join our forces. In that respect, the enlargement story is an excellent example for the future. We can solve the institutional problems and we can win the globalized economic competition if we tackle the issues with the same determination and political strength.

Part I

The Enlargement from Fifteen to Twenty-Five

The Brussels View

1

The Need for Enlargement and Differences from Previous Accessions

Eneko Landaburu

1. INTRODUCTION

The EU enlargement from fifteen to twenty-five members on 1 May 2004 is an unprecedented event due to its scope and its historical and symbolic impact.

It is an event of prime importance from a political point of view, as it brought together into a common entity states which used to belong, not so long ago, to rival or even hostile groups. But it is also important from a cultural point of view, as it offered the possibility of bringing together nations which are all important components of the European family. Europe is as present in Prague or Budapest as it is in London or Paris.

It is also a major event from an economic point of view, as it lays the foundations for a unique entity, a market composed of 450 million consumers, which will create greater economies of scale.

Finally, it is a historical event with global implications, as it is the first time that such a large number of sovereign states have freely decided to give up a substantial part of their prerogatives towards the attainment of a common ideal of peace, stability, and democracy.

What is at stake in fact is the reconciliation of Europe, which was artificially split into two parts in the past. This is a much wider scope than the mere enlargement of an economic entity, no matter how prestigious this entity is.

The enlargement on 1 May 2004 must also be understood in a historical perspective beginning just before—or at the very beginning of—the Second World War, i.e. when some of the regions concerned by our analysis started losing their freedom (for example, in the Sudetan region or in Poland). The Nazi–Soviet Pact and the disasters of the Second World War temporarily wiped reduced or alienated old nations off the map of continental Europe.

Following many convulsions, the divisions of 1944–5 only confirmed this de facto situation. The gradual freezing of the situation, despite the many attempts to recover democracy (in Budapest or Prague for example), lasted almost half a century.

The birth of European integration can itself be analysed from this perspective, since in political terms it had originally two ambitions. The official ambition was Franco-German reconciliation, which was a complete success. There was also a more implicit ambition to demonstrate the capacity of building an alternative democracy, which would attract the Soviet system, which had been maintaining its control over the eastern part of Europe. In that sense, European integration was the daughter of the Cold War.

The fall of the Berlin Wall brought an end to this parenthesis, which had prevailed since the late 1930s. An extraordinary hope then arose. Most observers quickly understood that it was the rise of a new era for Europe, which would hopefully allow all Europeans to live under a common system and to confidently look to the future. EU enlargement ultimately appeared to be the goal of this transformation.

There was nevertheless a long waiting period ahead, as the first steps in this transitional policy were particularly hard to accomplish for two reasons, namely the existence of the ex-communist system for almost half a century and the sudden breaking down of the previously existing relationship. The reorganization has been delicate. While EU enlargement appeared as a goal, there were numerous difficulties linked to the transition. The question was not whether this policy should be pursued, but when and how it should accomplished. In fact, fifteen years, or half a generation, have passed between the fall of the Berlin Wall in 1989 and the 2004 Union enlargement. Rather than being a speedy enlargement, as it is sometimes portrayed, it can be said on the contrary that it is a relatively long period.

The reality is that there was no alternative to responding to the political hope which had arisen in the East. It would have been at the same time politically unthinkable, morally impossible to defend, as well as an economic nonsense to search for a solution other than the obvious one, provided certain precautions were taken.

A semantic aspect however ought to be and still remains to be clarified. There is an implied notion of Messianism in EU enlargement, which is debatable. It aims at proposing the same model of European integration as has been applied so far to other peoples, other nations, tending towards 'the promotion of the *acquis*'. Enlargement implies de facto that there are candidate countries which are willing to assimilate to the existing centre by integrating its model. Like the founding states, these countries have however inherited European culture, although they have not participated in the launching of the Community construction. This is a disturbing terminological imbalance, as it refers to the export of a particular model rather than to the joint accomplishment of a common ambition on an equal basis. Some would have preferred the terms expansion or extension, which would not have been better. Central and Eastern European countries ought to have been recognized as components of the development of the construction of Europe, as their only mistake was that they were cut off from the rest of Europe by the advancing Soviet troops and by the Iron Curtain.

Changes occurring in the Community structure ought however to have been translated into terminology. It is striking to note today that the new Member States have brought along a heritage, a past, as well as a system of thoughts and behaviours which differ slightly from those of the other partners. This should have been transposed at a semantic level. Things however happened otherwise in practice and this empirical choice was confirmed by usage. Central and Eastern European countries bring a 'Slavonic' variation to the European construction, which has been missing so far, as it was dominated until then by its Latin, German, Anglo-Saxon, as well as its more recent Scandinavian components. It must be noted in this respect that the new members have always referred to EU 'accession' rather than enlargement, which they have banned from their vocabulary.

Having placed the issue of enlargement into its historical, cultural, and political contexts, I will demonstrate that this EU enlargement had relatively little in common with previous accessions and that it expresses a wider concept of reunification. I will go on to confirm that there was a real and profound need for enlargement, which still exists today. One cannot dismiss today the centrality of this policy, which is the very essence of the Community construction of peace, stability, and democracy.

2. THE NEED FOR ENLARGEMENT

This is inherent in European integration, which appears both at the political and economic levels, but mostly must be understood as a long-term phenomenon.

The satisfaction of a political hope

When the Central and Eastern European countries recovered their liberty, it was clear that their prime objective was to join the European Union as soon as possible. But the difficulties of the initial transitional period led to a slightly longer road towards accession than they had originally envisaged. It was only in the middle of the 1990s that the perspective of the Union enlargement started becoming clearer following the adoption of the Copenhagen criteria in June 1993 and of Agenda 2000 in July 1997.

From the point of view of the European Union of twelve (or of fifteen), even if some may have had second thoughts, there was no realistic political alternative and it was unthinkable to offer something other than accession to countries which had emerged from half a century of dictatorship imposed on them by the course of history and by geographical accident.

It is in fact a game where both parties are winners: to limit oneself to the mere consideration of immediate budgetary issues amounts to taking into account only one aspect of the question. If one looks at the example of the southern enlargement, it is obvious that both parties benefited from it: it is certainly the case of Spain and Portugal, which managed to relaunch their economies and to consolidate their recent democracy. It is also the case for other European states, in particular Spain and Portugal's immediate neighbours like France, which benefited from stability in the neighbourhood. They managed to enter new markets, which opened up to their economy.

What is at stake in the current enlargement at a political level is the stability of the continent. Would it have been thinkable not to seize this opportunity? What would have happened to the Central Europe zone, had no EU enlargement taken place? Can we imagine what type of relations the states of small Europe would have developed with their neighbours of Central and Eastern Europe? From an economic, political, but also cultural point of view, it is easier to establish good relations with neighbouring countries benefiting from a certain level of internal stability than with countries in the process of a chaotic transition, which would have resulted in uncontrolled convulsions, even in crises leading to war, as has been unfortunately demonstrated in the Balkans.

The early participation in European programmes in research or other areas has been an important factor contributing towards the integration of the future Member States and of their civil society as a whole. It allowed Member States to familiarize themselves with the various Community policies and instruments. Contributions by pre-accession funds, in particular the PHARE programme, helped the implementation of these activities. Similarly, their participation to the work of Community agencies proceeded from the same philosophy (for example with the European Environment Agency).

The type of action, which appears the most interesting from the point of view of the penetration of the European ideal in the various layers of the population and its dissemination, remains nevertheless the encouragement given to the mobility of young people and students (in particular through the SOCRATES, LEONARDO, and YOUTH programmes) or in a slightly different context with ERASMUS exchanges. Through these various actions, a European spirit is built via the exchanges of students, researchers, and other socio-professional groups. Spending a year in another Member State allows one not only to acquire the knowledge of a language, but also to familiarize oneself with a different way of thinking. Even if the initial objective is usually to come back to the country of origin with the benefit of an experience abroad, the practice shows that a significant number of participants to the exchanges remain in the host countries for various professional or personal reasons. Even in this latter case, an overall advantage exists, since these new migrants enrich the host country with their previous experience drawn from their country of origin.

Economic aspect

The overall benefit of enlargement is even more obvious in the economic field.

The enlargement on 1 May 2004 brought into being a group of 450 million consumers who were coming more to resemble each other, representing the largest market in the world. As the first commercial power in the world, it can play an important role on the international scene and impose its views, in particular during the WTO negotiations. Thanks to the communitarization of trade policy, it is a major trade partner facing American or Chinese competitors, for example. It may promote the development of Airbus against its rival Boeing as well as allow for a restriction on Chinese textile exports. The addition of 105 million citizens (with Romania and Bulgaria) brings in Europeans all the more eager to consume, produce, and be competitive since they were prevented from doing so for half a century. The new Member States actually represent a potential for growth slightly higher than that of their partners' economies, which have already reached maturity. This growth differential can be estimated at +/−2 per cent per year.

On an internal bilateral level with the European Union, enlargement to Central and Eastern European countries also had a beneficial impact on the old Member States. With the 2004 enlargement perspective and its achievement, the Central and Eastern European countries totally reoriented their commercial exchanges towards the European Union of fifteen. Even before 1 May 2004, the European Union had become by far their first trading partners, whereas Central and Eastern European economies were completely incorporated into the COMECON at the beginning of the transitional period.

At the time of accession, several of the Central and Eastern European countries were more integrated into commercial exchanges of the EU 15 than some of the old Member States. Overall, they became the second trading partner of the EU 15 after the United States, while the EU 15 constituted between 60 and 70 per cent of their external trade depending on cases, representing a very substantial market share.

Despite frequent affirmations to the contrary, the enlargement to Central and Eastern European countries strongly benefited the old Member States. Just before the date of accession they had a very significant overall bilateral surplus with all of the new Member States. Almost all Central and Eastern European countries were individually in deficit vis-à-vis the EU 15. Even sectors like agriculture had a surplus from the EU 15, which was not expected initially.

For the sake of comparison, Spain also had a rather strong bilateral deficit vis-à-vis its partners at the beginning of its accession period. Looking back, it cannot be said that this situation hindered the subsequent evolution of the Spanish economy. The initial deficit is not an obstacle, to the extent that the economies concerned are in the process of expansion. It is normal that they encounter an imbalance in this situation; the contrary would not be sound. One should only ensure, on the one hand, that this deficit is mainly due to imports of capital goods rather than consumer goods and that, on the other hand, this deficit can be financed more or less in terms of balance of payments through incoming capital movements. This seems to have been more or less the case for Central and Eastern European countries during this transitional period.

The perspective of enlargement and its achievement also constitute very important means of attracting foreign direct investments (FDI), which are the key for economic take-off. This economic growth would not be achieved without FDI.

In the early 1990s, there was no FDI in Central and Eastern European countries. Subsequently, thanks to the various association agreements, FDI started pouring in quite rapidly. This was due originally to the policies of privatization in force at that time, then to existing comparative advantages, which allowed the attraction of investments *ex nihilo*. Around €20 billion worth of annual investments have been realized in the last few years in Central and Eastern Europe, mainly in Poland, in the Czech Republic, in Hungary, in Slovakia, but also in the whole region. These investments allowed for the re-creation of poles of competitiveness in certain zones (for example in a quasi-quadrangle constituted by Silesia, Prague, Bratislava, and Budapest). These investments also saw the rebirth of the car industry, which existed previously in Slovakia and in the Czech Republic, thanks to the know-how of the local labour force.

This policy of attraction of direct investments has often been criticized in the old Member States of the European Union because of the so-called 'delocalization'. This does exist but it seems also certain that it would have taken place anyway, irrespective of enlargement, and that it would have most probably been merely directed to other countries. Moreover, the real relocations, where a site is closed down and reopened 'over there', seem to be relatively few. The future of the European economy does not rest any longer on labour-intensive industries or industries of low added value. There is also a certain correlation between the level of foreign investments and the level of development of the country (at least for comparable entities). In other words, Spain, which has a higher level of development, attracts more FDI than Poland, with more or less equal populations. France receives more investments per inhabitant and Belgium even more.

A last point must be made regarding foreign direct investments. They must be attracted by the comparative advantage of the country and not through doubtful practices, in particular fiscal ones. An FDI must not come to a specific country because of promises of full or part exemption on taxation or on the payment of customs duties. The integration of Central and Eastern European countries into the European Union has thus been particularly difficult to achieve as far as competition law is concerned. While aids and incentives are not totally prohibited by Community competition law, practices must be in accordance with this body of legislation. The Irish example and success in this area demonstrate that such a policy is certainly feasible and can be successful, provided it complies with the system.

From the point of view of companies, enlargement means more exports and more business with the new Member States, which have adopted the rules of the single market. Companies benefit foremost from the freedom of movement of goods, services, persons, and capital through a better allocation of resources, a more substantial investment, and a stronger growth in productivity. What is at stake is the removal of the last existing barriers towards the achievement of a large unified market of 450 million consumers, where all companies are competing under the same rules. The improvement of market access allows in particular a better efficiency through greater specialization and stronger competition. The zones of expansion are consequently broader from the point of view of companies.

The introduction of unified economic policies also improves economic and monetary stability in the new Member States, mainly through lower inflation and a stricter fiscal policy. This stability favours a better business environment and encourages investment.

The financial markets of the new Member States are also developing, which enables them to attract additional investments through the implementation of the Community rules of supervision. A wider range of financial products is available as well as better conditions of liquidity, which also bring financial opportunities.

Nowadays, the level of privatization and liberalization of the market is often higher in new Member States than old ones.

The opening of the continent can finally be observed in two sectors which have a meaningful economic impact: trans-European networks and tourism.

The incorporation of the ten new Member States in the construction of trans-European networks has led to substantial progress on the geographical coverage of the European continent. Under communism, the railway in these countries was very developed, although rather obsolete and inefficient. This network had therefore to be rationalized so as to become competitive. There was also a road network, which was in great need of modernization so as to be able to absorb the increasing flow of vehicles, through the financing in particular of new highways. The ISPA programme, the European Investment Bank, and subsequently the Cohesion Funds were used to finance these investments.

The current development of tourism in Central and Eastern Europe is also a consequence of enlargement, whether in historical cities such as Krakow, Budapest, or Prague, or soon in a more popular form on the beaches of the Black Sea. Tourism is an extraordinary vector of understanding and of knowledge of people, which can facilitate the achievement of a common ideal of belonging to the same European entity.

EU enlargement must not however stop at the current stage. There is a continuum in the process, which must benefit states and European citizens as a whole. The idea that there is a certain degree of 'fatigue' of enlargement among the populations must not be accepted.

Anyway, if one were to stop the enlargement policy for whatever reason, what incentive would one have to offer to countries like the western Balkans, which are still undergoing a transformation after years of communism and a very chaotic transition?

The principles, namely the will to build together one type of democratic society, the criteria for participation, and the mechanisms of membership, remain. There has been continuity since the creation of the common market of six in 1958; the enlargement to ten new Member States, former communist countries, on 1 May 2004, was only a particularly important step in this long-term policy.

The frequently mentioned opposition of enlarging versus deepening has not stood up to examination, at least until today. First of all, nobody had presented serious propositions of deepening before the last enlargement. Also every enlargement has been accompanied by the deepening of one European policy or another. The foundations of European social policy were boosted in the 1970s at the time of the first enlargement. The development of the Cohesion and Structural Funds policy was achieved at the time of the second enlargement to the Mediterranean countries through the successive doubling of the budget allocated to Structural Funds. The implementation of the EMU and the birth of the euro were achieved shortly after the third enlargement. Provided the same direction is kept, enlargement to Central and Eastern Europe should necessarily be accompanied by a major institutional reform, so as to adopt decision-making mechanisms adapted to this new context of twenty-five or twenty-seven Member States, thereby opening real perspectives of political integration.

The European Union is currently going through a serious crisis, perhaps the most serious since its origin, including in relation to the European defence policy and to the 'empty chair' situation, with the challenging of its institutional perspectives following the two negative votes to the French and Dutch referendums and the lack of agreement on the financial perspectives. These are real difficulties and it is no use trying to underestimate their potential consequences. It is even likely that there is a certain link between the enlargement policy and the results of the referendums in France and the Netherlands. If consultations of a similar type had taken place in other countries, they could very well have led to comparable results.

This link most probably exists regarding the perspective of future enlargements, in particular to Turkey. But it may even exist regarding the 1 May 2004 enlargement, on which many European nations did not have a direct right to speak and consequently felt frustrated by this lack of consultation. It is not possible to challenge the validity of this policy and of this strategic choice, the necessity and the fairness of which we have attempted to show. At best, certain tactical choices may be discussed a posteriori and be subject to changes in the future.

But the main criticism regarding the way in which this policy was carried out concerns the weakness in the explanations given to the populations. Provided the implications of such choices are clearly explained, it should be possible to change opinion that are initially reluctant. Provided the advantages and disadvantages of the various options are correctly set out, the public should be in a position to make a fully informed choice.

This weakness in communication constituted the main deficiency of the enlargement policy. One must constantly explain so as to convince public opinion of the validity and the fairness of such a policy.

There is no alternative to the overall policy undertaken if one wishes to achieve, in the long run, the maintenance of continental stability. Enlargement to Spain was a success, enlargement to Poland contains all the ingredients towards success. There is no reason why we could not in the future adapt this method to other countries needing it. This method has been applied so far to the benefit of all—whether old or new members—and should continue in the future through its application to other regions of Europe.

3. DIFFERENCES FROM PREVIOUS ACCESSIONS

EU enlargement on 1 May 2004 to the Central and Eastern European countries is different from previous accessions in nature. There is a global element, which did not exist before, whether it is considered from a historical perspective or through its general or sectoral economic aspects. This is a new phenomenon, which can hardly be said to follow previous accessions.

History of enlargement

The first enlargement in 1973 allowed the European Community to expand from six Member States to nine, while a tenth member, Norway, failed to ratify the existing treaties through a referendum. It was a laborious enlargement, since one Member State—France—had previously on two occasions opposed the candidacy of one country—the United Kingdom—following its initial rejection of the offer to join the first train of the Treaty of Rome. It was necessary to wait for the departure of General de Gaulle and the arrival President Pompidou to waive this veto and accept the British candidacy. Nevertheless, this enlargement did not raise any issues relating to the economic development of the newcomers, since the economy of two of the three of them had a level comparable to that of the then Member States. Moreover, some options of international politics (in particular with respect to the relations with developing countries) were common both to France and to the United Kingdom, even though the Atlantic side of the latter was a little too strong in the view of the former. The main difficulty was found in the initial selection of Community preferences, which were made at the origin of the Common Agricultural Policy and which caused huge problems to the United Kingdom. This controversy subsequently created numerous arguments among the nine members of Europe, until a settlement was found under Margaret Thatcher.

The second wave of enlargement can be analysed according to three key issues: first, the strengthening of democracy in three countries which had been subjected to dictatorial regimes over many long years; second, a redirection of Europe towards the Mediterranean area through the incorporation of three countries with more or less comparable economic structures; and third, European cohesion with three countries which lagged behind compared to northern Europe.

The first of the three accessions during the second wave of enlargement may have been achieved under a strong political constraint of consolidation of democracy, which most probably hampered Greece's economic integration for a number of years. The two other accessions were characterized by the fear of a massive flow of labour from Spain and Portugal towards the European Community, which subsequently appeared to be unfounded. The incorporation of Spain also led to the integration of Spanish fishing and to the development of a Common Fishing Policy. More importantly, the arrival of these three countries ushered in a quite efficient European cohesion policy, which resulted in the successive doubling of the budget allocated to Structural Funds.

The incorporation of East Germany into the European Union can be compared with other enlargements, despite its different nature from traditional enlargements. It is comparable to the previous enlargement to the cohesion countries as far as the size of the financial transfers created is concerned. It can also be compared to subsequent enlargements to Central and Eastern European countries which originate from the same type of political system.

EU enlargement to Scandinavian states and to Austria caused no major concern, as the countries involved benefited from levels of economic development at least comparable, if not superior, to the ones existing in the European Union. On this occasion, Norway rejected once more the offer to join the Community construction. The main potential divergence concerned the fact that they were not members of NATO and did not adhere to a policy of neutrality. However, the old concept of neutrality did not have much importance any more following the end of the Cold War and due to the fact that dangers have now developed in different directions.

The enlargement on 1 May 2004 is a different beast altogether. It is a qualitative step into the future with a relatively unknown element, as the challenge is to integrate ten (and soon twelve) countries, which not only come from totally different political and economic systems, but also initially present a standard of living much lower than the average of the countries they are joining. The gap is slightly bigger than the one which existed between the Community of nine and the Mediterranean countries when they joined.

On a political level, it is mostly a strong symbol sealing the reunification of the European continent and the end of the split into two caused by the Cold War. As in the case of the Franco–German reconciliation, the Community construction has reached its second initial political goal of spreading democracy in Europe.

The Differences

The differences in the approach towards this enlargement are so significant that they partly created the need for the establishment of objective membership criteria.

As far as the number of countries is concerned, it is the largest EU enlargement ever. While the Union had only fifteen Member States, there were thirteen candidate countries, the negotiations started with twelve of them and ten of them finally joined on 1 May 2004. In relative terms, this latest enlargement represents a two-thirds increase.

On previous occasions, there were four candidate countries in the first enlargement, of which three joined the six Member States in 1973, whereas in 1995, there were again four candidate countries, of which three joined the then twelve Member States. The 2004 enlargement therefore has had first and foremost an impact on the institutional framework, since the institutions must now function with twenty-five Member States (several of which are small, even very small states).

In terms of area, it is a significant enlargement although not extraordinary. The 'Ten' cover a total area of 736,000 km^2, whereas the 'Fifteen' cover a total area of 3,156,000 km^2. The addition of the Ten therefore represents an increase in the Union territory of 23 per cent. The first enlargement in 1973 saw the territory of the Community at that time grow by 30 per cent.

As far as the populations and a fortiori the level of economic development are concerned, the latest enlargement's impact must also be put into context, while keeping in mind the differences from previous experiences. On 1 May 2004, 74.2 million Europeans joined a Union of 379.5 million inhabitants, which represents an increase of 19 per cent. In 1973, 64.3 million newcomers joined the population of the Community, which then amounted to 194.6 million inhabitants, which represented an increase of 33 per cent!

The above figures therefore result in relatively comparable densities of population between the Ten and the Fifteen, since the Ten reported in 2004 an average density of 100.8 inhabitants per km^2 while the Union of fifteen showed an average density of 120.2 inhabitants per km^2 (on the other hand, the three countries that joined in 1973 reported an average density of 180.1 inhabitants per km^2, mainly due to the United Kingdom).

The most significant comparison is expressed in economic terms by comparing the total GNPs of the countries joining with that of the Union. In 2004 the GNP of the Fifteen was €9,687 billion in purchasing power parities, while the GNP of the Ten was merely €928.9 billion in PPP, thereby reaching only 9.5 per cent of the total of the Union. At current exchange rates, the ratio is even more significant, as the Ten only represented 4.6 per cent of the Union of fifteen.

For comparison purposes, in 1973 the three new countries represented 29.9 per cent of the GNP in PPP of the Community they were joining. If one takes into consideration the level of development per inhabitant, the per capita GNP of the Ten reached in 2004 49.6 per cent of the Community average in the EU of fifteen and 23.9 per cent at current exchange rates. In 1985, Spain reached 71.8 per cent of the average per capita GNP (in PPP) of the Community of ten, whereas Portugal was at 47.2 per cent and Greece at 54.3 per cent.

Even though these comparisons are of interest, they must however be put into perspective, to the extent that joining the Community in 1973 did not mean the same as joining the Union in 2004, due to the fact that European policies have greatly developed and diversified.

Nevertheless, the fact that there were so many candidates (thirteen) justified the adoption of objective membership criteria, so as to treat all candidacies on an equal basis. It was not possible any longer to proceed empirically, as was the case when four was the maximum number of candidates at once. Hence, the Copenhagen membership criteria were adopted in 1993.

Before turning to this issue, one must recall two basic principles, which have guided the enlargement strategy throughout. Any European state can join. This principle was already mentioned in the Rome Treaty. The difficulty came from the fact that even though it is possible to give a strictly geographical definition of Europe, the exercise becomes more delicate if political, historical or, even more so, cultural elements are introduced in the definition. Europe is a much more ambitious notion to define, when one considers it as a community of thought and a willingness to live together of states which share common democratic values.

The second principle concerns the level of development of the candidate country. At the Copenhagen Summit in 1993, the heads of states and governments of the twelve Member States agreed that any European state could join, irrespective of its initial level of development. This very laudable commitment nevertheless had two implications, which may not have penetrated public opinion as yet. This meant that the European Union would welcome within the Union countries with very different initial levels of development and with quite substantial average gaps. This also implied, in line with the philosophy of developing all regions of all Member States, that there would be financial transfers from the wealthier Member States to the less wealthy ones. This point might not be today completely acknowledged by certain portions of public opinion.

Thus, it is in the above context that the Copenhagen membership criteria were agreed in June 1993. Three criteria must be satisfied. The first one, a political criterion, is the most important of the three since it governs the starting of the accession negotiations.

The candidate country must have stable institutions, which guarantee democracy, the rule of law, human rights, as well as the respect and the protection of minorities' rights.

There is then a double economic criterion: the candidate country must have a viable market economy and the capacity to face competition and market forces within the Union.

The candidate country must finally be able to assume its obligations, in particular to commit itself to the objectives of the economic and monetary union. In this respect, it was clarified at the Madrid European Council of December 1995 that any candidate country must ensure it is able to join the EU through the adaptation of its administrative structures so as to implement European legislation in its national system. In particular, this legislation must be implemented in an efficient manner, based on adequate administrative and legal structures.

The existence of these common objective criteria applicable to all countries wishing to start accession negotiations allowed a relatively homogeneous treatment of candidacies, which although originating mostly from countries with the same politico-economic system, were nevertheless disparate. And what can be said about the differences between the post-communist Central and Eastern European countries, on the one hand, and the islands of Malta and Cyprus, and most of all, of Turkey, on the other hand?

The clear and harmonized criteria also brought into view differences existing from previous enlargements.

Sectorial aspects

If one refers to the Mediterranean enlargement to Greece, Spain, and Portugal, which seems a priori to be the closest to the current enlargement as far as the economic structures of these countries are concerned, some significant differences remain.

The structures in the agricultural sector are however rather close. In 1980 agriculture represented approximately 8 per cent of the GNP of these three countries and 17 per cent of their active population. In 2000 agriculture was also representing 8 per cent of the GNP of the ten candidate countries from Central and Eastern Europe as well as 17 per cent of their active population. But the comparison cannot somehow be drawn beyond this surprising similarity of data, due to the fact that the levels of productivity and of efficiency are much lower in Central and Eastern European countries. Moreover, the enlargement to the Central and Eastern European countries added much more potential agricultural resources (whether in the form of land or of labour force) to the Union of fifteen than the three countries had done vis-à-vis the Community of nine. Last but not least, another aspect must be taken into account. Whereas the enlargement to the three southern countries brought Mediterranean-type agricultures, which supplemented to a certain extent agriculture already existing in the Community of nine, the current wave of enlargement brought northern-type agricultures, which may well add to the already existing massive production.

A second major difference between the two groups, namely the education level in those countries as a whole, may well favour the Central and Eastern European countries. In 2002 more than 45 per cent of the 25–64-year-olds in Italy, Spain, Greece, Portugal, or Ireland had qualifications at the level of the first cycle of secondary education or lower; whereas more than 68 per cent of the same population had qualifications at the level of the second cycle of secondary education in Central and Eastern European countries, except in Lithuania, Bulgaria, Estonia, and Hungary.

The Eastern and Central European countries showed however weaknesses in tertiary education, which represents less than 15 per cent of the 25–64-year-olds almost everywhere (except Estonia, Lithuania, Bulgaria, and Latvia), whereas the average for the same population in the European Union of twenty-seven is 25 per cent.

The strong presence of an average level of qualifications in the Eastern and Central European countries may be an important factor of economic growth and may eventually lead to a quicker adjustment than was the case for the southern countries. The weakness of the higher level of qualifications is however a drawback.

The strong impact, which the current enlargement will have on the cohesion of the European Union constitutes the third significant difference from previous enlargements. Approximately 92 per cent of the nationals of the new Member States live in regions where the per capita GNP represents less than three-quarters of the average in the European Union of twenty-five, whereas more than two-thirds live in regions where the GNP is less than half of this average. Should Bulgaria and Romania be included, 153 million inhabitants would then live in regions where the GNP is lower than 75 per cent of the Community average, which would represent one-third of the new Union, as opposed to 73 million before the 1 May 2004 enlargement.

Due to the statistical effect (lowering of the Community average of the per capita GNPs and mechanical eviction of the regions exceeding the 75 per cent threshold of this average so as to be eligible for Objective 1 of the Structural Funds), seventeen additional regions of the EU Fifteen are excluded from this budget, whereas they are not intrinsically richer than before. Briefly, one can distinguish three groups of countries in this new Union in terms of revenues: the first group with twelve of the fifteen Member States of the previous Union; the second group with Spain, Portugal, Greece, Cyprus, Malta, Slovenia, and the Czech Republic with a revenue amounting approximately to 80 per cent of the new Union average; and a third group with the eight new Member States or acceding countries with a revenue amounting approximately to 40 per cent of the average of the Union of twenty-seven.

Taking into consideration these diverging characteristics, it appears that the impact on the Structural Funds policy and on the social policy is very significant. Structural Funds become to a large extent an operation of financial transfers from Western Europe to Central and Eastern Europe, while previously, the flows were rather north–south due to two factors: the eviction of numerous Western European regions from the old Objective 1 of the Structural Funds, as explained above, as well as the relative reducing of the budget allocated to the old Objective 2 of the Structural Funds.

In terms of social cohesion, the employment rate of the 15–64 year olds, which was already not so high in the European Union of fifteen (64 per cent in 2002), is particularly low in the new Member States (56 per cent in 2002). Unemployment is also higher on average in the new Member States (15 per cent in 2002) than in the European Union of fifteen (8 per cent in 2002), although this trend is not uniform. This rate is tending to drop. Certain newcomers which have already engaged in significant restructuring are, however, in much more favourable situations (6 per cent in Hungary and in Slovenia in 2002).

These diverging characteristics of the labour market must not, however, conceal a different conception of social relations between the new Member States and many of the old ones. The particularities of social relations and of the labour market for the new Member States must be considered as forming part of the comparative advantage they have vis-à-vis their partners within the EU. These divergences of interpretation have given rise to many misunderstandings between old and new Member States.

Fears of massive migrations have represented an important aspect of the debate on enlargement in certain countries, as was the case for the enlargement to Mediterranean countries. But as in 1985 and despite certain slightly stronger characteristics (bigger gap in development), these fears are unlikely to materialize to a great extent in common practice for the simple reason that most new Member States are countries with ageing demography. Some of these countries are already in the process of losing population and it is not when people are 55 or 60 years old that they will think of migrating, but rather when they are 25 or 30 years old. All available forecasts show potential cumulative levels of migration lower than 1 per cent of the active population in 2009, which is unlikely to destabilize the European Union labour market. Sectoral migrations could however take place (for instance, cross-border workers, seasonal workers in agriculture, truck drivers, young qualified workers, etc.); this is the reason why transitional periods of up to seven years have been put into place regarding the freedom of movement of workers.

A last significant difference must be mentioned regarding the recent enlargement, namely the privileged option of the newcomers in international relations. For an easily understandable reason, almost all of them prefer their integration into NATO and their relationship with the United States to any other policy. This choice differentiates them to quite a large extent from some of their partners within the European Union, as recent international events indicated. It also distinguishes them from the Member States which joined in the previous wave of enlargement (Sweden, Finland, and Austria), which have all made the choice of neutrality and of not belonging to NATO.

The differences from previous accessions are therefore numerous, but they should not however hinder the need for enlargement of the European Union, which must be considered as a central feature of its policy.

2

The Preparation of the Fifth Enlargement

Poul Skytte Christoffersen

1. THE START: THE FALL OF THE BERLIN WALL

The fifth enlargement process of the Union involving the Central and Eastern European countries as well as Malta and Cyprus started officially in March 1998, and ten states joined the existing fifteen member states five years later on 1 May 2004. Bulgaria and Romania, which were also part of the fifth enlargement, are expected to enter the Union in 2007 or 2008 at the latest.

Shipping metaphors have often been used in order to describe the fifth enlargement process. Words like 'waves' or 'regatta' have entered the vocabulary of the enlargement story. The saga of the latest enlargement of the Union has proceeded with different speed over the long period it has covered. Sometimes the winds were favourable, at other times they were failing. But even in periods with hardly any breeze or when the winds were blowing in the opposite direction good seamanship on the part of the Commission, individual presidencies of the Council, and not least the candidates themselves ensured that the process stayed on the right course.

The history of the fifth enlargement formally started in 1998, but its origin goes back to the end of the division of Europe after the fall of the Berlin Wall in 1989. From the very start the new democracies in Eastern and Central Europea placed the objective of becoming part of the Euro-Atlantic partnership (EU and NATO) at the top of their agenda. This was also the process that in the end crowned with success the ambition of Malta and Cyprus to become members of the European Union, as expressed through their membership applications in 1990 and in 1992.[1]

The European Union in many ways acted rapidly to consolidate the new-found freedom and democracy in Central and Eastern Europe. The Union quickly removed long-standing import quotas, granted trade preferences, and concluded trade and cooperation agreements with these countries. Through its PHARE programme, which was created already in 1989, the Union provided financial support for the countries' efforts to reform and rebuild the economies. PHARE soon became the world's largest assistance programme in Central and Eastern

[1] As described later, Malta during the process withdrew its application only to reintroduce it a later stage.

Europe. In fact the European Union, and in particular the Commission, was among the first to understand in full the significance of the historic change that took place and act accordingly.

Malta and Cyprus had already concluded association agreements with the Union in 1970 and 1972 respectively.

Openness and financial help were the order of the day but considerations on adhesion were definitively not in the foreground. The first years in the 1990s were a period where little attention was being paid inside the Union to the prospect of enlargement. The agenda was focused on ambitious internal reform. Plans for economic and monetary union as well as political union were moving forward culminating in the agreement on the Maastricht Treaty in December 1991. The financing of the Union was the next topic on the agenda. At the meeting of the European Council in Edinburgh in December 1992 a final agreement was reached on the financial perspectives for the period 1993–2000.

The Union, however, was not closed to the other states in Europe. In addition to political support, increased market access, and substantial economic assistance to the Central and Eastern European countries, the EU offered the EFTA countries (Austria, Finland, Iceland, Norway, Sweden, and Switzerland) access to the internal market through an agreement on the creation of 'the European Economic Area'.

For most leading politicians in the Union the perspective of enlargement was relegated to a distant future. Most leaders considered that it would take many years—if not decades—to bring the political and economic situation, in particular in Central and Eastern Europe, to a level where membership could be considered a realistic possibility.

The vision of the Commission President Jacques Delors of a 'European Village' with many houses, one of which would be the European Union, and other houses occupied by the Central and Eastern European countries, was shared by many leading politicians in Europe. But after a few years this vision was overturned by events.

Four of the EFTA countries (Sweden, Finland, Norway, and Austria) had hardly concluded the EEA agreement before deciding that this type of relationship could not be a substitute for taking part in full in the shaping of the future of Europe. They responded by applying for membership in 1991.

The Central and Eastern European countries broke down the barrier towards enlargement mostly by themselves, as they had done when they threw off the chains of communism. Political and economic reform in Central and Eastern Europe proceeded with a speed that few had expected. Economies which had tumbled immediately after the changeover picked up rapidly as did trade with the EU and inward investments, in particular from Europe.

The mood inside the Union was also changing. In particular for Germany it became more and more difficult to envisage a European Union expanding only to the north and the south. The new design for Europe would have to include its big neighbour to the east, Poland. Europe could not stop at the Oder-Neisse. In general the winds in favour of the fifth enlargement were picking up.

The Union's next move was to replace the association agreements with the more advanced 'Europe agreements' in which the Central and Eastern European countries' ultimate objective to become a member of the Community was recognized. But it took time before the Union responded without ambiguity to this aspiration. Only at the European Council in Copenhagen in June 1993 did a clear position emerge.

2. THE EUROPEAN COUNCIL IN COPENHAGEN, 1993; OPENING UP THE DOOR FOR ENLARGEMENT; THE 'COPENHAGEN CRITERIA'

For a moment the uncertainty on the fate of the Maastricht Treaty threatened to prolong the period of introspective, and to block progress towards enlargement. However, at the Copenhagen European Council the heads of state and government could note with satisfaction that the crises in the European Union created by the rejection a year earlier by the Danish people of the Maastricht Treaty had been overcome. In May, a month before Copenhagen, in a new referendum, the 'yes' to the Maastricht Treaty had carried the day. The Union was prepared to move forward on expansion.

Enlargement negotiations with the former EFTA countries, which had been put on hold awaiting the ratification of the Maastricht Treaty, could now gain momentum. This encouraged a more open mindset with regard to the other European countries that aspired to membership.

The enlargement file for the European Council in Copenhagen in 1993 had been prepared by the Committee of Permanent Representatives (COREPER) and by the General Affairs Council in the months preceding the meeting. The Commission, and in particular its Vice President Leon Brittan, responsible for external affairs, had taken the lead. Inside the Commission earlier reticence towards contemplating enlargement towards Central and Eastern Europe had been replaced by renewed openness.

The preparatory process had paved the way for important decisions, and the European Council in Copenhagen delivered after a fairly brief discussion.

The European Council welcomed that the Commission would present its opinions on Malta and on Cyprus. This ended a period where these two applications had been stalled inside the Commission. These opinions would then be examined rapidly by the Council, 'taking into consideration the particular situation of the two countries'. Even though not directly spelled out, there was no doubt that the division of Cyprus was a 'particular situation' to be taken into account.

The European Council language with regard to the Central and Eastern European countries was more straightforward. The 'associated countries' in Central and Eastern Europe 'that so desire, shall become members of the

European Union. Accession will take place as soon as an associated country is able to assume the obligations of membership by satisfying the economic and political conditions required.'[2] With this wording it was no longer a question of 'if' but of 'when' the Central and Eastern European countries would become members.

The European Council went on to define the 'economic and political' conditions that had to be fulfilled. These would from then on be known as the 'Copenhagen criteria'.

Membership will require

- 'That the candidate country has achieved stability of institutions guaranteeing democracy, the rule of law, human rights and respect for and protection of minorities' (political criteria);
- 'The existence of a functioning market economy as well as the capacity to cope with competitive pressure and market forces within the Union' (the two economic criteria).[3]

For the first time the conditions for membership of the Union (apart for being a European state and a democracy) had been defined. These political and economic criteria were later to play a crucial role in evaluating progress in the candidate countries with regard to fulfilling the conditions for membership.

The European Council added that 'Membership presupposes the candidate's ability to take on the obligations of membership including adherence to the aims of political, economic and monetary Union.'

There was nothing new in this message that a candidate country in order to become a member should accept the Union as it was and in its totality. No room was left for 'à la carte' adhesion.

Finally the European Council concluded that 'the Union's capacity to absorb new members, while maintaining the momentum of European integration is also an important consideration in the general interest of both the Union and the candidate countries'. This was a reminder that enlargement with so many new candidate countries could require further progress towards consolidation of the Union. The Union might have to change in order to accommodate the new members.

The European Council in Copenhagen took other important decisions. It established a structured relationship between the Central and Eastern European

[2] The associated countries were countries that had concluded or intended to conclude 'Europe agreements' with the EU: Bulgaria, the Czech Republic, Estonia, Hungary, Latvia, Lithuania, Poland, Romania, and Slovakia. Later on Slovenia would join the group after the dissolution of Yugoslavia. The Copenhagen European Council itself included the three Baltic republics (Estonia, Latvia, and Lithuania) as countries with a vocation to conclude Europe agreements.

[3] The Madrid European Council in 1995 added a fourth criterion on the necessary adjustment of the candidate countries' administrative capacity.

(CEE) countries on the one hand, and the institutions of the European Union on the other. This involved the holding of meetings between the Union and the associated countries on matters of common interest (e.g. energy, environment, transport R & D, common foreign and security policy, and home and justice affairs).[4] These meetings, which were to be held at regular intervals throughout most of the pre-accession, were not meant to function as decision-making forums. They had an important psychological and pedagogical function by inviting the future members of the Union 'inside the door' in the Council building and confronting them with issues which were being discussed in the Union.

The European Council also decided to help the preparation for accession by offering training in community law and procedure to officials from the associated countries. The success of future accession negotiations would depend very much on the capacity of officials in the candidate countries to fully understand community law and practices. The learning process initiated in Copenhagen and implemented in practice by both the Commission and the Member States over the coming years would become of great importance for the success of the enterprise.

Finally the European Council decided on further improvements in the market access of the associated countries and to reinforce the Union's assistance through the PHARE programme, in particular by greater emphasis on infrastructure developments.

The Copenhagen European Council all in all opened a new approach to enlargement:

- A strategy for enlargement was established before formal demands for accession had been received. Except for Cyprus and Malta, the formal applications for the other countries were only received later.[5] Until Copenhagen the Union had discouraged the submission of formal demands for accession.
- A precise yardstick was established for the fulfilment of the criteria for enlargement (the Copenhagen criteria). Such criteria had not existed in earlier enlargement processes.
- Enlargement negotiations and internal reform of the Union were included in the same agenda ('widening' and 'deepening' in a single package).
- Practical steps were taken to prepare the candidate countries for enlargement.

[4] This 'structured relationship' was put into effect after the Essen European Council in 1994 (see below). It was scaled down to only meetings between Foreign Ministers in 1998. However, as the enlargement process came closer to the end, specialized Council meetings enlarged to include the candidate countries were reintroduced, in particular on ECOFIN and home and justice affairs.

[5] Bulgaria: December 1995; Czech Republic: January 1996; Estonia: November 1995; Hungary: March 1994; Latvia: October 1995; Lithuania: December 1995; Poland: April 1994; Romania: June 1995; Slovakia: June 1995; Slovenia: June 1996.

Considering the later importance of the Copenhagen criteria it is surprising how little attention was paid in the media at the time to the Copenhagen European Council's conclusions on enlargement.

3. FROM 1994 TO 1997: FURTHER DEEPENING OF THE EUROPEAN INTEGRATION OF THE UNION AND REFINEMENT OF ITS APPROACH TOWARDS ENLARGEMENT

Following Copenhagen and after concluding the fourth enlargement round with the former EFTA countries, the Union again turned its main attention to its own internal development.

The rapid economic expansion which had characterized the Union in the second half of the 1980s gave way in many Member States to a period with slower economic growth and rising unemployment. The internal economic agenda took up much of the attention of the Union, including the preparation for the passage to the third stage of economic and monetary union and the introduction of the euro.

Much political energy and attention was also devoted to the institutional debate. From 1995 to 1997 the Union was engaged in a new treaty revision procedure, resulting in the agreement on the Amsterdam Treaty in June 1997.

There were two main inspirations to the negotiations on the Amsterdam Treaty: first, the continuation of the integration process building on the Maastricht Treaty. The Amsterdam Treaty carried further the European integration, in particular in the field of justice and home affairs and common foreign and security policy. Secondly: to prepare the Union for enlargement. On this account, the Amsterdam Treaty failed to live up to the aspirations. In the end the institutional set-up was left basically unchanged, and for instance the ambition to introduce more qualified majority voting (QMV) in the Council was not realized.

The European Council recognized its failure in agreeing a protocol to the Amsterdam Treaty spelling out the need to come back to the institutional questions before the fifth enlargement of the Union could take place. A distinction was made between two scenarios:

- A Union enlarged with five or fewer new Member States. In this case a reduction of the size of the Commission to one per Member State and a modification of the weighting of the votes in the Council was considered necessary.
- An enlargement with more than five new Member States. In this case a full-fledged intergovernmental conference dealing with all the provisions of the treaties 'on the composition and functioning of the institutions' (meaning i.e. also the provision on qualified majority voting in the Council) was called for.

This distinction between an enlargement with fewer and one with more than five members would play a certain role later on in the history of the fifth enlargement.

In parallel to the deepening of the European integration process, preparation for enlargement continued, without necessarily catching the headlines.

The European Council at Corfu in June 1994 clarified the inclusion of Malta and Cyprus into the fifth enlargement process by stipulating that 'the next phase of enlargement of the Union will involve Cyprus and Malta'.

The European Council in Essen in December the same year met for the first time with heads of state and government of the Central and Eastern European countries. It also implemented a number of the decisions taken in Copenhagen by launching an ambitious pre-adhesion programme of support from the Union in preparing for enlargement. The pre-adhesion strategy included formalized structural dialogue on various levels (heads of state and government, Foreign Ministers, and specialized ministers), dealing with issues like increased market access, specialized technical assistance in preparing for participation in the internal market, stimulation of investment from the Union, and extending the trans-European networks to Central and Eastern Europe.

As soon as the negotiations on the Amsterdam Treaty were put on track, the Union also started to confront the issue of when to start enlargement negotiations. This was initially done with great caution.

Malta and Cyprus were the first countries to obtain a firm undertaking. The Madrid European Council in June 1995 agreed that negotiations with these two countries would start six months after the end of the intergovernmental conference (on the Amsterdam Treaty).

For the Central and Eastern European countries Madrid limited itself to expressing the hope 'that the preliminary stage of negotiations will coincide with the start of negotiations with Malta and Cyprus'.

On the procedural level the European Council in Madrid asked the Commission to prepare its opinions on the various applications as well as to prepare an overall ('composite') paper on enlargement. It also called upon the Commission to undertake a detailed analysis of the European Union's financing system in order to submit, immediately after the conclusion of the intergovernmental conference, a communication on the future financial framework of the Union as from 31 December 1999, having regard to the prospect of enlargement.

4. FROM AMSTERDAM WITH ENLARGEMENT AND NEW WINDS IN THE SAILS

When the European Council in Amsterdam in June 1997 agreed on the 'Amsterdam Treaty' it also noted 'that the way is now open for launching the enlargement process'.

Since Madrid, the Commission had been preparing opinions on the various formal applications which had been received. Time had now come for the Commission to 'draw the main conclusions and give its views on the launching of the accession process'. A rendezvous clause was fixed for the following meeting of the European Council to be held in Luxembourg in December the same year.

The Commission responded to its mandate by submitting only a few weeks later a number of important documents that had been under preparation for some time under the responsibility of Commissioner Hans van den Broek. These were the Commission's opinions on the membership applications for each of the candidate countries and an overall report 'Agenda 2000', which covered general questions concerning the enlargement process and the Commission's proposal for the overall financial framework for the period 2000–6. The financial documents also contained proposals for reform of the Common Agricultural Policy and the Structural Funds. Enlargement and development of the Union's policies and finances were now intrinsically linked together.

Both inside the Commission and among Member States, the perspective of actually opening enlargement negotiations, and in this way engaging on the path of 'no return', launched a debate on which of the candidates should be invited to join in the negotiations. Both technical and political arguments were present.

In most Member States the dominant view was that negotiations should start with only a few countries. This 'first wave' could then be followed later with other groups, when they (and the Union) were ready.

The Czech Republic, Hungary, and Poland were the candidates mostly cited. The first two were the Central and Eastern European states which had achieved most progress on economic reform. However for many, and in particular for the Germans, Poland was the *raison d'être* for eastern enlargement and could not be left out—despite uncertain progress in many areas.

To the list of three countries was added Cyprus, which economically was much further advanced than the Central and Eastern European countries. Most Member States at the time, however, did not envisage adhesion of Cyprus until the division of the island had ended. Malta itself had decided to suspend its membership application when a Labour administration in 1996 replaced the Nationalist Party in government.

Besides the evaluation of the economic and political situation, institutional considerations also played a role. Enlargement with up to five new Member States could be handled without major institutional change, as spelled out in the enlargement protocol to the Amsterdam Treaty.

In the end the Commission decided on an objective approach, instead of a political one.

The candidate countries had been requested to provide the Commission with a host of information in response to Commission questionnaires and enquiries launched in connection with the examination of their membership application. The Commission had supplemented this database with information from IMF, OECD, OSCE, and the Council of Europe. For the first time an objective basis existed for an evaluation on how the candidate countries complied with the Copenhagen criteria.

It appeared from the Commission's examination of the facts that several of the Central and Eastern European countries had progressed further than had been commonly believed. Furthermore, differences in their preparedness for membership had been reduced. It would for instance be difficult to pretend that Estonia was less prepared than Poland. The Commission also recognized that the situation in Slovenia—the last country to apply for membership—was quite advanced. The Commission in the end proposed that negotiations should start with six countries: Cyprus, Czech Republic, Estonia, Hungary, Poland, and Slovenia.

In preparing its proposals on the selection of candidates for opening negotiations, the Commission had to take a position on when and to what extent the Copenhagen criteria had to be fulfilled. The Copenhagen conclusions had been clear on the economic criteria. They had to be fulfilled from the time of entry. The Commission's overall evaluation was that 'Hungary, Poland, Estonia, the Czech Republic and Slovenia could be in a position to satisfy all the conditions for membership in the medium term, if they maintain and strongly sustain their efforts of preparation'.

With regard to the political criteria the situation was less clear. Could a country that did not fulfil the political criteria start negotiations? The Commission concluded that it could not. The political criteria had to be fulfilled before enlargement negotiations could start. It found that in one candidate country—Slovakia—serious problems existed with regard to the fulfilment of the political criteria. It pointed *inter alia* to clear breach of the constitution by the Mecir government in power, insufficient independence of the judiciary, and unacceptable treatment of minorities. The Commission recommended on this background that Slovakia should not be included in the list.

5. THE LUXEMBOURG EUROPEAN COUNCIL: THE DECISION TO LAUNCH ENLARGEMENT NEGOTIATIONS

The Commission's recommendations were well received by the majority of Member States, in particular by those who preferred to start the enlargement process with a limited number of candidates. Those candidates that had made most progress should be rewarded through the opening of enlargement negotiations. By proposing six countries, the Commission went beyond the five envisaged in the Amsterdam protocol. But this number included Cyprus, and many Member States doubted that the implicit conditions for accession of Cyprus—reunification—would be fulfilled in the foreseeable future.

Others, and in particular Sweden and Denmark, supported by the UK, pointed to the difficulties in separating the candidates into two groups. Like the other Member States they thought it justified to eliminate Slovakia for lack of fulfilment of the political criteria. Eliminating candidates on economic grounds, however, was more doubtful. Differences in economic performance were not that great (in particular between the three Baltic countries). Leaving somebody behind—awaiting another 'wave' in an uncertain future—could take away the pressure for reform and modernization in the countries left on the shore. Denmark and Sweden proposed the regatta model, where all the candidates were allowed to 'set sail' and participate in the enlargement negotiations. Each country's efforts would then determine when they were able to conclude the negotiations.

It was the 'wave' approach, and not the 'regatta model', that won the day at the European Council in Luxembourg. The heads of state and government agreed on the Commission's proposal to start with six countries.

Several elements of the regatta approach, however, were introduced in the blueprint for the enlargement process agreed by the European Council:

The conclusions underlined that the accession process, involving the ten Central and East European applicant states and Cyprus, would be comprehensive and inclusive. All these states were destined to join the Union on the basis of the same criteria and would participate in the accession process on an equal footing. The European Council sought in this way to eliminate fears among the countries left behind that they might be subjected to stricter conditions when a judgement would be made in the future on the start of negotiations.

The inclusive process was substantiated through a number of practical steps, in particular:

- All eleven applicant countries would participate in the opening meeting on the enlargement negotiation process, planned for 30 March 1998. Many elements from the EU's general negotiation framework (though not the ones which dealt specifically with the conduct of negotiations) were to be presented by the EU to the candidates on that occasion, and would therefore apply to all the applicant states.
- All Central and Eastern European candidate countries would be offered accession partnerships, which would mobilize all forms of assistance in preparing for membership, including technical support and financial assistance through the PHARE programme. The partnerships linked the financial assistance to the country's progress, and to its compliance with its national programme for adoption of the *acquis*. They set out the key short- and medium-term priorities to be met in order to prepare for membership. A special 'catch-up' facility was foreseen for those initially left behind.
- From the end of 1998 the Commission would make regular reports on all the applicant states, and when appropriate propose the opening of enlargement negotiations for those that had been left behind in the first place. The same criteria would be used as those applied to the first group of countries.
- The five remaining countries would go through an analytical examination of the Union *acquis* (called '*acquis* screening' in the jargon) in parallel with screening conducted for the first group. The analytical examination is the first step in an enlargement negotiation process, where the Commission—together with the candidate countries—examines in detail how each country's laws, regulations, and administrative practices relate to those applicable in the European Union. The modalities for the *acquis* screening in the two groups of countries varied, but the process would allow the residual five to gain precious time. It also forced this group to mobilize its public administration to be able to cope with enlargement-related issues.

3

Organization of the Process and Beginning of the Negotiations

Poul Skytte Christoffersen

1. ROLE OF THE COMMISSION

Before describing the how of the Commission's involvement in the enlargement process, a brief reference to the why is in place, not least because the Commission's role is not self-evident.

Usually, in negotiations with third countries, the Commission is the EU's negotiator acting on the basis of a mandate from the Council. This applies also to the negotiation of association agreements and other bilateral agreements with candidate countries. Accession negotiations, however, do not aim to deepen the bilateral relationship between the EU and the candidate country but rather to transform an external relationship into an internal one, whereby a third country becomes an equal of the existing Member States. Here the Commission is *not* the EU negotiator. Ever since the creation of the European Community, accession negotiations have been governed by a specific procedure which is largely intergovernmental.

Formally, the role of the Commission in this procedure is limited to formulating a non-binding opinion. According to the Treaty on European Union, which lays down the accession procedure in its Article 49, this opinion must be delivered before the Council decides to admit a country to the Union. In the case of the fifth enlargement, this opinion was issued on 19 February 2003, shortly before the signature of the Accession Treaty with the ten.[1] This Commission opinion is short and formal, in stark contrast to the Commission's real role in the enlargement process.

[1] Commission opinion of 19 February 2003 on the applications for accession to the European Union by the Czech Republic, the Republic of Estonia, the Republic of Cyprus, the Republic of Latvia, the Republic of Lithuania, the Republic of Hungary, the Republic of Malta, the Republic of Poland, the Republic of Slovenia, and the Slovak Republic (COM/2003/0079 final). Published in *OJL* 236, 23 Sept. 2003, pp. 3–4.

In reality, the Commission has been deeply involved in enlargement long before and after the formal opinion. The Commission's key activities can be summed up as follows:

(*a*) The Commission manages bilateral relations with candidate countries, ranging from resolving commercial disputes to delivering large assistance programmes. These bilateral relations are part of the overall pre-accession strategy aimed at guiding the candidate countries towards membership and have become inseparable from the accession process itself. By way of example, the meetings of committees and expert subcommittees under the association agreement, where the Commission represents the Union, serve not only to administer the agreement in the narrow sense but also as a forum to review overall progress by the country in respect of the *acquis*.

(*b*) The Commission assists candidate countries with its expertise on the *acquis*. The most intense period of assistance is during the screening process at the beginning of the accession negotiations but as just mentioned this assistance continues in bilateral contacts in the association bodies and elsewhere.

(*c*) The Commission monitors the progress and performance of the candidate countries against the requirements for membership, most importantly the Copenhagen criteria, and against the commitments made during the negotiations. In-depth reports published every autumn by the Commission systematically record progress made by each of the candidate countries. These reports offer the public and policy-makers in the candidate country and in Member States an authoritative judgement on the commitment of each country to the accession process. They contribute strongly to the momentum of political, economic, institutional, and legal reforms in each of the candidate countries.

The basic task of a candidate country, and the basic aim of the accession negotiations, is to ensure the complete and timely adoption and implementation of the *acquis*. The task of checking compliance with the *acquis* in a candidate country is in the end similar to that of checking implementation of a new directive in an existing Member State. As this is one of the Commission's core competencies, it is well placed to apply its monitoring expertise to the pre-accession preparations by candidate countries. The main difference is that candidate countries must not only put in place new *acquis* but also catch up with whatever existing Member States have put in place over the past years and decades. Monitoring 'old' *acquis* has posed a challenge even for the Commission as its institutional attention has shifted to new tasks once older *acquis* had become a reality in the existing EU.

(*d*) The Commission prepares and proposes the EU's common positions during the accession negotiations. The subject matter of accession negotiations is vast. It is as large as the entire body of EU *acquis*, built up over decades. Member State negotiators, or even a group of Commission negotiators, would not be able themselves to undertake this task without the support of the entire spectrum of expertise in each of the Commission's departments. Many negotiating issues, be it waste water treatment or the size of fish which may be caught locally, are more technical than political.

Beyond its undisputed technical expertise, the Commission also plays an important political role largely due to its institutional position. Although the Commission acts outside the formal confines of the intergovernmental conference it has a clear and recognized responsibility within the EU, in both its present and future composition. In this capacity, the Commission advises both the Member States and the candidate countries on the feasibility of their positions, taking into account the requirements of the *acquis* and the specificities of each situation, quite similarly to a discussion on internal policies.

Although the Commission is rarely asked to negotiate *on behalf of* the Council, in practice it pre-negotiates most issues with the candidate countries. The Commission encourages candidate countries to submit acceptable positions to the EU, which it can support in Council. A firm Commission stance in favour of a tabled position helps to prevent divisive discussions among Member States and to focus discussions on the EU *acquis* rather than possible special interests. On the most political dossiers, the Commission would act in agreement with the presidency or, when the presidency decides to take the lead (such as in the end-game negotiations), in support of the presidency. For the key aspect of negotiations *among* Member States, the driving seat is occupied mostly by the presidency but the Commission works closely together with successive presidencies, as the navigator who delivers the necessary ideas and proposals at the right time.

The Commission is neutral in arbitrating the specific interests of existing and prospective Member States and, within the limits of its duty to uphold the basic principles of the EU, it is able to play a key role as an honest, and therefore trusted, broker. This is certainly the case in the relationship between the candidate country and the EU.

(*e*) Finally, at the strategic policy level, the Commission ensure a degree of continuity in a process that turned out to span eleven presidencies, from Luxembourg in 1997 to Copenhagen in 2002. The strategy papers which the Commission publishes every autumn based on the country progress reports referred to above are particularly influential in setting the enlargement agenda. They inform the December European Council meetings where the main political decisions on enlargement have traditionally been taken. Perhaps the most celebrated example is the Commission's proposal in autumn 2000 of a road map for completing accession negotiations over a two-year period with those countries which are ready. This proposal was endorsed by the European Council of December 2000 and successfully implemented, leading to the conclusion of negotiations with ten countries in December 2002.

Although the political impetus for the enlargement process comes from the Member States and in particular from the European Council, and despite the intergovernmental set-up of the accession negotiations, one may conclude that the Commission's de facto role is more typical of the 'Community method': the Commission proposes, the Council decides, and the Commission implements, controls, and evaluates.

2. THE ENLARGEMENT DIRECTORATE

In 1998, following the decision to open intergovernmental conferences and start accession negotiations with six countries, the Commission set up a task force known as TFNA (Task-force Négociations d'Adhésion). The mandate of this temporary body is to deliver the Commission's input into the intergovernmental process. For this purpose, TFNA coordinates and ensures overall control of negotiation work within the Commission. Although TFNA has only a few dozen staff, its head has the rank of Director General both for reasons of protocol vis-à-vis the candidate countries and to ensure effective lines of command within the Commission. Indeed, TFNA would rely strongly on the other Commission services, the 'line Directorates General', to provide the expertise for accession negotiations in each chapter of the *acquis*.

The German former Commission spokesperson Nikolaus van der Pas was chosen to head TFNA, under the political control of Commissioner Hans van den Broek. TFNA is modelled on similar bodies created for previous enlargements, notably the recent enlargement involving Austria, Finland, and Sweden. Several TFNA staff were involved in those negotiations and were able to transfer relevant know-how to this new round of enlargement negotiations.

Alongside TFNA, the Directorate General responsible for the countries concerned—known as Directorate General IA—continues to manage bilateral relations and assistance programmes as it has done for a number of years. Most candidate countries are beneficiaries of the PHARE assistance programme and are linked to the EU by far-reaching association agreements known as Europe agreements. Directorate General IA is also responsible for the Commission's delegations in the countries concerned.

The Prodi Commission, which took office in September 1999, created for the first time a post of Commissioner for Enlargement as a reflection of the political importance and of the unprecedented scale and complexity of the ongoing enlargement process. The first Commissioner to occupy this post was the former German Minister for European Affairs Günter Verheugen. The Prodi Commission decided to merge TFNA and Directorate General IA into a single Directorate General for Enlargement headed by the Spanish former Director General responsible for regional policy and Structural Funds Eneko Landaburu.

Commissioner Verheugen can thus rely on a single Directorate General whose mission and portfolio coincides with his own. The merger also reflects a shift in the focus of the accession process from diplomatic negotiations to a much broader-based preparation process. Most countries of the fifth enlargement have developed separate legal and economic systems over several decades and the adjustment to the EU regime is very demanding, particularly when compared to the preceding enlargement involving Austria, Finland, and Sweden. The accession process cannot be limited to negotiations on specific technicalities of the *acquis* and has to encompass a comprehensive transition process. Accordingly, the pace of progress in the accession negotiations proper is determined to a large extent by progress on the ground, in adopting and applying EU standards. In the very broadest sense, the accession process thus includes, besides progress on the *acquis*, efforts to implement correctly and successfully the association agreement with the EU, to improve the respect of the Copenhagen political and economic criteria, to upgrade public administration and the judiciary, and to promote these changes and adjustments by making full use of the EU's financial instruments PHARE, ISPA, and SAPARD.

As a result, the Commission's activity focuses predominantly on helping and monitoring the preparation of a candidate country to bring about this transition. Commissioner Verheugen's mission statement of 2001, as implemented by DG Enlargement, reflects these priorities:

- smooth conduct of the accession negotiations towards their closure with those candidates who have completed their preparation and are ready to assume membership responsibilities.
- efficient implementation of the pre-accession strategies.
- optimal use of financial instruments.
- continue the deployment of a communications strategy aimed at creating support for the enlargement process in the Member States and in the applicant countries.

Two dedicated instruments are created for the specific purpose helping candidate countries build the institutions needed to apply the *acquis*. First, in 1996 a special service is set up—the Technical Assistance and Information Exchange instrument (TAIEX)—to provide centrally managed short-term technical assistance by making EU legislation available along with the necessary appropriate tailor-made expert advice and training on its application, implementation, and enforcement. TAIEX is managed by Directorate General Enlargement. The peer-to-peer assistance from Member State experts over this period amounts to over 5,000 seminars, workshops, meetings, and exchanges and reaches over 100,000 officials in the candidate countries. The counterparts are not only those officials in the central administrations dealing with the drafting of legislation, but also those involved in the implementation and enforcement of legislation, namely at subnational level and in associations of local authorities, and for example parliaments and legislative councils, the judiciary and law enforcement authorities, private associations.

The second new instrument is 'twinning'. Launched in May 1998, twinning provides the framework for administrations and semi-public organizations in the candidate countries to work directly with their counterparts in Member States, notably through the long-term secondment of experts and practitioners from the Member States. The nature of the EU legal system is such that the implementation of most EU laws rests entirely with the national administrations of the Member States, who are thus best placed to help the candidate countries develop the structures, human resources, and management skills needed to implement the *acquis* to the same standards as Member States. In the period 1998–2004, around

700 twinning projects helped the ten candidate countries to implement specific areas of the *acquis* on the basis of a detailed work programme.

The success of both TAIEX and the twinning approach is increasingly being extended to other areas of Commission activity, such as the European Neighbourhood Policy.

In line with the mission statement referred to above, Directorate General Enlargement invests considerable resources in information activities. A specific communication strategy is developed to explain why the Union is undertaking its largest and most ambitious enlargement so far, and what the consequences of this step are likely to be. It targets citizens both in current and future Member States. Actions are undertaken through the media and in partnership with local government and civil society. The Commission's delegations in each of the candidate countries, together with a network of information and documentation centres spread throughout the countries, play a key role in making Europe accessible and understandable for citizens in the candidate country. Particularly during the pre-accession period, the delegations are a major source of information in the local language.

This enlargement is significantly more resource-intensive than past enlargements. At the height of activity, Directorate General Enlargement directly employs approximately 400 staff. Hundreds more work in the Commission delegations in the candidate countries and several dozen staff in the different specialized Directorates General in the Commission are largely occupied with the enlargement dossier.

3. INTERNAL DECISION-MAKING: COOPERATION WITH THE OTHER DEPARTMENTS

Directorate General Enlargement has been *chef de file* for enlargement, meaning that it is overall in charge of the enlargement dossier. Nevertheless, as in other policy areas the Commission services operate in close consultation with each other, reflecting the collegiality of the college of Commissioners itself. All policy documents and reports are adopted in agreement with the other competent Directorates General using the Commission's elaborate system of inter-service consultation. In the large majority of cases agreement can be found at technical level; in other cases, the issues are taken up at a higher level, with the most important issues being resolved between Commissioners. The use of a simplified non-bureaucratic procedure for the preparation and adoption of draft EU common positions gives Directorate General Enlargement considerable leeway to decide the timing and content of negotiating positions. Nevertheless, this freedom is constrained by the fact that other Directorates General may ultimately take the issue to the college of Commissioners to be arbitrated by the Commission President. Also, because of the intergovernmental context, the possibility always exists that in case the Commission prevaricates, the presidency of the Council could bypass the Commission and work out its own solution.

Within Directorate General Enlargement, a system of checks and balances is used. For this purpose, responsibilities are distributed over a matrix structure where some officials are in charge of a specific policy area (for example, the agriculture chapter of the negotiations) and others are in charge of relations with a specific country. Negotiating positions are drafted by the chapter desks but consulted with the country desk, whereas the annual progress reports are drafted by the country desk but consulted with each of the chapter desks. Not only does this approach ensure that the specificities of each candidate country are properly taken into account within a consistent approach over time and between different countries; it also creates a mutual interdependence between officials, units, and directorates within Directorate General Enlargement which contributes to the smooth and efficient functioning of this 'single-issue' Directorate General. Moreover, the in-house expertise built up by the chapter desks in each of the Commission's policy areas and their close relationship with experts from other Directorates General helps Directorate General Enlargement to fulfil its role as *chef de file* and uphold its views where necessary even in the most technical areas.

The large EU assistance programme too is implemented primarily by Directorate General Enlargement and by the Commission delegations in the candidate countries, subject to consultation with other relevant Directorates General and to approval by the management committee consisting of the Member States. This is particularly the case for the PHARE programme; in other programmes such as SAPARD and ISPA, the Directorates General for Agriculture and for Regional Policy play a central role as these programmes prefigure existing internal EU programmes run by those Directorates General. Nevertheless, over the years, the management of assistance programmes has been devolved to the delegations and then to the beneficiary countries themselves, with the Commission departments in Brussels retaining responsibility for overall programming, financial control and auditing, and monitoring and evaluation.

In line with its internal role in the Commission, Directorate General Enlargement is the primary interlocutor of both the candidate countries and the Member States. As negotiations on a given topic intensify and as accession draws closer, the other Directorates General gradually increase their direct contacts with the candidate countries. In particular during the period following the signature of the Accession Treaty in April 2003 and until accession in May 2004, Directorate General Enlargement gradually hands over responsibility for managing relations in each policy area to the respective Directorates General and intervenes mostly where coordination is still required. After May 2004 the activity in relation to the ten new Member States focuses on the implementation and phasing out of the remaining specific assistance programmes, notably the PHARE programme and transition facility.

Where in the past accessions were largely an ad hoc event, involving mostly the negotiation of specific details related to the *acquis communautaire*, enlargement has become a large and complex undertaking involving significant human and financial resources within the Commission. The Commission closely accompanies candidate countries during their entire ten- to fifteen-year journey towards membership. Since 1998 and as long as there will be candidate countries, this will remain a permanent activity with the Commission. Since the ten countries joined in May 2004, Directorate General Enlargement has responsibility for countries in different stages of the process: acceding countries Bulgaria and Romania, candidate countries Turkey and Croatia, and the potential candidate countries of the western Balkans. Directorate General Enlargement represents the institutionalization of EU enlargement as a lasting feature of EU integration.

4. COREPER AND THE GENERAL AFFAIRS COUNCIL

In Brussels the initial examination of the draft common position takes place in the Council's working group on enlargement, based on instructions from capitals. The members of the enlargement group are diplomats, with a solid experience in Union affairs. They play a key role in the whole process, since the majority of the problems that might arise are solved in this group. For the individual members of the group this requires both a clear understanding of the interests of his or her country in each specific matter, and a willingness to reach agreement, both with the delegates from the other Member States and with candidates.

If problems arise in the course of the definition of the common position the matter is referred to the Committee of Permanent Representatives (COREPER). COREPER is the senior committee of officials in the Council framework. It is composed of the EU ambassadors from the Member States and a senior official from the Commission. When enlargement matters are being discussed, it will normally be the Director General responsible for Enlargement that represents the Commission. Referral to COREPER is rare in the initial stages of the negotiations, where the 'easy' chapters are examined. It becomes more frequent as negotiations move into more complicated areas. At that stage of the negotiations it also happens that the Commission informally consults COREPER before submitting its draft proposals on particularly delicate matters. The Committee of Permanent Representatives has a long tradition and experience in settling difficult issues. Each member of the Committee knows that if he is helpful on a matter of interest to others, they in term will be helpful to him, when he has a problem on another issue. An important *esprit de corps* exists between the members of the Committee. The permanent representative can have a considerable influence in her own capital, and might be able to convince her authorities back home to modify the national position, if it is holding up agreement.

If an issue cannot be settled it will be referred to the General Affairs Council, which meets once a month and is composed of the Member States' Foreign Ministers and a member of the Commission. Even in cases where ministers cannot solve the issue, their discussion can offer insights to the political issues at stake, which can be useful when officials renew their attempts to find a solution after the Council meeting.

The matter might even have to be raised to the level of the European Council. In the fifth enlargement this happened at the end of the negotiations. The Union's negotiation positions on a number of financial issues were only agreed after difficult negotiations at the level of heads of state or government.

Once the Member States have defined the common position the negotiations with the candidate can be opened.

The negotiations normally begin at deputy (ambassador) level. The President of COREPER, who is assisted by the Director General of the Commission, leads the Union delegation. The other members of COREPER (or more often the members of the enlargement group) are present, but do not normally intervene in the discussions.

Negotiations also take place at ministerial level with the EU being presented by the members of the General Affairs Council as well as the Commissioner responsible for Enlargement. The candidates are represented by the minister appointed by each Member State for conducting the negotiations at ministerial level. Results of the negotiations on deputy level must be confirmed at the ministerial level. During each presidency, at least one meeting at deputy level as well as one meeting at ministerial level will take place. The conferences can even be held at the level of heads of state and government. This happened at the end of European Council in Copenhagen in December 2002.

The outcome of the negotiations on a particular chapter can be one of the following:

- All issues within the chapter are settled and the chapter is provisionally closed. This implies that at the present stage, there is no need for further negotiations. This can change over time, when the Union adopts new legislation in the same area that has to be taken over by the candidate. The chapter can also be reopened if the candidate does not conform to the obligations agreed earlier, for instance on the establishment of the necessary administrative capacity or adoption of planned legislation.
- When supplementary information or negotiations are needed, the chapter remains open.

Most of the enlargement conferences are of a purely formal character, characterized by the reading out of statements prepared in advance. Little real negotiation takes place in these formal meetings. The conferences nevertheless are useful, as they permit to register progress in the negotiations. The dates set for these meetings are important as target dates for adjusting positions and settling issues. At the same time they are the occasion for both the candidate countries and the Union representatives (the presidency and the Commission), in their general presentation at the start of the meeting, to convey messages to the other side on questions of particular importance.

Most of the real negotiations take place behind the scenes, in meetings between representatives from the candidate countries (often the chief negotiator) and the

Commission and/or the presidency. Frequently, direct contacts take place between a candidate country and a Member State with a particular concern, which is not shared by others, in order to find a bilateral solution which other Member States could find acceptable. Even more important are the negotiations that take place in capitals of the candidate countries. Often the chief negotiator or his team will be engaged in explaining the EU rules back home and try to convince the various parts of the national administration of the need for change. Most chief negotiators in the enlargement negotiations that have taken place will probably concur with the thesis that 90 per cent of enlargement negotiations happens at home.

5. THE MECHANISM OF ACCESSION NEGOTIATIONS

The first formal step in the accession procedure is the submission from the interested country of an application. Normally the next step is the acknowledgement by the Council of the application and a request to the Commission to prepare the opinion in the candidature as required by the treaty.

The Commission's opinion is a very detailed and thorough analysis of the economic and political situation in the candidate country. In order to prepare an opinion, intensive consultations take place between the candidate and the Commission. The opinion can run to several hundred pages, and provides an important source of information and analysis. It constitutes an important tool for the negotiations that follow. The opinion ends up with a conclusion as to the opening of accession negotiations. It is then up to the Council to decide when membership negotiations can start.

When deciding the launch of accession negotiations, the Council establishes at the same time the 'negotiation framework', which sets out the negotiation procedures to be followed. A key element in this framework is the establishment of the basic principle that 'nothing is agreed until everything has been agreed'.

The procedures and mechanism of the accession process have been developed over the years through the experience acquired in connection with the several rounds of enlargement negotiations in which the Union has been engaged over the past three decades.

The purpose of the accession negotiations is to define the terms and conditions under which each of the candidate countries will accede to the EU. The basis for accession is the *acquis* of the Union, that is the combined set of rules, regulations, and practices (including those established as case law by the EC Court of Justice) applied by the Union at the time of entry. While it is accepted that transition periods of limited duration may be necessary in certain justified cases, the objective of the Union is that the candidate applies the *acquis* on accession.

For practical reasons the negotiations are divided into chapters, representing the various parts of the *acquis*.

The negotiations in the fifth enlargement were based on the following list of chapters:

1. Free movement of goods
2. Freedom of movement for persons
3. Freedom to provide services
4. Free movement of capital
5. Company law
6. Competition policy
7. Agriculture
8. Fisheries
9. Taxation
10. Transport policy
11. Economic and monetary union (EMU)
12. Statistics
13. Social policy and employment
14. Energy
15. Industrial policy
16. Small and medium-sized enterprises (SMEs)
17. Science and research
18. Education and training
19. IT and telecommunication
20. Culture and audio-visual policy
21. Regional policy
22. Environment
23. Consumer and health protection
24. Justice and home affairs (JHA)
25. Customs union
26. External relations
27. Common foreign and security policy (CAP)
28. Financial control
29. Budget
30. Institutions
31. Miscellaneous

The enlargement negotiations always start with an analytical examination (called 'screening') by the Commission of the *acquis* for each chapter and the content of the relevant Union's legislation. The presentation is made to all the candidates that have embarked on the negotiations, at joint meetings. Subsequently, separate meetings are held with each candidate. At those meetings the candidates present their own relevant legislation and identify what changes are necessary in order to conform to the Union's rules and regulations, possibly after a period of transition.

In practice the 'screening' starts with a detailed presentation of the *acquis* by the Commission of the content of the Union's legislation. This multilateral part is followed by bilateral meetings with each candidate country, at which the applicant states are asked to set out whether they have in place the laws necessary to comply with community rules, or when they intend to introduce such legislation. Where necessary, the candidates will state that they intend to request transitional arrangements in the chapter under examination. The question of administrative structures and capacity is also examined. The candidates are asked to indicate whether they posses the administrative structures and other capacity needed to implement and enforce the Union's rules and regulations. Where capacity does not exist, they are asked to set out a time frame for putting such capacity into place.

The screening process provides the raw material for the negotiations that follow. It gives the Commission the basis for reporting to the Member States on problems which are likely to arise in the negotiations, and for its preparation of negotiation positions to be submitted in the course of the negotiations. Following the screening of each chapter with a country, the Commission presents a report to the Council indicating the main findings, including possible problems and potential requests for transitional periods.

Before negotiations can start on an individual chapter each side has to define its negotiation position. After completing the screening of a chapter, and normally after an informal invitation from the EU side, the candidate country will formulate a negotiation position. In this position the candidate explains how it intends to conform with the *acquis*, which changes to its laws will be carried out, as well as how and when its administration will be in a position to actually implement the rules. Any requests for transitional periods must be accompanied by a clear timetable for application of the *acquis*.

On the EU side, the Commission proposes draft common negotiation positions for each chapter and for each country, except for the chapters on common foreign and security policy, and on justice and home affairs cooperation. For these latter chapters the Council presidency 'in close liaison with the Member States and the Commission' is responsible for submitting proposals.[2]

The draft EU common position for each country sets out an 'action plan' and a timetable for the adoption and implementation of the *acquis* by the candidates, including the suggested response to requests for transitional periods, in cases where the implementation of the *acquis* will not be fully accomplished by the time of entry. It covers as well the question of administrative structures and other capacity needed to implement and enforce EU rules effectively. It enumerates questions that require supplementary clarification before proceeding further. The request for transitional periods can come from both the candidate and the Union. The candidate might need time to implement the *acquis* in national law or administrative practice. The existing Member States might want to reduce competitive pressure immediately after enlargement, by requesting transitional

[2] Even though the presidency is formally responsible for preparing the draft of the common position on Home and Justice Affairs it is in practice the Commission that does the work which the individual EU Home and Justice Ministers follow closely. During the fifth enlargement, a special evaluation mechanism was established. The evaluation included special visits by the presidency and the Commission to the candidate countries, and the sharing of information between Member States.

arrangements in particular sensitive sectors. During the fifth enlargement several requests for transitional periods came from the Union.

The draft is then submitted for examination by the individual national authorities of the Member States. This examination often involves consultation of technical ministries and interest groups. The national process also includes internal arbitration between on the one side the technical and economic interests and on the other side overall political considerations, including the national approach to the enlargement process. A Member State that desires to slow down the adhesion process can in theory draw out the technical examination. Despite the varying political sensitivities which existed in the Member States throughout the whole process of the fifth enlargement, there were however very few examples of such filibustering tactics. One of the characteristics of the Union machinery is that once it gets into motion it is in practice difficult to stop, and the political costs involved in working against the common objectives are great.

6. THE NEGOTIATIONS FRAMEWORK

The EU formally adopted this framework early in 1998 following a draft attached to the General Affairs Council's report to the Luxembourg European Council. It was based on texts drawn up in 1992 for the previous enlargement, but due to the unique nature of the fifth enlargement and the development of the EU since 1992, it diverted from this precedent in important ways. The ten Central and Eastern European countries came from a significantly different background from countries in earlier enlargements, particularly the last one with the EFTA countries. Special attention had to be given to the applicant countries' political, economic, administrative, and judicial systems to ensure that the *acquis* was not just transposed into national legislation, but that the administrations and national judiciaries were also able to implement and apply the rules.

The general framework stated the basic principle—valid for all previous enlargements—that accession implied the full acceptance by the applicant country of the actual and potential rights and obligations derived from accession to the Union system and its institutional framework (the *acquis*). The new Member States would have to apply this as it stood at the time of accession, and they had to come into line with the *acquis* before accession. Accession also implied effective implementation of the *acquis* by the applicant country, which required the establishment of an efficient, reliable public administration.

The acceptance of these rights and obligations by a new Member State might give rise to technical adjustments and exceptionally to non-permanent transitional measures, but could in no way involve amendments to the rules or policies of the EU, disrupt their proper functioning, or lead to significant distortions of competition. Any transitional measures would have to be limited in time and scope and accompanied by a plan with clearly defined stages for application of the *acquis*. Account would be taken of the interests of the EU as well as the candidate countries. It would be up to the Member States to decide in due course whether conditions were right for the conclusion of negotiations.

Any view expressed by either party on a chapter of the negotiations would in no way prejudge the position on other chapters. Agreements reached during the course of negotiations could not be considered final until an overall agreement had been established.

As decided by the European Council, progress in negotiations would depend not only on the applicants taking over the *acquis*, but also on their fulfilment of the Copenhagen and Madrid criteria. The EU stressed the need for administrative and judicial capacity as well as actual implementation of the acquis to a much higher degree than it had in earlier enlargements. Previously, adoption of the necessary legislation to bring national law into compliance with the *acquis* had been considered the most important part of a country's preparation. Now the focus shifted. Certainly, national law would have to be brought into line with the *acquis*. But candidates would also have to convince the EU that they possessed efficient and reliable administrations and judiciaries which would be able to ensure correct implementation and application of the many rules.

The unprecedented scale of the negotiations also led the EU to highlight the principle of differentiation. Negotiations with the different applicant countries would be conducted on the basis of the same principles and criteria, but separately and according to the individual merits of each applicant country. Their progress and conclusion were not required to take place in parallel.

To avoid applicants in the first wave blocking progress with countries in the second wave, the EU demanded acceptance by each applicant country of the principle that its application formed part of the inclusive process established by the European Council.

The prospect of a large enlargement led the EU to underline that it should be capable of absorbing new members, while maintaining the momentum of European integration. Every effort should be made to ensure that the institutional structures of the Union were not weakened or diluted.

Finally, the general framework contained provisions on organization and procedure of the accession conferences, in particular that the presidency of the EU would chair the meetings, that the Council secretariat would act as secretariat for the conferences, and that the negotiations would be conducted with each applicant on its own merits.

The general framework was presented to each of the six countries which started negotiations in bilateral accession conferences on 31 March 1998.[3]

It was the British Foreign Minister Robin Cook who opened each intergovernmental conference with the first six candidate countries. His statement included, *inter alia*, the principles of negotiation which became the framework for the negotiations with the then six negotiating countries.

[3] An identical text, only adjusted slightly to take account of new *acquis*, was presented to the six other countries at the first meetings of the accession conferences in February 1999.

Accession implied full acceptance of the *acquis* of the Union. It has to be applied, implemented, and enforced upon accession, which requires in particular the establishment of an efficient, reliable public administration. The *acquis* is made up of the entirety of EU legislation (some 80,000 pages). It is the shared foundation of rights and obligations binding on all Member States of the European Union and covers:

- the content, principles and political objectives of the treaties;
- legislation adopted pursuant to the treaties, and the case law of the Court of Justice;
- statements and resolutions adopted within the Union framework;
- joint actions, common positions, declarations, conclusions, and other acts within the framework of the common foreign and security policy;
- joint actions, joint positions, conventions signed, resolutions, statements, and other acts agreed within the framework of justice and home affairs;
- international agreements concluded by the Community and those concluded among themselves by the Member States with regard to Union activities.

The resulting rights of the application of the *acquis* cover a wide field, including the free movement of goods, services, capital, and persons as provided for in the EC Treaty. Moreover, they imply the termination of all existing bilateral agreements and of all other international agreements which are incompatible with the obligation of membership.

The *acquis* also includes all the commitments entered into under policies pursued by the Union externally. It is required to take on the Common Commercial Policy. The requirement to become a member of the European Economic Area is foreseen.

Finally it was pointed out that new members will be required to take on all the obligations of the Community and its Member States in these areas, including that of contributing to the European Development Fund.

In the candidate countries the first important step was the designation of the team that would be responsible for the negotiations with the Union, and in particular the chief negotiator. The chief negotiator would be in charge of the day-to-day negotiations with the Union. In some cases the negotiators were replaced during the process, but most remained throughout. The chief negotiators in the enlargement negotiations have normally been senior civil servants from the capital. This was also the case for seven out of the ten countries in the first wave of the fifth enlargement. In two cases they were politicians, and in one case the EU ambassador also had the title of chief negotiator.[4]

[4] The following chief negotiators were appointed:
Cyprus: George Vassiliou, former president of the Republic
Czech Republic: Pavel Telicka, career diplomat
Estonia: Alar Streimann, senior civil servant in the Ministry of Foreign Affairs
Hungary: Endre Juhasz, ambassador to the EU
Latvia: Andris Ķesteris, career diplomat, state secretary in the Ministry of Foreign Affairs

7. THE FIRST STEPS: FROM THE BEGINNING TO THE FINNISH PRESIDENCY

The screening process for the six 'first-wave' candidate countries started immediately after the opening of the enlargement negotiations in April 1998, and was concluded in July 1999.[5] Before the completion of the process, negotiations had started up on chapters examined early on in the screening process.

As agreed by the Luxembourg European Council a similar 'screening' exercise was conducted with the other candidate countries with whom negotiations had not been opened. At the start the Commission only intended to carry out the multilateral part of the process ('the explanation'), but later on agreed to do the full screening, including the bilateral part. The screening process for these five 'second-wave' countries began early in 1999 and was largely finalized by the end of that year.

The first few months from the formal start of the accession negotiation in March 1998 saw only limited progress in the actual negotiations, as screening of the first chapters had to be conducted, and principles for the first EU common positions had to be agreed. Furthermore, the Commission and most Member States were more focused on getting agreement on the financial perspectives than on seeing rapid progress in accession negotiations. From November on, the negotiations started for real. Seven of the easier chapters were first in line. They concerned (1) science and research, (2) telecommunications and information technology, (3) education and training, (4) culture and audio-visual Policy, (5) industrial policy, (6) small and medium-sized enterprises, and (7) common foreign and security policy. For the majority of the seven chapters the applicant countries indicated that they could accept the *acquis* and would be in a position to apply it by the date of accession. Most applicants based their position on the working hypotheses that they would join the European Union on 1 January 2003, while Hungary used 1 January 2002 as the target date.

Due to their nature, most of these chapters were easy. They contained only limited 'hard' *acquis*, which had to be transposed into national legislation, and in general required no extensive national administrative structures. Most discussion within the EU focused on finding general language for the common positions, which could serve as a precedent for future texts.

Two issues emerged as the most controversial ones among Member States. Monitoring of progress in the candidate countries, which did not figure prominently

Lithuania: Petras Austrevicius, carreer diplomat
Malta: Richard Cachia Caruana, chief of staff in Prime Minister's office
Poland: Until 2001 Jan Kułakowski, former ambassador to the EU, followed by Jan Truszczynski, also former ambassador to the EU
Slovakia: Ján Figel' politician
Slovenia: Janez Potočnik, former Professor of Economics.

[5] Throughout the negotiations new screening meetings between each candidate country and the Commission were organized to take account of new *acquis*.

in the general negotiation framework, became fundamental to many Member States. In the light of the unprecedented scale of the enlargement process and the Central and Eastern European countries' background, a particular monitoring mechanism had to be established so that Member States—and not just the Commission—could feel confident that preparations progressed as planned in the accession countries. The result was a formula whereby the accession countries' fulfilment of their obligations would be monitored not just through the Commission's yearly regular reports, but also within the framework of the Europe agreements, where numerous meetings would provide ample opportunity to keep track of progress or any lack thereof.

The second controversial issue related to the formula for closure of chapters. The principle that nothing was agreed until everything was agreed had already been established, but how would the EU indicate that a chapter was closed? Some Member States preferred a text which would allow Member States to return to any chapter easily, while others wanted more firm assurances that the process could not be dragged on indefinitely through frequent reopening. In the end, Member States agreed on the formulation: 'the EU notes that, at this stage, this chapter does not require further negotiation.' For some time, not all Member States accepted that this actually meant provisional closure of a chapter. But as the negotiations progressed, this reality became apparent, and in spite of much talk about reopening chapters, the EU did not demand the reopening of a single chapter for any other reason than new *acquis.*

Two of the supposedly easy chapters proved surprisingly difficult. Concerning common foreign and security policy, the issue of Cyprus (even though it was not formally raised by any Member State in this connection) prevented the chapter from being closed. Only after the European Council in Helsinki (see Chapter 8) were Member States able to overcome this problem, and the chapter was easily closed in early 2000. Concerning audio-visual policy, only Cyprus had adopted the directive on television without frontiers. The Commission, supported by some Member States, insisted that this legislation had to be adopted before the chapter could be closed. Assurances that this would happen before accession were not sufficient. As a result of this unusually strict approach, the chapter was not closed with most candidate countries until 2000 or 2001, and it was one of the last chapters to be closed with Hungary in 2002.

All candidates were able to quickly close the chapters on science and research, on education and training, as well as on small and medium-sized enterprises. Industrial policy proved only marginally more difficult with Cyprus closing immediately and the other countries during 1999, while telecommunication and information technology was closed with five countries during 1999 and with Hungary in 2000.

Finally, it should be noted that the objective of a high level of nuclear safety was also mentioned in the framework. Throughout the negotiations, this issue tuned out to be one of the more politically sensitive areas, as the *acquis* did not contain any definition of such a level, and Member States' interests differed widely.

4

From Helsinki to Seville, July 1999–June 2002

Poul Skytte Christoffersen

1. THE HELSINKI EUROPEAN COUNCIL: A NEW DIRECTION FOR THE ENLARGEMENT PROCESS

The year 1999 was important for the enlargement process in many respects: the financial framework for enlargement was agreed in Berlin in the early spring and the Union decided to tackle, as the next step, the institutional questions linked to enlargement.

In the Commission an important change of the guard took place. A new Commission under the presidency of Romano Prodi took office in the fall, replacing the Santer Commission. In formal terms the Commission has only a limited role in the enlargement process. In reality it is the most important actor. The attitude of the Commission, and in particular of its President and of the Commissioner responsible for enlargement, is crucial. The Santer Commission and the Commissioner responsible Hans van den Broek had carried forward the process with diligence in accordance to the orientations of the European Council, but without any great hurry. The Prodi Commission made enlargement a top priority for its term of office, and with the new Commissioner Günter Verheugen the candidate countries gained a fervent advocate for enlargement, and at the same time a person well trusted by the Member States.

Negotiations were gradually moving ahead: new chapters were opened.

During the German presidency the chapters on company law, free movement of goods, consumer protection, fisheries, statistics, external relations, customs union, and competition policy were opened. Under the Finnish presidency, the chapters on economic and monetary union, energy, environment, free movement of capital, free movement of services, social policy, taxation, and transport followed. As many of these chapters required much new legislation, adjustment of trade agreements, and extensive administrative capacity, their provisional closure naturally became more difficult.

Consumer and health protection, economic and monetary union, as well as statistics were the easiest chapters, and they were closed with everyone during the course of the year. The land-locked countries of Hungary and the Czech Republic also quickly closed the chapter on fisheries. But that was the end of the simple chapters.

Company law covered the complex issue of intellectual property rights, which included the fields of pharmaceutical products. Even though candidates presented only few and very limited requests for transitional periods concerning free movement of goods, implementing the rules, particularly on certification, posed a huge challenge for national administrations. In the chapter on customs union, several candidates wished to keep free trade agreements with some of the non-EU countries to which they had historical links. Competition policy demanded adherence to the strict *acquis* on state aid, an area which proved particularly problematic for countries with an economic legacy (sometimes including large state-owned and subsidized steel mills) from the years under communist rule, and which had attracted investors during the 1990s through the promise of tax breaks and the establishment of special economic zones.

The chapter on transport included the issues of road cabotage, where some Member States feared unfair competition from candidates. Maritime safety was a major public concern in several member countries due to the risk from outdated oil tankers. Taxation raised a number of questions concerning the implementation of the directive on VAT, and most candidates requested some transitional periods in this area as well as transitional periods for phasing in the required excise duties on cigarettes.

The chapter on social policy and employment led to a number of requests for transitional periods on work equipment and working time. The *acquis* on energy included rules on the building up of oil stocks which candidates could ill afford. It also demanded liberalization of the energy sector. The chapter on free movement of services demanded the establishment of an effective regulatory infrastructure, in particular to supervise the financial sector, and it placed new burdens on the countries' financial institutions which led to the request for transitional arrangements. Most candidates required extensive transitional periods for the chapter on free movement of capital as far as acquisition of real estate was concerned. And the chapter on the environment included a vast number of requests for transitional periods as the candidates did not possess the financial means for fulfilling the strict *acquis* in this area from day one of accession. Furthermore, the *acquis* on water, industrial pollution control, chemicals, and nature protection required the establishment of new administrative structures.

The process was growing increasingly complex. The need for dealing with the really difficult issues of transitional periods became obvious. Beginning with the overall report to the European Council in Luxembourg in 1997, the Commission submitted annual reports to the Member States on each candidate country's progress towards accession. These reports became a crucial instrument in the enlargement process. A detailed report was prepared on each of the candidate countries, setting out the status for preparation for enlargement. An overall report—the composite paper—contained the overall picture and the general conclusions.

The 1999 composite paper reflected the new attitude in the Commission. It proposed to the European Council a new approach to the enlargement process:

- The Commission proposed to open enlargement negotiations with all of the candidate countries. This meant that accession negotiations were to be also opened with Bulgaria, Malta, Latvia, Lithuania, Romania, and Slovakia. For each of the candidates particular reasons indicated this choice. In the case of Malta the Nationalist Party had once more replaced the Labour Party in government and had taken Malta's application for adhesion out of the freezer. Latvia and Lithuania had made important progress in their preparation for membership, including privatization, and had coped effectively with the crises in the aftermath of the breakdown of the Soviet Union. And Lithuania had agreed to close the Ignalina nuclear power plant, which could not be upgraded to European safety levels. In Slovakia a change in government had occurred and the new government was pursuing an ambitious programme of democratic reform. The country could now be considered to meet the Copenhagen political criteria. Furthermore, the Slovak government had agreed to close down its non-upgradable nuclear power plant Bohunice. In the case of Romania and Bulgaria the Commission was conscious of the fact that the two countries still had very important progress to make in order to become functioning market economies (in particular in the case of Romania). However both countries had suffered from the Kosovo crisis and needed the encouragement of the perspective of enlargement to promote and sustain internal reform. The recommendation to open negotiations with these two countries was conditional upon a promise from Bulgaria to close down the non-upgradable nuclear power plant Kozloduy, and for Romania to provide resources for a reform of its orphanages. Both countries fulfilled the conditions during the following months. For all of these 'second-wave' candidates, a risk existed that encouragement for progress towards accession would slow down after the end of 2000, unless new steps were taken. In accordance with the Luxembourg conclusions they had all been engaged in the '*acquis* screening' in parallel with the 'first-wave' countries. But the end of 1999 would terminate this process, which had been an important catalyst for internal preparation.
- The Commission was conscious of the risks inherent in enlarging the group of countries, in particular with those that were still far away from meeting the conditions of enlargement. It could create a precedent for future accessions. It could lead to a certain relaxation in the efforts to prepare for enlargement in those countries that had already started negotiations. Finally the negotiation process risked becoming very long for the weakest candidates. To counter these risks the Commission proposed greater differentiation between countries in the enlargement negotiations. It suggested what appeared to be more stringent rules for 'provisionally closing' chapters. Greater stress should be put on the actual preparation in the candidate countries, and no chapter should be closed unless the EU was satisfied that the candidate's preparation was in line with its commitments in terms of preparation for accession. In reality, though, this provision was not as stringent as it seemed. Only the easiest chapters had been closed provisionally

so far, and even among these the EU had demanded actual adoption of the required legislation before offering provisional closure of culture and audio-visual policy. Through its new language the Commission managed to appear strict while in fact ensuring that actual legislation did not have to be in place in order for a chapter to be closed. It established the principle that chapters from now on would be provisionally closed on the basis of *credible commitments*. The Commission suggestion to stress differentiation in the opening of chapters proved more important in the negotiations which followed. This meant that not all candidates would open chapters at the same time, as had been the case for the first wave. Now, the EU would only open a chapter for negotiations when conditions in each candidate country could be considered ripe for such a move.

- The Commission furthermore proposed a set of principles for transitional periods. For the areas linked to the single market the *acquis* should be implemented quickly, and any transitional periods should be few and short. For those areas of the *acquis* where considerable adaptations were necessary and which required substantial effort, including important financial outlays (such as environment, energy, and infrastructure), the EU could be more open towards allowing transitional arrangements. Even though the European Council did not endorse this part of the Commission's suggestions, the principles became, in practice, the basis for future deliberations on transitional periods.
- Finally the Commission suggested setting a target date for the conclusion of the negotiations. Various dates had been on the table for entry. Agenda 2000 operated with the year 2002. All the candidate countries that had started negotiations had fixed for themselves a target date for entry (2002 or 2003). The Commission did not propose an entry date, but stated its evaluation that it was possible to conclude negotiations with the most advanced countries in 2002.

The approach towards Turkey was another essential ingredient in the Commission's suggestion for the Helsinki meeting of the European Council. By opening negotiations with the remaining six countries, Turkey would become more isolated, if nothing else were done. Turkey had submitted its application for EU membership earlier than any of the countries which already were or soon would be engaged in negotiations. Turkey had a long-standing association agreement with the Union (dating back to 1963), in which the EU had referred to the possibility of Turkish membership. At several occasions over the years the EU had recognized Turkey's European vocation and its eligibility for accession. Time had now come, according to the Commission, to regard Turkey as a candidate for accession, in the same way as the twelve countries had been recognized as candidate countries by the European Council in Copenhagen. To place Turkey in a similar framework would include:

- The establishment of a pre-accession strategy, involving coordination of all EU financial assistance for pre-accession within a single framework.

- The opening up of the possibility of full participation of Turkey in all Community programmes and agencies.
- Adoption of an accession partnership with Turkey combined with a national programme for the adoption of the *acquis*, and the establishment of mechanisms to monitor the implementation of the accession partnership.

To the Commission it was clear that Turkey did not fulfil the political criteria laid down in Copenhagen. Human rights, the Kurdish problem, the lack of political control over the armed forces were some of the main problems. At the same time it was in the interest of Europe to have a stable Europe-oriented Turkey. It was time to move from a stage where the European vocation of Turkey was recognized, to one where Europe actively engaged with Turkey working towards the fulfilment of these criteria. A close and confident cooperation should also facilitate the solution to one of the major important outstanding issues in the enlargement negotiations: the reunification of Cyprus.

Both with regard to the new approach to the enlargement process and with regard to Turkey, the Commission's proposals were basically well received by the EU Member States, and the Commission's report became the basis for the conclusions of the European Council in Helsinki in December 1999. Four important decisions were taken with regard to the enlargement process:

- Enlargement negotiations with Bulgaria, Latvia, Lithuania, Malta, Romania, and Slovenia should begin in February 2000. The European Council underlined, in line with the Commission's new approach, that each candidate would be judged on its own merits. This principle would apply to the opening of chapters as well as to the conduct of negotiations. Candidate states in the second wave would have the possibility to catch up with those already in negotiations. The requirement not only to incorporate the *acquis* into legislation, but also to actually implement and enforce it, was reasserted.
- A target date was fixed. The European Council expressed itself in a more prudent way than the Commission and declared that 'the Union should be in a position to welcome new member states from the end of 2002'.
- The European Council affirmed that Turkey was 'a candidate country destined to join the Union on the basis of the same criteria as applied to the other candidate states'. Turkey like other candidate countries would benefit from a pre-adhesion strategy. With a view to intensifying the harmonization of Turkey's legislation and practice with the *acquis*, the Commission would prepare a process of analytical examination of the *acquis*. Even though the Luxembourg European Council had confirmed Turkey's eligibility for accession and had stated that Turkey would be judged on the basis of the same criteria as the other applicant states, a special strategy had been envisaged for this country, and it did not participate in the accession process. Now the EU unequivocally stated its intention to treat Turkey as a candidate country on an equal footing. There is no doubt that by this

wording the European Council had 'crossed the Rubicon' with regard to its engagement toward Turkey's adhesion to the Union.

- The recognition that the unification of Cyprus was no longer a precondition for accession of Cyprus to the Union. Until Helsinki most Member States had implicitly made the unification of the island a condition for accession. For Greece, however, the explicit elimination of this precondition was necessary to accept Turkey as a candidate country. Many also feared that Greece in any case would block any enlargement of the Union where Cyprus was kept from joining due to the division. It was also the expression of a recognition by the other Member States that it could be detrimental to the UN-sponsored talks on unification which all hoped soon would be on their way, if one party to the talks (Turkey) was given a veto on an EU enlargement with Cyprus.

2. THE PORTUGUESE PRESIDENCY: FIRST HALF OF 2000

The enlargement process had from the start been characterized by periods of rapid progress and periods where the movement slowed down. The year that followed the great sprint ahead, represented by Helsinki, was no exception to this law of alternations.

The attention of the Portuguese presidency in the first half of 2000 and the French presidency in the second were focused on the preparation for the Nice Treaty (see Chapter 6).

In particular the six countries that had started negotiations in November 1998 felt that their fear of a slowdown in the process after admitting six more countries to the process had been confirmed. The reason for the perceived slowdown was to be found elsewhere, however. The period of negotiations on easy chapters was over. The negotiation chapters now coming up for the more advanced candidates required more careful preparation by the Commission and by the Member States.

In February the first accession conferences with Malta, Slovakia, Latvia, Lithuania, Bulgaria, and Romania took place, and the EU presented its general negotiation framework. Substantial negotiations began in May.

Before the end of the year, sixteen chapters had been opened with Malta, Latvia, Lithuania, and Slovakia.[1] Bulgaria opened eleven[2] chapters and

[1] Freedom to provide services, free movement of capital, company law (not SK), competition policy, fisheries (not LT), transport policy (not M), EMU (not SK and LT), statistics, social policy and employment (only LT), industrial policy, small and medium-sized enterprises, science and research, education and training, telecommunication and information policy (not LV), culture and audio-visual policy, environment (only LT), consumer and health protection (not LT), customs union (only SK), external relations, CFSP.

[2] Free movement of capital, company law, statistics, small and medium-sized enterprises, science and research, education and training, telecommunication and information technology, culture and audio-visual policy, consumer and health protection, external relations, CFSP.

Romania nine.[3] Differentiation had become a reality not just in closing, but also in the opening stages. The position papers of Malta, Latvia, Lithuania, and Slovakia showed that these countries in general had no greater difficulties in implementing the *acquis* than many countries in the first wave, and that they did not request a larger number of transitional periods. On the contrary, Latvia and Lithuania, for instance, refrained from demanding transitional periods concerning acquisition of real estate. The chapter on competition policy also seemed easier for these two countries, as they—unlike Poland and the Czech Republic—had no coal or steel sector which needed restructuring, and—unlike Hungary and Poland—had not promised to companies that they would extend state aid that would be incompatible with the *acquis* beyond the accession date. Slovakia had embarked on an ambitious and successful programme of economic reform and legislative adjustment. Malta did not suffer from the legacy of communism and was consequently able to conclude a number of the easier chapters quickly. However, when the negotiations reached the more difficult chapters, the country's previous economic policy put it at a disadvantage in many respects, as it gave substantial state aid to its shipbuilding industry, had a sheltered agricultural sector, and had introduced a VAT system which differed significantly from the *acquis*.

Negotiations with the first-wave countries also progressed. By the end of the Portuguese presidency, the chapters on free movement of persons, agriculture, regional policy, JHA, and financial control as well as financial and budgetary provisions had been opened with these countries. Now all chapters except institutions and chapter 31 (other issues) were on the table. But the most important, and politically delicate, elements were still missing from the EU common positions.

On free movement of persons everyone expected the EU to ask for transitional periods, but at this stage Member States could agree to indicate that the mobility of workers was an area of special sensitivity to which the accession conferences would have to return. On regional policy the EU common positions only referred to the general principles of the *acquis* and did not include the actual amounts which candidates could receive.[4] However, the candidates would have to agree with the Commission on a provisional classification for the implementation of Structural Funds, demonstrate their programming capacity, and establish administrative structures. On agriculture—apart from direct payments—the candidates required a huge number of technical transitional periods as well as transitional periods for food establishments to upgrade to EU requirements. They also demanded quotas, base areas, and reference yields based either on potential production or on their most productive years in the late 1980s and early 1990s. The EU common positions did not react in substance to the demands but insisted

[3] Competition, statistics, small and medium-sized enterprises, science and research, education and training, telecommunication and information technology, culture and audio-visual policy, external relations, CFSP.

[4] The amounts would be dealt with under the chapter on budget during the final months of the negotiations.

that figures had to be based on historical production and requested information for production as well as base areas during years in the second half of the 1990s. The *acquis* on justice and home affairs placed huge demands on the candidates in the form of new administrative structures, the establishment of an efficient reliable and independent judiciary, and the strengthening of control on their new EU external borders. As in earlier enlargements, the lifting of internal border controls would not take place immediately upon accession, but would be subject to a separate Council decision at some time after accession. However, the candidates would have to present a Schengen action plan to demonstrate their preparedness and present a credible schedule for the introduction of the Schengen *acquis*. The chapter on budget, like the chapter on budget control, at this early stage of the negotiations focused on the candidates' administrative capacity.

In the autumn, the first chapter with transitional periods was closed provisionally. It was the chapter on services in the negotiations with Poland. The transitional periods were not spectacular—they concerned cooperative banks and investment companies—but the move marked a new milestone, although one which in the candidates' view was long overdue.

At the same time, some difficult subjects—not all directly part of the negotiations—caused problems. This, combined with the limited progress on tackling substantial requests for transitional periods, caused some nervousness among the first-wave countries. The issue of nuclear safety resurfaced as the Czech Republic started the first reactor on its new nuclear power plant Temelin in October. A meeting of the accession conference with the Czechs had to be postponed due to internal EU disagreement over the wording of the EU common position on energy. A bilateral agreement on the issue between the Czech Republic and Austria brokered by the Commission later in the year allowed the negotiations to continue, but did not solve the disagreement. To tackle the increasingly problematic issue of nuclear safety horizontally, COREPER in late 2000 decided to task an ad hoc working group to evaluate the situation in each candidate country.[5] Slovenia, otherwise one of the front runners, proved reluctant to close down its land border duty-free shops, which prevented it from closing several chapters. Political issues stemming from the end of the Second World War also resurfaced, even though they were not covered by the *acquis*. The Benes Decrees in the Czech Republic, which caused the expulsion of Germans and Austrians and the confiscation of their property in that country, and the Avnoj Decrees in Slovenia, which had similar effects for ethnic Germans in Slovenia, gave rise to criticism from some Member States, though others insisted they be kept outside the negotiations.

[5] The process eventually succeeded in depoliticizing the issue to a large degree. The report from the ad hoc working group was finalized in May 2001, and its recommendations on technical improvements and other necessary measures formed the basis for the EU common positions. As a follow-up, COREPER tasked the ad hoc working group with monitoring the candidate states' commitments through a peer-review process.

Still, the overall picture was fairly encouraging. By the end of the Portuguese presidency the list of provisionally closed chapters looked as follows.

Chapters provisionally closed by 30 June 2000:

Countries that started after Luxembourg	
Cyprus	16
Czech Republic	13
Estonia	13
Slovenia	12
Poland	11
Hungary	11

Countries that started after Helsinki	
Malta	7
Slovakia	6
Latvia	5
Lithuania	5
Romania	5
Bulgaria	4

3. SECOND HALF OF 2000: THE FRENCH PRESIDENCY

The French presidency in the second half of 2000 was the period during which the Union prepared the ground for the final effort for the essential negotiations in the following two years. Not many chapters were provisionally closed but the Union succeeded in defining its common positions and agreeing the priorities for 2001 and 2002.

By the end of the French presidency the list of provisionally closed chapters looked as follows.

Chapters provisionally closed by 31 December 2000:

Countries that started after Luxembourg	
Cyprus	17
Czech Republic	13
Estonia	16
Slovenia	14
Poland	13
Hungary	14

Countries that started after Helsinki	
Malta	12
Slovakia	10
Latvia	9
Lithuania	7
Romania	6
Bulgaria	8

Cyprus and Estonia had already passed the halfway mark towards reaching closure of thirty-one chapters. The countries that had been added after Helsinki and started on the enlargement negotiations on 15 February were rapidly catching up.

In its annual report, which as usual appeared in the late autumn, the Commission considered that the time had come to outline a strategy that would take the enlargement negotiations forward and point them towards conclusion. The most important element in this approach was the setting up of a detailed 'road map' providing a clear sequence for tackling the outstanding issues in the course of 2001 and 2002.

The Road Map

Priority schedule for the first half of 2001

In this period the Union would have as its priority to define common positions, including positions on requests for transitional measures, with a view to closing provisionally the following chapters:

- *Free movement of goods*
- *Free movement of persons*
- *Freedom to provide services*
- *Free movement of capital*
- *Company law*
- *Social policy and employment*
- *Culture and audio-visual policy*
- *Environment*
- *External relations*

Issues of substance to be considered in this period included, for example, coordination of social security schemes; recognition of diplomas; land acquisition; pharmaceuticals; freedom of movement for workers; health and safety at work; quality of water; pollution and treatment of waste; preferential trade regimes etc.; as well as general questions related to the capacity to implement and enforce the Community *acquis*.

Priority schedule for the second half of 2001

In addition to any element not yet addressed in the previous period, the Union would have as its priority, in this period, to define common positions, including positions on requests for transitional measures, with a view to closing provisionally the following chapters:

- *Competition policy*
- *Transport policy*
- *Energy*
- *Taxation*
- *Agriculture (in particular veterinary and phytosanitary questions)*
- *Customs union*
- *Fisheries*
- *Justice and home affairs*
- *Financial control*

Issues of substance to be considered in this period include, for example, proper implementation and enforcement of state aid legislation; land transport; maritime safety; internal gas and electricity markets; nuclear safety; customs code; VAT; excise duties; food safety; visa policy; Schengen *acquis* etc.; as well as general questions related to the capacity to implement and enforce the Community *acquis*.

Priority schedule for the first half of 2002

In this period, the Union would concentrate on any important questions from other chapters for which solutions had not yet been found and define common positions, including positions on all requests for transitional measures, with a view to closing provisionally the remaining chapters:

- *Agriculture (remaining questions)*
- *Regional policy and structural instruments*
- *Financial and budgetary provisions*
- *Institutions*
- *Other matters*

Like so many times before, the Commission's approach had a significant impact on the negotiations for the following two years. The tasks of each of the presidencies that would follow were spelled out, and the candidates received a welcome planning instrument. Any Member State that might be reluctant to go ahead on a specific chapter was placed in a difficult situation. If complete EU common positions were not ready by the specified timetable, the fault for the lack of progress would fall on the EU—and in particular on any country which blocked internal EU agreement.

The Nice European Council in December 2000 endorsed the Commission's road map. It also added further clarification as far as a target date was concerned.

The Council concluded that 'in the European Council's view that strategy [the "road map"] together with the completion of the Intergovernmental Conference on institutional reform [the Nice Treaty] will place the Union in a position to welcome those new member states, which are ready as from the end of 2002, in the hope that they will be able to take part in the next European elections'.

The Cologne European Council, which followed the Berlin meeting, concluded: 'In order to ensure that the Union's institutions can continue to work effectively after enlargement, the European council confirms its intention of convening a Conference of the Representatives of the Governments of Member States early in 2000 to resolve the institutional issues left open in Amsterdam that need to be settled before enlargement. The Conference should be completed and the necessary amendments to the Treaties agreed upon at the end of 2000.'

The distinction from Amsterdam between a situation with five or fewer and one with more than five new Member States obviously no longer made sense. It was becoming increasingly clear that the Union was heading towards a much larger expansion than originally foreseen.

The Nice Treaty

The negotiations on what became the Nice Treaty respected the time schedule set out in Cologne. They started during the Portuguese presidency in the first part of 2000 and ended under the French by the end of the year.

The Nice negotiations led to the fourth round of changes of the original Rome Treaty, following the Single European Act, the Maastricht Treaty, and the Amsterdam Treaty. In contrast to the former three treaty revisions the Nice negotiations concentrated on institutional change, leaving the Union policies or competences unchanged. The introduction of more qualified majority voting (QMV) in the Council, changes to the voting system in the Council, and limitation to the size of the Commission were the main challenges.

The negotiation on the Treaty of Nice will not go down in history as the Union's finest hour. In particular the end negotiations at the European Council in Nice were confused. They ended up with a result which on some points lacked logic and precision. Despite all the criticism, however, the Nice Treaty did provide important progress, in particular by changing the voting rule in the Council from unanimity to qualified majority in thirty areas of Union policy, including on trade in services and commercial aspects of intellectual property; Structural Funds; economic, financial, and technical cooperation with third countries; certain aspects of asylum, immigration, and frontier policy; financial regulation; and on the nomination of the President of the Commission and of the High Representative.

The main criticism relates to the voting system which emerged from Nice. The earlier simple system, which had survived since the Treaty of Rome, was replaced with one involving a recalculating of votes for the benefit of the bigger Member States, bringing them more in line with their relative population size. In addition three thresholds were introduced, which had to be reached in order to obtain a qualified majority in the Council:

- 72 per cent of the votes;
- Member States representing more than 62 per cent of the population should be voting for; and
- at least half of the Member States should support the proposal.

Besides the complexity of the system, it had the major inconvenience of making it more difficult to find a majority in the Council. This could hardly be described as the best way of preparing for enlargement.

The Nice conclusions spelled out the voting weights both for Member States and for candidates (see Table 1). It also set out the various thresholds needed for obtaining a qualified majority in the Council in the enlarged Union. Unfortunately, these thresholds were established for a situation where all the candidates (including Romania and Bulgaria) adhered at the same time. Since politics, rather than mathematics, had determined the thresholds, this left a difficult issue (in particular in the light of the acrimonious discussions that had taken place in the European Council) which had to be settled later on, with an enlargement with fewer than twelve new Member States.

Table 1. Voting weights in the Council adopted by the Nice European Council

Members of the Council	Weighted votes
Germany	29
United Kingdom	29
France	29
Italy	29
Spain	27
Poland	27
Romania	14
The Netherlands	13
Greece	12
Czech Republic	12
Belgium	12
Hungary	12
Portugal	12
Sweden	10
Bulgaria	10
Austria	10
Slovakia	7
Denmark	7
Finland	7
Ireland	7
Lithuania	7
Latvia	4
Slovenia	4
Estonia	4
Cyprus	4
Luxembourg	4
Malta	3
Total EU 27	345

The lack of clarity or logic behind the Nice agreement also meant that other issues would come back for discussion later on in the enlargement negotiations. The most glaring example was the number of seats in the European Parliament for the new Member States. Despite the fact that population size would be the only consideration in determining the number of seats in the European Parliament, Hungary and the Czech Republic were awarded fewer seats in Nice than Belgium or Portugal, two countries that had similar or lower population.

Even though not a formal timetable, the indications were quite explicit. The next elections to the European Parliament would take place in June 2004. Normally the new members would not be able to take part in those elections unless the enlargement treaties were ratified before then. Considering the time needed for the ratification procedure, the wording of the European Council implied that negotiations would have to be finalized at the end of 2002 or at the beginning of 2003 at the latest.

4. THE SWEDISH PRESIDENCY, JANUARY TO JUNE 2001

During the Swedish presidency the enlargement negotiations picked up speed. The Swedes, if anything, overperformed compared to the 'road map'. The internal EU discussions on some major transitional periods began to heat up.

The map was a timetable for completing the Union's position on the individual chapters, not for concluding the negotiations. Some of the most contentious issues among the Member States had to be settled, like the free movement of persons and the freedom to provide services. Both chapters touched upon fears that, rightly or wrongly, had been expressed in a number of Member States for a massive influx of workers on the labour market, from the new Member States.

The Union had already adopted a (partial) common position on the free movement of workers in May 2000, but with regard to the mobility question it had limited itself to underline 'that there are sensitivities over the issue of mobility of workers. The question of mobility of workers in the labour markets will have to be taken into account at a later stage of the negotiations.'

Now in the Swedish presidency the Union needed to come to grips with the issue and define its position in more precise terms. In March the Commission submitted an information note on the free movement of workers in the context of enlargement. Behind the technical analysis, two important messages emerged:

- the long-run migration potential from the candidate countries would be small (in the order of 1 per cent of the EU population). However,
- temporary problems could arise in certain Member States resulting in disturbances in the labour markets. Border regions could face particular problems.

The Commission had been prudent in its approach. Member States took a harder line, in particular Germany and Austria with extensive borders to Central

European candidates. Many Member States, however, were under internal pressure to adopt a tough line. This, combined with widespread understanding of German and Austrians worries, uncertainty over the projections for Eastern and Central European emigration after enlargement, as well as the precedent from the enlargement with Spain and Portugal, led the Union to adopt what was for all practical purposes a seven-year transitional arrangement for the free movement of workers from the new Member States, except for Malta and Cyprus.[6] The seven-year transitional period was broken down into several sub-periods:

- Two years' application of existing (or more liberal) national rules on the free movement.
- A review to be held before the end of the two-year period, but its prolongation for a further three-year period to be decided essentially by the individual Member State.
- Possibility for prolongation of a maximum of two years after the end of the five years, where serious disturbances of the labour market or threat of such disruptions existed.

The adoption of the common position was not without drama, though. Spain linked the issue to the question of continuing regional aid to poorer regions in the EU 15 after enlargement, as the relative wealth of Spain in relation to the EU average would automatically rise when the poorer candidates entered. After having blocked the chapter for several weeks, after an EU Foreign Ministers' meeting where tensions ran high, and finally after the Swedish presidency had to cancel a series of planned meetings in the accession conferences, Spain finally accepted the common position.[7]

Reaction in most candidate countries to the Union's negotiation position was characterized by a deep feeling of deception. The countries that had been living behind closed frontiers for so many years put particular stress on the freedom of movement. In the end, they however accepted that on this issue, the Union was unlikely to move. Hungary was the first country to accept the Union's position. This was done in the context of obtaining a similar transitional period—this time in favour of the Central and Eastern European countries—on another sensitive issue, the purchase of real estate.

The chapter on free movement of capital, which was up for negotiations, included the issue of land acquisition. The candidates feared that their land and property would be bought up after enlargement by individuals and firms from older Member States, in particular farm and forestry land as well as secondary

[6] The common position included provisions for Germany and Austria on the cross-border provision of services by companies established in the candidate countries. The two countries were allowed to apply flanking national measures to address actual or threatened serious disturbances in a number of specifically listed sensitive service sectors on their labour markets.

[7] At the same time, Member States agreed to ask the Commission to examine the impact of enlargement of regional funding, but the issue would not be linked to the accession negotiations.

residences. It was an explosive issue, which could swing public opinion against EU membership in some of the candidate countries.

Recognizing the high political sensitivity of the issue, the Commission presented a draft common position that would allow the candidates who wished to do so to limit the purchase of agricultural and forestry land for a period of seven years, with a review clause in the third year for determining whether the period should be shortened. For secondary residences a period of five years without revision was proposed.

The discussion in the Council revealed that not all Member States were prepared to accept restrictions on the possibilities to buy land. But in the end they gave in. It would be difficult to refuse to take these preoccupations of the candidates seriously in a situation where restrictions of the same duration had also been imposed, at the initiative of the EU, on free movements of persons.

Other contentious issues were discussed and agreed within the EU. In the chapter on company law, Member States found a solution to the complicated problem of extended patent rights for pharmaceutical products which were already on the market in the candidate countries. In the chapter on environment, Member States agreed to insist on transposition of the *acquis* into national legislation, on implementation of nature protection directives, and on implementation of the *acquis* in relation to product-related legislation as well as in relation to new installations, while accepting long transitional periods where substantial adaptation of existing infrastructure (requiring major financial outlays) was needed. One of the longest transitional periods related to the treatment of urban waste water, where the EU generally accepted that candidates would not fulfil the *acquis* until 2015. Other substantial transitional periods covered the quality of drinking water, air pollution from large combustion plants, recovery and recycling of packaging waste, as well as landfill of waste.

Agreements on transitional periods were also reached in chapters which did not fall under the Swedish presidency according to the road map. In the chapter on taxation Member States agreed to a number of transitional measures relating to the level of VAT and excise duties on specific products. On energy, the EU accepted transitional periods for the building up of oil stocks. On the customs union, Hungary was allowed an import quota on aluminium applying only a limited duty.[8]

Sweden had a successful presidency, not only in establishing negotiation positions for the Union, but also in achieving significant progress in the negotiations themselves. When its semester started on average between eleven and twelve chapters had been provisionally closed. When the semester was over the average had risen to seventeen. All in all, sixty-six chapters had been closed, including some of the most technically difficult ones. In particular the newcomers to the negotiation process made spectacular progress. By the end of the presidency Latvia, Lithuania, and Slovenia had opened all negotiation chapters and

[8] Malta, the only other country to be granted transitional periods under the customs union, did not close the chapter until December 2002.

Table 2. Provisional closure of negotiation chapters

	End December 2000	End June 2001	End December 2001	End June 2002
31				
30				
29				
28				CY–LIT
				SLOVE
27				EE–LAT
26			SLOVE	SLOVA
25				CZ–PL
24			CY–CZ–H	H
23			LAT	M
22		CY–H	SLOVA	
21			LIT	
20			EE–M–PL	BG
19		CZ–SLOVE		
		SLOVA–EE		
18		LIT		
17	CY	M		
16	EE	LAT–PL		
15				
14	H–SLOVE		BG	
13	CZ–PL			
12	M			RO
11				
10	SLOVA	BG		
9	LAT		RO	
8	BG			
7	LIT	RO		
6	RO			
5				
4				
3				
2				
1				
0				

Note: BG (Bulgaria), CY (Cyprus), CZ (Czech Republic), EE (Estonia), H (Hungary), LAT (Latvia), LIT (Lithuania), M (Malta), PL (Poland), RO (Romania), SLOVA (Slovakia), SLOVE (Slovenia).

Source: Peter Ludlow, *The Making of the New Europe*, (Brussels: EuroComment, 2004).

concluded negotiations on more chapters than Poland. Except for Romania and Bulgaria, the difference between the two groups had disappeared (see Table 2).

On the political level, Sweden also succeeded at the European Council in Göteborg in reaching agreement on even firmer language on the conclusion of the enlargement process. The European Council specified that it should be possible 'to *complete negotiations* by the end of 2002' (instead of 'welcoming new states which are ready as from the end of 2002'). 'The aim was to enable the countries concerned to take part in the 2004 elections to the European Parliament *as members*.'

5. THE BELGIAN PRESIDENCY, SECOND HALF OF 2001

It was well known that Sweden was very enthusiastic about enlargement, and it was only natural that it would pursue the process with great vigour. Many thought—and some hoped—that the following presidency would lower the speed.

The incoming presidency had declared that the preparation of the next round of institutional changes in the Union (preparation for what would later become the constitution) was placed as top priority for the semester. The ambition was to agree the 'Laeken declaration', named after the castle on the outskirts of Brussels where the December European Council was going to be held. The presidency followed this ambition through and agreement was reached in Laeken.

The world changed on 11 September 2001 with the terrorist attack on New York and Washington. So did the whole perspective for the Belgian presidency. Major attention had to be devoted to the building up of an anti-terrorist work programme for the Union, and on reaching agreement on urgent measures.

Against this background it was difficult to imagine that enlargement could also be given high priority. This turned out to be a wrong prediction. If the performance of the preceding presidencies on enlargement had turned into a beauty context, the Belgian one certainly also wanted to have a go at the prize.

The 'road map' had scheduled agreement during the presidency on EU common positions with regard to another series of difficult issues like implementation and enforcement of state aid legislation; land transport; maritime safety; nuclear safety; VAT; excise duties; food safety; visa policy; and Schengen *acquis*. These were all areas in which Member States were concerned over unfair competition from the candidates due to existing lower standards (e.g. on state aid control, maritime transport, food safety control, or external frontier control) or lower prices or rates (e.g. excise duties on cigarettes or prices for road cabotage). But once more the combined efforts of presidency, Commission, and Member States ensured that the road map was generally respected.

The chapter on competition was closed with some of the most advanced countries which did not request transitional periods. Likewise, the chapters on justice and home affairs as well as financial control were closed with some candidates without transitional arrangements. Under the chapter on energy, the Czech Republic obtained a transitional period for implementation of the gas directive, and the chapter was closed after a bilateral agreement between that country and Austria on conditions for assuring the safety of the nuclear power plant Temelin.[9] Slovakia also closed the chapter after the EU promised to provide financial assistance to the decommissioning of the nuclear power plant Bohunice. Taxation was closed with several candidates with transitional periods reflecting the principles established during the first semester.

[9] The issue resurfaced at the Copenhagen European Council, see Chapter 11.

The most controversial transitional periods related to food processing plants in the candidate countries and to the issue of road cabotage. The EU agreed on a formula under which certain identified food establishments in the accession countries were allowed to operate for a specified time after accession, even though they did not fully meet EU requirements. Products from these establishments would have to be marked and could not be sold in other Member States. On road cabotage Member States decided to demand a transitional period from most candidate countries. The period would vary in time according to the scope of transitional periods each candidate demanded in other areas of road transport.[10]

On average, between three and four negotiation chapters were provisionally closed during the Belgian presidency. Once more, the progress by the Helsinki group was particularly impressive.

The boldest move of the Belgian presidency was to suggest that the European Council in Laeken named, for the first time, the countries that—on the assumption that the present rate of progress in the negotiations and reforms in the candidate states was maintained—could be ready to conclude negotiations by the end of 2002: Cyprus, Estonia, Hungary, Latvia, Lithuania, Malta, Poland, the Slovak Republic, and Slovenia. The spelling out of such explicit ambitions was not to the liking of all and some members of the European Council suggested more caution. In the end the European Council agreed with the report of the Commission, and then followed the presidency text, including the names of the countries. The road was now cleared for a large enlargement, unless any of the ten countries presented unforeseen difficulties.

6. THE SPANISH PRESIDENCY, FIRST HALF OF 2002

Progress in the enlargement negotiations was maintained during the Spanish presidency. An average of four additional chapters closed for each candidate was the score. Looking beyond the mere statistics, some main achievements were obtained, like the agreement with Poland on the free movement of capital (including the vexed issue of purchase of agricultural land), energy with Lithuania (including a clear timetable for the decommissioning of the nuclear power plant in Ignalina as well as an EU commitment to provide financial assistance in this respect, a topic which had been subject to bitter controversy), taxation (in particular excise duties on cigarettes) with five countries. Justice and home affairs as well as transport were concluded with most of the front runner countries.

[10] Austria for some time blocked agreement on the transport chapter, demanding a solution to the problem of road transit through the Alps beyond 31 December 2003, when the so-called eco-points system was due to expire. The common position was only agreed after the Commission on 20 December 2001 at the request of the European Council in Laeken adopted a regulation prolonging the eco-points system to the end of 2004.

On the other hand, the statistics on the closed chapters included institutions and regional policy. On both of these chapters the most controversial parts were still outstanding at the end of the presidency, because the EU had not yet defined its negotiation position on these issues. The main challenge for the Spanish presidency was to establish a negotiation position for the EU 15 on these controversial issues. In the road map Spain had been allocated particularly complicated tasks: EU positions on regional policy and structural instruments; remaining issues in relation to agriculture (in particular quotas and direct income support); financial and budgetary provisions; and institutions.

In accordance with the road map the Commission presented a communication at the beginning of the Spanish presidency on the Common Financial Framework for the years 2004–6. The basis was the agreement reached in Berlin in 2000. However, since Berlin several things had changed:

- The Berlin conclusions were based on the assumption of an enlargement with six countries (Cyprus, Czech Republic, Estonia, Hungary, Poland, and Slovakia). Now the perspective was an enlargement with ten new countries.
- Berlin was based on the accession date of 1 January 2002. Now the perspective was l January 2004.
- Berlin had foreseen only a partial inclusion of the new Member States in the Common Agricultural Policy (CAP), excluding the farmers in the new Member States from direct income support. The candidates were hotly contesting this assumption. They saw it as an unacceptable discrimination from both a political and an economic point of view. Furthermore at least one of the reasons for excluding income support—a much lower level of agricultural prices in the candidate countries than in the present EU—no longer persisted. Prices had increased considerably in the candidate countries.
- The Commission also recommended a number of ways to adapt the rural development policy to the new Member States during a transitional period. The EU co-financing rate should be increased to 80 per cent, the policy should be managed according to the rules guiding the pre-accession instrument for agriculture (in particular roll-over of unused funds from one year to another), and some specific measures should be added to encourage the restructuring of semi-subsistence farms.
- New needs had been identified during the enlargement negotiations. This referred in particular to financial support for the decommissioning of nuclear power stations in Slovakia (Bohunice) and Lithuania (Ignalina). Furthermore, continued financial support for institution building would be needed after enlargement. Finally, funds would have to be reserved for the northern part of Cyprus in the case of a settlement.
- The phasing in of new Member States in structural actions would have to take place over three, rather than five, years. The starting point for the Commission was still the expenditures for the first years of membership as foreseen in Berlin, adjusted to take account of the larger enlargement.

In order to ensure a faster profile while accepting the limits to the new Member States' absorption capacity, however, the Commission proposed an increase in the Cohesion Funds available for new Member States, from 18 per cent to one-third of the total.

- The net budgetary situations of the candidate countries had to be taken into consideration. Applying the *acquis* without corrective measures would lead to a situation where several candidate countries would end up being net contributors to the budget from the first year of membership.

Despite the changed situation the Commission decided to stick to the overall ceiling agreed in Berlin for the period 2004–6. The Commission also rejected the idea, which had been floated by some candidates, that the amounts 'saved' in 2002–3 could be used in the following years. The Commission's proposal to keep within the Berlin financial ceilings for an expansion with ten instead of six new Member States was based on the facts that, first, the four countries that had been added to the 'first wave' envisaged in Berlin were comparatively small countries and represented only an increase of 20 per cent in terms of population. Second, experience from earlier enlargements showed that expenditure in the candidate countries would only increase over time. In particular, expenditure on Structural Funds would be built up gradually, as the new members' absorption capacity increased. The 2004 figures agreed in Berlin were based on expenditures for the third year of membership. Everything else being equal, the expenditure for the first year of membership would be lower, even after adjusting for the larger enlargement. Room was hereby created for additional countries and for additional expenditure for specific purposes.

In fact the Commission proposal fell considerably short of the Berlin figures. For the period 2004–6 its proposal for commitment expenditure (ceiling for entering into new commitments) fell on average about €800 million short of the Berlin ceiling per year (6 per cent below). For payment appropriations (amounts that can actually be used for paying expenditure) the difference was even greater (close to 20 per cent). The reason for these lower figures was that the Commission had taken into consideration the need for restraint in public finances, in order to avoid aggravating the worsening situation in the old members, and to parry the likelihood of overheating in the new members.

Table 3 sets out the financial framework now proposed by the Commission and compares it to the figures agreed at the European Council in Berlin.

One exception was agriculture. This expenditure category was the only one to exceed the Berlin ceiling. The Commission had come to the conclusion that it was untenable to exclude the candidate countries from direct income support. It proposed that income support be granted gradually to farmers in the new Member States over the period 2004–13. For the first three years it suggested support levels of 25, 30, and 35 per cent of the EU level respectively.

The Commission's proposals on introducing income support for farmers in the acceding countries immediately gave rise to heated and acrimonious discussions in the Council. In the end the Spanish presidency decided not to force the issue

Table 3. Commission proposal for the financial framework for enlargement 2004–2006 with accession of ten new Member States in 2004 (€m. 1999 prices)

Commitment appropriations	2004	2005	2006	Total 2004–6
Agriculture (Berlin)	2,048	3,596	3,933	9,577
	(2,450)	(2,930)	(3,400)	(8,780)
Structural operations (Berlin)	7,067	8,150	10,350	25,567
	(7,920)	(10,000)	(12,080)	(30,000)
Internal policies (Berlin)	1,176	1,096	1,071	3,343
	(790)	(820)	(850)	(2,460)
Administration (Berlin)	503	558	612	1,673
	(450)	(450)	(450)	(1,350)
Total commitment appropriations (Berlin)	10,794	13,400	15,966	40,160
	(11,610)	(14,200)	(16,780)	(42,590)
Total payment appropriations (Berlin)	5,686	10,493	11,840	28,019
	(8,890)	(11,400)	(14,220)	(34,510)

through a substantive discussion at the Seville European Council, fearing, probably rightly, that such a discussion would further complicate matters. Consequently, the EU common position on agriculture did not take a stance on the issue of direct payments. Instead it recalled that the financial perspectives agreed at the Berlin European Council did not cover direct payments to new Member States, but that direct payments were part of the *acquis*.

The presidency had greater success in establishing common positions on other aspects of the Common Agricultural Policy. It reached agreement on the Union's opening bid on agricultural quotas as well as rural development to be presented to the candidates. Usually, the Directorate General responsible for enlargement would be preparing the draft common position on any given issue with technical assistance from other relevant Directorates General. This procedure ensured that the draft common positions should be more or less acceptable for the candidate country. On quotas, however, the Directorate General responsible for agriculture was in the driver's seat. This position was a much better starting point for traditional horse trading than those normally reflected in the Commission's draft common positions, where an attempt had been made beforehand to come up with a proposal on which all could agree.

The Spanish presidency also faced difficulties in achieving agreement on the other important financial proposal from the Commission, concerning financial compensation. The Commission suggested that corrective measures should be taken to ensure that no new member would find itself in a situation where its net position under the budget would be less favourable than the situation existing in 2003 (where the country received pre-adhesion aid but paid no contribution to the EU budget). The amount needed to bring the candidate back to the pre-entry situation would be made in the form of cash payments. The amount would be calculated beforehand and inscribed in the adhesion treaty. According to the Commission's calculations, five of the candidates were likely to need corrective measures in order to bring them up to the 2003 level: Cyprus, Czech Republic, Hungary, Malta, and Slovenia. The Commission calculated that amounts in the order of €1.7 billion would be needed.

Several Member States contested the principle of compensating the candidates for net budgetary losses compared to 2003. The maximum that could be envisaged was a compensation to those of the new members that otherwise would become net contributors to the budget in the first years of membership. Furthermore the Commission's method for calculating the compensation was called into question. There was a broad feeling among Member States that the Commission had overestimated the benefit from pre-adhesion aid in 2003, and had underestimated the amounts the candidates would receive after entry. They consequently felt that the compensation amounts should be reduced. The Spanish presidency ended without agreement on the substance of this disagreement. The EU presented a new common position, but apart from specifying that the new Member States should pay full contribution from the day of accession (and that requests for gradually phasing in their contributions therefore were unacceptable) it only indicated that a temporary budget compensation might be necessary in some cases for 2004–6 to prevent a new member from becoming a net contributor.

On regional policy, the Spanish presidency succeeded in reaching agreement between the Fifteen on all issues, except the overall amount. The amount of the funds which each country would receive was expressed as a percentage of the overall amount available for the new Member States. This agreement also included the Commission's proposal to use a third of the allocation to the Cohesion Fund to increase the absorption capacity of the new Member States. Through the Cohesion Fund the Union would be able to contribute up to 85 per cent to major transport infrastructure and environmental protection projects to be undertaken by the candidate states. Most candidates agreed to close the chapter provisionally on this basis.

Finally, the institutions chapter was opened and closed with most candidates under the Spanish presidency. As it was limited to repeating the Nice provisions and stating that transitional arrangements would have to be agreed once it had been decided which countries would take part in the first enlargement wave, this did not constitute any substantial progress in the negotiations.

5

The Danish Presidency: Conclusion of the Negotiations

Poul Skytte Christoffersen

1. THE STRATEGY

The Swedish, Belgian, and Spanish presidencies had led to considerable progress in the enlargement negotiations. The road map established by the Commission at the end of 2000 had generally been adhered to. However, the Danish presidency, which started on 1 July 2002, had a huge task before it, if the ambition—to conclude the enlargement negotiations before the end of the year—should be crowned with success. The Seville European Council had failed to agree on the Union's negotiation position on financial and related questions. This also meant that crucial parts of the agricultural and Structural Funds chapters could not yet be negotiated with the candidates. Institutional issues were outstanding, and negotiations with some candidate countries on major chapters (in particular competition policy) had yet to be concluded. Finally, it was (not unfairly) expected that as in all earlier enlargement negotiations some tricky and politically sensitive topics would pop up when the finishing line was in sight.

The political landscape in Europe was not without its complications. France had held elections in June, just before the start of the presidency. Elections had taken place in the Netherlands in May, and the formation of a new government turned out to be exceptionally complicated, even by Dutch standards. Germany would be facing national elections in September, and it could be expected that the biggest Member State would be paralysed in European political terms for several weeks. This was a very long period of deadlock for a presidency in the second half of the year, which in terms of working days was much shorter than spring presidencies (in reality only ninety-nine days). In addition the Irish people had rejected the Nice Treaty in the preceding year. For many Member States, the coming into force of the treaty was a condition for agreeing to enlargement. A new referendum in Ireland was planned for October 2002, a few weeks before the first European Council.

Despite these difficulties, the Danish presidency did not shy away from declaring that the finalizing of the enlargement negotiations with the first group of countries (the number was deliberately not defined) would be the top priority. 'From Copenhagen to Copenhagen' became the motto.

The first difficulty was psychological. While fully subscribing to the goal in public statements, most of the Member States—as well as some in the Commission—believed that it was impossible to reach in practice. And why the rush? While all candidate countries subscribed to the ambition, several also expressed doubt about the feasibility in discussions behind closed doors.

The Danes pointed to a number of reasons why termination by the end of 2002 was crucial: First of all, this date had now become the target of the Union, with the Union's credibility in the candidate countries linked to the respect of this date. If it failed to be reached, there would be little credibility attached to a new date and a serious risk existed for prolonged delays, with negative consequences for the reform process in the candidate countries. In addition the intergovernmental negotiations on a new institutional reform, the 'constitution for Europe', would start up in spring 2003. The mixture of an enlargement process still open and a new institutional debate could be dangerous. (As it turned out, another issue that came to the forefront in the spring of 2003, and seriously divided the Member States—the Iraq war—certainly would have been even more detrimental to the ambition of an early conclusion of the enlargement negotiations, if they had not been concluded according to plan.)

When the outcome of the Spanish presidency became clear after the Seville European Council, the future presidency presented a detailed plan on how to bring the process to an end, and set out to convince delegations that conclusion by the end of 2002 was not only desirable, but also possible.

The plan of the six-month presidency was divided into two parts. Part one would start with the beginning of the presidency and end with the first European Council to be held in Brussels on 23–4 October. During this period negotiations had to be concluded on all chapters, except those linked to finance and institutional questions with the candidates that expected to terminate the negotiations by the end of the year. Two crucial decisions had to be taken by the European Council in Brussels. First, the Council should determine the list of countries that could be expected to be ready to enter into the Union in 2004. Second, the European Council should define the Union's negotiation position on finance and related issues (in particular agriculture, Structural Funds, and budgetary compensation) as well as on institutional questions.

Part two would run from Brussels to the European Council in Copenhagen, planned for 13–14 December. During these seven weeks intensive negotiations should take place with the candidates on finance and related issues, with a view to a final conclusion, at the latest in Copenhagen.

The Commission had already been convinced of the plan earlier. The conclusion of the negotiations presupposed that, as early as possible in the presidency, there would be a fair amount of clarity as to how many candidate countries would be ready for membership. This meant that the Commission's annual report on the enlargement process had to be available two months earlier than usual—by early October—instead of late November. Despite a number of technical difficulties, including the need for the Commission's staff to work over the summer holidays, the Commission early in 2002 promised the future presidency that it would submit the report in good time before the first European Council under the Danish presidency.

2. PREPARING FOR THE EUROPEAN COUNCIL IN BRUSSELS, AUTUMN 2002

Finalizing negotiations on non-financial issues

The first months of the presidency proceeded according to plan. Negotiations with ten candidate countries were—with a few exceptions[1]—successfully completed on twenty-seven out of the thirty-one negotiation chapters before the European Council of Brussels.

The competition chapter had been provisionally closed with a number of candidates throughout the negotiations, but of these countries only Cyprus was granted a minor transitional period on phasing out of incompatible fiscal aid by 2004. The main issues with Poland, Slovakia, the Czech Republic, Malta, and Hungary had not been settled. All of these countries gave fiscal aid to large companies which was incompatible with the *acquis*, and which had often been promised to the companies in question for a period beyond the date of accession. Some of these countries also had to restructure sensitive sectors (steel and shipyards), requiring state aid for a number of years. The EU agreed on a formula which allowed some of the incompatible aid to be converted to regional aid, acceptable under the *acquis*, and which gave the candidates a possibility of extending state aid to the sensitive sectors for a number of years under specified conditions in connection with restructuring. The breakthrough came when Slovakia and the Czech Republic accepted the EU common position in accession conferences just hours before the start of the European Council of Brussels.

The method for calculating new Member States' net budgetary position after accession was discussed among Member States during September and October on the basis of a note from the Commission. The most controversial issues related to advance payments of Structural Funds[2] and to the expected rate of payments as a percentage of appropriations for Structural and Cohesion Funds.[3] The debates in

[1] Hungary and Poland had not concluded competition policy, Poland also needed to settle issues relating to phytosanitary conditions in the agricultural chapter, and the Czech Republic had not yet concluded the transport chapter. Finally, Malta had agriculture, taxation, and customs union outstanding.

[2] As the *acquis* stood at the time of negotiations, Member States received advance payments in the order of 7% of the total contribution of the funds over their seven-year programming period. Member States agreed that new Member States in 2004 should receive advance payments of 16% of the total contribution of the funds over the period 2004–6. This improved the budgetary situation of the new Member States, but most of them objected to the increase, as they feared they would not be in position to actually spend the money even if it technically counted as a payment from the EU budget. The presidency, in its final compromise proposals, offered to split the 16% into 10% in 2004 and 6% in 2005.

[3] In both cases, the Commission envisaged that no funds would be paid in 2004. Member States, however, agreed that payments in the order of 3% of commitments should be foreseen for the year 2004.

the Council, where budgetary experts participated in the enlargement group, could not be settled until the General Affairs Council immediately preceding the European Council in Brussels. The actual amounts in question, however, were relatively modest compared to the whole package. After two months of acrimonious debate, the Member States agreed on a model that foresaw a reduction in budgetary compensations of less than €90 million. But the process ensured that the Member States' Finance Ministers had a stake in the negotiations.

Finally, chapter 31, 'other issues', had to be opened. It encompassed a number of largely uncontroversial elements such as implementation of pre-accession funds after accession as well as the provisions for the new Member States' participation in the European Development Fund, the European Central Bank, the European Investment Bank, and the Research Fund for Coal and Steel. The safeguard clauses, described below, were also negotiated under this chapter.

Establishing a negotiation position on institutional questions

The major challenge for the presidency was to reach agreement by the Member States on the outstanding chapters. It had decided to confront the institutional chapter early on in the presidency and not leave it to the end, as had traditionally been the case in earlier enlargement negotiations. Three major issues had to be settled on the institutional set-up in the enlarged union: the definition of qualified majority, the number of European parliamentarians, and the presidency rotation system. The two first questions were leftovers from the Nice Treaty negotiations. Nice had defined the number of votes to be given to the new Member States, but had not settled the issues of how many votes would be needed to reach a qualified majority in a Union of twenty-five. Disagreement between the Member States on a similar question had held up the end of the negotiations with the four EFTA countries in 1994 for three months, after all other issues had been settled. This time the Member States accepted a proposal by the presidency, as part of a final package. This package included the acceptance of two more seats in the European Parliament to Hungary and to the Czech Republic, thus correcting the clear injustice made in Nice. The package finally included the decision (taken in agreement with the candidate countries) that the new Member States should not be included in the list of presidencies for the first three years after entry into the Union.

Selecting the candidates that would be ready for 2004

The Commission presented its annual report on enlargement in early October, with its evaluation of the readiness of each candidate country to join the Union. According to the Commission, all the candidates, with the exception of Bulgaria and Romania, should be ready. Constant monitoring on how the candidate countries were meeting their obligations was however essential. It would also be necessary to introduce a general economic safeguard clause, as had been the case in all earlier enlargement negotiations. This clause could be involved where 'difficulties arise which are serious and liable to persist in any sector of the economy or which could bring about serious deterioration in the economic situation of a given area'. Both new and old members would be able to call for the application of this clause. In addition the circumstances surrounding the fifth enlargement, and, in particular, the need to allow for the real (if remote) possibility of a severe volte-face in the CEE countries necessitated the introduction of two specific safeguard clauses, one for the internal market and one for justice and home affairs. The internal market safeguard could be applied if a new Member State failed to comply with the accession obligation, causing a serious threat to the internal market. The justice and home affairs safeguard could be invoked in case of risk of serious shortcomings in the transposition or implementation of instruments in this area. The specific safeguard mechanisms would be introduced for a period of two years, and could be implemented by the Commission on the request of a Member State.

3. KALININGRAD

One highly political issue linked to accession but with wider political implications—Kaliningrad—required much attention by the presidency during the first part of the semester. The Union had known for a long time that the situation of this part of Russia, which after enlargement would become an enclave inside the Union, would pose problems. Kaliningrad was poor, and suffered from serious problems of environmental degradation and crime. In its relations with Russia, the Union had for several years paid special attention in its aid programme to the enclave. For Russia, any step that would affect the sovereignty of the enclave or its relations with the motherland was unacceptable. Russia considered the free flow of goods and persons between the enclave and the Russian mainland to be essential.

This simmering crisis was only brought out in the open late in the negotiations. While there was general understanding for the Russian situation, it was not possible for the Union to accept a hole in the Schengen system. This meant that Russians needed to be in possession of a Schengen visa in order to travel through the Union (through Lithuania, Latvia, or Poland) on their way to or from Kaliningrad. The passage through Lithuania was of particular importance. The question of transit was raised during the Russian–EU summit under the Spanish presidency. It became clear on that occasion that Kaliningrad was an issue where President Putin had strong views, which included the rejection of visa requirements for Russian citizens in relation to Kaliningrad.

The discussion among Member States after the summit revealed that Mr Putin's views had made a strong impression on a number of them, perhaps stronger than the plight of Lithuania, which risked finding itself caught between two stools. If Lithuania showed flexibility towards the Russians by an accommodation on the visa issue (which some Member States directly or indirectly invited them to do) the country risked being excluded from the Schengen area of free circulation of persons. Lithuania was keenly aware that the new Member States did not become full members of Schengen by entry. Full membership, including the possibility to cross borders inside the Union without frontier control, required that the Schengen members were satisfied that Lithuania's external frontier control was up to Schengen standards. The possibility that a Russian on his way to Kaliningrad without a visa would stop in Lithuania and from there move on to another Member State was not compatible with Schengen rules. If Lithuania took an accommodating stance, it risked becoming permanently excluded from Schengen.

From the start of the presidency, the Danes had talks with Russia. The main purpose was to explain that a transit regime for Kaliningrad which did not respect the fundamentals of Schengen was excluded. The talks also served to analyse the various elements of the problems. From this examination it became clear that the main practical problem was in relation to passage by train through Lithuania. For persons travelling with buses and personal cars, as well as transport of goods by lorries and trains, it turned out that Schengen-compatible solutions could be found. But the Russians insisted that passengers in transit by trains should be excluded from the visa requirement. If necessary the transit trains could be sealed, so that no persons left the train during the passage of Lithuania. The Commission, which had been asked by the European Council in Seville to analyse the problem and come up with solutions, rapidly rejected the idea of sealed trains. Trains with human beings travelling behind closed and sealed doors had nasty connotations in European history. Further, such measures would be ineffective in controlling the territory in a situation where the trains—because of poor infrastructure—travelled through Lithuania with an average speed of 15 km per hour.

In the Commission's paper, which appeared in late September, a new idea was presented: the facilitated transit document. A special type of transit permission, different from the normal Schengen visas, could be introduced for Russians travelling by trains to and from Kaliningrad. The document would not be valid outside the transit route, and would be issued by the Lithuanian authorities on the basis of full knowledge of the identity of the holder. Determining the identity of the person was a problem in itself. Very few Russians travelling on the Russia–Kaliningrad route had a passport. Many had internal passports, but most dated back to the Soviet era and were easy to falsify. The Union would be ready to accept that, for practical reasons, a certain transitional period in which these primitive ID papers would be accepted could be granted to the Russians until modern, internationally recognized passports could be introduced. The proposal for sealed trains was rejected, but the Union declared itself willing to examine, for the long run, transit by high-speed trains without visa requirements.

The discussion that followed was based on the Commission's suggestions. The initial debate between the Member States followed the earlier trend, with some countries very attentive to Russian sensibilities, while others primarily had the question of Lithuanian sovereignty, as well as the respect for Schengen rules, in mind. At the last General Affairs Council before the Brussels European Council, ministers agreed on a common line to be submitted to the European Council, with a view to defining the Union's position for the upcoming EU–Russian summit (in November):

- The facilitated travel documents would be introduced from 1 July 2003, and could be issued until the end of 2004 based on the existing internal Russian passports.
- A feasibility study would be launched on non-stop trains, once Lithuania had agreed the terms. A decision would only be taken after Lithuania had become a member of the Union.
- The Union would cover additional costs for Lithuania arising from the Kaliningrad package.
- The EU would assist Lithuania to fulfil the conditions for full participation in the Schengen regime with a view to ensure that Lithuania was among the first candidate countries to participate. Any development of the Schengen *acquis* to take full account of the specific situation of Kaliningrad would not in itself constitute a ground for delaying Lithuania's full participation in Schengen.[4]

4. FINANCE AND RELATED ISSUES

The General Affairs Council preceding the European Council in Brussels did not only settle the Kaliningrad question but was able to reach agreement on most matters, with the exception of the financial issues. These agreements were to be put to the European Council for formal approval. The work of the General Affairs Council might not have caught the headlines as much as the work of the European Council did. In reality, however, the Council under the chairmanship of Dr Per Stig Møller succeeded in settling numerous points, and allowed the European Council to concentrate on a few but important issues such as the financial issues that were still pending.

The preparation for a common position of the Member States on finance and related issues was complicated. Three issues were outstanding: (1) the question of direct income support to farmers in the candidate countries; (2) the funds to be provided for the new Member States for Structural Funds; and (3) the question on budgetary compensation to the candidate countries.

On budget compensation, the preparation at the level of COREPER and the General Affairs Council brought negotiations to the stage where agreement seemed possible, subject to the overall agreement on financial issues. This was based on the 'basic principle' of the Commission's proposal, according to which a

[4] This agreement formed the basis for the discussions with Russia at the summit in November, and was agreed with a few minor amendments.

new Member State that saw its net budgetary position vis-à-vis the Union deteriorate compared to the year before accession would receive a lump-sum payment to make up for the difference. During the internal EU negotiations important changes had been made in the financial forecasts on which the lump-sum compensations were based. The figures had been reduced, and fewer countries would benefit.

However, the question of the direct income support to farmers was still unsettled when the European Council met. For a number of Member States (Germany, UK, the Netherlands, and Sweden) income support to farmers in the new Member States was unacceptable unless it was accompanied by a general reform of the Common Agricultural Policy (CAP).

Discussions on changes to the CAP had been under way since the start of the presidency on the basis of a Commission report on the 'Midterm Evaluation of the CAP', which the European Council in Berlin had requested from the Commission for the second half of 2002. The changes suggested in the report were quite modest and did not meet the expectation of the reform-minded countries. Even though the presidency represented a country which was generally in favour of CAP reform, it was equally determined that the mid-term review should not be allowed to delay the end of the enlargement negotiations. It was convinced that the Council would not be able to reach early agreement on a reform of the CAP, and certainly not with a level of ambition similar to that called for by the countries that made the link between income support in the new members and agricultural reform.

Fortunately for the presidency and for the enlargement negotiations, one of the countries that had made the linkage—Germany—in the end agreed that time and political conditions inside the Union did not allow for a substantial change in the CAP at the present time. It demanded, however, that a limitation be put on farm spending in the enlarged community for the whole transitional period (up to 2013). In the weeks preceding the European Council bilateral talks were held between France and Germany in order to agree on such a ceiling. An agreement in principle was reached between the Federal Chancellor and the French President only hours before the start of the European Council.

5. THE EUROPEAN COUNCIL IN BRUSSELS

Some of the earlier worries of the presidency had been cleared away before the European Council met in Brussels. Chancellor Schröder had (unexpectedly) won the election and the blockage of policy decisions in Berlin had been of short duration. The referendum in Ireland on the Nice Treaty one week before the European Council had approved the treaty and cleared the way for its entry into force. On the other hand a new government had been formed in the Netherlands in July, but the new Dutch Prime Minister had been sent to Brussels with a very restrictive mandate. This was one of many hurdles on the way to agreement.

The negotiations in the European Council in Brussels focused on financial issues. The pre-summit agreement between France and Germany was important, but not enough. As the presidency was all too aware, fifteen countries needed to agree. Discussions in the European Council also revealed that the French–German agreement had not settled some important technical details like the inclusion of inflation or the starting point for calculating the ceiling on agricultural spending.

The remaining three countries (the Netherlands, UK, and Sweden) of those that from the beginning had objected to the introduction of income support to farmers fought hard to lower the financial ceiling. The Dutch, in particular, continued to fight until late. In the end the European Council agreed on a ceiling on farm spending based on the maximum level of expenditure for the Common Agricultural Policy for the year 2006 as agreed in Berlin. This ceiling would be increased in nominal terms with 1 per cent per year up to 2013. An inflation rate above this figure (which was likely) would consequently decrease the ceiling on agricultural spending in real terms.

As far as agriculture was concerned, this decision removed the opposition to income support. It also marked the confirmation of the Commission's proposed figures for CAP expenditure in the new Member States.

The next issue to be settled was funding for structural action. Several members of the European Council insisted on reducing the Commission's proposal, based on the argument that the candidate countries would not to be able to spend the amounts foreseen. The European Council decided to reduce the Commission proposal from €25.6 billion to €23 billion for the period 2004–6. The heads of state and government reached this agreement on structural expenses during dinner on the first day of the European Council. In accepting the cut for Structural Funds, Commissioner Verheugen and the Danish Prime Minister Fogh Rasmussen commented that these cuts would provide room for negotiations in other areas. Whether all participants in the dinner understood or agreed with this comment is unclear, but the Danish presidency would act as if they had in the last parts of the negotiation process.

The other issues on the table of the European Council were settled more easily. The Commission's choice of candidates for entering the Union in 2004 was accepted. The agreement already reached by the Foreign Ministers on the institutional issues was confirmed, and the mechanism for budgetary compensation agreed as part of the overall financial package. On safeguard clauses, the European Council reinforced the Commission's existing proposals. In particular, on the insistence of the Dutch delegation, the European Council agreed that the specific safeguard clauses, which could be invoked against a new member, should remain in application for three years instead of the two proposed by the Commission, and that the internal market safeguard should apply to all commitments concerning economic activities with cross-border effects.

An attempt was made by the Italian Prime Minister Berlusconi to reopen the agreement by the General Affairs Council on Kaliningrad, but he was turned down.

6. THE FINAL HECTIC MONTH: PREPARING FOR COPENHAGEN

The presidency finally had a negotiation mandate for the outstanding questions in the enlargement negotiations. The final negotiations could start.

Informal negotiations with the candidates

The presidency had organized a meeting in Copenhagen with all the candidates two days after Brussels at the level of Prime Ministers and Foreign Ministers. Danish Prime Minister Rasmussen and Commission President Prodi informed the candidates about the outcome of the meeting of the European Council in Brussels, and listened to reactions. These were quite outspoken. Candidates recognized the importance of the fact that agreement had been reached in Brussels, but at the same time they expressed serious misgivings on the financial and budgetary means that had been made available. Several issues specific to the individual candidates were also raised. The candidate countries insisted that the result of the European Council would be the subject of meaningful negotiations in the seven weeks that remained before the Copenhagen Council; the results of the Brussels Council would not be treated on a take-it-or-leave-it basis.

The presidency had already planned for an intensive series of informal negotiation meetings with candidates in Brussels starting early in November. It had decided that the time had come to replace the formal negotiation conferences with direct talks. These would be held in meetings with few officials present on each side. The President of COREPER, Ambassador Poul Skytte Christoffersen, would represent the Union together with Director General Eneko Landaburu from the Commission, and only a few officials from the presidency and the Commission would be present during the talks. The chief negotiator, who would be accompanied by a limited number of officials, would lead the candidate country delegation. From time, to time meetings between the three top officials—Christoffersen, Landaburu, and the candidate's chief negotiator—would be held.

The purpose of the initial series of bilateral meetings was first to start negotiations on the chapters where the European Council had finalized the Union's negotiation position, or where the candidates had not yet had a chance to react (agriculture, funding for Structural Funds, budget compensation, overall financial framework, and safeguards). Second, the meetings should serve to draw up, for each candidate, a complete list of outstanding issues.

The reaction of the candidates on the overall financial framework agreed in Brussels was in line with the views expressed by their Prime Ministers in Copenhagen. The common view was that the original Commission proposals on finance had already been too restrictive, and had not used up the resources within the financial framework set out in Berlin. The European Council in Brussels had made further cuts. Disregarding the financial restrictions imposed by the European Council, some candidates suggested that the Union should pay not just what was the result of the application of the *acquis* but also for costs linked to the introduction of the *acquis* (like setting up administrative structures). Dissatisfaction was further expressed on the fact that the new members were to contribute to the UK budget rebate.

With regard to budget correction, most of the affected countries preferred a different system, based on rebates on contributions to the Union instead of repayments. If the EU proposal should be carried forward, several candidates sought changes in the figures used for the calculation.

The presidency and the Commission were all too aware of the strict limits within which they had to move on financial matters. Any idea of choosing another compensation system was discarded. The presidency rejected the theory according to which the Union should be held financially responsible for the implementing of the *acquis*, but was prepared to recalculate (for the purpose of verification) the figures used in the calculations.

On agriculture, most candidates asked for a higher level of income support to farmers by entry and a shorter transition period than agreed by the European Council. A host of objections were expressed on the proposed production quotas and reference amounts. The size of the quotas determined how much could be produced in a new Member State with Community support. The EU proposals were based on a reference to historical production in 1997/8, the first years for which reliable statistical information was available, while the candidates' figures had been based on their production in the early 1990s. Most candidates argued that the choice of reference year placed them in an unfavourable situation, since agricultural production had fallen in the years following the regime change. Increases in quotas were therefore necessary in their view, even though this would mean greater expenditure for the Union.

The candidates regretted the cuts in regional policy allocations which had been made by the European Council. Their main preoccupation however was to ensure that the promised flow of funds would be forthcoming and not impeded by bureaucratic restrictions or delays.

On the proposed safeguards, the candidates expressed a measured fear that the EU would use them to restrict imports, and some even argued that the candidate countries should also reserve the right to be able to apply the specific safeguards.

Besides these points relating to the new negotiation positions, each individual delegation presented a long list of issues which they felt had not been adequately dealt with in the former negotiations, or where the situation had changed, for instance where the Union had offered concessions to other candidates, which they themselves had not been able to obtain. Some of these problems might seem minor to outsiders, but they could be of great political importance to the individual candidate country.

The following table sets out examples of the issues raised. This, as it turned out, was not the final list of problems and other issues were added later.

List of problems raised by the candidate countries in the last phase of the enlargement negotiations

Cyprus:

- Direct payments: possibility to top up with national support to CAP level
- Agricultural quotas: higher milk and beef quotas
- Compensation for increased cereal prices
- Subsidies to vineyards
- Change in database for calculating budgetary compensation
- Classification of the whole of Cyprus as regional policy Objective-1 area

Czech Republic

- Direct payments. Higher starting level or shorter transitional period. Possibility to top up nationally
- Agricultural quotas: higher quotas in particular on suckler cows, potato starch, and milk
- Higher advance payments on Structural Funds
- More members of the European Parliament

Estonia

- Direct payments: shorter phasing-in period
- Agricultural quotas: higher quotas in particular for milk, sugar, and arable crops
- Compensation for higher sugar prices
- Support for construction of Schengen-compatible border installations
- Limitation of duration of safeguard clauses
- Marketing rights of chemicals produced from shale oil
- Specific treatment on dioxin content of fish
- Subsidies for afforestation of agricultural land
- Derogation of sizes on Baltic herring eligible for consumption
- Less ambitious targets for energy from renewable sources
- Special treatment for steel imports from Russia
- Permission to continued managed hunting of lynx

Hungary

- Direct payments: much shorter transition period
- Agricultural quotas: higher quotas for arable crops, milk, and beef
- Safeguard measures for purchase of land by foreign EU nationals
- Temporary derogation for VAT on internal passenger transport
- Recalculation of budget compensation
- Conversion of existing national aid schemes
- Possibility for state aid to agriculture
- Longer transition period for duty on cigarettes
- Derogation for home-produced alcohol for consumption

- Reduced VAT on electricity and for SMEs
- More seats in the European Parliament

Latvia

- Land purchase: similar transitional period to Poland
- Direct payments: top up with national means
- Agricultural quotes: higher quotas with regard to milk, arable crops, sugar, suckler cows, mother sheep, and potato starch
- Derogation from state aid rules on financing of national water drainage system
- Baltic herring. Derogation on sizes eligible for consumption
- Transitional measures on VAT for heating
- Lynx: permission to continued managed hunting

Lithuania

- Land purchase: similar transitional period to Poland
- Direct payments. Much shorter transitional period and possibility of application of safeguards
- Agricultural quotas: higher quotas on milk, sugar, potato starch, flax, arable crops, suckler cows, and dried fodder
- Increased financial assistance for closure of Ignalina nuclear power plant
- Kaliningrad: legal, political, and financial guarantees

Malta

- Continued imports of agricultural products at world market prices
- Agricultural quotas: higher wine, tomato, and milk quotas
- Specific safeguard mechanism for agriculture
- State aid for transport of agricultural goods to Gozo
- Insurances on continues Structural Funds for Gozo
- Zero VAT on certain additional products
- Extra seat in the European Parliament
- Declaration on neutrality
- Protocol on abortion

Poland

- Direct payments: much shorter transitional period and higher starting rate
- Agricultural quotas: much higher quotas in particular for milk and arable crops
- Steel: equal treatment of investors
- Milk-processing establishments: transitional measures for eighty-two establishments
- Transitional measures for VAT on housing and in the agricultural sector
- Transitional measures for large combustion plants

Slovakia

- Land purchase: similar transition schemes to others
- Direct payments: shorter transition period

- Agricultural quotas: higher quotas on milk, sugar, suckler cows, sheep and goats, arable crops
- Budgetary compensation: need for recalculation
- Participation in 5 per cent reserve for rural development
- Confirmation of EU contribution for decommissioning of Bohunice nuclear power plant

Slovenia

- Land purchase: transitional period if only country left without one.
- Direct payments: possibility for national top up.
- Agricultural quotas: higher quotas for milk, arable crops, suckler cows and goats
- Temporary exemption on VAT for international passenger transport
- Budget compensation. Change in system and calculation
- Safeguard not to be applicable to Slovenia
- Classification of vineyards. Same treatment as Austria and Italy

The Union's leading figures in the negotiations realized how extremely complex and how time-consuming simultaneous negotiations with ten candidates would be. The first round had lasted more than forty hours in total, and the number of issues raised was much higher than had been foreseen.

Presidency and Commission prepare compromise proposals

The presidency and the Commission then started the meticulous exercise of examining each specific demand, to see what could be done. For the series of bilateral meetings that followed, the EU negotiation team had in its pocket suggestions for solutions to some of the minor problems that had been raised, as well as concessions on some of the agricultural quota issues. These were suggestions put forward on the presidency's own responsibility. The Member States were being kept informed about the development in the negotiations, but the presidency deliberately did not seek a negotiation mandate. It was firmly convinced that the nature of the final stage of the negotiations, as well as the short time available, did not permit the application of normal negotiation procedures. The Council's agreement would be needed in the end, but for the moment the presidency and the Commission preferred to move forward without asking for permission.

The presidency and the Commission also started to reflect on possible responses to the major outstanding problems on finance. Ambassador Christoffersen and Director General Landaburu brought ideas forward which were then discussed at the level of the President of the European Council, Commissioner Verheugen, and President Prodi.

Suggestions about improving the EU offer on direct income support were considered, but in the end rejected because of their budgetary consequences and the fear of rejection by the Member States. However, it was accepted to offer the candidate countries the possibility for 'topping up' by national means the income support to be provided to their farmers. It was also considered possible for candidates to use a part of their allocations for rural development (20 per cent), which they might have difficulties in using, for this topping up.

It was decided not to touch the financial ceiling on Structural Funds, but to offer financial compensation in other areas. Efforts were made to respond to the fear of candidates that they would not receive in practice the promised Structural Funds because of complicated administrative procedures. The presidency responded by offering better facilities for advance payments from the Union budget to the new Member States. It was also decided that the new Member States should be eligible for support for Structural Funds from the 1 January 2004 (even if entry took place a few months later) and that preparation for programmes would be concluded from 2003 on the basis of pre-adhesion information.

It was agreed to propose the establishment of a 'Schengen facility' that would help the new Member States to finance the expensive improvements in frontier controls which they were obliged to introduce. The existing Member States also had an obvious interest in an effective implementation in this area. An amount of €1 billion over three years was suggested. The funds were to be distributed to candidates according to the length of their third country borders.

The candidate countries had also complained that, while they were obliged to contribute to the financing of the CAP in the first year of membership, they would only receive CAP benefits a year later. The presidency felt that it was reasonable that they should be compensated through a refund for their first year of contribution to the CAP. An amount close to €1 billion was at stake.

Four of the new member states (Cyprus, Czech Republic, Malta, and Slovenia) would receive compensation payments in order to ensure that their net receipt did not deteriorate compared to the last year before entry. However, the compensation amounts would diminish as other community expenditure increased. Overall, they would therefore not profit from new funding facilities. The presidency considered that a lump sum should be kept in reserve for these four countries, to be offered at a later stage in the negotiation, when the budget compensation amounts had been fixed, thus leading to a net benefit for the four.

Additional funding would be necessary for the decommissioning of the Ignalina nuclear power plant in Lithuania and the Bohunice plant in Slovakia. At the same time, financial guarantees to Lithuania for costs incurred by the implementation of the Union's arrangement with Russia on the Kaliningrad transport regime would have to be paid by the Union.

Finally, the presidency and the Commission discussed the financial consequences of the entry date. Already for some time it had been clear to them that the working hypothesis of entry on 1 January 2004—on which all the financial calculations had been based—was unrealistic. Even if negotiations were concluded in substance in December 2002, time would be needed for technical tidying up and for final treaty drafting in the first months of 2003. This would leave unrealistically short time for national ratification of the enlargement treaty. A date of entry in the early spring of 2004 would be more realistic. A postponement of the entry date for a few months would financially be to the advantage of the candidates, since they would save some months of financial contributions to the Union, while receiving practically the same in payments. This was due to the fact that the large bulk of payment from the Union to the Member States would fall in the second half of the year.

Institutional issues pointed in the same direction as these financial considerations. The President of the Commission pointed out that the entry of Commissioners from the new member states on 1 January 2004 would necessitate a reshuffling of the portfolios of the Commissioners. This would create considerable turbulence in the work of the Commission in its last year in office. The obvious solution would have been to refrain from according portfolios to the new Commissioners for a full year, but this would be politically unacceptable to the new Member States.

The solution to these problems—a postponement of the entry date for a few months—had been discussed between Anders Fogh Rasmussen and Romano Prodi as early as September. It had been decided not to go public with the suggestion until after the European Council in October, in order to avoid the danger of easing the pressure for agreement in Brussels, and in order to avoid allowing Finance Ministries to cash in on the windfall profit from a postponement of the enlargement date by reducing the financial framework. Now, two months later, time had come to put forward the idea and suggest an entry date of 1 May 2004. At the same time, it was suggested that the date for taking office of the successor Commission should be advanced to 1 November and that the Commissioners from the new members would not have portfolios during this short six-month period (which included the summer break).

The Member States react

The next step was to inform Member States of the proposals for an additional offer to the candidates elaborated by the presidency. On 20 November the presidency reported to COREPER on the financial issues and its intention to present an offer to the candidate countries, with the various concessions agreed with the Commission. The presidency ran into a storm of criticism. The presidency's offer was going far beyond the financial package agreed in Brussels and some of its proposals, in particular the idea of refunding CAP expenditure for the first year of membership, were breaking basic financial principles. The presidency maintained its line of action, however, and it replaced the suggested repayment of first-year CAP expenditure with a 'cash facility' with the same amount. For the rest of the issues, it put forward the package to the candidate countries in unchanged form. The presidency was more than ever treading on thin ice in relation to the Member States.

By the end of November, Prime Minister Rasmussen had set out on his tour of capitals in preparation for the European Council in Copenhagen; during this tour, he was criticized in many capitals for the presidency's 'expensive' suggestions, but neither in Brussels nor in the capitals did anyone go so far as to reject outright the presidency's approach.

The European press reported that the presidency was increasingly being criticized for acting more as an honest broker between the candidate countries and the EU members than as a stern defender of the Union's position.

Member States were briefed on the position of candidates at a meeting held on 19 November on the level of Foreign Ministers. The dissatisfaction with what was on offer, in particular on finance and agriculture, was expressed in no uncertain terms, but there were significant points of convergence. In particular, the candidates agreed on the (new) working hypothesis of an accession date of 1 May 2004. At the same time, they welcomed the understanding that they would be able to participate on equal terms with the Member States in the intergovernmental conference on a constitution of Europe, which would begin its work in the second half of 2003.

The presidency's compromise proposals

The presentation of the presidency's compromise in the third round of the marathon bilateral discussion in the last week of November speeded up the negotiations despite some obstacles that were still to appear. Although a number of candidates were gradually moving towards accepting what was being offered, many issues—some more trivial than others—still required intensive negotiations.

By early December, several of the candidates were getting ready to conclude the negotiations as far as their substantive side was concerned. However, those ready to agree on a package feared that those who remained adamant on their demands would in the end be compensated for their endurance, possibly at the European Council itself.

The presidency then offered assurances that candidates who concluded an agreement before the European Council would also profit from any concessions that might be given in the end to those who had not agreed before. Candidates were also made conscious of the fact that it would be extremely difficult to negotiate technically difficult problems in Copenhagen. It would be to their advantage to settle the issues beforehand and have them included in the overall package which the presidency intended to present to the European Council for approval.

An additional round of negotiations, this time at ministerial level, was being held on 9 December. The presidency was surprised to discover that a number of issues which it considered settled through the many hours of talks were being reopened, but in a show of perseverance on all sides, a renewed effort that lasted throughout the day and the following night succeeded in bringing most rabbits back into the box.

The following day the presidency had to confront the General Affairs Council (GAC), at the same time as criticisms were being addressed to the presidency by the Member States on its 'financial irresponsibility'. It also became clear that the financial questions could only be solved at the level of the European Council. This was no great surprise. More importantly, the General Affairs Council gave its conditional endorsement (conditional of agreement on finance) of the hundreds of smaller or greater points—like agricultural quotas, home distillation of alcohol, or a protocol on abortion for Malta—where the presidency and the Commission had agreed to adjust the negotiation results.

The agreement was only reached after prolonged discussion that stuck on several issues. One example was the decision of the presidency to accord temporary derogation from the Union's habitat directive to permit continued hunting of lynxes in Estonia, as well as brown bears in both Estonia and Latvia, which gave rise to heated discussion before agreement was reached.

An agreement was indeed reached, however, and the presidency finally had the ingredients for the presentation of an overall package to the European Council in Copenhagen, with basically only the financial issues outstanding. The day after the meeting of the General Affairs Council, the final package, in the form of a 136-page long and detailed document, was addressed to the European Council. The presidency knew that this package was acceptable to a majority of candidates. It also knew that some others would negotiate to the bitter end.

More worrying to the presidency was the fact that the Council discussion had revealed that some Member States were starting to ask for concessions for themselves. If the presidency could adjust the milk quotas for the candidates, the argument would go, then the milk quota for Portugal was up for discussion as well.

7. THE EUROPEAN COUNCIL IN COPENHAGEN

The presidency is forgiven its sins

Most candidate countries went to Copenhagen prepared to settle on the basis of the package offered by the presidency, but were simultaneously determined that if others obtained more, they should be entitled to similar improvements. Four countries, Poland, the Czech Republic, Slovenia, and Malta, had expressly rejected what was on offer, in particular with regard to finance. The last three countries had profited the least from the various financial concessions which had been added by the presidency in the last part of the negotiations, because these had led to corresponding reductions in the budgetary compensation on offer. The situation for some candidate countries was unclear.

For the presidency the first objective in Copenhagen was to obtain approval from the fifteen EU members of the package, which it—to the great dissatisfaction of many—had been negotiating on its own responsibility with the candidates. The presidency decided, as it had done in Brussels seven weeks earlier, to confront the main issue head on, through a discussion with heads of states and governments at dinner during the first evening in Copenhagen. The reaction which Prime Minister Rasmussen received at table was very similar to the one he had received in capitals during his visits to colleagues over the preceding two weeks. Serious concerns were expressed on the size of the financial package, and in particular on the pressure which continued to be exerted by some candidates for further improvements. In the end, however, the President of the European Council was forgiven his sins and got the blessing for the package, but also a strong warning that this was the end of the road. No more funds would be available.

Negotiations with the candidates on finance

The next morning started with an early bilateral meeting on a Prime Minister level between the presidency and Poland. Poland had problems with the financial package on offer, as well as misgivings on several other issues. How many was unknown to the presidency, and possibly also to the Polish delegation itself. The meeting with the Poles was difficult. The presidency explained the attitude of the Council, as expressed at the dinner the preceding evening: additional financial concessions were impossible. This did not deter Poland from asking for more. Despite the stand-off, the meeting was useful because it created greater clarity on the nature of the Polish financial and budgetary problems. It turned out that, with regard to finances, the problem was not so much the size of the overall allocation, but the fact that the bulk of the support would go directly to farmers or local entities. The budget of the central government would receive little, at a time where it was confronted with heavy financial costs in preparation for enlargement. The meeting also served to circumscribe the remaining problems in other areas than finance.

At ten o'clock started the meeting of the European Council. In the margin of the meeting, the presidency and the Commission continued to reflect on how to bring the negotiations with Poland forward thereby unlocking the negotiations with the rest of the candidates. When COREPER President Christoffersen and Commission Director General Landaburu met later in the morning, they discovered that they had come across essentially the same idea for a solution to the Polish financial problem. The solution would be found in a limited shift from Structural Fund to the cash facility, which had been established in the latter part of the negotiations. A concrete suggestion for shifting 10 per cent of the structural funding for all candidates from structural funding to the cash facility was prepared by the presidency as the basis for the further negotiations.

A new bilateral meeting with the Polish delegation later in the morning showed for the first time some light at the end of the tunnel. The idea of the shift of funds seemed to offer a basis for making progress. Following the meeting with the Poles, and armed with the hope that the deadlock was about to be broken, the other 'difficult' delegations were called into bilateral meetings with the presidency.

In his next discussion with the European Council, which took place over lunch, the President suggested permitting all candidates to shift up to 10 per cent of the Structural Funds to the cash facility, and allowing the presidency to use an additional €200 million to conclude the negotiations. It was not possible to reach agreement on the first element as it was presented by the presidency.

Some delegations insisted that only Poland should be allowed to shift 10 per cent of its Structural Funds allocations. After much discussion, the heads of state and government accepted a proposal by the presidency to limit the transfer to Poland, but at the same time to allow the presidency a flexibility of a further €300 million to conclude the negotiations with the others. The presidency had not forgotten the promise it had made when concluding negotiations with a number of candidates before Copenhagen that concessions given at the end game would be extended to the others as well. It needed the extra €300 million to honour this commitment. Like the night before, all Member States agreed to more funds, but added that this was really the last money to be put on the table.

This was not going to be the case. A second round of meetings followed in the afternoon, this time with all the candidates, one at a time. The additional €300 million obtained over lunch were distributed to all the candidates (except Poland), but with a distribution key that favoured Malta, the Czech Republic, and Slovenia. These were the three countries that had gott less out of the earlier improvements in the financial package made by the presidency, since improvements were automatically equalled by reduction in their budgetary compensation. The presidency could add a further sweetener for the candidates' national budgets. It had obtained an agreement from the Board of the European Investment Bank to the distribution over a longer period of time of their contributions to the bank's capital than earlier foreseen.

The negotiations moved towards happy conclusions, but a final effort by the European Council would be needed to overcome the last hurdles. The heads of state were once more called together, and the presidency obtained an agreement to extend the application of the Polish model to the Czech Republic. The European Council also agreed to increase the amount offered to Poland under the Schengen facility by €108 million. This was done after obtaining firm promises from the presidency that this was really the ultimate concession.

The financial package agreed in Copenhagen

The result of Copenhagen was the shift of €1,100 million of the Structural Funds entitlement to Poland and the Czech Republic over the first three years. This did not change the overall allocation, but only the distribution between the Structural Funds and the cash facility. In addition, a further €408 million of fresh money was added to the financial package, of which €108 million went to Poland and €300 million to the rest, with particular attention to the Czech Republic, Malta, and Slovenia. The presidency was convinced that not only had it been able to get as much money out of the Member States as was humanly possible, but that it had also been able to assure a fair distribution among candidates.

Table 4 sets out the financial results of the negotiations at the European Council in Copenhagen

The overall financial result of Copenhagen represented an important improvement over the package of €37.5 billion foreseen by the Brussels European

Table 4. Financial results of the negotiations in Copenhagen (€m., 1999 prices)

	2004	2005	2006	2004–6	Commission communication 2004–6	Berlin European Council 2004–6
Agriculture	1,897	3,747	4,147	9,791	9,577	8,780
Structural Funds	6,070	6,907	8,770	21,747	25,567	30,000
Internal policies (including Schengen facility and nuclear safety)	1,457	1,428	1,372	4,251	3,343	2,460
Administration	503	558	612	1,673	1,673	1,350
Total	9,927	12,640	14,901	37,468	40,160	42,590
Cash flow facility	1,011	744	644	2,399	1,129	
Budgetary compensation	262	429	296	987		
Total	1,273	1,173	940	3,386		
Grand total	11,200	13,813	15,841	40,854	41,289	42,590

Council. The Copenhagen package seems on first look €400 million lower than the Commission's January proposal, which had been used as a yardstick by many of the candidates. However, if one takes into account the windfall gain accruing to the candidates by the postponement of the entry date from January to May 2004, a further €1,640 million benefit to the candidates can be added. This brings the value of the Copenhagen package to the candidate countries to a total of €42.5 billion, some €5 billion higher than what was foreseen in Brussels. Taking this additional benefit into account, the Copenhagen package exceeds the Commission's proposal, and comes very close to the ceiling fixed in the Berlin framework, another yardstick to which reference had been made throughout the negotiations.

However, as Member States, the new entrants have to contribute themselves to the financing of the Union. The net transfer of resources from the old to the new Member States would therefore be much smaller than the amounts indicated above. A calculation of the new Member States' net financial benefit for the first three years of membership showed a surplus of €8.2 billion after the Brussels European Council. After Copenhagen the net benefit had risen to €13.1 billion, by almost 40 per cent.

The presidency was convinced that through its various initiatives it had brought the Member States as far as they would go. In relative terms the amounts were small—the net transfer of €13 billion amounted to less than 0.05 per cent of the Union's GDP. For the new Member States, the amounts were more substantial in relative terms. Countries like Cyprus, the Czech Republic, and Slovenia would receive the net transfer in the first three years of membership amounting to 0.2–0.3 per cent of GNP annually. Hungary, Slovakia, and Malta would receive close to 1 per cent; Poland just above 1 per cent. The figure for the three Baltic states reached 2–3 per cent. These were in no way huge sums, but, as it turned out, they were enough to avoid serious problems for the new members' state budgets during the first years of membership.

As far as the matter of the 'quality' of the resources made available was concerned, there had been marked improvements seen from the candidates' points of view. More had been made available for the central governments in the form of cash, and greater flexibility introduced in the use of the various types of Union resources.

Settling the rest

Other outstanding questions had to be settled in the bilateral meetings with candidates in the margin of the European Council, in particular with Poland, but, finally, at seven o'clock in the evening, the President could report back to the European Council, whose members had been waiting for most of the day, that a deal had been reached with the candidates.

Other events at the European Council—or around it—also had a bearing on the final result of the enlargement negotiations. The UN-sponsored talks on the reunification of Cyprus had been on their way for some months, and UN Secretary General Kofi Annan had decided that a final attempt should be made at the time of the European Council to conclude the talks, at a meeting to be held at a separate location in Copenhagen. The Danish presidency had welcomed this final attempt, but insisted that the UN talks be concluded early on during the session of the European Council. The end game of the enlargement negotiations should not be linked to the UN talks on unification of Cyprus. Two versions of the negotiation package on finance for Cyprus were presented at the first day of the Council, one with and the other without unification. When the final package was presented at the end of the day, only the latter package remained on the table. The UN talks had for the moment failed to produce an agreement.

Turkey also was an important point on the agenda in Copenhagen, and the discussions had a direct link to the fifth enlargement process, indirectly through the Cyprus issue, and directly with regard to the relations between NATO and the enlarged Union, where Turkey had been blocking an agreement on EU–NATO cooperation which was essential for building up the EU security and defence policy (ESDP).

The new Turkish government had put the objective of enlargement negotiations with the EU at the top of its agenda, and had started an ambitious reform process in Turkey aimed at doing away with the obstacles (of which foremost was the matter of human rights) to achieving this objective. Turkey expected a sign of encouragement from the Copenhagen European Council, including a date for the start of negotiations. The presidency was therefore prepared to give due prominence to the issue. However, it was also determined that potential differences of view over Turkey among EU members should not be allowed to block agreement on enlargement in Copenhagen. Prime Minister Rasmussen had therefore agreed that discussions on Turkey should be concluded on the first evening in Copenhagen, and not reopened later. Over dinner, heads of state and government agreed a text on Turkey: 'The Union encourages Turkey to pursue energetically its reform process. If the European Council in December 2004, decides that Turkey fulfils the Copenhagen political criteria, the European Union will open accession negotiations with Turkey.' The discussions however did not end there, but continued between delegations in the margin of the European Council the next day. Somewhat to the surprise of the President of the European Council, a new text emerged the next day, in which the words 'without delay' were added to the already agreed text. What was most important, however, was that all delegations agreed to the new text, and that it allowed everybody, including the Turks, to unblock the EU–NATO agreement.

All the pieces of the puzzle were falling into place, but there were still difficulties to overcome.

The European Council reconvened at seven o'clock in the evening, after having been interrupted since the morning. The presidency had held bilateral negotiations with all the candidates throughout the day and had now reached an agreement with each one of them. Only the agreement of the European Council was outstanding.

Since the President of the European Council had consulted the heads of state during the day, the agreement on the enlargement package turned out to be no more than a formality. However, considerable time had to be spent on wrapping up some issues raised by individual Member States, which—while not being part of the negotiations—were linked to the enlargement process. The Austrian Chancellor insisted on a solution to two matters: agreement on the future regime for Alpine transport ('eco-points'), and assurances to Austria on the future of the Czech nuclear power station at Temelin that is situated close to the Czech–Austrian border. Portugal, in turn, insisted on a declaration recognizing the specific nature of Portuguese agriculture. After some discussions, compromise formulations were found on these points. Finally, this late session of the European Council also confirmed that the new Member States would participate fully in the upcoming intergovernmental conference (on 'A Constitution for Europe').

The European Council was presented with and agreed on a text 'One Europe', promising in particular Bulgaria and Romania that the enlargement negotiations with them would continue without delay on the basis of the same principles that had applied to the other candidates. During the Danish presidency, the European Council had gradually been reinforcing its message about future membership. In Brussels, the European Council had expressed 'its support for Bulgaria and Romania in their efforts to achieve the objective of membership in 2007' and foreshadowed an agreement in Copenhagen on a road map, including timetables, to advance the accession negotiations with the countries. The road map was prepared by the Commission and duly approved by the European Council in Copenhagen, together with a significant increase in pre-accession assistance.

The family is brought together

Finally, at around ten o'clock in the evening the candidates were allowed into the European Council room. First, the ten entered in order to confirm their approval of the text 'One Europe', and to formally conduct a short session of the enlargement conferences, which formally approved the negotiation result. This was the first—and the last—time the conferences met at Prime Minister level.

Then the thirteen (including Bulgaria, Romania, and Turkey) met with the European Council. It was time for official statements. It was a moving moment when Prime Ministers and Presidents from the candidate countries, many of whom had worked for decades to see the unification of Europe and the entry of their countries into the Union, saw their lifelong efforts crowned with success. Prime Minister Rasmussen had worked tirelessly and travelled to all candidates and Member States to prepare for a success in Copenhagen. He could now invite the new European family to the family photo, and pronounce in front of the assembled world press his concluding speech:

> Ladies and Gentlemen,
> This is indeed a historic moment and a day to remember, for the people of Europe and for the whole world.
>
> Today we succeeded in fulfilling the aim, which generations of Europeans have fought for. In 1989 brave and visionary people tore down the Berlin Wall. They would no longer tolerate the forced division of Europe.
>
> Today, we have delivered on their hopes. We have decided to heal our continent. We have decided to create 'One Europe'.
>
> Today we have closed one of the bloodiest and darkest chapters in European history. Today we have opened a new chapter. Europe is spreading its wings, in freedom, in prosperity and in peace.
>
> It is truly a proud moment for the European Union. It is a triumph for liberty and democracy.
>
> To our new members I say: 'A warm welcome to our family.'
>
> Our new Europe is born.

The meeting was over, but the celebrations were not. The Danish Queen had invited members of the European Council to dinner in the evening to celebrate the event, but the meeting had lasted too long, and the dinner had to be cancelled. In the end it was the Copenhagen riot police in full battledress, after having been engaged in controlling the demonstrations in Copenhagen (in the end very peaceful) during the day, that were invited to dinner in the royal apartments.

In much less luxurious surroundings, in the cafeteria in the Bella Centre, where the meeting of the European Council had taken place, another party came to life. Many were tired and hungry after the long day of work, and the rumour was spreading that the cafeteria had been resupplied, after having been raided during the day by the many delegates that were patiently waiting for the presidency to conclude the negotiations.

There was a renewed run on the cafeteria by everybody from Prime Ministers to secretaries, and soon a party was in the making. The candidates were bringing in national drinks (from vodka to Budvar beer, by special courtesy of the Czech delegation that had fought hard during the negotiations to preserve the national protection of this beer of Czech origin). Toasts and signatures were exchanged. The family had been brought together.

8. THE DRAFTING OF THE TREATY

While negotiations on enlargement at its final stage involved several rounds of discussions at the highest level, important technical work was proceeding with a view towards producing the text for the adhesion treaty.

Work had started up during the Spanish presidency on the drafting of the Accession Treaty, was intensified during the Danish presidency, and finally concluded during the Greek presidency in early 2003. It was entrusted to a group of officials known as the drafting group.

The drafting work followed the same procedure as the enlargement negotiations. The Commission, which once more had a central role, produced a draft text setting out in legal form the result of the negotiations. This text was then examined in the drafting group, and subsequently forwarded to the candidate countries for approval. If the candidate had amendments or comments, the process would start over again in the drafting group. This could imply several steps of 'back and forth' between the group and the acceding states. In practice, close contacts between the acceding states and the presidency, the Council secretariat, and the Commission allowed many problems to be solved outside the meeting room. The Council's legal service was an important actor in the drafting exercise.

The lessons learned from former adhesion treaty drafting were applied, in particular from the drafting of the latest adhesion treaty with Austria, Finland, and Norway. This precedent implied a model based on one treaty covering all the new Member States (as opposed to one with a treaty for each new Member State). Technical considerations were not the only reason for choosing this approach, as political considerations also came in play, No one wanted to find the Union placed in the situation where a national parliament during the ratification procedure started to pick and choose between the candidates.

It was also decided to create a legal construction comprising:

- The Treaty of Accession, with only three articles: Article 1 stated that the ten countries became members of the Union on the conditions laid down in the act of accession.
- The act of accession that formed the core part of the treaty complex and contained the very substance of the accession provisions. The act in terms referred to a number of annexes.
- The annexes and protocols with regard to individual accession country, where for instance temporary derogations were spelled out.
- The final act with attached declarations (unilateral or joint declarations).

The precedent was useful, but the challenges of drafting a treaty catering for ten acceding countries were huge. The drafting was supposed to be a purely technical exercise, but reality turned out to be different. The drafting group from time to time was confronted with filling out holes that the negotiations had left open or interpreting conclusion texts that were not clear. Particularly in areas where new mechanisms had been invented in the negotiations, problems could arise. This was the case for instance in the field of intellectual property, where the legal systems in the new members were very different from the existing EU. In the negotiations, it had been concluded that 'a new specific mechanism' should be established with a view to ensure the rights of patent holders. The accession conference had not left much guidance as to the content of this mechanism, nor to the conditionality of its application, if any. The drafting group suddenly found itself faced with heavy lobbying from industrial interests. The lobbyists, as well as the Commission, each had their particular ideas on how to fill the gap. After various informal contacts by the presidency and several rounds of discussions in the working group, agreement on a text was finally reached.

Besides transitional arrangements, the act of accession also contains numerous technical adaptations. Because these adaptations are technical in nature, they had therefore not been included in the negotiation process. The *acquis*, however, needed to be updated with names and addresses of authorities allotted responsibility.

As it turned out, not all adaptations were considered purely technical and some proved to be controversial. A typical example was the establishment of lists of mutually recognized professional qualifications. The question of mutual recognition of nurses from Poland had in the end to be settled by the European Council in Copenhagen.

The act of accession would also need to spell out how the new members should be brought into the agreements concluded by the Union with third countries, or how to settle possible problems which the candidates' existing third country agreements might cause in relation to the *acquis*. The so-called Bilateral Investment Treaties, BITS, proved to be particularly difficult to integrate.

In the early months of 2003, translations and jurist-linguistic work (safeguarding the proper terminology and the concordance of the various linguistic versions) had been completed, and the treaty was forwarded to the European Parliament for its assent.

6

Financing the Enlargement

George Vassiliou
Poul Skytte Christoffersen

Many generations of Europeans were dreaming to unite Europe; a dream that could not be realized as long as Europe was divided in two opposing blocs. In 1989 and 1990 the forceful division ended but huge social and economic differences remained between the ex-Warsaw Pact country members and the EU. Thus, the EU's first task was to help the Central and Eastern European countries to overcome the neglect of many decades and promote the reform of their economies and civil society.

This process of reform and its financing could be divided into two periods:

(*a*) the period of preparing for the enlargement, from 1989 to 1998; and
(*b*) the period of enlargement negotiations from 1998 to 2003.

1. FIRST PERIOD (1989–1998)

Practically immediately after the collapse of the Berlin Wall, the EU realized the need for urgent help and economic assistance.[1] This led to the creation of the PHARE project with Council Regulation 3906 of 1989. The original resolution referred to Hungary and Poland only, but shortly afterwards was expanded to cover all Central and Eastern European countries. The programme was put into practice in 1990 and in the period from 1990 until 1998 nearly €9 billion were committed. PHARE focused on two main priorities:

- Institution building and
- *acquis*-related investment.

[1] East Germany, the ex-DDR, was immediately reunited with West Germany and therefore is not included in the group. The cost of its reconstruction was huge and was undertaken by the German government. It amounted to €1.25 trillion for that period and it is doubtful whether all money was wisely spent. All these funds were not included in the programmes created by the EU in order to support the Central and Eastern European countries. Rightly, Germany considered that the reunification of the country was what all Germans aspired to and the support and help was an internal German problem.

First priority: institution building

This accounted for some 30 per cent of the budget. It is defined as the process of helping the candidate countries to develop the structures, strategies, human resources, and management skills needed to strengthen their economic, social, regulatory, and administrative capacity. To serve that purpose an innovative tool was introduced: the long-term twinning of administrations and agencies. Ever since its inception, this new instrument has occupied a central place in pre-accession assistance. With EU support, the vast body of Member States' expertise was made available to the candidate countries, through the long-term secondment of civil servants and accompanying expert missions, in order to support them in their efforts to adopt and implement key areas of the institutional infrastructure.

The process worked as follows: the Commission identified lacunae in the administration in the candidate countries. The candidate country was asked to come up with a concrete project to reform the administration and then the Commission asked the Member States to mobilize a team of experts, led by a project leader and a pre-accession adviser, in order to help the candidate country to reform its administration. It is a very pragmatic, case-by-case method of reforming public administration.

Initially, twinning focused on the fields of agriculture, environment, public finance, justice and home affairs, and regional policy; later the twinning instrument covered the whole body of the *acquis* in all its diversity. During the 1998–2001 period, more than 500 twinning projects were programmed. Their implementation often involved more than one EU Member State.

Second priority: *acquis*-related investment

This accounted for 70 per cent of the total economic assistance and consisted of two major types of activities:

1. Co-financing of investment in the countries' regulatory framework to strengthen the regulatory infrastructure needed to ensure compliance with the *acquis*. In other words, investment needed to operate the internal market, such as putting the food safety structure in place, making frontiers secure, procuring testing and measuring equipment related to the internal market, or for laboratories and control equipment in the field of consumer protection.
2. Co-financing of investment in economic and social cohesion, initiated in PHARE 2000 programmes, through measures similar to those supported in Member States through the European Regional Development Fund (ERDF) and the European Social Fund (ESF). This promoted the functioning of the market economy and the capacity to cope with competitive pressure and market forces within the EU. It represented about one-third of each national PHARE programme.

Table 5. Commitment of funds by country

Country	Commitments (1990–1998) in millions of euros	Population 1998 (000)	Commitments/capita
Czech Republic	389.73	10,282	37.8
Estonia	162.83	1,429	116.9
Hungary	864.04	10,116	84.1
Latvia	206.57	2,424	85.3
Lithuania	272.03	3,694	76.4
Poland	1,731.51	38,718	64.8
Slovakia	253.23	5,377	47.0
Slovenia	131.29	1,993	66.1

Sources: (1) The PHARE Programme Annual Report 1998, Annual Report 1998; (2) Eurostat.

In Table 5 we are giving an analysis of the various sums committed by country. Infrastructure for energy transport and telecoms absorbed the biggest amount, 24 per cent of the total, followed by the private sector (private and restructuring, SMEs) (13 per cent) and education and training (11 per cent). The analysis by country clearly shows that in absolute terms Poland received most of the money followed by Hungary. On a per capita basis, however, the Baltic states, Estonia and Latvia, received the highest allocation.

2. SECOND PERIOD (1998–2003)

PHARE's total 'pre-accession' focus was put in place in 1997, in response to the Luxembourg Council's launching of the enlargement process. PHARE funds focused entirely on the pre-accession priorities highlighted in the road maps and the accession partnerships which established the overall priorities the country had to address in order to prepare for accession and the resources available to help them do so. The National Programme for the Adoption of the *Acquis* was the candidate country's timetable for preparing for accession. It estimated the timing and cost of the steps needed to prepare the country for membership and the implications for staff and financial resources.

These orientations were further refined in 1999 with the creation of SAPARD and ISPA, which took over rural and agricultural development (SAPARD) and infrastructural projects in the environmental and transport fields (ISPA) allowing PHARE to focus on its key priorities on all other fields.

In financial terms this period could be subdivided into the years 1999–2001 and the second period, the so-called Agenda 2000 period, for the years 2002 to 2006, i.e. covering the first two years after accession as well.

1999–2001

Accession negotiations with the six countries of the so-called Luxembourg group, (Poland, Hungary, Czech Republic, Slovenia, Estonia, Cyprus) started in March 1998. Nearly two years later, in December 1999, at the Helsinki Summit, it was agreed to include four more countries, Slovakia, Malta, Latvia, and Lithuania.

The financial assistance, however, covered all ten countries during the whole period. This was provided through the PHARE programme, in operation since 1990 covering Bulgaria and Romania as well, although they did not accede in the Union with the other ten countries in 2004. During these three years, 1999, 2000, and 2001, altogether €4,768.6 million were committed for various projects within the agreed framework.

3. AGENDA 2000: THE UNION FINANCES COPING WITH THE ENLARGEMENT

The negotiations on the economic and financial aspects of Agenda 2000, which was initiated in 1998 and concluded at the meeting of the European Council in Berlin in the spring of 1999, was different from earlier financial negotiations in the Union by directly integrating the enlargement perspective.

The basic principle in all earlier enlargement negotiations had been that the candidate countries would adapt to the Union's *acquis*, while the Union budget would remain the same until the enlargement. The challenges of the fifth enlargement however were such that part of the burden of change had to be borne by the Union. At earlier enlargements the consequences with regard to the Union's budget had been evaluated and absorbed after enlargement. For the fifth enlargement the budget discussion was initiated with the Agenda 2000 proposal, almost six years before the enlargement took place.

The background to this change in policy was that the Union was facing an enlargement without precedent. With regard to the number of countries, the accession of the ten Central and Eastern European countries plus Cyprus and Malta would exceed those of all previous enlargements taken together. The total area of the Union would increase by a third and its population by almost 30 per cent. In terms of gross domestic product, however, the increase would be modest—less than 10 per cent—as compared to almost 30 per cent with the first enlargement with UK, Denmark, and Ireland. The explanation was to be found in the low gross domestic product of the candidates. The Union taken together would become less affluent. If all the candidates (including Romania and Bulgaria) had entered the result would be a fall in the overall domestic product per capita by 16 per cent. This was not an unknown consequence of enlargement of the Union. Except for the 1995 enlargement with Sweden, Finland, and Austria all other enlargements had led to a fall in the GDP per capita, including the enlargement with East Germany. However, this time the difference between the older and the newer states was much greater. When negotiations started GDP per capita in most of the candidates was below 30 per cent of the Union average.

The Commission was in no doubt. The Union had to adapt to this new situation and changes had to be made to its policies, in particular to the Common Agricultural Policy and the Union's cohesion policy, first and foremost its Structural Funds.

On agriculture, not just enlargement but also the World Trade Organization (WTO) called for change in order to reduce the distorting effect of the Common Agricultural Policy on world trade. The main thrust of the Commission's proposals was to move away from price support of specific agricultural products to income support for farmers. Such a change would make life easier in WTO, but would also be much less expensive in relation to enlargement. Income support was in principle given to compensate for price cuts. Prices for agricultural products in the candidate countries were at the time much lower than in the Union. There would therefore be no price cuts to compensate in the new countries. On the contrary, farmers in the new members would benefit from a price increase. The Commission also argued that farmers in the candidate countries in addition would see a huge increase in economic support to agriculture by the application of the existing *acquis*. As a result there would be a major increase in production of the entrants and the formation of surpluses in the enlarged Union. Such a step would distort the economies of the new Member States, by unduly supporting agriculture, compared to other economic activities.

The Commission's proposals underwent change during the discussion in the Council. The shift towards income support in the existing EU became less ambitious than that proposed by the Commission. But the exclusion of income support to the new entrants was maintained. It was on this basis that the Commission determined the amount to be inscribed in the new pluriannual financial perspectives for agricultural support to the new Member States.

Reform on Structural Funds was also necessary, in order to avoid an explosion in expenditure in the enlarged Union. The main objective was to concentrate support to regions with the greatest need. Support for structural adjustment for regions lagging behind or affected by decline in traditional industries, which under the previous regime had covered 51 per cent of the Union's population, should be concentrated on 35–40 per cent of the population in the existing EU. The Commission further proposed an overall ceiling on aid to a country, corresponding to 4 per cent of the country's GDP. The ceiling was justified by experience in the existing Union, which had shown that very large transfers were difficult to absorb, and could create problems of overheating to the detriment of a stability-oriented macroeconomic policy.

The Commission's proposals on geographic concentration in the existing EU were watered down in the negotiations in the Council and the European Council. The final result was a concentration on 40 per cent of the population. The country ceiling of 4 per cent of GDP remained.

On finance the Commission proposed to keep the overall financial framework below the existing ceiling on the Union's financial resources. Agenda 2000 was the third multi-annual framework established by the Union. The two former frameworks (Delors Package I and II) had involved substantial increases in Union expenditure. But times had changed. Public expenditure was coming under increased pressure in the existing Member States, not least in the light of the need to reduce deficits on public finance in preparation for entry into force of economic and monetary union.

According to the financial system, the Union's resources increase annually in line with real growth in GDP. Maintaining the overall ceiling meant that, within the automatic increase, resources had to be found for financing the development of the existing Union' policies, and for the new entrants.

In the end, Agenda 2000 ended up with a framework for the Union's finance where total expenditure for the enlarged Union by the end of the financial perspectives (2006) would remain stable as a percentage of overall Union GDP compared to the year 1999. The total amount set aside for commitments (the limit on the financial engagement of the Union in a given year) for the last year of the financial perspectives would represent 1.13 per cent of Union GDP, the same percentage as in the first. For expenditure appropriations (the amount which could actually be paid out in a particular year) the ceiling in real terms in the last year of the financial perspective would be lower than in the first. This result was achieved after heavy cuts in the Commission's original proposals on EU 15 expenditure.

Agenda 2000 spelled out the direct financial costs of enlargement in the various spending categories. For this expenditure Member States endorsed the Commission's proposals. The Union reserved €4,140 million in 2002 rising to €14,220 million in 2006 (14 per cent of the budget) for commitments on Union expenditure in the new Member States.

In addition the Union would provide €3,100 million in pre-adhesion aid every year. The yearly sum would remain constant over the period, also after the first candidates became members. Pre-adhesion funds that were liberated when a country became a member would be channelled to the remaining candidate countries. Pre-adhesion aid would be concentrated in three areas: agriculture, structural policy (in particular transport and environment), and PHARE support, mainly for technical assistance in preparation for membership.

In order to make its calculations the Commission had to make an assumption as to how many countries would accede during the period 2000–6, and on the year in which accession would take place.

With regard to the number of countries, the Commission based its proposal on the entry of the six countries it had picked out for the first wave. On the date, the Commission made the assumption that entry would take place in 2002.

With hindsight this seemed an ambitious date. Nor did it reflect a deep conviction inside the Commission that entry at such an early date was unlikely. However a number of Member States had started to talk about early entry dates. Both the German Chancellor and the French President had mentioned the year 2000 in public speeches. The Commission could not be seen as dragging its feet compared to the Member States by proposing a much later date. As we all know the facts on the ground imposed their own solution. Ten and not six countries joined not in 2002 but in 2004. The Agenda, however, in essence did not change.

Table 6 sets out the agreement reached in Berlin.

Table 6. Berlin agreement: financial framework EU 21 (€m., 1999 prices)

Appropriations for commitments	2000	2001	2002	2003	2004	2005	2006
1. Agriculture	40,920	42,800	43,900	43,770	42,760	41,930	41,660
2. Structural operations	32,045	31,455	30,865	30,285	29,595	29,595	29,170
3. Internal policies	5,900	5,950	6,000	6,050	6,100	6,150	6,200
4. External actions	4,550	4,560	4,570	4,580	4,590	4,600	4,610
5. Administration	4,560	4,600	4,700	4,800	4,900	5,000	5,100
6. Reserves	900	900	650	400	400	400	400
7. Pre-accession aid	3,120	3,120	3,120	3,120	3,120	3,120	3,120
Agriculture	520	520	520	520	520	520	520
Pre-accession structural instrument	1,040	1,040	1,040	1,040	1,040	1,040	1,040
PHARE (applicant countries)	1,560	1,560	1,560	1,560	1,560	1,560	1,560
8. Enlargement			6,450	9,030	11,610	14,200	16,780
Agriculture			1,600	2,030	2,450	2,930	3,400
Structural operations			3,750	5,830	7,920	10,000	12,080
Internal policies			730	760	790	820	850
Administration			370	410	450	450	450
Total appropriations for commitments	91,995	93,385	100,255	102,035	103,075	104,995	107,040
Total appropriations for payments	89,590	91,070	98,270	101,450	100,610	101,350	103,530
Of which: enlargement			4,140	6,710	8,890	11,440	14,210
Appropriations for payment as % of GNP	1.13%	1.12%	1.14%	1.15%	1.11%	1.09%	1.09%

4. OVERALL APPRAISAL

Overall in the period between 1990 and 2003, €11,370 billion were spent by the EU to help the future members bring up their institutions and infrastructure to a level that would permit accession to the EU.

In absolute terms this is a significant amount of money but compared to the economic strength of the fifteen member countries and the EU budget it is surprisingly small. It hardly accounts for 1.3 per cent of the EU budget for the same period. This amount sounds insignificant if we relate it to the budgets of the fifteen members. On average, for the whole period, the EU budget absorbed just over 1 per cent of the members' budgets. In other words, only about 1 per thousand of the members' budgets for the period was spent on enlargement.

As a result of the enlargement, however, the GDP increased by at least 10 per cent and, what was even more important, new dynamism was injected in to the Union. It is not surprising that the new members attracted significant investments not only from the other member countries but from the whole world. As a result GDP growth in the first years after enlargement, i.e. 2004 and 2005, was three to five times higher in the new countries.

In Table 7 we are providing an overview of total commitments for the period for all ten countries. As expected PHARE, which was already operating in 1990,

Table 7. Total commitments to the ten candidate countries, 1990–2003

Country	PHARE commitments (1990–2003) in millions of euros	SAPARD commitments (1999–2003) in millions of euros	ISPA commitments (1999–2003) in millions of euros	Total commitments (1990–2003) in millions of euros	Population 2003	Total commitments (1990–2003) per capita in euros	Per capita GDP in PPS 2002 (euros)	Total commitments to total GDP (1999–2003) for each country
Czech Republic	881.14	93.30	290.30	1,264.74	10,203,300	124	14,820	0.0012
Estonia	328.32	51.10	121.20	500.62	1,356,000	369	9,650	0.0055
Hungary	1,442.95	160.60	371.70	1,975.25	10,142,400	195	12,830	0.0018
Latvia	403.21	92.80	196.60	692.61	2,331,500	297	8,370	0.0050
Lithuania	772.75	125.70	215.16	1,113.61	3,462,600	322	9,570	0.0054
Poland	3,879.23	712.17	1,553.97	6,145.37	38,218,500	161	10,010	0.0020
Slovakia	687.81	77.50	201.25	966.56	5,379,200	180	11,340	0.0025
Slovenia	340.85	27.00	63.60	431.45	1,995,000	216	16,710	0.0019
Cyprus				79.00	715,100	111	18,380	0.0013
Malta				50.00	397,300	126	16,530	0.0016
Total	8,736.26	1,340.17	3,013.78	13,219.21	74,200,900	178	11,370	0.0023

Note: Total commitments to accession countries as a percentage of total EU budget for the period 1990–2003 = 1.3%.

Sources: (1) General Report on Pre-accession Assistance (PHARE—ISPA—SAPARD) in 2003; (2) The PHARE Programme Annual Report 2003; Annual Report 2003; (3) Eurostat Yearbook 2004; (4) Partnership for the Accession of Malta and Cyprus (**http://europa.eu.int/scadplus/**).

accounted for nearly two-thirds of the total amount, but the amounts spent on infrastructure (ISPA) and agriculture (SAPARD) were also significant.

In absolute terms Poland absorbed nearly half of the commitments, followed by Hungary and Czech Republic. On a per capita basis, however, the Baltic states absorbed by far the highest amounts (€369 for Estonia, €321 for Lithuania, and €297 for Latvia) and Cyprus and Malta which were not entitled to PHARE funds the lowest.

7

The Public's Attitude to Enlargement

George Vassiliou

1. ANALYSIS BASED ON THE EURO-BAROMETER

Generally speaking the prospect of EU enlargement from fifteen to twenty-five members was accepted by the EU public both in the fifteen member countries and the candidates as a fact. The issue did not create any great animosity but neither enthusiasm. From the moment the so-called Iron Curtain collapsed it was accepted as a sine que non that the EU would be enlarged. This feeling was strengthened with the incorporation of East Germany in the Federal Republic. From there on it was a matter of time as to when the various Central and Eastern European countries, in addition to Cyprus and Malta, would be invited to join. It is characteristic in this respect that during the whole period of the negotiations the media gave limited attention to the issues of enlargement while they pointed out various other issues with which the fifteen dealt at their summits.

2. ATTITUDES OF THE PUBLIC IN THE MEMBER COUNTRIES

During the whole period of the accession negotiations, from 1998 to 2003, the public attitude in the fifteen member countries was more or less equally divided between those supporting the enlargement and those indifferent or opposing. Attitudes varied significantly, however, from country to country. Overall, the north and the south (Scandinavian and Mediterranean countries) were much more enthusiastic than citizens of the UK and other Western European countries.

As can be seen from Table 8, based on the Euro-barometer data, support in Denmark and Sweden was as a rule above 60 per cent. The same was true for Spain and Italy. Greece had an overall higher acceptance rate, around 70 per cent, which however was due to the special importance attributed to the prospect of Cyprus's accession to the EU. What is significant is the fact that from 1998 until the end the percentage of those in favour increased substantially while those who had no opinion declined substantially.

The main worries of the public in countries like the UK and France, with a low percentage of acceptance, were related to the prospect of unemployment. They

Table 8. Percentage of support for enlargement, EU 15

	Autumn 1998	Autumn 1999	Autumn 2000	Autumn 2001	Autumn 2002	Autumn 2003
Greece	61	57	70	74	76	65
Sweden	63	62	56	69	65	54
Denmark	61	60	56	69	71	63
Spain	51	48	58	61	63	62
Italy	48	49	59	61	64	61
Ireland	41	47	52	60	67	59
The Netherlands	51	55	40	58	58	50
Portugal	42	40	52	57	60	52
Finland	52	49	45	54	58	53
Luxembourg	36	41	46	53	56	45
Belgium	28	42	45	49	53	43
Germany	34	38	36	47	46	38
Austria	30	35	32	46	51	41
UK	44	41	31	41	42	38
France	35	34	35	39	41	34
EU 15						
In favour	42	43	44	51	52	47
Against	34	35	35	30	30	36
Don't know	24	22	21	19	18	17

were afraid that accession particularly of the Central and Eastern European countries would lead to massive emigration, mainly from Poland, leading to negative results on both the level of salaries and the employment of the local population. As a result, the EU leadership considered it necessary to ensure a transitional period, for the first time ever, not by the acceding but the member countries. Thus free movement of persons was postponed for a few years.

Interestingly enough, however, the reality proved to be entirely different as:

(*a*) there was a very limited immigration, and
(*b*) it not only had no negative impact but, on the contrary, a positive effect on the economies of all countries that permitted free immigration.

3. ATTITUDES OF THE PUBLIC IN THE CANDIDATE COUNTRIES

When negotiations started in 1998 there was a lot of scepticism among the public of the candidate countries regarding the prospect of accession, despite the very favourable position taken by their political leaderships. Practically all political parties (with only a few exceptions) were enthusiastically in favour. Probably this is why there was no large outright opposition to accession and overall those in favour were five times as many as those against.

Table 9. Support for membership according to the Euro-barometer

Country	% Support for membership				Referendum result
	Oct. 2001	Oct. 2002	Nov. 2003	Mar. 2004	
Slovakia	58	58	58	46	92
Slovenia	41	43	50	40	90
Cyprus	51	47	59	42	no referendum held
Poland	51	52	52	42	77
Latvia	33	35	46	33	67
Lithuania	41	48	55	52	90
Malta	39	45	55	50	54
Czech Rep.	46	43	44	41	77
Hungary	60	67	56	45	84
Estonia	33	32	38	31	67
EU 10					
In favour	50	52	52		
Against	10	10	12		
Don't know	12	10	7		
Neither good nor bad	28	28	29		

Note: The Euro-barometer started producing data for the candidates as from 2001.

The public's reservations are easy to understand. All Central and Eastern European countries had only recently become fully independent, with the collapse of the Soviet bloc, and were uncomfortable with the prospect of joining another bloc about which they knew very little. This is clearly proved by the fact that more than one-third of the respondents were not able to express an opinion, 28 per cent taking a neutral position (neither good nor bad) and another 12 per cent saying 'don't know'.

As can be seen from Table 9 attitudes remained remarkably steady over the years for the ten candidates together. On a country-per-country basis, however, there were remarkable differences, from a high rate of approval of over 60 per cent in Hungary and around 50 per cent in Poland, Slovakia, and Cyprus to a low rate of 30 per cent to 40 per cent in the Baltic states.

These reservations, however, were abandoned when the public was invited to express its opinion on the accession. At the referendums at the end of the negotiations, the results were indeed impressive. In all countries, percentages between 75 and 90 per cent were recorded, i.e. practically doubled compared to the Euro-barometer figures.

The population recognized that membership of the Union ensured peace and greater security but also economic development, a higher standard of living, and unlimited opportunities for the young.

The lowest level of approval was recorded in Malta, an attitude easy to explain. Malta has two major political parties, the Labour Party and the Nationalist Party, which traditionally share between them the votes. The Maltese Labour Party has always been against membership the EU, while the Nationalist Party was in favour. This attitude never changed and as a matter of fact when the Labour Party gained power in the mid-1990s it went to the extreme in freezing Malta's application for membership. The Nationalist Party returned to power in September 1998 and renewed the negotiations, which were successfully completed together with the other candidate countries in December 2002. At the referendum in March 2003, accession was approved by 53.6 per cent as compared to 46.4 per cent against.

The results of the referendums in the three Baltic states were also interesting. Only 67 per cent were in favour in Estonia and Latvia but 90 per cent in Lithuania. The reason is that both the Estonian and Latvian publics were always sceptical concerning the accession, which implied becoming a member of a large Union and losing a part of their sovereignty. Both Estonia and Latvia for centuries were annexed by their neighbouring powers. They became independent for a few years only at the beginning of the twentieth century and were subsequently absorbed in the Soviet Union. Thus when in 1990 they gained their independence, they were very anxious to protect it. All three states were very small countries and considered their newly found independence as their most valuable asset. Fortunately, at the referendum two-thirds voted in favour because they realized that the best way to protect their freedom was to become part of a larger union.

The attitude in the third Baltic state, Lithuania, was entirely different, as 90 per cent voted in favour. History again played a decisive role. Lithuania was practically always independent and for several centuries together with Poland controlled a significant part of Eastern Europe. Accordingly, Lithuanians were not afraid of joining together with the other European countries.

4. SUPPORT FOR EU MEMBERSHIP CURRENTLY

Generally speaking, the realities of accession have proved to be in accordance with the expectations of the public. Those against continue to be a small minority, while those in favour are at the same level as the pre-accession Euro-barometers indicated. In some countries there is a slight decline but in the majority there has been an increase of support.

The figures for the spring 2005 Euro-barometer (the most recently available) for the twenty-five members this time clearly show that those in favour are nearly four times as many to those against (Table 10 and Fig. 1). Furthermore, irrespective of whether they are old or new members they judge the EU according to the prevailing attitudes in their respective country. At the time of the barometer, thus the UK and Sweden have the highest percentage of 27 per cent and 28 per cent against while Luxembourg, Ireland, Slovakia, and Poland have the lowest.

We should also point out that one-quarter of the respondents took a neutral position. This in itself proves the need for an even more intensive and systematic effort to present the many advantages offered by the EU to its members.

Table 10. Support for EU membership

Country	% Support for EU Membership		
	Oct. 2002	Oct. 2004	Mar. 2005
Slovakia	58	57	54
Slovenia	43	52	49
Cyprus	47	52	43
Poland	52	50	53
Latvia	35	40	42
Lithuania	48	69	59
Malta	45	45	40
Czech Rep.	43	45	49
Hungary	67	49	42
Estonia	32	52	48

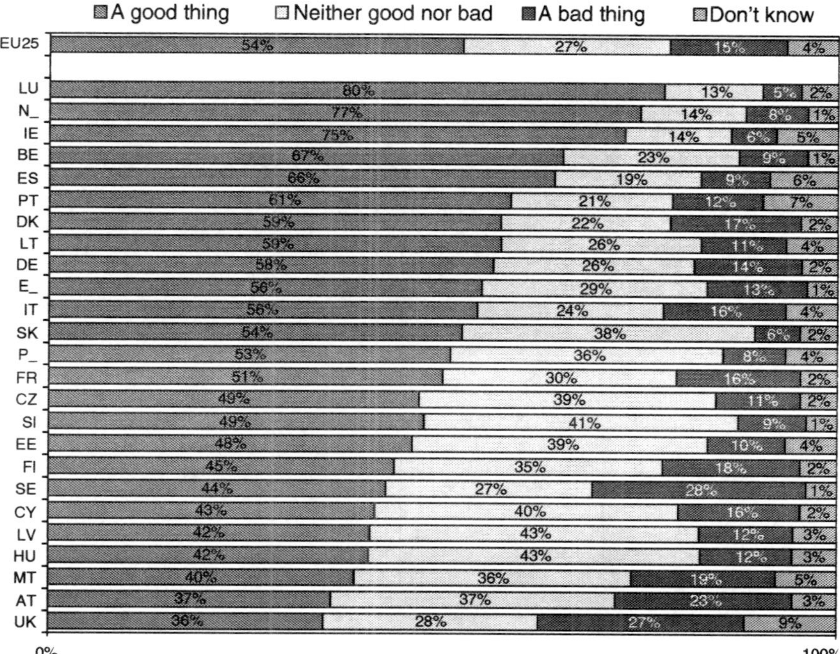

Figure 1. Support for membership of the EU

To assess the attitudes of the citizens to Europe they were all asked as to whether they are proud to be Europeans. The overwhelming majority of nearly 70 per cent answered positively. Attitudes, as expected, vary greatly from country to country; from a maximum 87 per cent in Hungary to only 50 per cent in Britain.

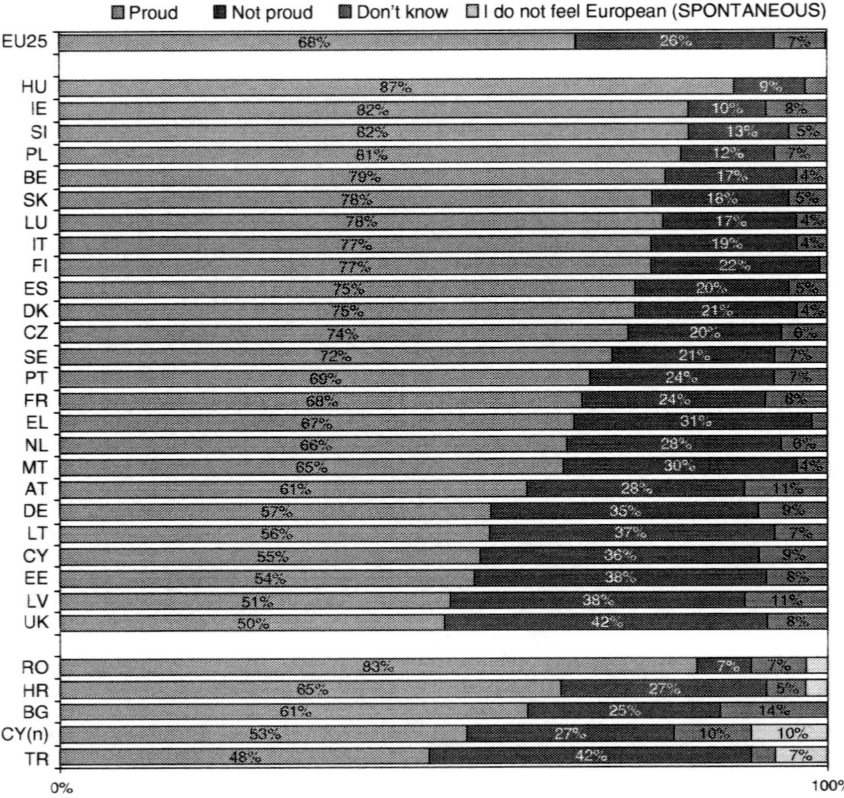

Figure 2. Would you say you are ... to be European?

In six out of the twenty-five countries less than 60 per cent claimed to be proud of being Europeans, out of which four were new members, the three Baltic states and Cyprus (Fig. 2).

Part II

The Ten Countries' Story

8

The Accession of Cyprus to the EU

George Vassiliou

1. INTRODUCTION: THE POLITICAL BACKGROUND

The Republic of Cyprus was established in 1960 after gaining its independence from Britain. Unfortunately, only three years later, intercommunal strife erupted and the Turkish Cypriots resigned from the government and withdrew into a number of enclaves where they lived all together. The UN had to intervene, and intercommunal negotiations followed, but the efforts to reach an agreement failed. In 1974, the Greek junta staged a *coup d'état* against President Makarios, which was followed a week later by a Turkish invasion, under the pretext of 'restoring the constitutional order'. As a result, Turkey seized more than 37 per cent of Cyprus's territory, which it still occupies today.

During the thirty years since the invasion, there have been several UN and Security Council resolutions and a series of intercommunal negotiations under UN auspices but unfortunately no solution has been reached. The lack of a solution and the continuous occupation of part of Cyprus by Turkish troops created a strong need for security, despite the significant economic progress of the Republic since 1974. It is accordingly easy to understand that the accession of the Republic of Cyprus to the European Union, which was everyone's objective, was by far the most important event since independence in 1960. On 13 December 2002, Cyprus was accepted into the European Union. The dream of all Cypriots, which looked unattainable when the application for accession was submitted in 1990, became a reality. For a very long period it was obvious to everybody that the European Union could not accept the accession of Cyprus before the solution of the Cyprus problem. Obviously, the Union was not willing to take over such a difficult problem that remained unsolved for such a long time and caused serious tensions between Greece and Turkey.

They all agreed, however, that the accession process would benefit the search for a solution. Accordingly, we pointed out to all concerned parties that we desired and worked for the reunification of our island more than anybody else. In the past, many mistakes were committed but we wanted to finally close this chapter which opened with the intercommunal conflicts of the 1960s, the Greek junta *coup d'état* in 1974, and the subsequent invasion by Turkey. Our ardent and honest desire was to secure the reunification of our island and the accession of a united Cyprus into the European Union; a simple and straightforward message welcomed by all.

During the whole period, from the submission of our application in July 1990 until accession, Greece was our faithful, valuable ally and supporter. The role and support of the Greek political world and in particular Prime Minister Simitis and the Foreign Minister George Papandreou during the whole period cannot be overestimated. Greece's position from the very beginning could be summed up in one phrase: 'we will not accept a different treatment for Cyprus because Turkish troops occupy part of it. You should judge Cyprus's application on its own merit and of course follow closely the negotiations under the UN auspices. If, despite the UN efforts, a solution cannot be found, Cyprus should not be punished twice; once by the invasion and continuous occupation and subsequently by treating it differently from the other applicant countries and denying its accession.'

In December 1997, at the European Council in Luxembourg, the application of all ten candidate countries was carefully considered and the decision was taken to open accession negotiations with six of them, namely Cyprus, the Czech Republic, Estonia, Hungary, Poland, and Slovenia, usually referred to as the Luxembourg group. The decision concerning Cyprus pointed out:

> 28. The accession of Cyprus should benefit all communities and help to bring about civil peace and reconciliation. The accession negotiations will contribute positively to the search for a political solution to the Cyprus problem through the talks under the aegis of the United Nations which must continue with a view to creating a bi-communal, bi-zonal federation. In this context, the European Council requests that the willingness of the Government of Cyprus to include representatives of the Turkish Cypriot community in the accession negotiating delegation be acted upon. In order for this request to be acted upon, the necessary contacts will be undertaken by the Presidency and the Commission.

The European Council thus sent a very clear message. It wished to see one delegation negotiating the accession of Cyprus in which Turkish Cypriots would also participate irrespective of the fact that the problem of the division of the island was still unsolved.

Immediately after, the government of Cyprus tried to fulfil this request. First of all, we had to decide who would appoint the Turkish Cypriot members of the negotiating team. Some Greek Cypriot politicians wanted the President of the Republic to appoint them. Fortunately, the opinion of the moderate forces prevailed and President Clerides early in 1998 informed the UK presidency of the Union that:

> having in mind Paragraph 28 of the Luxembourg Conclusions, which states, inter alia, that the accession of Cyprus should benefit all communities and help bring about civil peace and reconciliation ... I repeated my wish that the Turkish Cypriot Community nominate representatives to be included as full members of the Cypriot team, which will conduct the negotiations.
>
> Regarding the participation of the Turkish Cypriot Community on the Delegation, I am making an earnest and solemn invitation to my Turkish Cypriot compatriots to

participate; for I firmly believe that they should take an active part and make their contribution to the negotiating process for acceding to the European Union.

Should the Turkish Cypriot Community respond favourably to this proposal they may rest assured that the points of view and the opinions of their representatives will be discussed freely, seriously and in good faith and that the conclusions reached will constitute an important element in formulating the negotiating positions of the Cyprus team.

I hope that the response of the leadership of the Turkish Cypriot Community will be positive.

The significance of President Clerides' proposal was that although the Cyprus problem was not solved, the government acknowledged a relative independence of the Turkish Cypriot community institutions and that among others it was their task to decide who would represent them in the negotiations.

This decision by the Cyprus government was enthusiastically received both by the UK government, which held the presidency of the EU during the first semester of 1998, and all the Member States. Unfortunately, it was rejected outright by both Turkey[1] and Mr Denktash, the leader of the Turkish Cypriot community. Despite this rejection, at the Edinburgh European Council, 14 March 1998, it was decided to go ahead with the negotiations with Cyprus, as was originally agreed in Luxembourg.

Before starting negotiations, the government had to decide whether the Cyprus delegation would be negotiating on behalf of the Turkish Cypriots as well, despite their non-participation in the delegation. Fortunately, the tragic mistake to try and provide information on the prevailing conditions in the Turkish-occupied areas was avoided. As long as the Turkish troops controlled that part of the island, we could not provide any information. We expressed the hope that the accession process would facilitate and contribute to the solution of the Cyprus problem. This position was fully understood and considered fair by the Commission, enabling us to start negotiations on 31 March 1998, together with the other five countries.

The prevailing view at the time was that reunification would have to come first and accession second. Greece and other countries correctly pointed out that there should be no differentiation between Cyprus and the other candidate countries and that negotiations should start with all of them on an equal footing and were sincerely hoping that the new perspective of EU membership would help the process of reuniting the island. At the same time, of course, we were not prepared to accept any Turkish blackmail and in the event that, despite our efforts, a solution could not be reached, we were expecting that the whole island would join the EU but that the application of the *acquis* in the occupied areas would be suspended. On Cyprus' part, it was most important to appreciate the reluctance and anxieties of the EU Member States and, at that stage, to avoid pushing for a decision concerning the accession of Cyprus, if we

[1] Turkey was at that time greatly annoyed with the EU because it was exempted from the group of candidate countries destined to become members of the EU.

had failed to reach a solution as a result of Turkish intransigence. It was vital to start the negotiations and we purposely refused to discuss what would happen if there was no solution. We placed all emphasis on the fact that we were cooperating fully with the United Nations and we were hoping that intercommunal talks would start shortly and be successful. This attitude was welcomed by the EU Member States. Characteristically, the then permanent representative of Germany to the Union, Ambassador von Kyaw, told Mr George Vassiliou, at a meeting in early 1998, 'You are right, let's cross the bridge when we come to it.' The issue, however, was there and it was for this reason that all positions of the EU concerning the provisional closing of the thirty-one chapters started with the following declaration:

> The EU recalls its statement relating specifically to the negotiations with Cyprus made at the opening of the Conference as well as point 6 of the General Affairs Council Conclusions of 5 October 1998; in this context the EU notes that the invitation of the Cyprus government to include representatives of the Turkish Cypriot community in the negotiations has so far not been taken up, and that the Conference may therefore return to this chapter at an appropriate moment. The EU underlines the importance for Cyprus of compliance with the Association Agreement as well as with the Accession Partnership, which constitute basic elements of its specific pre-accession strategy. The EU encourages Cyprus to continue the alignment of its policies with the acquis and its effective implementation.

This policy was followed consistently over the years while at the same time Greece laboured to improve its bilateral relations with Turkey. The opportunity was given after the earthquakes in Turkey in 1999 and the so-called 'earthquake diplomacy' that followed. Subsequently, Greece took the wise decision to give up its veto policy vis-à-vis the perspective of starting accession talks with Turkey and created the conditions for the Helsinki decision in December 1999, in which it was clearly stated that

> The European Council welcomes the launch of the talks aiming at a comprehensive settlement of the Cyprus problem on 3 December in New York and expresses its strong support for the UN Secretary-General's efforts to bring the process to a successful conclusion. (b) The European Council underlines that a political settlement will facilitate the accession of Cyprus to the European Union. If no settlement has been reached by the completion of accession negotiations, the Council's decision on accession will be made without the above being a precondition. In this the Council will take account of all relevant factors.

Thus, the issue of the relationship between the solution of the Cyprus problem and the accession to the EU was clearly and finally clarified.

The perspective of accession to the EU was supported by all political forces in the government-controlled areas of the island without exception. The reason was very simple. There was a consensus that the accession process would contribute towards the solution of the Cyprus problem. For the first time ever, membership in the EU would offer real security and certainty for the future to all Cypriots and particularly to Greek Cypriots.

2. ORGANIZATION OF THE NEGOTIATIONS

Managing the effort

The perceived need for accession was so great that it justified every effort and any necessary sacrifice. We realized that we had to perform impeccably in the accession negotiations and we could not afford the luxury of delays. We had to convince everybody that we were doing our utmost to satisfy the Union's requirements and adopt the *acquis* while at the same time working closely with the United Nations in order to promote a solution of the Cyprus problem.

The above requirements made it necessary to combine the role of the negotiator with that of the coordinator within the country and entrust one person with this task.

The job included, among others:

- negotiations and continuous contact with the Commission in Brussels and the Member States' several envoys in Cyprus;
- harmonization and implementation of the *acquis* in Cyprus;
- full and continuous cooperation with all ministries and government services and departments and modernization of the government machinery;
- on-time drafting and subsequent approval by Parliament of the hundreds of new laws required;
- creation and development of harmonious relations with all interested parties and in particular trade unions, farmers' organizations, and businessmen;
- successful cooperation with the public at large and all political parties; and
- promotion of relations and presenting Cyprus' case in Brussels and all member countries.

The whole effort was guided and coordinated by the former President of the Republic, Mr. George Vassiliou, assisted by a small committee consisting of seven persons and using the services of the Planning Bureau and a special unit in the Law Office of the Republic. The Foreign Ministry had no supervisory role, as was the case in most other candidate countries, but in order to be able to contribute to the whole effort it had a representative in the seven-member committee. The amount of legal harmonization work was indeed huge. It is enough to mention that, altogether, Cyprus had to prepare and have approved 1,080 laws and regulations. The number of legislative changes by chapter was as follows:

Chapter 1—Free movement of goods	200
Chapter 2—Free movement of persons	21
Chapter 3—Freedom to provide services	58
Chapter 4—Free movement of capital	15
Chapter 5—Company law	18
Chapter 6—Competition policy	24
Chapter 7—Agriculture	253

Chapter 8—Fisheries	11
Chapter 9—Transport policy	64
Chapter 10—Taxation	16
Chapter 11—Economic and monetary union	4
Chapter 12—Statistics	2
Chapter 13—Social policy and environment	74
Chapter 14—Energy	23
Chapter 17—Science and research	4
Chapter 18—Education, training, and youth	2
Chapter 19—Telecommunications and information techniques	35
Chapter 20—Culture and audio-visual	4
Chapter 22—Environment	135
Chapter 23—Consumer and health protection	15
Chapter 24—Cooperation in justice and home affairs	66
Chapter 25—Customs union	25
Chapter 26—External relations	6
Chapter 28—Financial control	3
Chapter 29—Financial and budgetary	2

In order to succeed in carrying out this task on time, a very large department was set up within the Law Office of the Republic, comprising more than thirty experienced lawyers. Even so, some of the laws, for example those relating to the institutions of telecommunications and energy regulators and regulation of the respective market, company law and protection of intellectual property, credit institutions, and certain aspects of the environment, were commissioned to outside lawyers, either in Cyprus or abroad, specializing in the respective fields.

In each ministry a special team was set up to coordinate and implement all related harmonization. Their tasks included:

- the cooperation with the Law Office for the drafting of the necessary legislation;
- making all necessary changes and taking all necessary steps to implement in their ministry all harmonization-related tasks.

To ensure that the various tasks were being carried out on time and to help address the unavoidable hiccups, Mr Vassiliou scheduled regular meetings in all ministries to review the situation and decide on any necessary steps. The accession process itself created the need to push for the restructuring and modernization of the significant part of the government machinery, as well as the change of attitude within the various government departments. New organizations had to be set up, for example the Paying Agency for Agriculture—which had to be completely detached from the Department of Agriculture—the State Aid Commission, the simplification of the tax system, the restructuring and strengthening of the Monopolies Commission and the Shipping Department, etc.

One of the most demanding and unpleasant challenges that Cyprus had to face was the sorting out of overlapping in competencies, as for a number of activities there were several ministries involved. This was a basic requirement of the EU which specified that for every task there should be one and only one responsible body. The fact that I had served as President of the Republic, a few years before, and I was not answerable to any specific ministry, in other words that we had no 'axe to grind', helped me carry out this task successfully. It required, however, a lot of time and effort as well as all my 'diplomatic' capabilities.

Coordination with the House of Representatives (Parliament)

A special department was set up in the House of Representatives in order to coordinate the work necessary for the adoption of the several hundreds of laws and regulations that had to be enacted. In addition, to succeed in our efforts two important initiatives were introduced: first, all laws, irrespective of the subject, were discussed and approved by the Committee on European Affairs and not, as with all other legislation, by the various specialized committees, such as labour, finance, etc.

Second, all hearings from outside organizations were abolished. Only the representatives of the relevant ministry and the Law Office were present and could give the necessary explanations and clarifications to the Committee, in addition to the overall presentation made by the chief negotiator and other members of the coordinating team. However, at the drafting stage the various interested parties were invited by the relevant ministry and the Law Office to express their views and present any objections, which to the degree possible were taken into consideration. The views and any objections of all those outside organizations and interested parties were communicated to the Committee of European Affairs and therefore there was no need for it to call them again for their views.

Of course, if parliamentarians felt obliged to discuss certain legislation at their committee they could do so, although the Committee on European Affairs had the final word and responsibility of preparing the submission to the Plenary Meeting. By making this theoretical concession we ensured that all MPs representing all political parties were satisfied and at the same time no delays occurred. By the end of the five-year period there were only a few isolated cases for which this parallel examination took place. As soon as the law was drafted, it was submitted to the Committee for examination and approval. Voting in the Assembly was a mere formality. Usually, it was the first item on the agenda and there was no discussion. During the whole period we also arranged to have regular meetings with all relevant organizations, trade unions, farmers' unions, employers, and other interested bodies.

Presenting the Cyprus case

The negotiations as such were conducted on the Union side by the Task Force and the Inter Directorate General for Enlargement of the Commission assisted by experts from the relevant Commission departments, and on our side by the chief negotiator and his team assisted by officials from the relevant ministries. The accession conference meetings, which took place twice a year at Foreign Minister level, were simply a necessary formality.

Many people believe that it was the meetings in Brussels—the formal negotiations—that were important. On the contrary, the real work was carried out at home. Brussels presented the *acquis* and asked questions. It was our task here in Cyprus to understand and implement it. The EC officials frequently visited the island, personally examined how things worked in the ministries, and inspected the various establishments and institutions. As a rule, this was a lengthy and elaborate process during which the EC officials became acquainted with our system and were convinced that the *acquis* was being implemented and our various requests for transitional periods were justified. Subsequently, at the semi-annual meeting at COREPER and chief negotiators' level, the official documents were presented, pre-prepared statements made, and if already agreed, the chapter provisionally closed.

We should point out that on the part of the Commission we found both understanding and the relevant goodwill but we never for a moment got the impression that we could be exempt from adhering to and implementing the EU requirements. Any requests for transitional periods had to be submitted after serious study and fully justified with detailed documentation. It was important to distinguish those issues on which we would have to insist until the end and hopefully convince our counterparts that our requests were justified and those we might have to abandon and withdraw. It was obvious that for practical reasons we could submit neither an unlimited number of requests nor too few.

All requests, irrespective of whether they were to be withdrawn later or not, had to be fully justified. Furthermore, once commitments were made we had to make sure that we stuck to those commitments and implemented them in the best possible way. If there were delays it was of no use to try and hide them. On the contrary, it became very quickly obvious that it was to our advantage to be open and honest with the Commission, explain the difficulties faced, and clarify how and when we expected to overcome them. Honesty was indeed the best policy, and we consistently pursued such a policy: tell them the truth and try to stick to our commitments. Furthermore, we had decided, from the beginning, not to try to blame Brussels for any problems or difficulties we might encounter. It was much better to explain the situation and mobilize our resources.

Evidently, the success of the effort depended mainly on the competence of our people at home as well as on our ability to present our case convincingly, develop good relations, and gain the confidence of the officials involved on the Commission side. At home we were sometimes criticized by certain individuals and political parties for being too soft and not very demanding or aggressive during the negotiation process. The results, however, regarding our overall performance, if judged by the transitional periods, quotas, etc. granted to Cyprus, in comparison to the other applicant countries, disprove that argument.

Parallel to the work on the implementation of the *acquis*, we had to convince the Member States and the Commission that Cyprus's accession would not cause too many problems or be a burden to the Union. Fortunately, the Cypriot economy was in good shape, social peace prevailed, and the level of unemployment was low and the rate of inflation insignificant. We were confident that with accession we would contribute positively rather than negatively to the Union. Among others, Cyprus would help in the improvement of safety and better protection of the Union from illegal immigration and drug trafficking, and with the addition of the Cypriot shipping fleet, the EU would have by far the largest merchant fleet in the world.

Finally, we pointed out that we could contribute to the development of better relations with our neighbours, Israel and the Arab countries, and act as a bridge of the EU to the Middle East. As was correctly pointed out to us by the former Prime Minister of Israel, Mr Netanyahu, Israel was supporting Cyprus's application because with Cypriot accession, Europe would come nearer and become part of the eastern Mediterranean area.

3. NEGOTIATIONS

The negotiations followed the same pattern for all six countries of the so-called Luxembourg group. They started in March 1998 with the screening phase and were completed in December 2002. However, this is where the similarity ends, because for every country there were different problems and issues that had to be addressed and the significance of the various chapters varied from country to country.

For each chapter, we had to decide whether there were any issues for which we would have to request transitional periods. It was extremely important in this respect to realize that nothing could be taken for granted; a lot would depend on how convincing we were in presenting our case and on what tactics we followed in order to achieve our objectives.

In this book it is neither possible nor advisable to deal with every single aspect of the accession process. Instead, we concentrate on presenting the negotiations on some of the issues for which harmonization was more problematic and where particular difficulties were encountered. These are:

The single market
Competition policy
The cooperative movement
Agriculture
Shipping
Taxation
Environment
New status for the British bases
Protocol No. 10 on Cyprus

The single market

The creation of the single market is by far the most important achievement of the European Union and its continuous development and strengthening is indeed the backbone of the Union. Cyprus, as well as all other candidate countries, had no reservations whatsoever in joining the single market. The main challenges we had to face were not in Brussels but at home. This was a much more difficult task than it looked. We had to negotiate with our own people. We had to:

(i) Harmonize with the EU and adopt all standards, HACCP regulations, etc.;
(ii) Gradually abolish all forms of protectionism, i.e. any legal or other advantages Cypriot products enjoyed vis-à-vis those imported from the EU;
(iii) dismantle monopolies of certain agricultural products; and
(iv) create all those institutions and services that were absolutely vital in order to permit the functioning of the single market.

The concept of the single market is composite. In order to have a single market, it is necessary to ensure the free movement of goods, persons, services, and capital. Monitoring of the proper functioning of the single market is ensured by the harmonization of company law and adhering strictly to the free competition requirements. Overall, the volume of work related to the introduction of all single market requirements was huge and had to be a continuous effort over a long period of time. It is enough to mention that in order to meet the EU requirements we had to prepare and adopt more than 300 new laws and regulations.

Free movement of goods (chapter 1)

The formal negotiations lasted for eighteen months, from June 1999 to December 2000, when the chapter was provisionally closed. Our limited requests, after some discussions, were met. We secured a transitional period until December 2005 for all the pharmaceutical products that already had a permit to circulate but did not fully conform to the new EU regulations. The Commission also agreed to our decision to prohibit the import of any products containing boron in order to protect our underground water resources and agricultural products. The hard work was to adopt the EU standards and implement the HACCP regulations.

Adoption of EU standards

The first challenge we had to face in order to ensure the free movement of goods was the adoption of standards. In the Ministry of Commerce and Industry, a Standards Organization was functioning but with a very limited output. Over several years, it only succeeded in adopting a few hundred standards when the need was to introduce and adopt well over 10,000. If we were to continue working at that tempo, we would need at least ten to fifteen years to meet the EU requirements.

Shortly after the start of the negotiations, this weakness became evident and despite the efforts to strengthen the Organization it became obvious that they would need many years to do everything by themselves. As in the case of the 'Gordian knot', a radical solution was needed. We decided to stop developing the standards ourselves and entered into an agreement with the British Standards Institute. As a result, within a few months it became possible to electronically transfer from the UK to Cyprus all the EU standards. The fee paid to BSI was hardly equal to the annual salary of two low-grade staff in the Organization.

HACCP

The task of introducing the HACCP regulations for manufacturing, warehousing, and retailing of meat, dairy, and other food products was extremely demanding and difficult. As far as the Union was concerned, the rules were clear and we had to implement them. In Cyprus, however, we knew that there were hundreds of meat and milk producers working in conditions totally unacceptable to the EU We had to explain to all those manufacturers that it was to their advantage to change and that we would give them every possible assistance to upgrade their establishments. Time was of the essence as in the 'Contre le montre' race in the Tour de France.

In addition, there was considerable overlap, but no cooperation, between the Department of Sanitary Services of the Ministry of Health and the Animal Husbandry Department of the Ministry of Agriculture. Both departments claimed to be responsible for this function and we had to sort out, after a number of meetings and consultations with them, the specific competencies of each department.

To succeed we had to be ruthless. We made it clear to all producers that they either had to meet the EU requirements or stop producing. Considerable subsidies were offered but that was not enough. Many were too small and inefficient. So at the end of the day we had to close down hundreds of meat and milk processing establishments and ensure that only those capable of investing and meeting the HACCP requirements would remain. As an example we mention that out of thirty-two abattoirs, only three were allowed to stay in business. The largest one at Kofinou, which accounted for nearly 70 per cent of the total production, received close to €2 million in order to be modernized and meet the EU requirements. Even so, however, we spent too much time explaining to the officials that changes had to be made.

Free movement of capital (chapter 4)

The free movement of capital is the other side of the coin in the functioning of the single market. Unfortunately, while Cyprus was in principle ready to accept and adopt the EU requirements, in practice we had to overcome many difficulties. One of them was the fact that Cyprus was the only country in Europe, and probably in the world, that still had in operation a law introduced by the British colonial powers during the Second World War, limiting the interest rate that could be charged to a maximum of 9 per cent. The original intention was to protect the population from usurers who used to charge well over 10 per cent even for short-term loans. However, it ended up being a serious impediment to the development of the economy and the adoption of the single market. The EC officials made it quite clear that this law had to be abolished. The Commission was prepared to give us some time in order to take the necessary measures, but nothing more. The problem for us was that within the country, practically all political parties were in favour of maintaining the law, considered by many as a God-sent gift for the population at large. It took a lot of pressure and many months of discussions, both in Parliament and publicly, to obtain agreement for the law to be abolished as from 1 January 2001. Fortunately, the overall reduction of interest rates during the last few years enabled banks in Cyprus not only to avoid increasing the base rates above 9 per cent, which was the main fear expressed by all those who insisted on maintaining the previous law, but subsequently to reduce them significantly. We should also point out in this respect that many Cypriots, even among bankers, were expressing the fear that with the abolition of controls there would be a significant outflow of capital from the island. Fortunately, as the experience of the other countries had shown, this fear was also baseless. If anything, there was capital inflow rather than outflow subsequent to the abolition of this law.

Money laundering

One of the most difficult challenges we had to face in ensuring the closure of this chapter was the image of Cyprus as a money-laundering centre. This image was partly due to the fact that in the 1980s Cyprus had become a major offshore centre. Accordingly, through Cyprus hundreds of millions of dollars were transferred around the world, as we had a very favourable tax system and we were the only country that had double taxation agreements both with the Soviet Union and the USA. In the early 1990s, Cyprus was also extensively used for investments in Russia. Furthermore, partly due to the traditional close relations with the ex-Yugoslavia, there were many offshore Yugoslav companies registered in Cyprus, in addition to the Beogradska Banka, which had offices on the island as well.

It is by now well known that in the early 1990s there had been a number of cases of improper use of Cyprus for money transfers. This is why we had established a special unit (MOKAS), under the Central Bank's jurisdiction to combat money laundering and drug trafficking. However, the bad image was there and the EU rightly was very strict and demanding on this issue. They wanted to be convinced that we had indeed implemented all those measures that were absolutely necessary in order to stop money laundering practices and apprehend any individuals that were responsible for such crimes. We therefore had to invest a considerable amount of time and money in the building up and strengthening of the MOKAS unit. It took a lot of hard work for the unit to succeed in setting up an effective anti-laundering mechanism and to convince members of the Union and other countries that we were successful in our efforts. This work had finally borne fruit and was recognized in the 2003 EC progress report which pointed out that we succeeded in fully implementing satisfactory controls through the adoption of the necessary legal infrastructure and also by supporting and strengthening the operations of MOKAS.

Purchase of holiday houses

The free movement of capital implies, among other things, that any citizen of the EU is free to purchase a second residence anywhere in the Union on the same conditions as any citizens of that country. In Cyprus this was not the case. Non-Cypriots had to obtain a permit to purchase a house after the Council of Ministers (cabinet) considered and approved any such request. The political parties made obvious their desire to maintain these controls after accession as well. The EU, however, was not prepared to grant such a permanent exception. After long and demanding negotiations, we ensured a transitional period of five years up to 1 January 2008. This compromise was accepted as fair, although criticisms were heard by some due to the fact that subsequently the EU agreed to also grant such derogation for Malta. My personal view is that the Union's approach is correct; the free movement of capital is a sine qua non, although some exceptions, as for Malta due to the very small size of the island, are justified.

Company law (chapter 5)

This was a relatively easy chapter, which did not require too many changes on our part. Cyprus, having been a British colony, had introduced the British company law system, which was compatible with the EU's requirements. I refer to this chapter, however, because it is a typical case of the applicant country insisting wrongly on securing an exception.

It is a basic requirement of the EU law that every company should publish the names of its shareholders. This measure is considered necessary for the protection of all persons that may have any dealings with the various companies. We tried to ensure the right to continue with the established practice which permitted the offshore companies not to publish the names of their shareholders if they so desired. The Commission, however, was not prepared to agree to such an exception. For a time, it looked as if we might have serious problems as some of the offshore companies, particularly in the shipping sector, implied that they might be obliged to relocate should the law change.

In the end, we had no choice but to withdraw our request. It is interesting, however, that this was a typical case of 'much ado about nothing'. The rule was implemented, but there were no negative repercussions for any company and the sector continues to thrive. The companies were simply used to a practice which we were obliged to abandon.

Competition policy (chapter 6)

Undoubtedly this was one of the most difficult chapters, and we did not succeed in closing it until June 2002. It required complicated and demanding negotiations with both the Commission and some member countries, as well as at home. In Cyprus we had to deal mainly with the farmers' organizations and, at a different level, with the offshore sector, which includes the international companies and ancillary activities such as legal and accountancy services.

We had to address three issues, each one requiring different approaches and skills. These were:

- The need for legal harmonization and creation of the relevant institutions in order to be able to implement the competition policies;
- Our request for the introduction of a 'grandfather' clause in order to ensure the continuous existence of the offshore sector; and
- The abolition of trade monopolies for a number of agricultural products.

New institutions

The first issue did not involve any difficult negotiations with Brussels. The *acquis* was given and well known. The problem was not in preparing the relevant laws but in giving substance and power to the relevant institutions.

The Competition Authority was already in existence since 1990, but needed restructuring and strengthening. It also needed to deliver a few decisions in order to prove both to the Commission and Cypriot businessmen that it was a real and effectively functioning institution. With the help of outside consultants, continuous follow-up, and also a decision to impose a penalty of £20 million on the Telephone Authority for anti-competitive behaviour, the Authority convinced everyone of the need to respect the competition rules.

The State Aid Authority had to be created afresh and had a substantial task to fulfil, as state aid in various sectors was the rule rather than the exception (in 2001 it represented 2.1 per cent of the budget). Within a short period, however, after intensive training, the Authority was able to clear the backlog and ensure the proper functioning of the market.

The need to abolish the special treatment of the offshore sector

The existence of the offshore sector and two different tax systems presented a major problem. In vain we argued that this issue would be satisfactorily handled within the taxation chapter. COREPER was not prepared to agree to the closing of the chapter unless they saw proof of substantive action. We had no choice but to speed up the whole process. Thus, while the relevant legislation was only submitted on 30 May 2002, within two days it was unanimously approved by the parliamentary Finance Committee. Brussels was immediately informed and the green light for closing the chapter was given.

Another difficulty was related to our request for the 'grandfather' clause. We agreed that the distinction between offshore and onshore should be abolished, but we wanted to ensure a transitional period during which the original tax of 4.25 per cent would remain in effect for all companies registered no later than 31 December 2001. The Commission did not agree. We knew, however, that our request was justified as such a 'grandfather' clause had been granted for two other members in the past. After several years of discussion, with both officials of the EC and member countries, a compromise was reached and a transitional period until the end of 2005 was granted.

Literally at the last moment, two days before the meeting, three member countries objected to granting the transitional period. We reacted with hectic last-moment negotiations with them which fortunately ended well. The whole issue was due to a misunderstanding caused by the existence of a relevant agreement between the member countries. Cyprus, however, was not one of the signatories and therefore we could proceed with the original agreement.

Abolition of trade monopolies

For several major agricultural products, state monopolies were created shortly after the establishment of the Republic. The most important ones were those for:

wheat and grains
milk products
wines
potatoes
olives and olive oil.

All these monopolies had to be abolished and replaced by voluntary producer organizations. Both the farmers affected and the civil servants involved were dead against such a move and tried by all means to avoid any action. This was a typical case where it was easy to agree with the EU, but extremely difficult to implement that agreement. Because of the farmers' and others' reaction, considerable delays occurred. At the very last moment, after a lot of effort, and at a significant cost, we did what had to be done. Fortunately, the new arrangements are functioning efficiently, proving once more that sticking to the old familiar system is not necessarily the best solution.

The cooperative movement

The cooperative movement had very deep roots in Cyprus with the first societies having been established at the beginning of the twentieth century. By the time the accession negotiations started, they had become the major source of financing for the low- and middle-income population and, in general, all activities related to farming. There was practically no village or suburb of the urban areas without its own Cooperative Society. In total, they were responsible for about a third of both the deposits and loans. The societies were extremely proud and outside the control of the Central Bank. Last, but not least, they were very important politically because of the size of the movement serving the needs of nearly half the population. Therefore, it was of the utmost significance to ensure their cooperation and smooth transition to the new conditions, which we knew would be radically different from the prevailing ones.

We should point out in this respect that the coops were enjoying a number of privileges; they were exempted from paying income tax and their clients were exempted from paying the required mortgage fees. As a result, there was a continuous undeclared war between the commercial banks and the cooperatives. The banks demanded the abolition of the coops' special privileges and, at long last, they were now hoping that this would be achieved with the help of the EU. Therefore, we were facing a very difficult task, to say the least. We knew that we had to meet the EU requirements for banking institutions and safeguard of competition, but we also knew that we had to carry with us the cooperative movement and retain the maximum possible benefits for their members.

There were two separate sets of problems that had to be addressed:

(*a*) The need to ensure the special treatment of the cooperative movement which was not, under any circumstances, willing to accept the direct supervision of the Central Bank but also conform to the very stringent banking directives of the Union.

(*b*) To find solutions for the special privileges that the societies were enjoying up to that moment.

It was obvious a gradual approach was needed. It had to be seen that we were trying to protect the cooperatives and we assured everybody that during the whole process, which we knew would last several years, no initiative would be taken without discussing and agreeing it with the leadership of the movement. At the same time both the Central Bank and commercial banks had to be assured that the EU regulations would be implemented.

Accordingly, in our first paper submitted in 1999 we requested the exception of the cooperatives from the banking directives. We justified this request by pointing out that the coops are servicing the low-income population and are not profit-making organizations. We knew of course that this first position, although rational and justifiable in the eyes of the coops, could not be fully accepted by the EU.

After the submission of the initial positions, a three-year period of intensive negotiations followed. Gradually, the coop leaders familiarized themselves with the requirements of the Union and understood that despite the initial difficulties, they would be able to face successfully competition from the banks while also safeguarding their members' privileges. At the same time we succeeded in convincing the Union's officials that special treatment for the coops was both required and possible. In this respect, it should be pointed out that the leadership of the cooperative movement was directly involved in the negotiation process and was thus kept informed of any developments. This helped in building a mutual trust between the coops and the chief negotiator. The final agreement ensured the following:

(*a*) The cooperative movement accepted the banking directives but was given a transitional period of five years within which to gradually adapt itself to them. At the same time, the Commission agreed to the continuation of the independence of the cooperative movement and did not insist that every single coop would come directly under the supervision of the Central Bank.

(*b*) We ensured that the exemption from paying income tax would continue. To achieve this, we had to accept that coops would pay normal taxes for any business done with non-members. (This, anyway, did not create any serious problems since the bulk of the coops' activities were carried out with members.)

(*c*) Finally, we also achieved the continuation of the exemption from mortgage charges. However, in order to meet the competition rules this exception applied to all mortgage takers, whether they were being financed by coops or commercial banks. To safeguard against any considerable reduction of income by the Treasury, it was agreed that this exception would apply only to mortgages of up to £60,000. This arrangement covered the bulk of the coop clients' needs and satisfied everybody.

Agriculture (chapter 7)

Agriculture in Cyprus is not as important as it used to be. For many farmers it is a part-time activity, as most inhabitants of the rural areas work in either the construction industry or government services until early in the afternoon and they are thus able to spend some time every day plus the weekends on their small plots. Only those working in the milk and dairy sector and potato-growing tend to be full time, in addition of course to the retired persons who continue working on their plots until a very late age.

Because of its importance, as well as the many products and policies involved, the chapter on agriculture required several years of negotiations covering practically the whole period from 1999 until the very last moment in 2002.

The strategy followed by Cyprus in the negotiations was based on a maximalistic approach for the following reasons:

(*a*) We prioritized our requests so that, if necessary, we could withdraw a number considered to be of secondary importance, giving us a stronger position to insist on the more important ones.

(*b*) To ensure the cooperation of all agricultural organizations and farmers, we included in our position paper all requests submitted by the agricultural organizations in cooperation with the Department of Agriculture. Both the negotiating team and the agricultural organizations were aware of the remote chances of the EU accepting certain of our requests. The inclusion

> of these requests, however, served in avoiding any mistrust by farmers and possible accusations of not fighting hard enough to get the best possible results in the negotiation process.

The general impression in Brussels, after we submitted our position paper, was that Cyprus's requests far exceeded those submitted by any of the other nine accession countries. Cyprus therefore was asked to withdraw a number of requests and concentrate on the more important issues.

On issues where we felt that we were treated unfairly, we were very firm in presenting our case again and again, supporting it with sound argumentation. For example, on the issue regarding the yield per hectare on arable crops, we insisted that it was not fair to calculate the average yield by including the years of drought, as these would have given an unrealistic and unfair average, which would be detrimental to the Cypriot producers. We reiterated our position that yields should be as representative as possible of the true average situation and free of distortions caused by the high variations and uneven distribution of rainfall. We strongly opposed the inclusion of the years 1997, 1998, and 2000 for calculating the average because, during these years, Cyprus was plagued by an unprecedented and persistent drought. To prove our case, we submitted official data on rainfall and production, which proved beyond any doubt that our argumentation was reasonable. This led to its final acceptance.

Another example, also related to a large extent to the climatic conditions, was the fat content of cow's milk. The minimum fat content set by the EU is 3.5 per cent, a target that could not be easily reached by Cyprus due to the lack of grazing pastures. Finally, a 3.2 per cent rate was agreed for a transitional period of five years with the provision to be re-examined at that stage through the appropriate Community procedures.

Equally intense were the negotiations concerning the quotas for certain of our agricultural and dairy products. In particular, quotas relating to cow's milk, total arable land, and beef production were of crucial importance and we had to insist on achieving our targets.

On the whole, through our persuasiveness supported by factual information, we ensured that the overall quotas set for Cyprus were as a rule fair. In fact, for a couple of products, like the number of goats and sheep, the quotas were beyond our original expectations. These negotiations proved that EU officials were ready to modify their initial ideas and accept the candidates' requests, provided that these could be justified by hard facts. The importance of collecting detailed statistical data cannot be overestimated.

However, it also became obvious that under no circumstances would the EU meet requests if these would be in direct conflict with basic principles relating to the functioning of the relevant common market organizations for agricultural products. As a result, a number of our claims could not receive a more favourable treatment (for example, there is the special subsidy of €25/tonne on coarse grain imported from the EU due to long distance and tariff-free imports of 35,000 tonnes of wheat from third countries).

On the issue of direct payments, we insisted that the rationale for not granting them in full was of no immediate relevance to the conditions of Cyprus. Cyprus could not be penalized once by not receiving sufficient pre-accession aid and then a second time by being treated as if it was a CEEC country and being given only 25–35 per cent of the direct payments.

Unfortunately, Brussels insisted that all countries should be treated the same way and the Commission proposition was that a lump sum be paid back to new Member States to offset any deterioration of their net budgetary position in comparison with their situation in the year before accession. This was a typical case in which even the best statistical data and convincing arguments were of no help. The overall logic of the CAP realities imposed the policy of treating all the ten candidates differently, and this could not be altered.

Accordingly, we had no choice but to provide supplementary payments from national funds. Even so, we had to secure the EU's approval. Thus, at the very end of the negotiations, when practically all issues were agreed upon, we had to convince the Commissioner of Agriculture that we should continue paying subsidies for certain agricultural products from national funds at the pre-accession level. Thus, unlike other countries, for a number of products Cyprus would be entitled to a 'top-up 2' subsidy, i.e. continue paying subsidies above the level of those prevailing in the EU Member States for a transitional period up to the end of 2008. At the same, time Cyprus was asked to provide substantial state aid to certain sectors.

The question of subsidies on irrigation water had to be solved differently. The EU made it abundantly clear that, as a matter of principle, no state aid would be accepted for water. We therefore had to withdraw our requests. Subsequently, we initiated a new study of costs with the help of invited experts, who proved that the cost of water in dams was substantially lower than previous estimates. Therefore there was no need to increase the price of water supplied to farmers.

Shipping (chapter 9)

Cyprus was indeed, as the EU had also indicated, one of the largest shipping nations in the world. This had been achieved because we were pioneers in introducing favourable tax policies for shipowners but also due to the fact that we were rather tolerant on issues of ship safety. As a result, there were a number of over-age ships under the Cyprus flag and the incidence of arrests of ships was relatively high, something that led to Cyprus being placed on the blacklist of the Paris MOU. This was unacceptable to the European Union. It is indicative to point out that whilst the rate of arrest of EU ships was under 4 per cent, for Cyprus it was well above 12 per cent in 1998. The need to radically revamp the conditions under which Cyprus' flagged ships were operating was obvious. The task was entirely different from all other chapters. In all chapters, negotiations implied that we had to understand the *acquis*, compare it with the prevailing conditions in the country, promote harmonization, and try to achieve transitional periods where necessary. In this case, however, we had nothing to negotiate about with the EU. We were very happy to accept the *acquis* and implement it. But we had a tremendous amount of work to do with our own people, changing the attitude and work practices of our Department of Shipping. The emphasis until then had been on trying to recruit more and more ships to the Cyprus flag. From now on, it had to shift to safety. As it proved, it was very difficult to change this attitude and it took several years of hard work to achieve the turnaround.

The experience gained from the negotiations proved that one of the major advantages of our application to join the Union was that it helped us to improve the supervision and security of the standards as well as the overall management within the country. I have no doubt whatsoever that had it not been for this application, Cyprus would still be well behind the Paris MOU regulation standards. The various commercial interests would be exercising a disproportionate influence and a more relaxed attitude would have prevailed. Today, however, as a result of our determination, the Cyprus flag has been removed from the Paris blacklist.

Ship management

The problem with the ship management companies was entirely different. While in the case of shipping the task was to fight within Cyprus to change attitudes and improve standards, for ship management we had to convince the Commission and some member countries that their approach to ship management companies had to change radically. Ship management was considered as an ordinary service, like all other services, and was taxed accordingly. This attitude did not take into account the fact that shipowning had radically changed in the last decades; that the days of famous shipowners, like Onassis, Niarchos, etc., were over. Nowadays, because of the costs and responsibilities involved, more and more ships were owned by not one but several shareholders and, furthermore, the responsibility of managing the ships was taken up by specialized companies. In the past, the aim was to ensure a single cargo at a good price. Today the aim is, rather, to efficiently manage the ship on a medium-and long-term basis in order to satisfy the demands of both the users and the owners.

Therefore, we tried to convince the EC officials to treat shipowning and ship management companies in the same way. In other words, to be permitted to use the tonnage tax system instead of the income tax if they chose to do so. This was not easy to achieve, but at the end we did it. We were thus able to preserve Cyprus as the centre for ship management and safeguard the employment of thousands of professionals and also offer an important service to the ship industry at large. According to the new guidelines, put in force as of January 2004, shipping companies and ship management companies could be treated equally as far as taxation is concerned.

Taxation/offshore sector (chapter 10)

By far the greatest challenge posed by the EU was the need to create a unified system of taxation and abolish the existence of two separate tax systems; one for the offshore companies of only 4.25 per cent and the normal tax of the onshore companies of 20–25 per cent corporation tax and 20–40 per cent income tax. The EU made it quite clear that under no circumstances would they accept the continuation of a double tax system, particularly since the special rates for the offshore companies were considered as a form of state aid and hence unfair competition.

Clearly, we had no choice but to harmonize our two tax systems. This was easier said than done. We could not possibly abandon the international business sector which was one of the most important sectors of the economy, employing thousands of highly competent professionals, in addition to being a very large source of income. Neither could we however jeopardize the prospects of Cyprus' accession to the EU. In other words, we were faced with a dilemma of having to 'square the circle'.

Obviously a drastic approach was needed. To succeed we needed the understanding and help of the offshore sector companies in the island as well as of the Cypriot political parties, which was of particular importance because the government did not have a majority in Parliament. The situation became even more difficult, as a number of people in the government and the business community were under the impression that in some way we could more or less maintain the international business sector without radically changing the tax system. We knew that this would be practically impossible, but it would have been a grave mistake if we did not start by trying to convince the Commission.

As a first step, we therefore submitted a detailed study to the Commission with which we were proving the importance of the offshore sector to the economy. We also changed the title 'offshore sector' to 'Companies of International Activities' and argued that a special tax system could not be labelled as state aid. We also pointed out that these companies did not present unfair competition to local firms and that the economy would suffer heavy losses if we were to abolish the offshore sector as nearly all these companies would leave Cyprus for other territories outside the EU.

Despite our efforts and arguments, the Commission was not prepared to change its position. They insisted on the need of adopting a unified system. We had no choice but to radically revise our whole tax system. For this purpose, we created a think-tank in which all interested parties participated in order to make sure that:

(*a*) they were aware of all the work that was being carried out; and
(*b*) that they were contributing to the best of their abilities.

To design the new tax system, we used the expert advice of the Austrian and International Tax Law Department of the University of Vienna under Professor

Gassner. After several months of serious and hard work, we came to the conclusion that the best approach to solve the problem without reactions from the political parties and the public at large was to go for an overall revision of the tax system. This was the opportune time because it could link changes in the direct taxation with changes in indirect taxation (mainly VAT). The basic elements in the new revised tax system were the following:

(*a*) a unified corporation tax of 10 per cent was introduced instead of the 4.25 per cent for offshore and 20 per cent to 25 per cent for local companies;
(*b*) a special dividend tax of nearly 10 per cent was also introduced for all companies based in Cyprus and distributing profits within the island (accordingly the real corporation tax for local companies remained more or less at the same level as previously); and
(*c*) the personal income tax was reduced from 40 per cent to 30 per cent maximum.

The basic concept was to have a neutral tax reform, i.e. balance the increase in incomes from the VAT (15 per cent instead of 10 per cent until then) with the expected reduction from the income tax reform. While it looked as if we were all in agreement, at the last moment some political parties insisted on increasing the special discounts and social benefits to the population at large. As a result, the original concept of a neutral tax reform had to be abandoned. We were obliged to accept that at least in the first two years, there would be a loss of income from taxation. As we could not possibly jeopardize the whole tax reform, we introduced some special tax measures for 2002 and 2003 to cover part of the loss. Overall, the reform was successful and everybody was pleased: the offshore business sector appreciated our efforts to ensure the 'grandfather' clause and accepted the small increase in corporate tax because Cyprus was still offering better rates than other countries. Our businessmen and the population at large were also satisfied as the tax burden decreased.

During the negotiations we were also able to ensure that for a transitional period of five years the 0 per cent tax rate of VAT on foodstuffs and medicines would be maintained. Originally, we wanted to continue with a 0 per cent tax rate on children's clothing as well, but this was considered to be an excessive demand by the Commission and we had no choice but to abandon our request. We also ensured that the local spirit 'zivania' become 'appellation contrôlée' but we had to accept that the same excise tax would be applied to spirits whether local or imported.

Environment (chapter 22)

The chapter on environment presented a different kind of challenge. The only subject on which there was no concurrence of opinions and which was followed by long and rather unpleasant negotiations with the Commission was regarding the level of emissions at the two power stations of Dhekelia and Vassiliko.

According to the EU Directive 80/609, large combustion plants authorized (licensed) after July 1997 had to comply with the levels of emissions stipulated in the directive.

Concerning the Dhekelia power station, we succeeded after long discussions in proving that a few years ago we had carried out some minor improvements, while the station had been licensed (and started operating) in 1982 and therefore was well within the limits specified by the Commission. This position was finally accepted by the Union.

With Vassiliko, however, the situation was quite different, as the two units of the station were licensed and put in operation after 1997. Cyprus considered each generation unit as a separate plant within the meaning of the directive and had set the emissions accordingly. The European Union, on the other side, was of the opinion that the two units should be considered as a single plant because although they vent through separate ducts, these are located in a single chimney and consequently emission limit values had to be set according to the overall thermal capacity.

If the Union's view had prevailed we would have had to invest at least €50 to 60 million, in addition to nearly €75 million of annual cost, and, as a result, the price of energy would have increased by 6 per cent with a serious impact on inflation.

Fortunately, after nearly three years of negotiations, in May 2002, i.e. only a few months before the closing of the accession process, an agreement was reached which stipulated that:

> The E.U. having carefully examined Cyprus's requests considers that it is sufficiently limited in scope, since it applies at the current plants of Vassilikos and Dhekelia and is limited to SO2 emissions for which specific limit values will be respected. Given also the specific geographical situation of Cyprus, the E.U. can therefore agree that by way of derogation from Article 4(3), Annex III A, emission limit values of 1 700 mg/Nm3 shall apply to the boilers currently in operation at the combustion plants at Dhekelia and Vassilikos until the first of the following conditions materialises:
>
> - there is an upgrade or a significant change to the Power Stations currently in operation
> - natural gas becomes available on the island
> - Cyprus becomes an exporter of electricity
> - The currently operating boilers are closed.

On all other environmental issues, and there were a great number of them, there was an extensive and very close cooperation and exchange of views between the Commission and our services in defining and promoting the implementation of policies. Some of the most important tasks were the following:

(*a*) the need to create sewage systems in all towns and villages with a population of over 2,000, as well as to process the waste. As this was a huge and very expensive task, a transitional period of ten years was agreed upon.

(*b*) The protection of underground water was ensured through a number of measures that aimed at controlling the use of fertilizers.
(*c*) The implementation of the Natura 2000 programme.
(*d*) The protection from genetically modified organisms, etc.

The prospect of accession was a good opportunity to rationalize our public service as there was a great amount of overlap between various government bodies and ministries and strengthen the Department of Environment.

One area where agreement was not easy to reach, and where we had to compromise, was that of the protection of flora and fauna. There was a serious conflict between the Department of the Environment and the Game Fund Service which was an independent agency under the Ministry of the Interior. In Cyprus we probably have more hunters than birds. It is estimated that more than 50,000 persons, i.e. more than 15 per cent of the male population, have a hunting licence. All these hunters were supporting the Game Fund Service, whose main task was to breed thousands of partridges and hares every year, which are subsequently set free in the forests for the hunters to shoot. This was a battle that could not be won by rational arguments. As the Game Fund Service was doing a good job, in the end it was agreed that it could maintain its independence and continue to be responsible for the breeding and protection of game. However, the overall policy formulation regarding wildlife would be in the hands of the Department of the Environment.

Finally, in this presentation of the environmental issues we should make a special reference to the issue of 'Akamas'. The Peninsula of Akamas is the last part of Cyprus which has been protected from destruction by developers and which at the same time has a very great environmental value, being, among others, one of the few parts of the Mediterranean where turtles came on shore to give birth. For many years, development was impossible in that area because the British, as part of their sovereign bases agreements, had an exclusive right for army training and fire exercises. Ironically, it was these rights of the British that protected the area from destruction by controlled tourist development projects. For this reason, the government declared the Akamas Peninsula as a protected area in 1990 and this policy won the support of both the EU and all environmental organizations in Cyprus and Europe. As expected, however, this created conflicts with the owners of real estate and the few hundred inhabitants of the small villages in the area who naturally would like to see a fast development as in the rest of Cyprus. The government was under great pressure from local interests and political parties to modify its policy. Fortunately, however, the attention of the Union, and particularly of the European Parliament, saved Akamas. The insistence of the Commission that the government should not modify its preservation plans and proceed with the creation of the national park contributed greatly in resisting the pressures from the various lobbies and helped the government avoid changing the already agreed policies. This issue is still pending but it looks as though now, after Cyprus' accession, the area will indeed be saved and the various nature protection plans fully implemented.

New status for the British bases

The sovereign British bases (SBA) at Dhekelia and Episkopi cover an area of 255 square kilometres in which about 8,500 Greek Cypriots live in addition to several thousand British soldiers. When the UK became a member of the Union, they ensured that the bases in Cyprus and Gibraltar remained under special status. In Cyprus the arrangement was that, although sovereign, the Cypriot inhabitants of the bases would retain the same rights as all other Cypriot citizens and all residents were free to move around the SBA the same way as in the rest of Cyprus. The prospect of joining the EU was exciting, but obviously the last thing we wanted to accept was a Schengen border separating the bases from the Republic. It was therefore absolutely necessary to come to an agreement with the British authorities and hopefully ensure that with accession to the Union the extraterritorial status of the bases would be amended accordingly. For this reason, we took up contacts as early as 1999, but it became obvious that the British government was not ready to discuss the issue during the first years of the accession talks. Only in 2002, i.e. the last year of the negotiations, were we able to conduct in-depth negotiations. The European Union was neutral on this issue. They wanted to help the Republic but were ready to accept whatever agreement the British government would have reached with our government.

After intensive lobbying and long negotiations we succeeded in ensuring that there would be no Schengen controls, Cypriots' freedom of movement would continue, and the sovereignty of the Union, if not in theory at least to any practical extent, would cover the bases' area also. Specifically, it was agreed that the bases would be included in the Union's custom area and the same tax regime as for the rest of the island would apply to them. All regulations agreed on the CAP for the rest of Cyprus would apply also to the bases area. In practice, therefore, the degree of control on the SBA area by the British authorities was reduced. Probably this was the main reason for which the British authorities expressed readiness to return practically half of the sovereign area to the Republic if the Annan Plan was accepted.

Protocol No. 10 on Cyprus

With the conclusion of the negotiations we also had to agree on how to handle the issue of the occupied areas. For us it was vital that the entire area of the Republic of Cyprus would join the EU irrespective of the fact that nearly 37 per cent of the Republic's territory was under Turkish control. As a result of many bilateral meetings and discussions in Brussels, and of course the performance of Cyprus during the accession negotiations, we succeeded in concluding the so-called Protocol No. 10. The Protocol made it clear that 'the application of the acquis shall be suspended in those areas of the Republic of Cyprus in which the government of the Republic does not exercise effective control' but it will be lifted in the event of a solution to the Cyprus problem.

4. CONCLUSIONS

After five years of tough and continuous negotiations the accession talks were successfully concluded in December 2002. From the first moment we were optimistic that they could be successfully concluded, but this was not automatic. We had to mobilize all our resources, convey the message to all civil servants and the population at large that this was our primary task for the next few years, and be consistent in our cooperation with the UN and the efforts to reunite our island. To succeed we needed:

- a high level of coordination;
- to set short-, medium- and long-term targets and make sure by continuous follow-up that they were met;
- to adopt an open and frank policy towards Brussels and to home. In case of hiccups, delays, or omissions we should admit them and try to correct them rather that wait for Brussels to find out—never try to cover up;
- to ensure the smooth functioning of the Statistical Office and upgrade data collection;
- to develop good working relations with Brussels and the Member States. Keep them informed continuously and gain their confidence;
- to prepare our position papers in cooperation with all parties—trade unions, employers' associations, organized interest groups, etc.; and
- to aim high but be prepared to compromise and lower our expectations. Never be dogmatic.

What did harmonization imply? The need to implement hundreds of legal acts summarizing the collective wisdom of Western Europe. To try to catch up in a few years (and with the support of pre-accession assistance) with what the others have achieved in decades. This need was obvious from the beginning of the accession process and there were clear benefits from the first to the last day.

- The process itself was an incentive to reform in all fields and had the added advantage that everybody accepted the need to introduce the various changes since this was an EU requirement.
- We were given the opportunity to modernize our government structure and create a series of independent agencies (like, for example, the Paying Agency, the State Aid Commission, the Commission for the Protection of Personal Data) as well as strengthen and restructure the Monopolies Commission, the Shipping Department, etc.
- It created the need to move fast, not to postpone even unpleasant tasks simply because we could not afford any delays (e.g. the steps for the introduction of HACCP controls).

- Protect the consumer and ensure the better functioning of the market mechanisms.
- Ensure better organization of the civil service and overcome the diffusion of tasks and overlap of competences.
- Speed up technological upgrading and the introduction of IT methods in all fields of government.
- Pay greater attention and improve the protection of the environment (recycling, emission controls, animal welfare, etc.).
- Strengthen monetary discipline and prepare for joining the Eurozone.
- Ensure equal rights of men and women, anti-discrimination, protect the handicapped, improve the social security system.
- Promote police cooperation with other EU Member States and provide better protection for the citizens.

Probably, however, the most important benefit of the five years, from 1998 to 2002, was that both the civil service and the public at large gradually realized that Cyprus is becoming a full member of the EU with all the advantages and responsibilities that this process of modernizing the whole fabric of the Cypriot society entails.

9

The Accession of the Czech Republic to the EU

Pavel Telicka
Karel Bartak

One of the most particular, unique, and incomparable eras of Czech history was that during which the Republic first prepared for accession negotiations with the EU, and, later, carried out those negotiations to their ultimate success. Only a few years after the fall of the communist regime and, later, the division of Czechoslovakia, the government and Parliament voluntarily open themselves to the scrutiny of fifteen other European states and their watchdog, the European Commission. Of course, there was an overwhelming willingness to do so; it was widely understood as both a necessity and a healthy exercise for the new democracy. However, at the same time, it was psychologically difficult to become a pupil in the European classroom. The Czechs were not willing to assume the role of exotic tribesmen only recently accustomed to civilization, which was attributed to them by some of the more ignorant commentators of the West. At the same time, many were unready to acknowledge that in several respects they badly needed to take some political lessons in democracy and economic policy, among other matters. This period was thus characterized by high expectations and hopes, but was also full of anxieties and frustrations.

A very special element of the Czech approach was, from the beginning, a cunning mixture of nationalism, a feeling of superiority, and pro-American liberalism. Politicians like Vaclav Klaus displayed astonishment at the duration of the enlargement process for a country which was, in their view, ready from the first day. At the same time, they showed increasing discomfort with the EU's regulatory role. Publicly, they voiced suspicion about the EU being some kind of a leftist plot; in reality they rightly imagined that the enquiring eye watching the messy transition from communism to capitalism would with time deprive them of the advantages they could reap from the chaos which accompanied the early stages of the capitalist come-back and the huge property shift.

On the other hand, the EU also had to learn from us, and it did so voluntarily. The fifteen and the Commission were obviously in a position of control, since it was the Czechs who were banging on the door of their club. But they also had to find the means—money, people, and organizational arrangements—to prepare for the process and push it through. There were sceptics on their side, too, and they were not unimportant ones; just remember the 1993 push of French President François Mitterrand for 'European Confederation' which would have embraced most of the continent with the then twelve (later fifteen) EU members as its hard core, 'noyau dur', an idea immediately rejected by the Czech President Vaclav Havel.

At the same time, both sides were forced to get acquainted with each other. This turned out to be a quite difficult exercise. The Czechs were sometimes hesitant to abandon their prefabricated ideas about the EU, and, especially, to acknowledge that the integration train that they were trying to catch was much longer and more complex than foreseen. They had had a high opinion of their own qualities and felt quite justified in expecting an early membership. They disliked the reflection of the reality that the EU forced them to ponder during the process; they argued often that the conditions set up for the newcomers were tougher than for the Member States themselves.

If the Czechs were unprepared for their accession, the EU was starting from scratch—they only had a faint idea who their interlocutors were. Even many years after the first contacts, the general tendency in the European institutions was to throw all the 'post-communist PECOs' (the abbreviation used for Pays de l'Europe Centrale et Orientale) into the same basket and apply the same one-size-fits-all remedies for everybody. Unsurprisingly, this was a source of permanent frustration. The officials used to have some trouble in becoming more aware of the difference between a Czech and a Hungarian in terms of history, behaviour, but also, for example, in terms of the needs of SMEs or agriculture. The EU, however, produced with impressive speed a solid group of very well-informed and motivated civil servants, but for many years they remained a small minority, whereas the vast crowd of vaguely informed individuals followed a very slow course, and, indeed, are still to be fully aware of the particularities of their new partners.

1. FIRST STEPS

The screening was a moment of truth for both sides and also one of the best means of coming to know each other. The Czech side adopted, theoretically without reserve, the Commission dogma that this was supposed to be a technical, non-political exercise and thus that there is no reason to use diplomatic and other tools to improve the reality or to hide some of its ugly aspects. Michael Leigh, the then Commissioner in charge of enlargement, maintained this position very clearly, repeatedly calling for full openness, a frank approach, and no zigzags, for the sake of smoothness of the future 'real' negotiations.

Like all other candidate countries, the Czechs proceeded 'chapter by chapter', starting with the easy ones and moving gradually towards the more difficult topics. After a decision during 1998 not to wait until the end of the screening exercise, the simpler chapters were gradually opened for negotiations. The analytical comparison of legal systems was an arduous task on more levels than the intellectual one. Many tend to forget today that in the late 1990s, state administration in a country like the Czech Republic was still far from a high-tech computer workplace. Laws had to be flown to Brussels and back on paper. The then ambassador Josef Kreuter took pleasure in showing to visitors metre-high heaps of 'dossiers' piling up in the offices of the Czech mission to the EU. It was physically demanding work.

Many of the laws which were supposed to be compared with the *acquis communautaire* had never before been translated into English; at the same time, much of the *acquis* was still non-existent in Czech, despite some effort during the 1990s. In many cases, former translations were incorrect or flawed, for the rules of translation of juridical texts had only started to settle down. The use of terminology was still volatile and the translation of some expressions varied from one ministry to another.

Because of this, and the uneven quality of negotiators from different sectors of the government, the screening turned often into a delicate exercise. There were many misunderstandings and it became more and more obvious that on the Czech side a higher level of initial coordination was needed so that the delegations would be able to present a common and coherent position to the Commission negotiators. In their turn, the Commission negotiators experienced some problems in understanding some of the explanations and means of legal reasoning presented to them by the Czech teams.

The screening process produced results, usually in the form of undertakings—the Czech side would engage itself to adopt this and that directive, to adapt local laws to this and that regulation, to change the interpretation of this and that legal norm, usually within a time frame. These engagements were duly put on paper and signed by both sides at the end of the 'X-raying' process of each chapter. But were the screeners, usually senior officials from both sides, competent to do so? Could they promise in the name of the government that purely political steps would be carried out, like the adoption of specific laws by the Parliament? There was an obvious contradiction in the system and the method promoted by the Commission to reach conclusions, a fact that led directly to breaches in the functioning of democratic institutions.

It was not always easy to make people realize that the legal harmonization to which they were giving their consent has often very concrete impact on economy, finances, in some cases on social conditions or on the administration itself. The Ministry of Foreign Affairs and the Chief Negotiator's Office tried to assess this impact. Some of the undertakings were put on the programme of the EU Integration Council, a government body theoretically composed of ministers. In reality, it was never clear whether it was a political organ with decision-making powers or just yet another coordination committee. It was in any case seldom attended by ministers and its results were rather weak.

The Commission was often very willing to offer a helping hand, to give advice on how to proceed or how to avoid obstacles. Other times, it took a more stubborn stance, when it came, even at this early stage, to transition periods. The negotiators from Prague sometimes felt that this tool would be the best means to get rid of seemingly unsolvable problems. On the side of Brussels, the answer was always a rigid refusal. This obstinacy was not only a result of discipline, but, in some cases, of genuine lack of understanding—and interest—for the real problems with which their counterparts were struggling.

2. THE REGULAR REPORTS

With the exercise of regular reports, the Commission managed to produce, at regular intervals, a state of hysteria and panic; the Czech Republic was no exception. Some people suspected that the EC overstepped its competencies and interfered in the internal affairs of sovereign states. Every sector of political, economic, and social life of the country was scrutinized and assessed. The Commission stayed cool—it had its mandate from the 'Fifteen' and its conclusions were merely background information for the Member States not political decisions. If it had to poke its nose into so many Czech activities, it was because all these are covered, fully or partially, by the *acquis*, with the rest coming under their scrutiny as part of the 'Copenhagen criteria'.

With hindsight, one can responsibly say that it was a necessary and healthy system. Some even wish that it could have continued—since 2004, some Czechs miss the yearly very precise and rather objective mirror, in which the pluses and minuses were shown bluntly, but without aggression and always with a advice or a hint of solution. It is always easier to get the correct picture from outside than to establish it yourself.

The EU is an exclusive club; it behaved accordingly in this exercise, not only for the sake of the future members, but, above all, to defend its own interests; one of the most important such interests was the ex ante exclusion of all problems the newcomers might bring with them into the club. That was why it was always quite sharp in cases when it felt the candidate country was trying to cheat. The Czech Ministry of Affairs never encouraged any 'rose painting', although, from time to time, some ministries tried to improve their own image by submitting false or incomplete information. It usually backfired.

The Commission, on the other hand, also made mistakes, either factual ones or political. In these cases, it was much more difficult to make it acknowledge its mistake and change it. In some cases, one could feel political pressure behind certain formulations, especially in the effort to improve the image of Poland, which was not supposed to be seen to be lagging behind the others. The comparison between candidate countries, especially those from Central and Eastern Europe, created usually a lot of tension. It was clear that the EC did this deliberately. It often led to more earnest efforts on the side of the 'losers', although it also tarnished the image of the EC as 'honest broker'.

For the Czechs, this ordeal was perhaps tougher than for the others, because they fell from the highest pedestal. Until 1998, they were seen as the front runners, as the most innovative, the most liberal, and the most dynamic of the new members. When it became clear that the Czech transition method was littered with mistakes and misdoings, the evaluation changed radically into a negative picture across the board. That is why Prague insisted that the overall picture should be taken into account, not only the recent record, because, in general terms, the country which had had the best starting position of the ten candidates was still doing relatively well compared to those who had started from behind.

What happened in 2000 was a typical case—whereas Poland and Hungary were evaluated as 'functioning market economies', the Czech Republic (together with Slovenia) got a supplementary formula 'can be considered as' a functioning market economy. The difference, voluntarily introduced by the Commission, was interpreted by the Czech press as a disaster, despite the fact that, overall, the regular report was better than in previous years. Günter Verheugen, Commissioner charged with enlargement, tried to control the damage done by the regular report by giving several interviews to the Czech media, but with limited success. The Commission this time clearly underestimated the communication impact of its comparisons.

3. THE NEGOTIATIONS

The negotiations started in autumn 1988 and lasted until the end of 2002. In the beginning, six countries (Czech Republic, Poland, Hungary, Estonia, Cyprus, and Slovenia) started discussing the conditions of membership with the Member States and the Commission, but after the Helsinki Summit in 1999 the other four (Slovakia, Lithuania, Latvia, and Malta) joined the negotiations. Given their size, it was quite easy for the EU to arrange their 'catching up'; from 2000 onwards, it was increasingly obvious that there was politically no other way to organize the enlargement but the 'big bang': a very different scenario compared to the initial vision of the mid-1990s.

No chapters were particularly easy to close, but there were many where the negotiations went smoothly enough to be forgotten today. In objectively difficult chapters, like free movement of goods or competition, the Czechs lived through an experience that was typical for all the potential new members. The Czech Republic had a lot in common with the other post-communist states when it came to free movement of people and of capital, as well as the state aid systems. But it also had very specific controversial issues, which were politically explosive. The conflict with Austria about the Temelin nuclear plant or the historic controversy again with Austria and with Germany about the post-war expulsion of the German minority from the border regions became extremely sensitive issues which took years to solve, with great help from the European Commission.

From this point of view, the Czech negotiation was more *political* than that of any of the other candidate countries.

4. FREE MOVEMENT OF PEOPLE

It was clear from the beginning that there are important internal political reasons which disable the Austrians and the Germans from opening their labour markets to workers from new Member States. Their sensitivity was cunningly used by the Spanish government for other reasons—Madrid paraded as a big protector of the future new members, but, in reality, it was trading its agreement with the German position for gains in matters pertaining to regional policy.

The EU was bluntly brutal about this, despite the fact that one of the four liberties was at stake. The Member States concerned never produced any convincing impact assessment, any study confirming the danger for their markets. Although they normally stressed the differentiation principle and the 'according to merits' approach, in this case nobody dared to compare Czechs or Slovaks to the Poles. It was clear to everybody that the concern was, above all, about the Polish workers; fears of Czechs or Slovaks were never expressed. The Commission's study showed that the inhabitants of these countries would seldom move. On the whole it predicted 350,000 people to search for jobs abroad from the eight new Member States after enlargement, should all the Fifteen open their markets.

In Austria, there was some anxiety about Czech and Slovak pedlars crossing the border every day; that's why the Austrians also banned a number of services which can be provided in this way. Behind Berlin and Vienna hid most of the others—at the end of the day, only Britain, Ireland, and Sweden let the newcomers search freely for jobs inside their borders. None has reported any significant problems; on the contrary, the experience has been very positive. Nevertheless, as the first phase of the possible transition period expires in May 2006, there do not seem to be many countries wishing to join London, Dublin, and Stockholm. This is a typical reflection of the bad mood the EU has been in since the rejection of the constitution in France and the Netherlands in 2005, and thus a new tendency of the governments to listen to what the people have to say—and the people often think that the new members are one of the causes of the continuing high unemployment in many parts of Western Europe.

The transition periods during which the new Member States may prevent citizens from the 'old' EU from coming over to buy real estate were often seen as a counterweight to the ban on workers. In reality, the companies or individuals from old Member States can use several other forms to obtain houses, flats, or secondary residences in the new countries. There are no statistics, but it is obvious that this obstacle does not have much impact in practice.

5. COMPETITION

This chapter was a typical example of the Czech negotiation process in the sense that the Czechs started with an excellent reputation, which then gradually went from bad to worse. It became a perfect illustration of what the country looked like from the outside by the end of the era of the ODS (Klaus) government and of the shocks that followed when the real picture started emerging. On the other hand, the situation was no worse than in Poland or Hungary; the problem was that it was unexpected and the Commission had the unpleasant feeling of having been taken in.

There were two basic problems in this chapter—state aid to the banking sector and the steel industry. Both were immensely complex, with many players involved, including foreign investors, involving huge amounts of money and an important social dimension. Any collapse of a big bank would have put at risk the savings of hundreds of thousands of people. Likewise, bringing the huge steel mills to a halt would have led to massive lay-offs in regions like northern Moravia which had already been heavily hit by the restructuring of the political regime.

The Commission ordered and paid for a study by the Eurostrategy group, which proposed to concentrate all the local steel industry into one holding; the Czech government agreed, but later changed its mind and announced it would prefer to sell the companies to individual foreign investors. The Commission was annoyed and kept asking for a comprehensive restructuring plan; Prague promised a set of subsequent dates, but repeatedly failed to meet them. The tensions ran high and there was a huge lack of understanding on both sides. The Commission was under enormous pressure from Member States like France, Luxembourg, or the Netherlands, which had painfully restructured their steel industry with huge social consequences and would not allow any new competitors supported by public money to destroy what was left of it. Even when the Commission was satisfied with the Czech responsiveness, these countries continued for some time to prevent the closure of the chapter.

The story of the banking sector is a rather typical and sad part of the short history of Czech transformation. The EU could not have been insensitive to a situation in which bad loans prevailed, government guarantees covered all kinds of mischief, and the banks were kept alive by state subsidies. The Commission regularly suggested privatization and foreign involvement, but for a long time it went unheeded. When this turned out in the end to be the only option available, the banks had to be stripped of bad assets and made attractive to investors, which cost the taxpayers additional billions of Czech crowns. One of the EU negotiators used to call these events 'the biggest theft from people by their own state' and wondered why the Czechs had not rebelled.

In the end, after thorough examination and through a painful restructuring exercise, the EC gave the green light to one bank after another, except for one which is still today under investigation. It also swallowed the final balance of the

Konsolidacni banka, an unorthodox state institution created to buy and sell the bad assets in the privatization turmoil. The Czechs started too late to privatize the banks, for political reasons, and most of them paid hard cash for these mistakes; some made fabulous profits. Thankfully, however, the accession process accelerated the transformation and rendered the new situation irreversible. The Czech banking sector is today close to EU standards.

6. TEMELIN

There were two uniquely Czech cases in the negotiations, which differed radically from the experience of the other nine candidates. They greatly contributed to the conviction that the process was more complicated in the Czech case than in any of the other ones. Poland negotiated in a more stubborn way, its situation was objectively more difficult, problems were enormous, and the way forward was both difficult and painful. But they did not have on the agenda such explosive topics as Temelin and the Benes Decrees, which drained enormous amounts of energy and could potentially have derailed the whole exercise.

In principle, the Austrian government did not have any valid reasons to introduce the Temelin nuclear plant, then close to completion, as a topic of the accession talks. Energy policy is a traditionally national domain and there is very little *acquis* on nuclear reactors; each country is free to choose its own 'energy mix' without outside interference. At the same time, during the enlargement process, supplementary attention was drawn to the problem of Soviet-made reactors in the candidate countries. Slovakia, Lithuania, and subsequently Bulgaria were forced to decommission some of their older plants. The Austrians were fully aware of this new EU tool and found themselves under heavy pressure from their public opinion which is very hostile to atomic energy. Despite the fact that there was formally nothing to discuss, they turned Temelin into a huge issue, leveraging their policy on their liberum veto rights on the closure of any chapter.

The mood in Europe at the turn of the century was still quite anti-nuclear. Governments in Germany and Belgium promised to get progressively rid of nuclear plants. There was not a single reactor under construction. This atmosphere played in favour of the Austrian position, especially in the European Parliament. On the other hand, the country's reputation was still shaken by the deal the Chancellor Wolfgang Schüssel had struck in 2000 with the far right FPÖ party, which aroused pitched criticism. At the most crucial moment, the helm of the EU was taken over by France, traditionally a pro-nuclear country and for many reasons hostile to any harmonization of rules in this area. Because of the French presidency, the Austrians did not get full backing in the Council; on the contrary the reaction of most of the other Member States was lukewarm, hesitant, and irritated by this new complication.

The Czech side did not always behave according to the advice repeatedly given by the Enlargement Commissioner Günter Verheugen, who played an eminent role in the resolution of this imbroglio. There were unnecessary provocations, communication was lacking, and the Czech diplomacy neglected to mobilize its friends, especially in the European Parliament. And, while the French presidency was trying to play the whole matter down, the Austrians managed to push through another resolution in the EP, urging the Czech side to make an environmental impact assessment before Temelin entered its testing period. There was enough discussion for the Austrians to block the closure of the energy chapter. The Czech negotiators were concerned that to finally get rid of this chapter, they would have to 'consume' a lot of the goodwill they had with the others, which could then be lacking when other important Czech requests arrived on the negotiating table within the next chapters.

Austrian activists repeatedly blocked border crossings and the Czech side complained about the matter to the Commission. The tensions ran high when Prime Ministers Schüssel and Zeman met in December in the castle of Melk in Austria; Verheugen offered his good offices. The agreement was about solving the outstanding problems on the basis of the state of the art common in Member States; it immediately gave birth to a variety of different interpretations. In any case, it started a double-track negotiation about the nuclear security of Temelin, and about its impact on the environment, which lasted for nearly a year. In the meantime, the attack came again through the European Parliament—its regular report about the Czech Republic mentioned in September the closure of Temelin as an option and asked the Commission to organize an international conference about the subject, which was flatly refused by Verheugen.

In the end, the Commission was so irritated and tired by the Austrian obstructions that it clearly supported the Czech side. Even Romano Prodi, its President, came publicly to the conclusion that this matter was not a subject for accession talks, because it simply was not covered by the *acquis*. Prime Minister Schüssel could not escape Günter Verheugen's invitation to Brussels on 29 November 2001; he was expected to reach a final solution with Prime Minister Zeman. Their agreement, reached after several hours of negotiations, included a protocol which engaged the Czech side to upgrade the security of Temelin. It was supposed to be added to the Accession Treaty later on, should all the other Member States agree. They didn't.

7. THE BENES DECREES

Whereas Temelin was somewhat palpable, visible, and at least somehow linked to the accession negotiations, the issue of the Benes Decrees was a completely different cup of tea, much more bitter and unpleasant. Only the actors were, partially, the same—the Austrian government was joined by the Bavarian representation. The means used were also familiar—the European Parliament. Whereas the governments in Berlin and also partially in Vienna put on a neutral face, the MEPs rushed into the battle, led by German and Austrian right-wing parties.

Czechoslovakia was overrun by Nazi Germany in 1939 and turned into a German colony. One of the reasons for this was the Munich agreement from 1938, where France and Britain gave Hitler the right to annex the Czech border regions inhabited mainly by a German minority, which at the brink of the war was as pro-Nazi as the 'Reich' itself. This minority was, after the war was over, expelled to Germany and Austria with the consent of the victorious powers. The conditions under which this was done were fairly inhuman and cruel, an unnecessary revenge for the enormous suffering during the six-year war period. The legal basis for this expulsion was a series of decrees signed by the Czech President Edvard Benes shortly after the war was over.

Of course, these historic events had nothing to do with the accession talks. The temptation was great to use this opportunity, however, for the first and last time, to repair a historic wrongdoing. The vast majority of MEPs did not really know what was going on when the House adopted a resolution about the Czech progress in negotiations which included one inoffensive-looking request—to remove the decrees from the Czech legal system. It looked simple and just. That's why it was very difficult to counter. Didn't the Copenhagen criteria from 1993 include above all the rule of law, democracy, and human rights? The decrees seemed to be in breach of all these principles.

The Czech side had some trouble explaining that the decrees are virtually dead, 'extinct' was the expression, that they are no longer in use and cannot constitute a base for any new legal action. But their removal from the juridical system would create a huge vacuum and destroy an entire network of legal relations created after the war. It would lead to considerable legal uncertainty for people whose lives had been based upon them for five decades. At the same time, the German and Austrian MEPs did not, at least publicly, demand restitution or material compensations. But, for example, Bernd Posselt, MEP for CSU and President of the Sudetendeutsche Landsmannschaft, acknowledged that this would be the next step the moment the decrees were stricken off. The MEPs charged several times in different directions—they wanted the EU to compare these laws with the *acquis*, they complained, without any proof, about discrimination of Germans living currently in the CR, etc. In any case, they managed to secure the inclusion of the issue in the negotiation process. It had to be tackled by the parties and the Commission.

The Commission acknowledged that although the decrees were not a part of the negotiations, they filled in a part of the 'wider political context' which had to be in any case taken into consideration. Very discreetly, a working party comprised of EC and Czech officials was put together. The Commission and the Parliament legal services were set to contribute. One of their tasks was to assess whether the decrees still had any legal implications, which was one of the arguments put forward by German and Austrian MEPs. Whereas the rest of the EP completely and rightly ignored the subject, a few individuals were trying to use it to boost their political careers at home.

The affair culminated in the Parliament in April 2002, with a row between this group and Verheugen, who came up with a well-argued and skilful opposition.

The socialists and greens finally took the Czech side and hindered the adoption of a proposed resolution which contained a series of paragraphs about the Benes Decrees, all of which were unacceptable for the Czech side. Finally, a compromise was found, according to which an independent 'wise man' group would offer its legal opinion. After a series of ups and downs, including some very clumsy statements and actions in Prague during the election period, the report came into being in September, just weeks before the end of the negotiations. It noted that the abolition—or not—of the decrees did not and could not be an obstacle to the entry of the Czech Republic into the EU. A few days later, in October, the Commission published its own findings saying that from the point of view of the *acquis communautaire*, the decrees were not an obstacle to the Czech accession. Some MEPs still tried to revive the topic, but it was dead. The Czechs could at last concentrate on the final events of the negotiations which took place in Copenhagen in December.

8. IN COPENHAGEN

The question of funding came up regularly during the four years of negotiations. It played an overwhelmingly central role in the long and arduous talks about the agriculture chapter. Finally, all ten candidates were obliged to agree to quite unsatisfactory conditions under which their farmers were entitled to just 25 per cent of regular direct payments in 2004 and a very slow rise reaching the full amount only in 2013, at the end of the next financial perspective. The Commission also played hardball when it came to the quotas on the basis of which these payments are handed out, for instance for milk or beef. Most of the statistics provided by Prague were scaled down, unproductive years were taken as a basis, and the officials would not listen to any reason about possible future developments—for instance in the case of meat cows, the introduction of which into Czech farming had only just begun.

The farmers protested, and there were even some incidents in Prague, something that had never happened before in a country where agriculture represents just 2 per cent of national income and employs 3 per cent of the workforce. But finally, when the dust settled, the late Commissioner Franz Fischler was proved to be right, at least partially. Those who rely on direct payments from the EU are better off than ever before, because despite the above-mentioned disparity, their income has actually risen, also thanks to the higher intervention prices and government subsidies (allowed under the scheme). The opening of the market created tension in the cases where the Czech farmers turned out to be uncompetitive—for instance in non-subsidized vegetable production.

But when it comes to money, one's mind immediately switches to Copenhagen and its preparation. The direct payments were of course a part of the famous 'package' proposed on 25 November by the Danish presidency. To compensate for the losses in agriculture, it contained some supplementary payments in the form of lump sums and other sweeteners, altogether €2.5 billion for ten countries for the period 2004–6. The Danes never really tried to have it adopted before the summit—on the contrary, they negotiated on this basis without a mandate from the other fourteen members, hoping to present their solution to the heads of state in Copenhagen as a fait accompli, which it would be difficult and foolish to kill. In the very last moments of a four-year intensive effort, after an enormous 'spider web' negotiation of fifteen states with another ten, there were just these ten, the Danes, and the Commission around the table, as if the others had vanished.

The Danish 'package' contained €40.5 billion for the ten new members for two and half years; a limit had been set at €42.5 billion, so there still seemed to be some money at stake which could become the object of a trade-off at the summit. In the end, things did not develop this way. The Danish Prime Minister Anders Fogh Rasmussen, under direct influence from Germany's Gerhard Schröder, emerged as a tight-fisted and shrewd negotiator, sticking to every penny. The summit finally turned into a fight about peanuts, with the candidate countries not willing or able to create a common front, despite their earlier propensity towards concerted effort. Some were willing to sell their soul for a handful of euros and others seemed happy in their corner even before the meeting got under way.

The Czech Prime Minister Vladimir Spidla came to Copenhagen with one obsession, because of media reports in the previous days—to get a better deal per capita than richer Slovenia and a substantially better one than Hungary, which, according to the press, could expect twice as much as the CR. The calculations (€69 per capita for the Czechs, €100 for Slovenes, €134 for Hungarians) were correct, but the comparison was at least partially flawed—the Czech Republic could not expect, unlike the other nine, any monies earmarked for enhancing the protection of EU external borders, because it does not have any. There was also no need for help to decommission nuclear plants, the issue of Temelin having been solved. In any case, Spidla's argumentation was very badly perceived by Rasmussen, who after the second encounter became irritated.

The breakthrough came, as foreseen, from Poland, whose Finance Minister Leszek Balcerowicz very quickly understood that there was little fresh money to be got. He thus cheerfully accepted an ingenious offer, invented by the Danes and endorsed by Schröder, to convert €1 billion from the structural funds foreseen for Poland into a lump sum. In other words, to change virtual money which Poland would have had to merit by preparing good projects into real money paid out in cash. The Czech delegation quickly understood that this was the trick of the day and asked for €100 million to be transferred in the same way. This is what finally happened, not without teeth grinding on the side of the presidency and of countries like Hungary, who were not fast enough to react and do the same.

There were many other milestones and episodes in the process, but the above description covers the most outstanding events, concentrating on those where the Czech experience was unique or at least differed from the others. It was a very demanding adventure, physically and psychologically, and not necessarily a rewarding one. Whenever a problem surfaces since May 2004, politicians—primarily those in opposition—rush to blame the conditions enshrined in the Accession Treaty and thus the negotiators, much more than, say, ministers who at that time held political responsibility for the process. This also reflects the fact that in the Czech case the negotiations were much more in the hands of the chief negotiator and his team and the politicians did not interfere either in the daily matters of the negotiations, or in more substantial parts of the process. Sometimes, it was quite difficult to involve them and force them to take responsibility for the process, absorbed as they were by internal political struggles. On other occasions, however, their intrusions and sudden zeal risked derailing the process or damaging the results of long months of work. It must be said that most of the top-class politicians, including members of governments, imagined Europe for a long time as something quite distant and unreal; their participation with real interest and knowledge became more obvious only in the last stages of the accession process.

During the four years of the process, there were so many disagreements with Member States that it was not always easy to maintain a positive attitude. The argument often used was that if an outsider wants to join an exclusive club, he should forget about his wishes and conditions—these are set up exclusively by the members of the club. This is only partially true and application of this 'proverb' helped from time to time to create a feeling that the negotiators were entering a hostile territory, when it came to sit face to face. The Czech and Polish conflict at the Ecofin Council over the prolongation of transition periods for lower VAT rates, for example, reflected quite well the conditions under which chapters were concluded and the very limited manoeuvring space the applicants had.

In this context, it must be stressed that the Commission in most cases played the role of honest broker, was always at the side of the applicants to give advice and help out technically, and, sometimes, politically. The Czech side found valuable allies in extremely hard-working and dedicated civil servants like Michael Leigh and Rutger Wissels, heads of the Commission negotiating team, in Klaus van der Pas, and above all in Eneko Landaburu, Director General for Enlargement, and also very often in Günter Verheugen, whose role in the politically sensitive dossiers was irreplaceable. On the other hand, when it came to defending some of the interests of old Member States, which were difficult to swallow not only for newcomers but also from the point of view of the treaties, the Commission did not hesitate to flow with the prevailing tide and support the majority. This was significantly the case with the transition periods for the free movement of workers.

10

The Accession of Estonia to the EU

Alar Streimann

1. INTRODUCTION

Relations between Estonia, a small country on the northern coast of the Baltic Sea with slightly more than one million inhabitants, and the rest of Europe have been full of controversy for centuries. The fact that Estonians, who are considered one of the most ancient populations in Europe, have lived at their current habitat for thousands of years and retained their own distinct language and culture is indeed a miracle in today's fast-changing world where whole civilizations have perished without trace.

Violent crusades launched against the 'heathen' nations on the Baltic Sea shores at the turn of the twelfth and thirteenth centuries brought Estonians for many hundred years under several alien conquerors and introduced a medieval feudal system where native people were almost exclusively doomed to poverty and later on to serfdom. During the wars, which ravaged in the region almost constantly through the sixteenth to eighteenth centuries, the Estonian population was on several occasions reduced to less than half of its original size. On the other hand, this era meant intense cultural exchange with Germany and the neighbouring Scandinavian countries, as well as with Poland and Russia. National awakening in the nineteenth century laid the ground for uniting the Estonian people on the basis of a strongly rooted common and distinct language and a similar social status. When the revolution of 1917 shattered the former Russian Empire, the independence of Estonia was restored as a matter of course after a brief war with Bolshevist Russia. In the 1920s and 1930s Estonia was actively engaged in European political and cultural life, becoming a member of the League of Nations.

However, the rise of totalitarianism in Europe in the 1930s, and the agreements between leading European governments at the cost of smaller nations, which finally led to the Second World War, proved to be fatal for Estonia. By a secret protocol of the so-called Molotov–Ribbentrop Pact agreed in 1939 between Nazi Germany and the Stalinist Soviet Union, the country was assigned to the zone of influence of the latter. Immediately after that, Soviet troops occupied the country and the following year (1940) they staged a fake election which brought to power a puppet regime, which in its turn annexed Estonia to the Soviet Union. Mass killings, persecutions, and deportations to Soviet labour camps in Siberia of mostly elders, women, and children, which followed both before and after the Second World War, reduced the population again. In comparison, the human losses caused by war itself in Estonia were much lower, although both warring sides—the Soviet Union and thereafter Germany—forcibly recruited men from occupied Estonia into their troops. Altogether, an estimated 17 per cent of Estonians fell victims of the Second World War and Soviet repressive measures immediately before and after it. After the war, between the 1950s and the 1980s, large numbers of Soviet citizens were relocated to Estonia by the authorities in order to solve the problem of labour force shortage and thus allow industrialization.

Small states often have to rely more on their foreign relations than bigger ones, and this has been especially true with Estonia. The disadvantages of its small size, its relative poverty, its lack of resources, and its position as a 'frontierland' at Europe's margins had to be compensated by intense diplomatic activity—finding as many friends and allies as possible and binding the country to Europe with every possible thread, including politics, economy, and security. It was widely felt that this had to be done as quickly as possible, as a revival and entrenchment of expansionist or revisionist thought and policy in the general area was feared. Time was crucial for cementing the independence and this greatly influenced the Estonian positions on the speed of the EU accession negotiations.

Thus, from the very beginning, the Estonian accession process to the EU had a strong political component related to foreign policy, although the main driving factor was still the desire to simply become a part of a normal, democratic, stable, wealthy community with shared values. Never, during the ten years of accession process, did the desirability of EU membership come under question among the country's political decision-makers. The successive parliaments or cabinets neither questioned this goal nor did they introduce any major changes in the process. Obviously, because the Soviet rule had left the country almost in ruins and bankrupt,[1] the common wish to improve the people's well-being was also certainly there. Nevertheless, later opinion polls, as well as general atmosphere, showed that financial aspects of the accession still came second to the Estonians' wish of 'being part of Europe'—deciding for themselves about their own future now that they had the (historically rare) chance to do so.

2. ORGANIZATION, GETTING STARTED, AND THE COURSE OF NEGOTIATIONS

Circumstances at the start of negotiations

The Estonian application for EU membership was submitted on 24 November 1995, virtually at the eleventh hour before the EU Council of Ministers on 4 December took a decision on which countries the Commission was to present

[1] It is worth mentioning that even the environmental damage in Soviet military sites in Estonia amounted to an incredible €4 billion in 1999 prices, comparable to the whole Estonian annual GDP then.

its opinion or *avis* on. In fact, the letter of reply, signed by the then Council President Javier Solana, was also dated 4 December 1995. Subsequently, the Commission adopted its *avis* on 15 July 1997, recommending that the Union start membership negotiations with Estonia (and five other candidate states). That recommendation was later confirmed by an EU Council decision taken in December at Luxembourg.

At home, Estonians not only did not rest with this success, but reacted to the Commission *avis* as early as October 1997 with a working document titled 'A Road Map to Reform', which tried to summarize what was being done by authorities to remedy the problems pointed out in the *avis*. The Estonian message was that they 'recognize [their] shortcomings, and [they] start immediately working on them'. Circulated to experts from the Member States on the very eve of the Luxembourg Summit, this document proved to be another helpful argument in favour of Estonia.

The Commission recommendation, as well as the later Council decision, caused public discontent in the Baltic states, as Estonia was the only one among the three Baltic applicant states to be considered ready to start negotiations. Emotions in Latvia and Lithuania varied from criticisms of partiality to blaming domestic politicians for underperformance. Though official reactions in both countries were reserved, there were some accusations of Estonian diplomacy having beefed up the country's performance (of which Estonians were obviously, even if undeservedly, proud). Although the Commission was able to argue both forcefully and convincingly in favour of Estonia (especially its capability to meet the competitive pressure of the internal market), emotions were hard to die and they never actually fully disappeared.[2]

When the Commission presented its individual country *avis* for the first time in September 1997, Greece demanded that negotiations be simultaneously opened with all three Baltic countries, and both France and Greece demanded that Russian complaints on minorities in Estonia be closely investigated. The Commission, on its behalf, pointed out Estonian distinct advantages: rapid, coherent, and continuous reform process; high rate of integration with the EU; privatization practically completed; a solid legal basis; strong banking sector; and very high confidence of foreign investors. On the negative side, the Commission pointed out the Estonian high foreign trade deficit, which remains a matter of concern to this day.

Nevertheless, a number of comments in both Latvia and Lithuania pointed out the objectivity of the conclusions and, instead of criticism, called for intensified domestic action. They were proven right very soon when in 2000, after the Helsinki Summit, the EU opened negotiations with all remaining candidates.

[2] On 11 December 1997, the Irish MP and former Foreign Minister Spring, asking in Parliament, questioned the current Foreign Minister Andrews why Lithuania, which had a similar economic performance to Estonia, was not included in the negotiations. Minister Andrews replied that he did not know the exact reason.

Diplomatically, Estonia tried not to put salt on wounds and remained as silent as possible as the decision had been against many odds. There were among the then 'old' EU Member States some who were strongly against the inclusion of any Baltic countries, the reason, among others, being that interference with the 'immediate neighbourhood of Russia' was deemed to be undesirable at the time.

The camp supporting that negotiations be started with six countries was in turn wholeheartedly supported by Commissioners van der Broek, Silquis, Bangemann, Wolf-Maties, and Sir Leon Brittan. In a curious way, Estonia also found support from the fact that Cyprus, a candidate country since 1992, was on its way to begin negotiations. Estonia argued that balancing the south and north dimensions of the EU enlargement was another good reason for starting the negotiations with six candidates. On the other hand, objections raised to accepting Cyprus also threatened the chances of Estonia, so the two countries worked towards the parallel goal at the two ends of Europe.

However, in private discussions both in the EU capitals and with their Baltic neighbours, the Estonians stressed their view that the inclusion of at least one Baltic state in the negotiations automatically increased the chances of the other two joining soon as well.[3] On the other hand, they pointed out, if no Baltic states were to be included, it would immediately give a clear signal that these countries were still a 'grey zone' of Russia, leaving the future stability of the whole Baltic Sea region in question.

As a matter of fact Russia raised the issue of Estonian accession with the EU Member States at this early stage, but in a rather relaxed way.[4] The issue was of course the naturalization process of the Russian-speaking diaspora in Estonia, a matter raised by the OSCE and in the Commission *avis*.[5]

The situation changed almost immediately with the new administration in 2000. Russian policy vis-à-vis Europe became proactive and that of *demandeur*. Claims with Russian national interest in the EU enlargement and compensation for hypothetical losses, interests of Russian diaspora in candidate states, etc. were frequently circulated in Member State capitals. All such claims bore an undertone of ownership vis-à-vis former Soviet 'satellites' and were difficult to take seriously.[6]

From the domestic viewpoint, the opening of negotiations with Estonia meant an enormous change, from immense media attention both at home and abroad to

[3] German Foreign Minister Kinkel also made the same argument to the press after the Luxembourg Summit.

[4] For example, Russian Foreign Minister J. Primakov in a letter to his Finnish colleague T. Halonen in December 1997.

[5] Commission President Santer also discussed it when in Estonia in November 1997 and again when receiving credentials from the new Estonian ambassador on 15 January 1998.

[6] That did not prevent Russia from applying double import tariffs to Estonian products from 1995 to 2004 (Estonia was the only third country they did not grant MFN status). Direct losses of about €150 million were caused to the Estonian economy as a result. Indirect losses to enterprises and individuals in both countries were much higher. However, this proved to be a strong motivation for economic integration with the West.

a huge amount of extra work to be done with very limited resources available. As early as summer in 1997, when the final decision by the EU Council was still pending, the Foreign Ministry engaged in internal discussions on how to handle an invitation to start negotiations. At the ministry's brainstorming session at a nice south Estonian farmhouse on a sunny summer afternoon in August, I was privately approached by the then Foreign Minister Toomas Hendrik Ilves with the proposal to become the head of the team for negotiations, which would probably have to be set up soon. Officially, the cabinet set up the whole negotiating delegation on 3 February 1998. That obviously caused some raised eyebrows among friendly western diplomats. One of them, possibly reacting to the team's young age, remarked that we lacked the most important person, the 'bullshit man'. He then went on to explain that this particular character would need to be an elderly, preferably retired, easygoing gentleman with a good handshake, who would permanently travel around in Member States and promote the cause of Estonia. We were much amused by the naive story of European relaxed and retired fireside diplomacy, which had nothing to do with our own, so different, realities.

Structures and getting started

When the decision was taken by the EU Council at the Luxembourg Summit in December 1997 to open negotiations with Estonia, the first concern was to immediately set up necessary structures and goals for negotiations and to organize our work.

We had to do everything practically from zero. Estonia, with its relatively limited staff resources, with young and devoted, but mostly inexperienced, civil service, had scant know-how on diplomatic operations of such a vast scale. In 1998, everything still had to be learned by doing. Furthermore, the most important lessons could not be learned ahead of time, as the best know-how was only available on the other side of the negotiating table.

Beyond identifying the problems to be negotiated, the whole country had to be set on a course for accession. It was clear from the outset that most of the work was to be done on the domestic front, with thousands of new legislative acts to be adopted or amended. A number of activities had to be pursued in parallel: set up and consolidate a strong and stable economy and political system, choose ways and practices that best suited Estonia in all functions of a modern state, train and gain experience for the young civil service while learning on the job, draft legislation, debate with the public even while educating it. An ambitious government action plan for the EU accession had already been adopted in 1996. However, little if anything had happened by the time the negotiations started.

In the Estonian administrative system, where the ministries are rather small and everyone is overburdened with work, it was essential to bring 'draft' decision-making as close to actual experts as possible. Obviously, the cost of doing so was that political participation was weakened, but this could be compensated for by establishing a regular and close working relationship between experts and parliamentary committees. About thirty inter-authority working groups were established; they first analysed the implications of the EU *acquis* in their area of responsibility (this was also partly done via the so-called 'screening' operations with the Commission) and secondly made proposals for negotiating requests. Importantly, by being involved in the accession process, the different authorities were also more motivated to progress in their homework. As it was clear that Estonia never had human resources comparable to bigger countries, every expert had to be involved from the very early stage and to develop his or her skills in the course of events. That also meant sending as many people as possible to screening meetings in Brussels. With the same purpose we arranged regular study-visits of experts to Member States and EU institutions. Such visits were of enormous importance to understanding how to implement the EU requirements in real life because the Estonian administration often adopted (and still does even today to a very large extent, unfortunately) a very rigorous interpretation, which was unnecessary and caused much public criticism. For the practically minded Estonian civil service, it was difficult to understand that most EU legal documents are a result of complicated political compromises between Member States and not always the single best and objective solutions. But in general, by the date of accession Estonia had in most areas a devoted team of experts whose awareness and professionalism by far outperformed that of political decision-makers at home.

The composition of the working groups was left to the discretion of the group leaders, whereas every authority or NGO had the right to be represented, if they so wished. With open-ended working groups, we tried to achieve at least two goals: to get transparent and independent expert assessments in order to be better prepared for political debates in sensitive issues at home, and to take into serious consideration the wishes of those to be affected by the accession.

This kind of expert assessment in working groups was horizontally coordinated by a supervisory team of about fifteen top government officials, including our ambassador to the EU, and was led by a deputy head of delegation, or, as commonly called, the chief negotiator. The official head of the Estonian delegation throughout the accession process was the Minister of Foreign Affairs, while on a daily basis the work of the whole negotiating set-up was managed by the chief negotiator in the MFA. Therefore, the Estonian negotiating structure was not quite similar to that of the other candidates, e.g. Poland or Slovenia, where chief negotiators sometimes had their office under the PM, or even Hungary, where the chief negotiator was the ambassador in Brussels, while at home a state secretary at the MFA was the main coordinator.

There was also a small but devoted team at the Office of European Integration within the Estonian State Chancellery. They had a relatively limited, though important task of coordinating harmonization of laws and preparing the country for accession, although formally and primarily it was the task of every ministry itself. This bureau also helped the Prime Minister privately in 'boosting' line ministers on lawmaking and implementation, while its head was also a member of the negotiating delegation.

Any provisional agreements with the EU were only made by the Foreign Minister and the chief negotiator. A task force of five or six persons was set up at the Foreign Ministry in order to assist the different working groups and create a daily link between them and the chief negotiator. In many critical or novel negotiating issues, this core group at the MFA actually had a brainstorming role in looking for and drafting ideas for solutions, or acted simply as broad range troubleshooters for every kind of situation which the course of negotiations created. As closest partners of both the chief negotiator and experts, members of this task force certainly had the heaviest burden during all the accession years without much reward, and deserve to be separately highlighted.

A separate small secretariat at the Foreign Ministry took care of logistical support—documentation, archives, travels, hotels, etc. In order to better prepare our experts for the screening and negotiating meetings, and also for their frequent visits and stay in Brussels, we compiled a handbook for experts, where people could find answers to FAQs about negotiations and practicalities and also explanations of what was expected of them. It should also be mentioned that a complete set of negotiating archives was well organized and is now part of the ministry's archives in Tallinn.

Obviously, the total number of people more or less involved in the negotiations on the Estonian side was much bigger—roughly up to 700 experts working on a daily basis. Then, as the negotiations progressed, and as the need was, other set-ups appeared. In the margins, I proposed as early as 1997 to establish a special public advisory body to the minister, with the task of debating different key problems and advising solutions, but also explaining critical issues to the public. They functioned as a kind of 'safety valve'. This advisory council, very successfully led throughout the accession process by the President of the Estonian Chamber of Commerce and composed of about forty business leaders, media editors, academicians, and simply well-known, outstanding public opinion leaders, was crucial in confidence building with NGOs and the broader public, especially in the run-up to the membership referendum in 2003.

As to the official negotiating positions, these were based on problems singled out in the working groups, further discussed and cross-analysed at core delegation level, and then taken to the cabinet to be adopted. Even if there was no particular negotiating position to be discussed, we informed the cabinet approximately once a month. In selecting our negotiating requests, efforts were made to concentrate only on the most important issues on which it was possible to predict realistically at least some progress, although not a single issue that had been identified as a problem ever passed unnoticed. Before the positions were taken to the cabinet, the chief negotiator, together with relevant experts, discussed them in detail with the parliamentary EU Affairs Committee. Although the Parliament had no formal right of confirming or vetoing negotiating positions, the relevant procedure gave the possibility to all parties represented in Parliament (the Riigikogu) to express their opinion. Behind the scenes, and informally, we had to secure their maximum support by close dialogue. Aware of the draft negotiating position they could also take subsequent action regarding the proposals made if they deemed it necessary. In the final stages of the negotiations, where a number of finance and agriculture-related issues were at stake, discussions in the Parliament were crucial in defining the best course to pursue and, for example, position papers for agriculture were discussed in great detail and copied for the Parliament. It is worth mentioning that never during the years of negotiations did any composition of the Parliament or its committees question the course of negotiations or Estonian positions as such. However, occasional mud-throwing occurred before and after elections. Excellent cooperation with the Parliament, as well as the unanimous support given by the latter to the negotiation delegation, was crucial at all these times, not least because it helped to increase the confidence of the people.

The media were regularly briefed at least once a month, and I made an explicit point that, in order to avoid all misunderstanding and false alarms, all media interviews and comments on our positions and agreements would remain the sole responsibility of the chief negotiator. We were able to keep this line to the very end of negotiations. With few exceptions, during the whole period of negotiations, the Estonian media were very helpful and reliable. Perhaps most useful, strange as it may seem, was their criticism, as it enabled the chief negotiator to highlight the problems whose solutions lay beyond the negotiating team. Media criticism was ultimately to our own advantage, enabling us to pinpoint mistakes and fairly and honourably admit and correct them.

It is therefore appropriate to touch upon one of the most challenging issues of Estonian accession—a very low public support for the accession. In fact, through all the accession years Estonians were among the most sceptical of all candidate peoples. There is no single reason for this. Many generations in Estonia have been brought up in tacit opposition to anybody in power in the country, as these were almost exclusively foreigners. Brief occasions of independence have been sharply contrasted by atrocities of foreign decision-making apparatuses. The Brussels megamachinery is notorious for its distance from the man in the street. Even worse, for many Estonians, it seemed (even if undeservedly) that the EU would be a new 'Soviet Union'. There is much formal similarity between the EU and the former SU supranational structures—perhaps a very reason to closely study what went wrong with the latter. Comparisons of this kind frequently appeared in publications of Estonian anti-accession groups. Worse still, a number of European politicians and Commission members visiting Estonia arrogantly failed to give fair answers on the difference between the two Unions. Some of them had to be warned informally to avoid such delicate discussion but self-assuredness sometimes still took its toll. This 'do as you wish, get in or stay out' attitude made our own public relations even more difficult.

On the other hand, it was clear that Estonians with their practical approach to life, with their clarity and simplicity of mind, would need some time to learn about things. Direct contacts with EU Member States on all levels—be it students, farmers, business partners, especially local governments, etc.—were crucial. Free movement of people was, for Estonians, not a matter of helping diplomats and functionaries to travel more comfortably; it was about educating people. Therefore, when the Estonian delegation appeared in Brussels at the opening of the negotiations on 31 March 1998, I proposed that in addition to acting nicely with a nice speech on a nice spring day, we try to make an immediate gain for the public and press on the abolition of visas. Thus, at the end of his speech the minister solemnly declared to an astonished Europe that Estonia was the only country among the six whose delegation and experts still needed a visa to come to negotiations in Brussels. I wish to believe that this timely move on such a huge public occasion, if not decisive, then at least speeded up the possibility for Estonians to travel freely again—something which we all had been so cruelly deprived of for many decades.

There was also another important difference between Estonia and the other five countries who started accession negotiations in 1998, and which caused us much concern. At least all three Central European states had, since the conclusion of association treaties with the EU in early 1990s, systematically prepared for the accession. Enormous analytical work had been done, perhaps most of all in Hungary where preparations started at least two years earlier than in Estonia, not to mention the superior economic situation and resources made available for this purpose. A few months before the opening of accession negotiations, we had practically nothing on the basis of which we could at least draw some preliminary conclusions on where the economy stood and what the problems were. The Commission *avis* of 1997 has already drawn a modest but telling conclusion that 'the Estonian authorities themselves believed... that of about 900 existing EU Single Market legislative acts, about 300 Estonian ones had... some degree of compatibility'. And even of these 300, almost half fell under technical regulations of customs control and others mostly under financial services—areas on which Estonia was traditionally strong. The compatibility gap was largest in agriculture, product safety, and environment, to say nothing of the fact that Estonia had never practised almost any of the numerous EU foreign trade instruments. But the internal market was of course only one part of the EU bulky *acquis*.

Thus, the first task for the delegation and its working groups was to produce within a few months at least something substantial to be put into our opening statement on 31 March 1998, something that would possibly stand the test of time for the years to come until the end of negotiations, something which would also meet the expectation of the public, while being based on a thorough analysis. There were unanswered questions like what will be the *acquis* to be negotiated, its precise legal meaning, and where to get its updated and consolidated version for hundreds of experts, many of whom had little understanding of foreign languages. Such challenges had to be solved within a few days and were innumerable.[7]

[7] As a reference, it may be recalled that the Commission, as the guardian of the treaties, provided to candidates some previously undiscovered parts of old, but still valid, *acquis* as late as 2002, the very last year of negotiations.

Setting the course: start of negotiations and tackling first problems

Screening started on 27 April with the science and research chapter being the first one. Spring and summer, with the screening exercise gaining speed, gave us necessary time to take a breath and prepare our home front for the autumn. In fact, everything was open and we were still optimistic about speedy progress of negotiations. In our analysis to the cabinet in spring 1998, we were still forecasting that negotiations 'might last well until the end of 1999 and beyond', which later proved to be very over-optimistic.

Immediately after the Luxembourg Summit and well before the start of negotiations, consultations were started between the chief negotiators and delegations of the group of the six first candidates.[8] These meetings, which rotated in six capitals during the next five years, taking place approximately every two months, turned into most intense and effective, open, and frank exchange of opinions, where joint steps were agreed, positions were coordinated, and 'best practices' learnt from each other. Being the youngest in this eminent group I was always impressed by the exceptional personalities of my five (and later of course nine) colleagues, their experience, integrity, modesty, and their unpretentious help.

Within a year, by May 1999, we had presented positions in as many as fifteen of the thirty-one negotiating chapters, and in four of the 'easier' chapters, provisional agreements had already been reached and the chapters were closed.[9] An interesting situation emerged in the telecommunications chapter where Estonia already had such a high level of mobile telephony that we were able to persuade the Commission that it would more than compensate for the lower amount of fixed telephony and thus fulfil the universal service requirement.[10] There were no particularly complicated problems in these first chapters, but we were keen to be very detailed in order to set good practice for the future and more difficult issues. However, two issues were raised in the company law chapter—patent protection of generic pharmaceuticals from new Member States by the EU, and precedence of Estonian pre-accession trademarks over analogous EU ones. The latter was relatively easily agreed by a legal formula, whereas the former was rather a problem for those candidate countries that had a significant pharmaceuticals industry, which was not the case for Estonia.

In addition to the issues raised at the negotiating table, we had immense problems with lawmaking and implementation at home. Administrative capabilities to implement EU requirements in some crucial sectors were almost non-existent in Estonia. Among them were customs, competition policy, state aid in the free

[8] On 9 December 1997 in Prague, at the invitation of Deputy Foreign Minister Svoboda.

[9] Some Member States opposed the principle of provisional closure of negotiating chapters. Therefore, a very complicated and solemn wording was agreed for this purpose, which basically gave the EU the right to return to any issue at any moment, which both sides could do anyway.

[10] Today, when 93% of Estonians are mobile phone subscribers and more than 50% regularly use the Internet, it no longer surprises anybody but it certainly sounded incredible in 1998 in Brussels where quality of mobile telephone service was far from excellent and our phones never worked properly.

movement of goods, and fisheries administration. In a number of sensitive areas like quotas for home production of TV programmes, social sector, and labour laws, it was difficult to find a political compromise for new laws. A specific problem was also the need to secure independence of internal market regulators. In Estonia, these are mostly state agencies operating under a line ministry without being directly subordinated to it. The agency director was usually nominated by the cabinet. However, in everyday work, agencies are closely related to ministries, which also set their budgets. The EU had quite reasoned fears that in theory political ministers were able to exercise partisan influence over regulators.

In some areas there were only one or two experts in Estonia to cover some specific EU competencies. For example, we had to find someone who knew well crystal and glass making, and we had but one person qualified for aviation accident investigations. Another horizontal problem was that very few people in Estonia could understand foreign languages well enough in order to participate in negotiations at par with their European partners[11]—that was further aggravated by a shortage of translators for transposing the EU resolutions. In some cases, novel solutions had to be found, as, for example, in the case of the requirement for translating thousands of EU product standards, where finally it was agreed that we translate only the title page of every specific standard. For years, the Commission remained justifiably critical of the Estonian administrative capabilities. However, they were wrong in expecting that we would develop huge structures similar to other Member States. That was out of the question, and although we made efforts to improve the situation, we could not jump over our shadow and the whole matter reminded one of a game of cat and mouse of sorts.

In contrast to other candidates, Estonia had no problem with the sale of land for foreigners, which had always been one of the most difficult issues of accession negotiations. Although we had to deal with it later—for different reasons—we were spared the complication in the beginning. On the other hand, in Estonia a unique restitution process had been carried out in the beginning of the 1990s, which was partly still ongoing, by which all real estate and lands previously nationalized by the Soviet regime were returned to former owners or successors, or compensation was offered to them. That could have meant discrimination vis-à-vis EU nationals, a problem that was solved by a relevant agreement that did not pose a substantive negotiating problem.

In a report to the cabinet in spring 1999 I was, however, extremely critical of the ability of the political establishment to take responsibility for the accession process. I said, 'in comparison to civil service, but also to NGOs and business community, who have all actively contributed to defining Estonian positions, political circles are far behind despite availability of a huge amount of information

[11] That was perhaps one of the heaviest blows delivered by the Soviet system—in order to minimize every possible contact with foreigners the quality of language teaching was very low and travelling abroad almost totally forbidden. Even at Tartu University in the 1980s linguists had hardly ever in their life been to a country whose language they were teaching! There was general reluctance among many Estonian cabinet members to travel to Brussels during accession negotiations to defend their positions and it has changed little since then.

and they deal with it with great reluctance. Among reasons for this are . . . also that they lack clear, objective, realistic visions of what Estonia needs for the future.' This situation put an enormous pressure on the civil administration and the negotiating delegation, who frequently had to analyse, discuss, propose, decide, and persuade the public without any clear vision from the politicians. In the same report I criticized the inability, or unwillingness, to implement the promises given recklessly and without budgetary coverage to the Commission by line authorities and the delays and endless debates in the Parliament over lawmaking, and warned against attempts to use negotiating problems as election weapons.

Difficult years

But more difficult times were ahead by the end of 1999 and in 2000. Developments abroad and in the EU were seriously undermining the credibility of the whole enlargement process. In March 1999 the Commission had resigned in the face of accusations of financial mismanagement. At the accession negotiations, the Member States had adopted a slowdown approach and during 1999 this became more and more evident.[12] That in turn nourished criticism and misunderstanding among decision-makers and the public in Estonia. On the other hand, the cabinet was demanding quick progress and the closure of the negotiating chapters, even at the cost of unnecessarily losing ground in tactics. On the other end, the Estonian media accused negotiators of closing negotiating chapters too quickly, and the public was increasingly losing sight of what was going on.

In spring 1999, we felt that if the EU would open negotiations with the second group of another five (or even six, as Malta had renewed its application) candidates, then it would be probable that the countries will be split into smaller groups for gradual accession. We grew afraid that the pre-*avis* situation of 1997 would repeat itself and Estonia might again, together with Latvia and Lithuania, be pressed into the second group of accession. From that point of view we had no options but to press ahead with speed and towards closing chapters. On the other hand, if we were to be in the *arrière*, simultaneous accession or so-called 'big bang' would be in our interest. Such ideas were still theory in 1999 but, when defining our strategy and tactics, I had to take care that we had good options for anything that might come upon us. While speaking at numerous seminars in Estonia and abroad I generally characterized the situation among members and candidates as 'everybody against everybody and everybody in favour of everybody'. Mathematically, that gave almost innumerable scenarios.

[12] For comparison, it is worth recalling that accession negotiations with Austria, Finland, Norway, and Sweden lasted only six months, with almost daily intermittent meetings. When Great Britain negotiated its accession in 1970–2, there were twelve meetings during half a year on the level of chief negotiators, six times more than in our case (2+1 ministerial level). Altogether, thirty-two official negotiating meetings during five years of negotiations took place with Estonia. The number of expert meetings in different format was, of course, much bigger.

By the end of 1999, the prospect of opening negotiations with all the rest of the candidates became very clear and Estonia had the lowest number of chapters provisionally closed among the first group of negotiating countries. Additionally, we were very much behind in domestic lawmaking and implementation and we had a long list of 'promised to do' things. In order not to lose ground in eventual regrouping, we decided to withdraw some less important requests. Importantly, the one regarding the Baltic Free Trade Agreement was withdrawn now that Latvia's and Lithuania's accession perspectives had cleared.

When, after the Helsinki Summit, negotiations were opened in 2000 with all remaining candidates, the criteria for progress were applied in a much less rigorous way than in the case of the six first countries in 1997. In Estonia, however, the only fear was that such an expansion of the group might give a good excuse for those EU Member States who argued for a postponed accession date (especially for the reason of financial implications). At the very end, the accession was not significantly postponed. It had been agreed already in autumn 1998, while preparing the first position papers, that the common goal for accession was 1 January 2003. In reality, it proved only a year's miss of its actual 1 May 2004.

Most of 2000 was spent on positioning and repositioning, Member States pressing on 'catching-up' of the first group by the four newcomers. In spring 2001, during the Swedish presidency, the EU made a proposal to maintain temporary restrictions on free movement of labour, which was very soon accepted by Malta and Cyprus (who were not covered by restrictions), Hungary, Latvia, and Slovakia. That put us in a difficult position as we had expected to set up a common front of all candidates for this purely political issue. On the other hand, all evidence showed that workers from small Estonia would hardly be of any threat even to the labour market of neighbouring Finland and we argued for individual treatment. In fact, as time went on and new studies predicted no substantive labour market problem, we felt less and less hurried to accept the EU proposal. Estonia and Poland were the last to agree to it, and I made a point to previously secure a bilateral agreement at least with Germany on log house builders who were competing on the German market with the Finnish and Swedish ones on unequal terms.

Last efforts

The turning point in negotiations came when at the Laeken Summit at the end of 2001 the Member States finally decided that the enlargement with those countries that were ready would take place in 2004. That automatically opened the way for agreements in more sensitive chapters. For Estonia, this amounted to a prospective closure in energy, taxation, and of course in agriculture and the financial package. As the two former two will be discussed separately below, it is worthwhile to briefly touch upon the two latter ones.

The Common Agricultural Policy (CAP) of the EU embraces almost 40 per cent of the EU budget and is therefore a non-negligible financial issue. For Estonia it also had an important social undertone. During the Soviet period, in Estonia, as well as in two other Baltic states, the agriculture had been flourishing. In Estonia collective farms were set up on the Soviet model of extensive dairy cattle and pig farming, and private farms had been effectively forbidden. Since 1991, practically no Estonian government had granted any significant support to the farming or food industry. That was considered to be in contradiction to the liberal economic doctrine, which was a dominant thinking among the country's politicians. An additional practical reason was also the lack of money for such subsidies.

Since 1991, Estonia has gone through a sharp decline in agricultural production, and by 2001, when more serious negotiations started over agriculture with the EU, Estonian agriculture had practically reached its bottom. There was a big income gap between rural and urban population, and the former was nostalgic for past times. That made a good basis for a political farming lobby. By 2000, the general wealth of society had to some extent increased again and polls showed an increasingly more sympathetic attitude within society for granting support to the farming sector. The EU was seen as a kind of saviour of Estonian agriculture and life in the countryside. The added value was also a face-saving opportunity for those politicians who had until lately been strictly against any support to farming. When the EU for the first time presented its positions in the agricultural chapter, the reality proved to be quite different from expectations.

For Estonia the main disagreements with the Commission were over the years to be used as a point of reference, which would automatically quantify the subsidies to be paid. By proposing the immediate years before accession, the lowest in Estonian agriculture, the EU effectively cut down the figures for the number of cattle (and in turn milk quota) and cultivation area, thus minimizing regional payments. We (and also Latvia and Lithuania) tried to argue that our situation was substantively different from the other candidates, who all had had an uninterrupted agricultural support policy and were therefore more or less satisfied with the suggested reference years. The EU obviously had no nostalgia for the Soviet Union and that brought us nowhere, although at the end certain buffers were agreed for increasing milk quota. However, a large number of issues under the agriculture chapter were similar for all, or most, candidate countries and thus received horizontal solutions, phasing in of direct payments being the most eminent one.

Another specific problem for Estonia was sugar. The sugar regime is one of the few elements, if not the only one of the EU agricultural and trade policy, which has been left unchanged in all successive CAP reforms. A remnant of political vote-fishing, it has no economic reasoning whatsoever, apart from the wish to maintain uncompetitive production. The lobby for maintaining the common market organization for sugar has been impossible to overcome in spite of all successive Commission reform attempts. The EU maintains the sugar production by way of a combination of sugar levies on imports and domestic production quotas and subsidies. As a result, in 2000 the price of sugar on the EU internal market was almost three times as high as on the world market and five large companies held more than 50 per cent of the total EU sugar quota.[13] The price differential is covered by the EU consumers. Some of these monies are returned to Member States via workplaces in the sugar beet growing and processing industry.

Estonian consumers had for many years benefited from the subsidies that the EU paid on sugar that was exported to us from the EU. As a result, the price of sugar in Estonia was much lower than in Latvia, where relevant import restrictions were applied. We were the only candidate country who had no sugar beet growing and sugar production; therefore our attempt to get a sugar production quota was bluntly rejected by the EU. That meant in broad terms that after accession the Estonian consumers, among the poorer ones in Europe, would pay an estimated €20–30 million annually[14] into the pockets of European sugar producers in wealthier Member States. Increased production costs were foreseen for the soft drinks industry and confectioners and bakeries. The EU turned a deaf ear on all our arguments and proposals and on the very eve of the Copenhagen Summit we gave up the price increase issue in order to defend our other positions. That battle was lost, but it left Estonia the most devoted adherent of abolishing this EU anachronism.

Unfortunately, we were wrong in thinking that the issue could be settled by simply accepting the price increase; the EU sugar fund would not settle for lower sugar profits. In 2005, the Commission concluded that, panicking for a price increase in the run-up to accession in 2004, the Estonian consumers had bought an extensive amount of sugar, and violated the provisions of the Accession Treaty on excessive stocks. It is true that acceding states were to take measures to avoid excessive stocks, and it is true that much of the sugar in Estonia had been bought for speculative purpose.

The conclusion, however, marked a last-minute and rigid adoption by the Commission of the formula for calculating stocks without listening to the opinion of the new members. As it is less and less customary in Europe to do domestic reserves it is perhaps less remarkable, though unfortunate, that the Commission also turned a blind eye to the fact that almost half of the so-called extensive sugar stock in Estonia was bought by private persons (many of my own relatives did!) of especially elderly families in rural areas for domestic consumption. Thus, the sugar bought before accession by private persons and perhaps consumed long since was defined by the Commission as a still existing excessive stock on the internal market.

The EU rigid rules on jam making had already been widely ridiculed by Estonian media. The Commission message was rather unequivocal; it amounted to saying that by buying cheap sugar before accession, Estonians were 'stealing' future profits from the EU in the form of more expensive sugar that would go unsold in the future.

[13] Cf. special report of the EU Court of Auditors No. 20/2000 on management of CMO on sugar.

[14] Approx 0.3–0.4% of annual GDP of Estonia. We estimated that as a result, sugar would make almost 6% of our current account deficit after accession. At the same time, the EU had criticized Estonia for years for its high current account deficit. This struck the Estonian negotiators as particularly unjust.

It is worthwhile recalling that already since 1998, at several association councils Estonia had explicitly invited the EU to abolish its export subsidies on sugar vis-à-vis Estonia. Even at that early stage, we were already worried about the effect of accession on lower-income families. The EU, however, did not act on these concerns. The *facit*—the price of sugar for Estonian consumers—almost doubled on average after accession, and the country further had to pay a penalty to the EU for having bought too much of the EU-subsidized sugar before accession. Of course, during negotiations we were unable to foresee such dramatic development occurring as a result of implementation gaps both in Tallinn and in Brussels before immediate accession. Nevertheless, the big facts remain and the Estonian case will hopefully serve as a textbook example for future accessions.

A few points are also worth noting on the financial package. As is well known, the EU took a horizontal approach in negotiating the financial package, and finally it was a matter of simple political compromise. All candidate countries had to accept that financial transfers from the EU funds would remain lower than for the 'old' Member States for many years. For various reasons, for Estonia the calculated revenue was still among the highest.[15] Obviously, as much of the transfers depend on the absorption capacity, co-financing, etc., precise receipts could not be predicted. The EU negotiating aim was rather simple—to make the envelope of 'hard money' (e.g. agricultural direct payments) as slim as possible and instead offer commitments or 'virtual' money (i.e. project-based funding, which was depending on a number of extra factors). An undeniably positive move by the EU was the establishment of the so-called Schengen facility whereby the new members received a substantive financial package to set up modern border controls.

As there was not much flexibility on the EU side regarding agriculture and financial issues, Estonia decided to increase the stakes and raised some other small but important new issues. Among these were restrictions on the sale of land to foreigners.

As noted above, Estonia initially had no problems in closing the relevant chapter as we had already abolished restrictions for all sales of land and real estate to foreigners. On the other hand, during all the years of negotiations there had been a political lobby in Estonia arguing for the need to have such restrictions. The transitional agreements granted to other candidates served, of course, as a good example. Approximately three months before the end of negotiations I learned from my Lithuanian colleague that they would most probably change their position and request a transitional period. That would have immediately left Estonia with Latvia under strong public pressure. I warned the FM and the PM that if Lithuania did so and their request was granted, it would be impossible to hold back the political forces in Estonia willing the same. Indeed, the situation developed in this way and at the very last hour relevant transition periods were requested and agreed also with Estonia and Latvia.

[15] Our estimate showed €365.4 per capita net revenue for Estonia from the EU for 2004–6. Figures for Lithuania were slightly higher because of EU funding to dismantle the Ignalina nuclear plant.

Among the most important issues for Estonia to be agreed on the very eve of the Copenhagen Summit was the issue of hunting of bears and lynx.[16] Unlike many other European countries, more than half of Estonian territory is covered by thick forests where large animals like elk, deer, bear, wolf, and lynx abound. All of them are hunted under strict management plans. Almost five hundred bears, more than one hundred wolves, and a thousand lynx wandering free in a country with a size of Denmark or the Netherlands sounded unbelievable for the Commission, which initially resisted our requests. Hunting, however, serves a bigger cause than leisure; it is also necessary to keep in balance certain food chain patterns as carnivorous animals often kill other protected species and as it sometimes proves to be necessary to eliminate ill animals. With some last-minute emotions, our requests were mostly met. Vitally important had been the fact that experts involved in nature protection in Estonia had prepared an excellent file and done good work in briefing the delegation.

3. OUTSTANDING ISSUES FOR ESTONIA

Shipping and tax free

A few problems specific to Estonia deserve to be mentioned separately from overall developments in the negotiations. The first one had to do with the need to abolish tax-free sales on ferries calling at the Port of Tallinn mostly from and to Helsinki and Stockholm. Traffic of cruise tourists from these two Scandinavian capitals to Tallinn had virtually exploded in the late 1990s and in its turn nourished the tourist industry especially in Tallinn. To the great dismay of the authorities, especially in Finland, many of the tourists returned from Tallinn with heavy cartloads of alcohol, purchased from the ships' duty-free shops. As a side effect, the Finnish authorities got permission from the EU to prolong restrictions on import of alcohol from third countries, something they had obtained at their own accession negotiations a few years before. It was argued as a health matter, although it seemed to be more related to the protection of the Finnish state alcohol monopoly company Alko and alcohol tax revenue. As the tax-free sales had been abolished on routes between Helsinki and Stockholm, obviously the Estonian route offered many advantages.[17] At least two large companies—Hansatee (Tallink) in Estonia and Silja Line in Finland—and a number of smaller ones were commercially very much interested in maintaining the tax-free shops. Although I had already (in 1998) alerted the Minister of Transport that it would

[16] Hunting of wolves had already been agreed.

[17] The route from Tallinn to Stockholm is almost equal to the one from Helsinki. However, because of restricted duty free, ferries from Finland were calling at Mariehamn port at the Åland Islands in order to exit the EU tax territory and thus sell goods tax free. That gave some advantage to Estonian shippers who could go directly. Today, ferries from Tallinn also call at Mariehamn.

be necessary to study the issue and find out whether we should expect to face serious problems, nothing happened until the ferry operators themselves discovered in 1999 what was coming to them. Instead of starting a dialogue with the cabinet or negotiating team, a heavy public relations campaign was launched. All media outlets were involved, and a number of clearly inclined articles with distorted arguments were published. As the ferry operators were under heavy loan obligations to large banks, the pressure was immense and no nasty language or recourse was spared in order to lobby for a transition period until the derogation given to the Åland Islands was in effect.

The derogation granted to the Åland Islands on the accession of Finland in 1995 was something which was most frequently quoted by the advocates of tax-free shops in Estonia while the details and background of this derogation on indirect taxes were mostly unknown for the public. The Åland Islands derogation had its roots in the history of the islands and was argued not on economic grounds but rather on its special status under international law (1921 League of Nations convention, which also Estonia had been a party to).

In order to establish the exact size of the problem and expected losses of the ferry operators as a result of abolition of tax-free sales, I requested a detailed study from the KPMG consulting firm in the autumn of 1999. In order to be on the safe side, I had the macroeconomic effect methodology of the study separately assessed by the Estonian Central Bank analysts, which was acceptable to all sides. The results of the study showed that at worst some reduction of passengers could be predicted, at best revenues could even increase, and that the most likely scenario was that any possible losses would be outweighed by positive developments and no significant change would occur. Such a study obviously did not reflect the operators' perception of the issue as a very serious problem. However, the unpredictability of the outcome was a valid argument, something that all parties to the debate had to admit.[18] However, ferry operators had managed to activate the whole Estonian tourism sector, especially the smaller companies, with horror scenarios of ferry traffic closing down and the ensuing chain reaction affecting not just tourism but the whole Estonian economy.[19] Therefore, four options were proposed for the cabinet:

- to request a transition period for up to seven years to maintain tax- and duty-free sales on ships calling at Tallinn port (a similar transition period had been granted when tax free was abolished within the EU in 1992–9);
- to work for the abolition of the Åland Islands derogation;
- to combine both previous requests; and
- not to raise the issue at the negotiations and comply with the EU rules by accession.

[18] Several other European shipping companies had reported reduced passenger numbers and economic losses when the tax-free sales were abolished.

[19] In a country with 3–4 million tourists annually and more than 80% of them arriving by ferry, it is a serious argument.

There was a loophole in the Finnish Accession Treaty, which momentarily seemed for us as the possible way out. Namely, the treaty safeguarded also that 'if the Commission considers that the provisions... are no longer justified, particularly in terms of fair competition or own resources, it shall submit appropriate proposals to the Council'. We even had some indications that the authorities in Finland and the Ålands might not immediately object to such an initiative for the abolition of the Åland Islands derogation. However, that would have implied another referendum in the Åland Islands, which was clearly unthinkable.

I also saw the possibility of getting a transition period or derogation for tax-free sales for ships as a remote one, but I was prepared to take it up for later trade-offs, having initially in mind the chapters on energy or free movement of workers—both equally 'political' issues. In any case, there were tax-free areas in some other EU Member States, which set some precedence[20] but that was far from the Baltic Sea, where many shipping companies in many countries had fought their big fight and lost it by 1 July 1999, when the tax free was abolished. It would have been unthinkable that competitors in neighbouring countries would have agreed to such an advantage granted to Estonian shippers.

But there was another side of the coin: the hefty subsidies paid by the EU governments to their shippers, which in turn helped to keep salaries high—something their Estonian colleagues could only dream of. In Finland in the autumn of 1998 the trade unions had even launched a boycott against Estonian cargo ships calling at Finnish ports, claiming that their lower salaries constituted social dumping. That was clearly in breach of the association treaty and we immediately raised it with the Commission.[21] We also raised the issue of discriminative port fees both in Sweden and Finland. Such proceedings were to last for years, of course, but at least at this moment I felt that we had plenty of reasons to protect our shippers against the state-supported sector of the Scandinavians. My arguments did not weigh enough with the cabinet at this moment and the decision was made not to request the transition period for the abolition of duty-free sales.

Perhaps it was a good decision in substance but a failure as regards public relations. The attacks on the negotiating team in the media grew worse. Popular slogans thrown out at these debates did, perhaps unwillingly, deepen the overall scepticism among the public, something that hit back only days before the accession referendum.

In early 2001, when the negotiations had come to a stalemate and Brussels showed no progress in 'difficult issues', we decided to return to the issue. With the hope for speedy accession fading, I proposed to revise the whole package of requests in the taxation chapter and include some new ones, among others the tax-free sales. This time the cabinet agreed. Our arguments proved to be right and it unexpectedly became a handy trade-off when in early 2002 we had to solve another complicated taxation issue, the corporate income tax. The long and

[20] The Canaries and Channel Islands, e.g. were not part of the EU tax territory.

[21] The issue was also raised with the government of Finland but with no effect.

emotional duty-free saga came silently to its end when the taxation chapter was finally closed as a package deal in June 2002.[22]

Corporate income tax

When the new cabinet was formed in Estonia after elections in 1999, one of the main political changes was the amended income tax law, whereby all profits reinvested in Estonia were made free from corporate income tax from 2000 onward. The aim of this measure was to attract and promote foreign investment in the Estonian economy in order to reverse the outflow of financial assets which had left the country through several Estonian-owned offshore companies.

In the beginning we did not expect it to become a problem at the negotiations, apart from political repercussions arising from the lack of consistency in the relevant national laws across the EU. The Ministry of Finance, in an internal memo in 2000, expressed fears that this might lead to enterprise shopping from other EU Member States and label Estonia as an offshore company haven.[23]

Apart from worries about the fate of our bilateral double taxation agreements, I was confident that the Estonian case was sound, despite these fears, and I confirmed to the cabinet that we should be able to argue our case and that the EU would be unable to prove non-conformity with any EU acts. The income tax regimes are not harmonized at the EU level, although this has been a matter of debate for many years. The Commission on its behalf made a stake on the Code of Conduct, but that was a non-binding instrument and we were not particularly worried.

Things took a sharp turn in October 2001 when the European Court of Justice in Luxembourg made a decision in the Athinaiki case against Greece.[24] That case showed similarities with the Estonian situation and we had followed its development with some concern for some time. I had previously believed that if the issue passed unnoticed and the taxation chapter was closed without any reference to our income tax, then the matter would be settled and the decision would be left for a later stage at court, if raised. But now, after the decision in Luxembourg, it was clear that we needed at least a transitional measure, if not a permanent derogation. The opinion of the Commission was that the Estonian income tax

[22] In 2005, more than a year after the accession, the number of incoming tourists to Estonia had, in fact, been increasing, and the boom in the tourism sector, as well as in cruise shipping, continued. The optimistic scenario proved to be the right one and Tallink shipping group reported a 100% year-to-year profit increase.

[23] In November 2002, the Belgian Ministry of Finance included Estonia on a provisional list of countries with an 'advantageous tax regime', threatening to suspend tax-free profits earned by Belgian companies in Estonia.

[24] Usually, no one in Estonia regularly followed cases pending before the ECJ. There was simply no resource for that. I therefore took time myself occasionally for late night reading on recent cases and found useful arguments for discussions both at home and abroad, as when the issue of imposing Estonian language requirements for public and private sector was discussed, etc. Monitoring the legal aspects of the EU law and its theory was one of our major problems during the years leading to accession.

suspension was in contradiction with at least two EU requirements: the so-called EU parent-subsidiary directive (redistributed profits from subsidiary to parent company are not allowed to be taxed) and the free movement of capital (profits distributed to Estonian resident companies were left untaxed whereas the ones distributed to non-resident companies were taxed).

At the same time, because of a number of sensitivities, both Estonia and the EU carefully avoided exaggerating the issue as the taxation chapter was already full of controversial requests from Estonia. In March 2003, after several unofficial meetings and discussions, the Commission was concerned that the issue had caught the attention of the media in Estonia. Low public support in Estonia for the accession was well known at all levels in the Commission and any new problem raised by the EU would have only aggravated the situation. In Estonia, people were mostly satisfied with a simple, transparent, and reliable tax system and the European attack on the cornerstones of our economic success might easily have become the last drop against accession. We were well aware of that and to a certain extent found comfort in it, as it made the Commission more interested in finding a positive solution and thus worked to our advantage. The issue was of enormous political importance, as it was also clear that it would be impossible for Estonia, and especially the Reform Party cabinet, to accept any deal which would have jeopardized the corporate tax incentive. Corporate tax incentive had been the main political message of the Reform Party for many years.

As usual, complicated problems have simple solutions. In order to avoid further tangling in legal formulae after both sides had equally ably proven and defended their arguments, a five-year transition period was agreed at a lunch meeting between Commissioner Verheugen and PM Kallas. Together with this, all our remaining requests in the taxation chapter (except the request for a derogation on wind energy) were accepted by the EU in June, a couple of days after the Estonian traditional midsummer holiday.

Energy and oil shale

The energy chapter was, for Estonia, perhaps the most complicated and also the most important one. The problems with the energy sector were further aggravated by the fact that by the start of negotiations the country had practically no policy or vision on energy and the relevant department in the Ministry of Economy was undergoing a thorough reformation.

Therefore, during the years of negotiations, much of the groundwork on energy had to be done by the members of the MFA negotiating task force. Even when preparing for our opening statement in 1998, our energy experts pointed out that oil shale-based energy production might require special attention and perhaps derogations in the course of negotiations. However, the problem was such a complex one, covering several parts of the EU *acquis*, that no single state authority was able to deal with it alone. Therefore, we were absolutely unaware with what parts of the EU *acquis* our ways and practices might be in contradiction.

In order to understand the unique situation of Estonia one has to know some basic facts. Estonia has a long tradition of oil shale mining and research. The first geological oil shale investigations in Estonia were made as early as 1858. The mining of oil shale began in 1918 near Kohtla-Järve in north-east Estonia. After the Second World War, the Soviet authorities turned it into a large-scale industrial operation with all accompanying problems. Oil shale was excavated mostly in order to feed two big power stations, located near the Estonian border town of Narva, which provided electricity not only for Estonia, but also for neighbouring Latvia and the St Petersburg region in Russia. It was also a raw material used by chemical factories in the area, which produced shale oil out of it. Vast areas all over the north-eastern part of the country were turned into mines or open-pit excavations. In several places huge mountains of oil shale waste were formed, which sometimes caught fire because of the low quality of enrichment technology. Poisonous substances leaked from oil shale waste deposits into surface water. Tens of thousands of mostly uneducated workers were brought from other mining regions of the Soviet Union into the area. By the 1990s, it had virtually been turned into a Russian-speaking area. The environment had been spoiled and polluted on a large scale in these areas, but the whole country had cheap electricity and no questions were ever allowed to be asked.[25]

In 1999, the share of oil shale in the Estonian primary energy balance was 58 per cent. Most of the oil shale was used for production of electricity and the rest for production of heat, oil shale oil, and coke as well as by the chemical industry. In 1999 more than 92 per cent of the electricity of Estonia was produced from oil shale. The Estonian oil shale has unique characteristics as a technological raw material: its thermal processing enables the production of by-products that are impossible to obtain from oil or coal, or from oil shale of other regions of the world. Estonia possesses the largest and best-defined oil shale reserves in Europe. According to the 1998 World Energy Council Survey of Energy Resources, citing the Geological Survey of Estonia, proven and surface-minable oil shale deposits amount to 3.8 billion tonnes.

Oil shale can be used mainly as:

- direct fuel for power generation;
- raw material for production of oil shale oil and/or gas or other chemical products; and
- direct fuel in the cement industry.

Estonia is the largest oil shale mining country in the world (84 per cent of total mining volume in 1999). The production of oil shale in Estonia peaked in 1980 at approximately 30 million tonnes a year. However, during the last decades, the extraction of oil shale had significantly decreased, mainly due to a decrease in electricity production. In 2000, oil shale extraction amounted to 11 million tonnes.

[25] It is worth recalling that in 1988, when the new plans by Soviet authorities to start another large-scale mining operation of phosphor in north Estonia leaked out, it led to general public protest, consolidation of opposition, and finally restoration of independence of the country.

A situation occurred in the second half of the 1990s whereby the oil shale producing sector was unable to cope with the almost threefold decline in the demand for oil shale. As a result, the effectiveness and the technology of the main enterprises in the sector suffered considerably.

In 1998 the Estonian government took a firm stance with a view to restructure the whole sector, thereby increasing its efficiency and decreasing emmissions of pollutants from oil shale production. The chemicals industry, based on oil shale, was privatized. By 1999, when Estonia presented its position on the energy chapter, there were ongoing negotiations with the American company NRG Energy with a view to also privatize the two power stations.[26] The Finnish state-owned company Fortum andw German Preussen Elektra showed interest in the purchase of the power stations as well.

After the start of accession negotiations, and having had some time to look into the matter, we realized that the situation was characterized by the following actors and problems:

- the Commission, pressed by lobbies from Finland and Germany, was concerned by the privatization plans of power stations to the US firm; informally they showed indignation that no public bidding was organized and they were also confident that NRG Energy was only interested in the transit of electricity and not in improving the whole range of problems related to the oil shale;
- the US government was concerned by the slow privatization process of power stations and never failed to demonstrate its interest at high level (on the eve of decisions on NATO accession it was a non-negligible argument);
- influential Estonian entrepreneurial lobbyists were interested in selling the power stations to Estonian investors, later to be offered for sale on the stock exchange;
- the whole north-eastern part of the country had the highest unemployment rate and the lowest number of private enterprises in Estonia; it was a region of high social tension with a large Russian-speaking minority which led Russia to take an interest in what happened in the area;
- huge deposits of oil shale ashes were in contradiction with the EU waste depositing directives;
- huge deposits of shale oil extraction waste were in contradiction with the EU waste water and surface water protection directives; and
- as the two power stations provided about 92 per cent of electricity in Estonia, there was virtually no alternative production except for imports from Russia (which were out of question for security reasons), from Finland (where there was no physical link), or building nuclear power stations (which lacked any public support as we had only lately got rid of the waste of the former Soviet nuclear marine base in Paldiski and a radioactive waste water deposit in Sillamäe).

In EU terms, this situation meant that we were unable to meet the criteria for the EU electricity market liberalization.

[26] They both operated within a single power generation company.

There were, of course, some positive elements in this situation. As the only future EU Member State to possess scientific knowledge on oil shale, Estonia was globally recognized as having unique know-how and cooperated closely with other leading countries, including the USA. We recognized that this might be a positive asset for the whole EU. We were also totally independent with regard to electricity, something that has become more and more important with recent failures and price fluctuations on liberalized electricity markets in different parts of the world. We had promising ground for developing a modern chemicals industry on the basis of shale oil, which could also be a strategically useful substitute in case of oil crises.

The problem, however, was still that we did not know where to start from and what exactly to request from the EU. So I decided that we should wait and see until some opportunity presented itself to us as a pretext; meanwhile, we should keep our request on the table in the energy chapter with some general language. Thus, in 1999 we made a small start, only noting that a 'special status' for the oil shale would have to be agreed.

Soon, the Commission (perhaps unwillingly) gave us the clue. In the privatization talks with the American company, one issue that was raised concerned state guarantees for a purchase of a certain amount of energy by the state-owned distribution company (the so-called Power Purchase Agreement). The Commission, who had carefully followed the developments, officially turned to us in autumn 1999, pointing out that such a deal might be in contradiction with Estonian obligations under the association treaty and, more importantly, the EU requirements on state aid. Of course, as the details of these negotiations were not public, the Commission had to guess and their message was a vague political warning rather than a formal notification.

The privatization did not concern the EU, and we had solid legal arguments even for the case of PPA, but the government was eager to secure that it would give no pretext to slow down the accession negotiations. A quick study in the MFA on the draft terms of privatization revealed an almost certain conflict with the EU electricity market and competition requirements. In our letter to the cabinet, we therefore pointed out that the issue has to be negotiated with the EU, leaving open the spectrum of possible results.

Meanwhile, although the privatization deal with the American company had fallen through,[27] the problem as such remained: we had a huge power generation complex, with a number of technical,[28] social, scientific, economic, strategic, and

[27] The deal could not be completed for reasons which had nothing to do with the EU. There was, among others, a huge public campaign initiated by some politicians, and some 180,000 (one-eighth of the population) signatures were gathered against the privatization of the power stations, which was considered to be a threat to national interests.

[28] Producing electricity in certain amounts requires complex back-up power generation for eventual fluctuations, etc. That, in turn, cannot be achieved by simply turning the system on and off. The Estonian power stations serve as a reserve system for the whole power network of the three Baltic countries and north-western part of Russia.

political reasons for keeping it in service. It was a clear monopoly and a pollution champion and it needed a PPA.

Under these conditions, we were able to start putting together piece by piece an all-inclusive package on oil shale for the accession negotiations. Very instrumental was the fact that during the preparations for privatization, several detailed and reliable studies on technology, finance, pollution, and market issues for the Estonian oil shale complex had been ordered from eminent European consultancy firms, which we could draw from. We also studied the former German Democratic Republic, where lignite mining had caused similar problems. The picture that emerged was very clear in that if we wanted to keep our energy independence, and especially the security of stable supply, while also making necessary and huge investments in overall renovation of the oil shale energy complex, the monopoly had to be maintained for at least ten years, independently of the type of ownership. The only matter on which the studies were not unanimous related to the length of such a period.

In November 2001 we had finally completed our almost three years of brainstorming and tabled the following official request to the EU:

- agree a transitional measure for electricity market liberalization until the end of 2012;
- provide Community financing to the regional development measures for the north-east;
- provide Community financing for elaboration of the 'best available technique' (BAT) for the oil shale industry;
- enhance the certification of oil shale oil and chemicals produced from oil shale in the European List of Notified Chemical Substances; and
- recognize and grant Community financing to oil shale research, especially with a view towards extending the possibilities of using oil shale, and for modernization of the technologies of processing oil shale.

Some of these requests we were able to solve outside the framework of the Accession Treaty, but the core of the matter was inevitably the question of market liberalization. As the EU was simultaneously discussing the amended, earlier targets for opening of European electricity markets, we had to carefully monitor these developments as well in order to avoid some new obstacles. Finally, in July 2002, after almost a year of negotiations, a transition period until 2009 was agreed with Estonia on market liberalization. In an additional declaration it was recognized that due to the specific situation related to the oil shale sector in Estonia, only a gradual market opening for non-household customers is necessary until 2012.

The social aspects were simultaneously addressed by adopting a North-East Estonian Employment Action Plan, which was later approved by the Commission. In the environmental chapter, agreements were simultaneously secured for transition periods on the EU directives on landfill of waste, surface water, and emissions of pollutants to air. We finally also agreed (under the other issues chapter) with the EU on including oil shale research among activities to be funded by the European research fund for coal and steel.

Fisheries

Estonia was unique among the candidates as a traditionally seagoing nation—Hemingway's quote about at least one Estonian in every world port is well known. During the Soviet era, Estonia had a big fishing fleet, which, at the start of negotiations, still numbered almost 200 vessels, many of whom went fishing on the high seas in the Atlantic. Estonia was also a member of major international quota sharing agreements (including the Spitzbergen agreement) and maritime organizations.

The fisheries chapter was among the first to be provisionally closed with Estonia. However, we received news that we had a huge problem with the implementation and administrative capability in the fisheries sector, even while the news of having closed the chapter was still fresh. It was mostly related to record keeping on catches, especially as regards coastal fisheries, and setting up lists of fishing ships and measuring their capacity.

The problem was aggravated by the fact that the fisheries *acquis* was, in Estonian administrative structures, divided between the Ministry of Environment (who dealt with resource policy, i.e. quota distribution and negotiation) and the Ministry of Agriculture (who dealt with processing, landing, and marketing requirements). That in turn made it difficult to make effective improvements, especially in matters related to staffing. Although all successive Prime Ministers tried to place the responsibility under a single authority, or otherwise clear up disagreement, they almost equally failed. Inside the negotiating delegation, we had to find a *modus vivendi* to make people in Brussels happy and continue working with our deficiencies. Throughout the negotiations, the fisheries chapter was the most likely to be reopened in the case of Estonia, something that we tried to avoid at all costs.

In the end, the fisheries chapter had to be negotiated again in order to agree on certain quotas and reference bases. We then also raised—and agreed without major problems—the issue of higher than permitted dioxin content in local fish (as had been the case with also Finland and Sweden) and smaller than permitted size for local herring.

Tariffs and other foreign trade instruments

Estonia had practically no restrictions on imports prior to accession. Even the few quantitative restrictions that were in place had been abolished at the beginning of the 1990s. In parallel we had concluded a number of free trade agreements with several European countries who luckily were either members of the EU, or candidates for membership, or members of the EEA.[29] The only exception was

[29] FTAs with candidates were with Hungary, Poland, Czech Republic, Slovakia, Latvia, Lithuania; with the EEA with Norway, Iceland, and Switzerland.

the FTA with Ukraine. Thus, we had three problem areas: what to do with these agreements, when and how to start adopting and implementing numerous EU trade instruments, and how to address these issues in the negotiations. It became a big issue in international media as Estonia was well known for the small number of import tariffs and other trade restrictions.[30]

From the beginning of the accession negotiations we raised two important issues under the external affairs chapter. First, the need to maintain provisionally the Baltic Free Trade Agreement we had concluded only a few years before with Latvia and Lithuania. We were well aware of its economic importance for Estonia. It gave free access for the Estonian farm products to the markets of Latvia and Lithuania where the level of protection would otherwise be very high. We had to keep in mind that in theory, any one of the three countries (including ourselves) could also finally stay out of the EU, be it for the result of referendum, a failure in the negotiations, or a number of other reasons. Theoretically, if Estonia stayed out, we would have lost all access to Latvian and Lithuanian markets, while having to keep our market open to their products.[31] At the same time, the prospect of the other two countries joining Estonia in the membership negotiations was also somewhat vague. Thus, the issue had to be at least marked and frozen in some way until the situation became clearer. Meanwhile, we had to politely fight back the proposals of our neighbours to establish a common Baltic customs area, which might have complicated our situation even more. As was explained before, we withdrew our request for maintaining the Baltic FTA in late 1999, when Latvia's and Lithuania's accession prospects had cleared.

With a slightly different language we raised the issue of the free trade agreement between Estonia and Ukraine. This agreement also gave free access for Estonian farm products to the Ukrainian market and was especially important for the export of canned fish products. It gave Estonian exporters a big advantage over the other Baltic and even EU producers of similar products. Additionally, political relations between Estonia and Ukraine were very close and there was a lot of goodwill towards helping to bring the country closer to Europe. So one element of our thinking was also to use this as an opportunity to promote Ukraine–EU relations in general. We proposed to the EU that we find suitable compensatory means to alleviate the impact of cancelling this agreement. Quite unpredictably, at the end of negotiations we had to return to this issue from a different angle.

30 When drafting first free trade agreements with Scandinavian countries in 1992 at the MFA, we never expected it to lay ground for a broader Estonian trade policy 'experiment'. We simply had no competitive home products to defend, no well-trained customs officials, and no money to recruit them. In addition, we also had none of the necessary statistics, staff, or funds to run complicated models for calculating the necessary level of protection. We also believed that such competition promotes economic efficiency in the initial phase of economic development. It was certainly not a deliberate, long-term political master plan but a simple reaction to Estonian reality.

31 Estonia had no import tariffs vis-à-vis the EU. At the end of 1997, in November when the time was running out for introducing these under FTA, the cabinet failed to do it, partly because of fears of losing the invitation to negotiations, although it was contemplated.

In the customs union chapter, the EU seriously questioned the ability of Estonia to participate in the customs union and implement numerous EU trade instruments. This was largely because of the absence of import tariffs, which translated to a lack of experience. These fears proved to be well grounded some years later. At this moment, we had to accept a formula under which we were to start gradual application of EU foreign trade instruments no later than 2001. As a country bound under WTO treaty, we had extremely limited possibilities to do so. Not a single Estonian border checkpoint met the EU veterinary control requirements at the time, and huge investments were needed. Controversy arose over the fact that most of our imports came from the EU and if we applied restrictions, then it would have been mostly against products originating in the Union.

On the other hand, Estonia was bound by its accession negotiations with the WTO, which were going on in parallel. In these negotiations, the EU position was very clear and opposed any wish by Estonia to bind our tariffs on the same level as the EU. Nevertheless, the EU did not miss any opportunity to remind us of the need to start applying the EU trade measures, while effectively refusing us agreement to do so under the association treaty. Finally, the new government, which took office in 2000, made a relevant decision and tariffs were introduced against third countries. Imports from these countries were of course negligible and it made sense only as a limited exercise for the post-accession period.

Another problem was the wish of some Estonian local governments to set up custom-free zones. There were even wishes to request transition periods for a number of them, which the cabinet decisively resisted. As we had four customs zones in operation and the EU agreed to only two, the Solomonian agreement was that there will remain three.

We briefly and quite unexpectedly had to revisit the earlier issue of trade between Estonia and Ukraine because of one particular product: steel. By 2001, a modern steel galvanizing facility had been set up in the port of Paldiski in Estonia. The business plan included importing steel from Ukraine, Russia, and Kazakhstan, processing it in Estonia, and exporting it to the EU. Competition among the world and European steel producers is very tough and such development combined with a fall in steel prices on the world market made several European producers nervous.[32] For us, the problem mainly came from the fact that after accession we were to introduce import quotas on steel from Russia and Ukraine, which would have immediately jeopardized this novel investment.[33] On the other hand, we were clearly swimming upstream with no support or understanding of what the request we made to the EU entailed.

In the beginning of the negotiations we had for some time kept open a 'window of opportunity' in the customs union chapter, by vaguely saying that for certain

[32] The US government decision at the end of 2001 to limit steel imports from the EU did not help our cause, although Estonia could still continue exporting to the USA.

[33] Another problem was that the Estonian producers of canned fish, who were successfully exporting their products to Ukraine under the FTA, were also in turn dependent on cheap Ukrainian and Russian steel imports for their cans. Also, shipbuilding and repair factories in Estonia were concerned.

products we might apply a gradual phasing-in of duty rates after accession. It caused much concern for the EU, but the Estonian economy was developing very quickly and trade patterns and new investments were almost impossible to predict. That window of opportunity ended in 2001, when it became more and more difficult to persuade the cabinet, without any facts,[34] especially as we were fighting to close the customs chapter, where we had immense problems with implementation and IT. Before that, we also looked well into the relevant *acquis* concerning steel imports, and found that our problem fell under external affairs rather than the customs chapter (which covered only tariff quotas).

Thus something else had to be done. At last, we argued with the Commission that Estonian pre-accession imports both from Russia and Ukraine need to be taken into account when new quota adjustments will be negotiated with these countries. As the EU had rejected all ideas of granting an individual steel import quota to Estonia, it was obviously far from a perfect solution, but we had made a point, we had framed it for future action as a Member State, and it was the most we could do at this very last minute. We also made a declaration to such a purpose in the Accession Treaty.

4. CONCLUDING REMARKS

During the five years of accession negotiations, Estonia went through immense changes. Many of these were directly or indirectly due to the accession itself. Perhaps these changes would have taken place anyway, but the accession gave a powerful impulse and it was easier to stay on track. The biggest changes were in competition policy, environmental policy, agriculture, internal market, and foreign trade; but perhaps the biggest of all the changes was the feeling that the country was for the first time coming out of mental seclusion.

There were perhaps not so many negotiating situations in the traditional meaning. It was rather a process management, which required from the negotiating team to ensure that all major deviations or obstacles both at home and abroad were predicted well in advance and kept under control. It was impossible to cover here everything that happened during five years of accession negotiations and I have mentioned only the most eminent issues and circumstances. But even in those cases covered here, it has only been possible to describe the tip of the iceberg. There were thousands of other issues where very substantive work was needed. Estonia came out of these negotiations as a totally different country, with a European legal system and a modern and efficient administration.

[34] EU position on 27 July 2000: 'Estonia is invited to confirm that... no post-accession approximation of duty rates will be necessary. The EU recalls that it could not accept transitional arrangements in the implementation of the Common Customs Tariff, as these would lead to distortions of competition and could negatively affect the functioning of the internal market.'

I have been asked several times whether during all these years we made mistakes or something went wrong in the negotiations.[35] There were obviously mistakes made, but they were mostly of a tactical nature; problems of managing everyday work with an extremely small and overloaded staff. There were sometimes gaps in legal analysis. In many areas, it became obvious that the administration lacked a dialogue with the implementing sector—for example, enterprises. That meant that problems were brought to the chief negotiator at the very last minute, sometimes directly from the NGOs. But as the process was slow, we had time to compare our records with the others, learn, and make corrections. So finally I do not think things could have been done much differently. Perhaps we went too much into detail but this was mostly because of the closeness of the Commission's scrutiny, although the Commission was also our only ally.

We were often held hostage to negotiations with other countries and developments in Europe and in the world. Our red line was that we do our homework as best as we can, and not look into our neighbours' back yard. Should circumstances so permit, we had to secure that accession would not be stopped by our own shortcomings. We wanted to minimize as much as possible the biggest problems in the negotiations. But that in turn required that thousands of minor issues had to be kept on the stove. This was where the daily frustration came from. And then we tried to work as hard as we could on these few big ones—energy, environment, taxation—and make them really matter for us and others. This was where the rewards came from.

It was extremely encouraging that through all these years until accession, and despite our difficulties, our team had the full support and trust and mandate of the Foreign Minister, the cabinet, the main political parties, and even public opinion. I feel that we managed to reciprocate this support and trust. Minor disagreements were never allowed to dominate relationships. Public opinion was regularly monitored with regard to how the accession negotiations were managed and the polls showed persistent high confidence of about 70 per cent. I felt that this was the highest credit we could ever get.

On 16 December 2002, two days after the accession negotiations had come to an end in Copenhagen, the President of Estonia, the Speaker of the Parliament, and the Prime Minister issued a brief but emotional and telling statement, from which I take the liberty to quote:

> Five years of accession negotiations may be considered as one of the most complicated tasks that the Estonian state has ever managed. During these negotiations we proved not only to our future partners, but also primarily to ourselves, that we are ready for future challenges and we wish and can shape our own future as free people....
>
> But freedom in itself makes nobody happy or the state rich. How and for what purpose the freedom is used, is vital. We are convinced that accession to the EU is the best guarantee for the development of a free society in Estonia and Estonian future existence. Now the people will have their say.

[35] No one can beat Estonians in being suspicious.

Last but not least, a few words have to be said on the contribution made by the average Estonian himself. The whole accession process was certainly no honeymoon for anybody and left almost no one untouched. I personally had a few moments of despair when I asked myself why I was doing all this. And at these few moments of a mix of domestic political ignorance, media attacks, and lack of progress in Brussels I was deeply moved how much simple and unpretentious support the ordinary people whom I met at numerous meetings, seminars, or even privately without any single exception, without compromise, were willing to give. This is the only reason why I believed in a successful end for my country and my countrymen and I will be ever thankful to all of them and keep that trust in my memory.

11

The Accession of Hungary to the EU

Peter Gottfried
Peter Györkös

1. INTRODUCTION

The change of the political and economic system in 1989–1990 has led to a fast restructuring of the country's institutions. Nevertheless, the historic target, namely the accession of the Republic of Hungary to NATO and to the European Union, has been achieved.

The historic target of Hungary and the countries undergoing radical reform after the collapse of the Soviet bloc, was their intention to become equal members of the democratic integration structures in the transatlantic family from the beginning of 1989. It is significant that the majority of the political and social forces fully supported this goal. In Hungary, their overall consensus had been preserved during the whole accession process, and it continues to be maintained even after accession.

Even with a view to the historic importance of the democratic revolution in Central and Eastern Europe, the European Community was rather reluctant to specify the perspectives. We had to learn that the road to the institutional framework of Europe is not only long but also rather complex, consisting of several successive stages.

In December 1991 Hungary signed the association agreement which entered into force three years later, in February 1994. The Member States were hesitant as to whether or not to officially offer the chance of accession to the CEECs. This, however, eventually happened in June 1993 in the Copenhagen Council, when the EU sent an official invitation to our countries naming, at the same time, the precise conditions of membership. These conditions became famously known as the Copenhagen criteria.

Hungary then applied for membership on 31 March 1994. The evaluation of this application lasted till July 1997, when the European Commission published its *avis* recommending the start of accession negotiations with six candidate countries in spring 1998. The Luxembourg European Council confirmed by December 1997 the start of accession negotiations with the group of the 'Luxembourg six', which happened on 31 March 1998.

The accession negotiations continued under ten presidencies and were concluded in December 2002 in Copenhagen. After a ratification process that lasted almost two years, the Accession Treaty entered into force on 1 May 2004.

It is now abundantly clear that the last enlargement was properly prepared, as the internal market is functioning properly and the institutions are functioning without significant problems. The EU 25 is, at the least, manageable, and the new EU 10 have been fully absorbed.

The recent crisis in the context of the ratification of the constitutional treaty has not been generated in or by the new Member States. Indeed, the conflict which led to the failure of the negotiations on the next financial perspectives 2007–13 erupted in June 2005 among old Member States.

We deem it important to develop a balanced picture about our long and often difficult way into the institutional family. We do not regret the efforts; we *had* to go through all these obstacles. However, after having reached this historic goal, it would be unfair to state simply that this enlargement is the problem or at least one of the reasons for the existing difficulties Europe has to face.

2. THE START

In the initial stages, Hungary had two basic dilemmas. The first question was what kind of attitude to maintain towards the necessary transitional measures. In general, we accepted that the transitional periods should serve so as to allow a soft landing of sorts for both sides, avoiding abrupt changes. In order to accommodate the potential requests of the line ministries, Hungary originally indicated that there would be about ninety potential areas for transitional measures, despite the basic intention to be integrated into community policies as soon as possible. Slowly, this number was later reduced substantially for various reasons.

The second big question concerned the target date for accession. Some hours before the opening of the IGC, the negotiating team was informed that the other five candidates would opt for 1 January 2003. The Hungarian side decided to formulate officially 1 January 2002 as our own target date.

The reason for doing so was rather simple. The draft package 'Agenda 2000', submitted by the Commission, suggested a new structure for the Community budget which included a special heading for enlargement. This heading started in 2002. Even if the proposed amount was very small, in principle it would be possible to set the enlargement date in 2002.

Albeit theoretical, the Hungarian point of view was clear nonetheless: the candidates should neither opt for later dates than necessary, nor explain away any delays. It should be noted that this heading had not even been touched in the Berlin Summit in March 1999 and that the Helsinki Council stated that, for institutional reasons, the EU would be in a position to welcome new members in 2002. However, we determined that this earliest possible date should also be the target date rather than a mere point of reference.

Having established both the general strategy to follow, and the targeted date for accession, Hungary then moved to an organizational preparation of the accession process. This organization was not particularly complicated, as it followed three basic principles:

- first, portfolio responsibility; this meant that all the ministries would be responsible for the draft negotiating mandates and the internal preparations chapters of the *acquis* relevant to their domain;
- second, strong central coordination. Thus the single State Secretariat for European Integration was established in the summer of 1996 under the umbrella of the Foreign Ministry; and
- third, Hungary should be able to speak with a single voice in Brussels. One country, one government, one position.

The daily domestic work was coordinated by the Inter-ministerial Committee for European Integration chaired by the Foreign Ministry and involving senior officials from all the ministries. The responsibility for the actual negotiations was delegated to a series of working groups which reflected the structure of the *acquis* chapters.

The accession negotiations were coordinated by the negotiating team, headed by the Foreign Minister, assisted at the operational level by the State Secretary for Integration, and involving senior representatives of some (but not all) ministries. The chief negotiator was the ambassador in Brussels. The government was regularly informed and it adopted the starting negotiating positions in all chapters, and, when necessary, the Prime Minister approved the modified mandate. This arbitrage played an important role in two cases: once in June 2001, as Hungary provisionally closed eight chapters, among which were the four basic freedoms which involved matters of labour and agricultural land. The second arbitrage at the highest political level took place in the final marathon on the financial package.

The parliamentary parties were regularly informed within the framework of the so-called 'six-party consultations', in the Committee for European Integration, and, once a year, at the plenary session of the National Parliament.

Further, the Integration Strategy Task Force provided academic support, and the relevant social partners became involved through the Council for European Integration, a new pillar in the tripartite system.

As noted above, the general and everyday conduct of the accession process and the accession negotiations were managed by a small staff headed by the State Secretary for Integration in Budapest and the ambassador in Brussels. They, and their direct collaborators, ensured that the negotiating efforts would enjoy the benefits of both daily coordination and consistency, as they cooperated with the line ministries and consulted with the relevant institutions and with the other candidates and Member States. This group of people prepared the dossiers for political approval, suggesting the options and solutions. The consistency and the continuity, starting from the beginning of the accession process and lasting until the very date of the signature of the Accession Treaty, provided the necessary institutional memory, thus providing a solid basis for well-considered national positions which took into account the broader national and international environment.

3. THE STRATEGIC DILEMMAS

The fifth enlargement was particular in its nature for a variety of reasons. Among them was the fact that the EU was now absorbing countries of the former Soviet bloc. There were many hidden concerns as to whether these countries would ever be able to function in the same mode as the developed and established western democracies. The Copenhagen political and economic criteria intended to ensure that the candidates could fully guarantee the rule of law and free market conditions. History proved that our countries rose to the task. The fifth enlargement had another particularity: beyond the legal harmonization, the building of the adequate *administrative* structures became an ex ante necessity in order to proceed with the accession negotiations, as without it, adoption of the *acquis* would be impossible.

The institution building aspect was the biggest part of the internal preparation and monitoring. Hundreds of questioners, peer reviews, and monitoring missions had to prove that the candidates were ready and able not only to take over but also effectively implement and enforce the *acquis communautaire.*

A second aspect of the fifth enlargement that was different from earlier ones was the geographical dimension. The fifth enlargement was a 'transit' enlargement of sorts. Once started, it would be impossible to stop. Nowadays, one can find many comments concerning the dilemmas related to the external borders of Europe. It was evident at the time that, should Hungary apply for membership, Romania would follow; should Slovenia become a member, Croatia and Serbia would try to do the same. The task of structuring a relevant strategy for the Union took a long time, and, at the end, several categories of aspiring members emerged: acceding states, negotiating countries, candidates, potential candidates, and countries covered by the neighbourhood policies.

A third matter that is characteristic of the fifth enlargement, but not earlier ones, was the political dilemma of the 'big bang' scenario. This dilemma had two sides. We faced the first question in Bonn by 1997 when we were asked whether we intended to take over the whole *acquis* from the very date of accession, or could accept, or intend to ask for, longer transitions or even opt-outs. Our answer was clear—full membership was the only option. We were, of course, aware of the necessity for transitional periods in some areas, but wanted to limit such periods to the absolute minimum possible. The agreed transitional measures allowed a 'soft landing' both for the EU and for the new members; since these transitional periods will someday expire, however, they also ensured that a second-class membership would not be considered.

The second matter relating to the 'big bang' scenario was linked to the number of new members that would be included in the enlargement. Our countries were squeezed by the question of who would be in the first round of enlargement. The strategy of the EU was rather ambiguous. The opening statement of the Union introduced the principles of 'individual treatment' and 'own merits'; these principles were later confirmed by all official statements in Brussels and the Member States' capitals. Nevertheless, it was evident that the EU did not intend to prepare for twelve or even more *individual* enlargements including ratifications, and that the enlargement would happen in a big format ('big bang') and, within the framework of the 5th enlargement maximum, a minimum differentiation could happen.

In December 1997, the Luxembourg European Council decided to start the accession negotiations with six candidates ('Luxembourg six'). However, in parallel with them, the other six also started the analytical examination of the *acquis* by spring 1998. Two years later, in December 1999, the Helsinki European Council revised the enlargement strategy, stating that all twelve candidates are in the same box, all negotiate on accession based on their own merits, and that the EU would take a decision only at a later stage on who and when could join the club. The matter of 'when' the enlargement would take place was settled when the Göteborg European Council approved the timetable in June 2001, thus leaving two questions still pending: who would participate in the enlargement, and under what conditions.

The first of these latter questions was officially clarified by the Laeken European Council in December 2001, according to which ten candidates had the chance to keep the Göteborg timetable. The second one, relating to the (financial) conditions of enlargement, was settled in the course of 2002.

4. THE COOPERATION AMONG THE CANDIDATES

The confusion around the strategic framework created a lot of troubles for the candidates. How to cooperate, when do we compete with each other? How could we call upon the EU to start with the accession process if we do not specify which countries would be included and which ones would not?

Even under the tension of some mutual suspicion, the 'Luxembourg six' became a club of sorts. The regular meetings at the level of the negotiators and ministers created a very nice atmosphere. Although the six never established common negotiating positions, we discussed together the relevant chapters on the agenda, analysed the real content of the concrete problems, and interpreted the potential consequences of the various available options. The regular joint statements on the strategic aspects of the negotiations may have played a significant role by urging the EU to move forward the enlargement dossier.

After the Laeken European Council, this framework changed as the consultations took place among ten candidate countries. Given the—by then—established and amicable relationship between the Luxembourg six, however, the social-cultural gatherings only between them did not end until October 2002, before the end game.

5. THE HUNGARIAN ISSUES IN THE CHAPTERS

As mentioned above, the negotiating partners—for different reasons—wanted to limit the number and scope of the transitional measures. Whether the final agreement is good or bad, or whether the number and scope was adequate or not, is a matter for debate, depending on one's point of view. The first year after accession proved that the deal was balanced and both sides survived the biggest ever enlargement without major difficulties. In our view this is the best proof of the success of the negotiating strategies of the parties.

It is important that in one of the biggest chapters, on freedom of movement of goods, no transitional measures were needed. This reflects the very high level of substantial integration that was already in place at the time of negotiations, and irrespectively of accession.

Freedom of movement of persons, however, proved to be more controversial, and remains an issue even after accession. The story started with the presentation of the 'road map' by the Commission in November 2000 by which the Commission suggested a strange but logical division of chapters. It was strange because we expected a linkage between the labour issue on the one hand, and the financial package on the other. And it was logical because it separated these two dossiers both in time and in substance, delegating the four freedoms to the Swedish presidency in the first semester of 2001, leaving the financial package to 2002.

In December 2000, the Member States agreed on the Nice Treaty, thus eliminating the last obstacle before enlargement on the Union's side. Six days later, the German Chancellor Gerhard Schröder visited Bavaria and launched the idea of a seven-year-long total transition for free movement of labour. After six months of tough negotiations, the scheme changed substantially and the provisional deal became possible.

One of the most important elements of the deal was the so-called '2+3+2 system': until the end of the two-year period following the date of accession, the present Member States would apply national measures, or measures resulting from bilateral agreements, regulating access to their labour markets by Hungarian nationals. The present Member States were allowed to continue to apply such measures until the end of the five-year period following the date of accession. Before the end of the two-year period following the date of accession, the Council shall review the functioning of the transitional provisions on the basis of a report from the Commission. On completion of this review, and no later than at the end of the two-year period following the date of accession, the present Member States shall notify the Commission on whether they will continue applying national measures. For the last two years, there should be a 'serious reasoning', with a higher level of scrutiny than in the earlier period. The first review was due before 30 April 2006.

A second element of the deal is the 'twelve months ruling' by which Hungarian nationals legally working in a present Member State at the date of accession, and admitted to the labour market of that Member State for an uninterrupted period of twelve months or longer, will enjoy access to the labour market of that Member State but not to the labour market of other Member States applying national measures. Hungarian nationals admitted to the labour market of a present Member State following accession for an uninterrupted period of twelve months or longer shall also enjoy the same rights.

Third, the principle of reciprocity was also agreed on. Whenever national measures, or those resulting from bilateral agreements, are applied by the present Member States, Hungary may maintain in force equivalent measures with regard to the nationals of the Member States in question. Additionally, even if none of the 'old' Member States apply such a transition period, Hungary may resort to the procedures with respect to the Czech Republic, Estonia, Latvia, Lithuania, Poland, Slovenia, or Slovakia.

A further element of the deal on the freedom of movement of labour was the free choice for old Member States: any present Member State may grant free movement for labour under national law. The United Kingdom, Ireland, and Sweden decided to do so from 1 May 2004 and the first year indicates a clear economic advantage for these countries.

Lastly, it was agreed that in specific sensitive service sectors (construction, industrial cleaning, horticultural services, social work activities, etc.), Germany and Austria were entitled to a derogation from the rules governing the freedom to provide services.

In the chapter on freedom to provide services, Hungary successfully broached two requests for derogation. The first was over the minimum level of compensation which should not apply in Hungary until 31 December 2007. It was requested that Hungary could ensure that its investor compensation scheme provided for cover of not less than €3,783 until 31 December 2004 and of not less than €7,565 from 1 January 2005 until 31 December 2007. The second concerned the initial capital requirement for cooperative credit institutions until 31 December 2007. Hungary wished to ensure that the initial capital requirement for these cooperative credit institutions would not be less than €378,200 until 31 December 2006 and not less than €756,500 from 1 January 2007 until 31 December 2007.

Freedom of movement of capital also proved to be politically a very sensitive chapter, as Hungary raised two issues. Hungary was entitled to maintain for five years from the date of accession the restrictions on the acquisition of secondary residences. The matter concerned nationals of the Member States and nationals of the states which are a party to the European Economic Area Agreement who have been legally resident in Hungary for at least four years continuously; these individuals would not be subject to the provisions of the chapter. During the transitional period, Hungary may apply authorization procedures for the acquisition of secondary residences based on objective, stable, transparent, and public criteria. As per the EU modus operandi, these criteria shall be applied in a non-discriminatory manner and shall not differentiate between nationals of the Member States residing in Hungary.

Hungary also negotiated a model by which it was entitled to maintain in force for seven years from the date of accession the prohibitions on the acquisition of agricultural land by natural persons who are non-residents or non-nationals of Hungary and by legal persons. However, nationals of another Member State who want to establish themselves as self-employed farmers, and who have been legally resident and active in farming in Hungary for at least three years continuously, shall not be subject to these provisions. A general review of these transitional measures shall be held in the third year following the date of accession. The authorization procedures for the acquisition of agricultural land during the transitional period shall be based on objective, stable, transparent, and public criteria. If there is sufficient evidence that, upon expiry of the transitional period, there will be serious disturbances, or a threat of serious disturbances, on the agricultural land market of Hungary, the Commission, at the request of Hungary, shall decide upon the extension of the transitional period for up to a maximum of three additional years.

In the competition policy chapter, no derogation was possible. Nevertheless, the negotiations on fiscal aid schemes lasted until the very end of the negotiation process, and were only concluded days before the Copenhagen Summit.

In chapter 7 on agriculture, the parties had two types of issues: the 'technical' derogations, which were negotiated individually, and the market support issues, which were included in the final financial package.

Concerning the fat content of drinking milk produced in Hungary, for a period of five years from the date of accession, Hungary may market milk with a fat content of 2.8 per cent (m/m) as drinking milk. Drinking milk which does not comply with the requirements relating to fat content may be marketed only in Hungary or a third country, but it may not be exported to a market within the Union.

Similarly, for a period of ten years from the date of accession, a minimum natural alcoholic strength of 7.7%/vol. for table wines shall be allowed in all Hungarian wine-growing areas.

By way of derogation, the use of the name 'Rizlingszilváni' as a (not correct) synonym for the variety 'Müller Thurgau' is allowed until 31 December 2008 for wines produced in Hungary and exclusively marketed in Hungary.

In the area of veterinary legislation, forty-four slaughterhouses are unable to apply the structural requirements before 31 December 2006, and are allowed to function in the meantime, while the necessary changes are concluded. As long as these establishments benefit from that derogation, products originating from those establishments shall only be placed on the domestic market or used for further processing in the same establishment, irrespective of the date of marketing. These products must bear a special health mark. Additionally, Hungary shall ensure gradual compliance with the structural requirements. Hungary shall ensure that only those establishments which fully comply with these requirements by 31 December 2006 may continue to operate.

Until 31 December 2009, twenty-one establishments may maintain in service cages not meeting the minimum requirements, provided that they were brought into service no later than 1 July 1999 and provided that they are at least 36 cm high over at least 65 per cent of the cage area and not less than 33 cm high at any point.

In the chapter on transport policy, the Hungarian Railway Company received a derogation according to which, until 31 December 2006, only 20 per cent of the annual total capacity of the Trans-European Rail Freight Network in Hungary shall be reserved for railway undertakings other than MÁV, and all origin-destinations shall allow for journey times comparable to those enjoyed by MÁV. The actual capacity of each railway line shall be indicated by the infrastructure manager in the network statement.

Hungary also allowed some aircraft that produce excessive noise to operate in Hungarian airfields until 31 December 2004. These aircraft are of the register of, and operated by, Azerbaijan, Kazakhstan, Moldova, the Russian Federation, Turkmenistan, and Ukraine.

In the area of national road haulage services (cabotage), until the end of the third year following the date of accession, carriers established in Hungary are excluded from the operation of national road haulage services in the other Member States, and carriers established in the other Member States are excluded from the operation of national road haulage services in Hungary. Before the end of the third year following the date of accession, Member States shall notify the Commission as to whether they will prolong this period for a maximum of two additional years. Member States also reserve the right to apply safeguard measures.

Concerning the maximum authorized weights in international traffic, respective vehicles may only use non-upgraded parts of the Hungarian road network until 31 December 2008 provided that they comply with Hungarian axle-weight limits. At the same time, Hungary shall adhere to its own timetable for the upgrading of its main transit network. Any infrastructure investments involving the use of funds from the Community budget shall ensure that the arteries are constructed or upgraded to a load bearing capacity of 11.5 tonnes per axle. In line with the completion of the upgrading, there shall be a progressive opening of the Hungarian road network for vehicles in international traffic complying with the limit values of the directive.

Temporary additional charges for the use of non-upgraded parts of the network by vehicles in international traffic that comply with the weight limit shall be levied in a non-discriminatory manner. Vehicles in excess of the Hungarian axle load limits of 10 tonnes for vehicles without, and 11 tonnes for vehicles with, air suspension systems shall obtain a Hungarian route permit in order to ensure that certain road structures and bridges are bypassed. Hungary shall accept a deviation of 0.5 tonnes when measuring axle weights of vehicles with air suspension systems and will only impose temporary additional charges if the axle weight exceeds 11.5 tonnes. No temporary additional charges shall be levied upon vehicles complying with weight limits when using the main transit roads.

In the area of taxation, Hungary may maintain a reduced rate of value added tax (VAT) of no less than 12 per cent on the supply of coal, coal-brick and coke, firewood and charcoal, and on the supply of district heating services until

31 December 2007, and a reduced rate of value added tax of no less than 12 per cent on the supply of restaurant services and of foodstuffs sold on similar premises until 31 December 2007. Hungary was further authorized to maintain a reduced rate of value added tax of not less than 5 per cent on the supply of natural gas and electricity until one year after the date of accession. Hungary is also permitted to maintain an exemption from value added tax on international transport of passengers.

Concerning the approximation of taxes on cigarettes, Hungary was allowed to postpone the application of the overall minimum excise duty on the retail selling price (inclusive of all taxes) for cigarettes of the price category most in demand until 31 December 2008, provided that during this period Hungary gradually adjusted its excise duty rates towards the overall minimum excise duty. In parallel to that, Member States may, as long as the above derogation applies, maintain the same quantitative limits for cigarettes which may be brought into their territories from Hungary without further excise duty payment as those applied to imports from third countries. Member States making use of this right may carry out the necessary customs controls provided that they do not affect the proper functioning of the internal market.

Last but not least, an important issue was how to maintain the system of hired distillation which is a very popular scheme in Hungary. According to the agreed solution, Hungary may apply a reduced rate of excise duty of not less than 50 per cent of the standard national rate to ethyl alcohol produced by fruit growers' distilleries producing, on an annual basis, more than 10 hectolitres of ethyl alcohol from fruit supplied to them by fruit growers' households. The application of this reduced rate is limited to 50 litres of fruit spirits per household per year, destined exclusively for their personal consumption. This arrangement will be reviewed in 2015.

Environment was a chapter in which it would be in the best interest of a candidate country to align its national framework with the *acquis* as quickly as its capacity would allow. A 'willing but not able' dilemma arose in the following well-considered derogations which corresponded to the objective limits of performance of Hungary.

In the area of waste management, the competent authorities shall be notified of all shipments of waste for recovery to Hungary. This waste should also be processed as quickly as possible.

On packaging and packaging waste, Hungary was obliged to attain the recovery and recycling targets for the following packaging materials by 31 December 2005, in accordance with the following intermediate targets:

- recycling of plastics: 11 per cent by weight by the date of accession, and 14 per cent for 2004;
- recycling of glass: 14 per cent by weight by the date of accession, and 15 per cent for 2004; and
- overall recovery rate: 40 per cent by weight by the date of accession, and 43 per cent for 2004.

Hungary may set an overall recycling target of 46 per cent from 2005 onwards.

In the area of water quality concerning urban waste water treatment, the requirements for collecting systems and treatment of urban waste water shall not fully apply in Hungary until 31 December 2015. The following intermediate targets were set for the meantime:

- by 31 December 2008, compliance with the directive shall be achieved in sensitive areas for agglomerations with a population equivalent to, or more than, 10,000; and
- by 31 December 2010, compliance with the directive shall be achieved for agglomerations with a population equivalent to, or more than, 15,000.

The requirements for biodegradable industrial waste water from plants belonging to the industrial sectors shall not apply to ten plants in Hungary until 31 December 2008.

On the quality of water intended for human consumption, Hungary may provide for derogations from the parametric value for arsenic until 25 December 2009. This derogation could be extended and does not apply to drinking water intended for food processing.

Concerning the incineration of hazardous waste, the emission limit values and the requirements for measurements shall not apply to five incinerators of waste oils and other liquid waste, to fourteen incinerators of hospital waste, and to eighteen incinerators and co-incinerators of solid and liquid hazardous waste in Hungary until 30 June 2005.

On the limitation of emissions of certain pollutants into the atmosphere from large combustion plants, the emission limits for sulphur dioxide, nitrogen oxides, and dust did not apply until 31 December 2004 to eight plants in Hungary.

Finally, a small derogation in the customs union chapter, saying that Hungary may, until the end of the third year following the date of accession, or until 31 December 2007, whichever is the earlier, open a yearly tariff quota for non-alloyed aluminium, in accordance with the following schedule:

- a quota of a maximum of 110,000 tonnes, at a rate of 2 per cent *ad valorem*, or one-third of the prevailing EU duty, whichever is the higher, during the first year;
- a quota of a maximum of 70,000 tonnes, at a rate of 4 per cent *ad valorem*, or two-thirds of the prevailing EU duty, whichever is the higher, during the second year; and
- a quota of a maximum of 20,000 tonnes, at a rate of 4 per cent *ad valorem*, or two-thirds of the prevailing EU duty, whichever is the higher, during the third year.

These derogations were contingent on the requirement that the goods in question:

- are released for free circulation in the territory of Hungary and are consumed there or undergo processing conferring Community origin there; and
- remain under customs supervision pursuant to the relevant Community provisions on end-use.

6. THE END GAME

The Göteborg European Council indicated the readiness of the EU to conclude the accession negotiations with the prepared candidates by the end of 2002, so that they could participate in the elections of the next European Parliament as full members.

The Laeken Summit six months later essentially confirmed that the first wave would consist of ten countries. One question now remained open: what will be the financial offer of the Union? The candidates had to negotiate the twenty-nine chapters in a way by which all questions and answers with financial implications had to be postponed.

The European Commission tried to launch the budget debate in due time, publishing its financial proposals by the end of January 2002. Nevertheless, the Member States were not eager to start the final round too early. The financial offer of the EU 15 had only been published in the second half of October, after both the German elections and the Brussels agreement on the CAP during the October summit. The Danish presidency did not officially submit the financial proposals until as late as 28 October. That was the starting point of the final marathon, whose results reveal how limited the room for negotiations was.

7. THE FINANCIAL PACKAGE AND THE QUOTAS

The financial package was not negotiated till the very end of the process. The overwhelming majority of the chapters had been provisionally closed by early 2002 and, at approximately that time (end of January 2002), the Commission submitted its proposals on the financial issues. Then, a period of inactivity ensued until October 2002.

That hiatus was caused by the fact that all players first waited until the outcome of the German elections in September. After the end of the German elections came the Brussels agreement on freezing agricultural spending (first pillar) until 2013, after which the EU made official the offer on the financial package. In the coming five weeks, the room for negotiations was very limited, and even the Copenhagen Summit was, albeit tense, devoid of surprises.

Once the offer was officially made, there was much commentary on it. It is true that it was marginally worse than had been anticipated. The new Member States had to learn that the level of solidarity decreased. In many Member States, the share of the Community resources with the newcomers appeared as a new chapter in the 'charity policy' rather than as a long-term investment for Europe.

While there were minor differences in the solutions offered to individual candidates, the ten candidates have been basically treated in a package.

In the matter of regional policy, the political decision was to introduce in the cohesion policy a three-year-long phasing-in period starting from 1 January 2004 (and, strangely, not from 1 May). The total commitment was €7.5905 billion in 1999 prices broken down to three years (€2.6168 for 2004, €2.157 for 2005, and €2.822 for 2006). The indicative allocation for Hungary of the total resources of the Cohesion Fund was between 11.58 per cent and 14.61 per cent in total.

The entire territory of Hungary became eligible for Objective 1 of the Structural Funds. Resources available under this heading amounted to €14,155,900 at 1999 prices for the ten countries. From the total amount foreseen for Objective 1, the share of Hungary was €1,765,400. This amount had to be used from the date of accession (i.e. 1 May 2004) to 2006.

Two community programmes have been extended to the newcomers. Hungary's share of allocations to the EQUAL initiative is €26.8 million and for INTERREG €60.9 million.

Within the scope of agriculture, the biggest issue was that of the direct payment. Based on the decisions of the Berlin Summit in March 1999 and the original ideas of the European Commission on the financial perspectives for 2000–6, it is evident that the starting point was 0 per cent until the end of 2006 even if enlargement started earlier. When the Commission suggested in January 2002 the introduction of a ten-year-long transition starting with 25 per cent, some Member States protested that this was against the political agreement of Berlin, while the candidates embarked on a long period of complaining. The end game, however, did not contain surprises. In this very complex and sensitive dossier, no real negotiations took place; the bitter agreement was the following: in the new Member States, the direct payment shall be introduced in accordance with the following schedule of increments expressed as a percentage of the then applicable level of such payments in the Community:

- 25, then 30, and finally 35 per cent in the 2004–6 period;
- a gradual 40–50–60–70–80–90 per cent increase in the period from 2007 to 2012; and
- 100 per cent as from 2013.

The only instrument of flexibility agreed was the possibility of national 'top-up', adding yearly a maximum of 30 per cent from the national budget in order to decrease the gap between the level of payments to the farmers in the old and new Member States.

In this process, there were many technical issues and technical adaptations with political content and economic importance, some of which were the following:

- the name 'grape marc' and 'grape marc spirit' may be replaced by the designation *Pálinka*;
- the name 'fruit spirit' may be replaced by the designation *Pálinka* solely for the spirit drink produced in Hungary (and for apricot distillates in four counties of Austria: Niederösterreich, Burgenland, Steiermark, and Vienna);
- the quality wine 'Tokaji esszencia' is not considered as grape in fermentation;

- special treatment for the wines from the Tokajhegyalja region such as 'Tokaji fordítás', 'Tokaji máslás', 'Tokaji édes szamorodni', 'Tokaji aszú', etc.; and
- the preservation of the term 'Termelői pezsgő' for quality sparkling wines produced in Hungary.

It's worth mentioning briefly the basic reference quantities and base areas for Hungary:

- milk (tonnes): 1,782,650 (deliveries) and 164,630 (direct sales);
- national guaranteed quantity for dehydrated fodder (tonnes): 49,593;
- rice: 163,215 (EUR/ha) with a base area of 3,222 hectares;
- processing thresholds: tomatoes: 130,790 tonnes; peaches: 1,616 tonnes; pears: 1,031 tonnes;
- maximum guaranteed areas in receipt of the supplement to the area payment for durum wheat: 2,500 hectares; and of the special aid for durum wheat: 4,305 hectares;
- national base area and reference yields: 3,487,792 hectares and 4.73 tonnes per hectare (which is the biggest success for Hungary in negotiating quotas);
- slaughter premium: bulls, steers, cows, and heifers: 141,559; calves: 94,439;
- national ceiling for suckler cow premium: 117,000; and
- the individual rights to ewe and goat premium: 1,146,000.

Additional provisions were agreed to over matters relating to the budget. A special lump-sum payment was introduced in order to ease the net position in the first year after accession. In the case of Hungary, the following amounts of a special lump-sum cash flow facility were fixed: €155.3 million for 2004, €27.95 million for 2005, and €27.95 million for 2006.

The payment to the Research Fund for Coal and Steel does not start until 2006 and the €9,993 million allocated to it is broken down in instalments: 15 per cent in 2006, 20 per cent in 2007, 30 per cent in 2008, and 35 per cent in 2009.

A special transition facility has been established between the date of accession and the end of 2006 in order to provide financial assistance to the new Member States to develop and strengthen their administrative capacity to implement and enforce Community legislation. This instrument covered €200 million in 2004, €120 million in 2005, and €60 million in 2006.

Although the process of accession was set for May 2004, the date for accession to the Schengen zone remained open. Both the new Members and the EU 15 recognized the need to satisfy certain preconditions. The Schengen facility was set up in order to help the new Member States to finance actions at the new external borders of the Union, thus allowing the implementation of the Schengen *acquis* and external border control. In this context, Hungary will receive €147.9 million at 1999 prices between 2004 and 2006.

8. THE INSTITUTIONAL PROVISIONS

The long night in Nice by mid-December 2000 led to an agreement on the institutional provisions for the enlarged Union by which the EU 15 fulfilled the conditions for the entry of the new EU 10. (One should keep in mind the language of the Helsinki European Council: when the Treaty of Nice enters into force the EU will be in a position to welcome the first new Member States.)

The institutional provisions regulated, on the one hand, the transitional measures between the date of the entry into force of the Accession Treaty and that of some Nice provisions (Commission, European Parliament, and Council). On the other hand, transitional solutions were also agreed for the EU 25 and EU 27 in the period between 2004 and 2009 should Romania and Bulgaria accede in that period.

There is one particular point that concerns Hungary: the number of seats in the European Parliament. The long night of Nice created a big problem. Three old Member States (Greece, Portugal, and Belgium) received twenty-two seats while two newcomers with the same population only twenty each (Czech Republic and Hungary). The Accession Treaty remedied this issue by granting the old and new members with similar population the same number of EP seats (twenty-two) and thereby correcting the upper limit of seats from 732 to 736. Between 2004 and 2009, Hungary will have twenty-four seats, since the quota of Romania and Bulgaria has been distributed among the EU 25.

Hungary also received five votes in the Council; from 1 November 2004, this weight will increase to twelve votes under the new scheme.

9. SAFEGUARDS

In order to handle potential difficulties after enlargement, the accession act contains three safeguards. The *economic safeguard* is designed for the new Member States to take protective measures in order to rectify serious problems in any sector of the economy and to adjust the relevant sector to the economy of the common market. Eighteen months after the accession we can take note that this instrument has never been invoked.

The *internal market safeguard* is targeted at serious breaches of the functioning of the internal market, including any commitments in all sectoral policies which concern economic activities with cross-border effect, or an imminent risk of such breach. This safeguard can be applied until the period of three years after the date of entry into force of the act on accession.

The third, the so-called JHA-safeguard, was linked to potential shortcomings in the transposition or implementation of commitments relating to mutual recognition in the area of criminal law.

The matters that arose during the negotiations can be summarized into four or five categories. We have had a lot of areas, in particular in the sector of environment and infrastructure, where it was clear that Hungary would not be able to apply the *acquis* by the time of accession. In these cases, we agreed upon reasonable transitional measures. In the second category, we had some items that were specific to Hungary; in these issues, we sought presentable and secure derogations. In that category the hottest potato was the acquisition of agricultural land and partly the real estate issue. But we can also list the hire distillation scheme and the fat content of milk. The final result demonstrates that the negotiating partners were ready and able to come to balanced solutions.

The issue of state aid in the form of tax benefits can be categorized separately from others. A direct conflict arose between, on the one hand, the big investments, which have played a definitive role in the economic change after 1990, and, on the other, the clear language of the *acquis communautaire*. This conflict was only solved at the very end of the negotiations, one week before the Copenhagen Summit. The last (but not least) group of issues concerns the financial elements of accession. There is no intention to say that in this category our countries have been treated as second-class future members. In all areas (agriculture and regional policy) we agreed upon transitional periods which one day or another will expire, and the equality between Member States will hence be sealed. Nevertheless, the offer and even the final outcome were much lower than originally expected. We had to learn the parallel track of developments in Europe. On the one hand, the net contributors decided to break with the old traditions and all individual members were forced to witness a declining sense of solidarity. This phenomenon became evident in a period when the newcomers were arriving, ten new members from which seven or eight were clearly below the Community average.

At the end of the day, the conclusion was clear: we have to look at the outcome as a global package. There may be legitimate complaints over the financial elements of accession, but, viewed overall, the end result is satisfactory and presentable.

10. THE DAY AFTER

The negotiation project was successfully completed by 8 p.m. on 13 December 2002 in Copenhagen. After the drafting exercise, the Accession Treaty has been signed and, following the two-year ratification process, it entered into force on 1 May 2004. As predicted in June 2001 in Göteborg, the new Member States participated on equal footing in the European Parliament elections in June 2004.

In Hungary—perhaps in other acceding states as well—the general conclusion was that the negotiators' job had been well done. This feeling of relaxation, however, was short-lived.

One week after the Copenhagen Summit, the so-called Interim Agreement entered into force. This created the legal basis for the passive and active observer period. Between Copenhagen and the Athens Summit, when the Accession Treaty was signed, the ten new members of the Union enjoyed a passive observer status, allowing them to receive all the internal documents of the Union. The paper flow reaching our capitals gave the first insight of what life would be inside the EU.

The signature of the treaty opened the way for active participation in the EU, as the acceding states not only received the internal documents of the Union, but could also enter the negotiating rooms with an institutionally protected voice. With the conferring of voting rights, the new EU 10 became part of the institutional family, participated in all working groups and parties of the Council, at COREPER and in the Council configurations, including the European Councils. The national parliaments delegated observers to the European Parliament.

11. LESSONS

Do we have lessons which could be useful for the future of enlargement, for current and future candidates or the current Member States? We think it could be worth to put on paper several of them, but special attention should be drawn to the fact that enlargement was—and remains—a dynamic process and all lessons should be adapted to the actual circumstances.

It's very important to recall the starting point of the 'eastern' enlargement. It enlarged the *acquis communautaire*, the common values and rules, to the countries of the former Soviet bloc. The common borders are protected by Estonian, Hungarian, etc. border guards and not by tanks. The historical dimension of this change is so radical that it is perhaps difficult to fathom. Indeed, many are not aware that the entire continent is now following a set of rules that were initiated by Robert Schuman, and that there is no longer a valid reason for the pessimism of the Cold War under such stable and peaceful conditions.

The second lesson is that Europe has to face the challenges of globalization irrespectively of enlargement. The loss of jobs and the decreasing competitiveness are not the consequence of an uncontrolled enlargement process but a universal phenomenon, partly caused by the slow reaction on behalf of the majority of EU Member States. The biggest reserve for competitiveness is the zone of the new Member States and that of the future acceding states. New markets, new resources, new human capital, and bigger mobility are at the disposal of the Union, while the economic and social standards have also been extended to these countries. It's a win-win process and not a zero-sum game. It is vital that Europeans do not forget this lesson.

Coming to the tactical area, we have to recognize that the accession negotiations constitute a very special kind of bargaining. They are, frankly, not negotiations, at least not in the classical sense. The reason is that the basis for these negotiations is the *acquis communautaire*, which is not negotiable. The Hungarian experience has demonstrated that 99 per cent of the *acquis communautaire* was not negotiated. In the case of the overwhelming majority of the community legislation, Hungary either was ready by the time when the talks started, or committed itself to take over and enforce the *acquis* before accession. One can say that accession is essentially a process of internal preparation. Only a small, if important, part of the *acquis* was actually negotiated, in the form of transitional measures which served as creating the foundations and conditions for the 'soft landing' on both sides.

If so, then the candidate has to elaborate his very personal relationship to the *acquis*. The Hungarian interpretation was rather simple: the *acquis* is not a poison. The transposition of the Community legislation is, irrespective of accession itself, in our interest. If we want to develop a modern country, a normal country, then the implementation of European rules is not against our national interest. If our economy is absolutely integrated into the internal market, then 'their rules are our rules'. The challenge was, therefore, to identify that part of the *acquis* where the immediate adjustment would have gone beyond our capacities (environment) or affected direct national interests (agricultural land). In all other cases, the task was to have a dynamic internal preparation plan for the adoption of the Community *acquis*.

There were some areas where either the candidate or the Member States were unwilling or unable to fully implement the *acquis* on the very date of accession. As we finalized our positions, we faced the limited but not negligible room for manoeuvre at the IGC. If we have a look at the labour issue or the agricultural land, or analyse the transitions in the environmental sector, then it becomes clear that both sides were realistic enough to negotiate a deal which could be digested by both.

All in all, we can draw two conclusions. The first is that the *acquis* is not against the fundamental interest of a candidate country and that its adoption is basically in the candidate's own interest. Of course, the candidate has to establish a reasonable sequence of steps in order to avoid unnecessary overburdening of the economy and society. The second conclusion is that the negotiating process is, in reality, little more than an internal preparation process, a real domestic task and challenge. A candidate should realize that the internal preparation is not for the sake of the Union. It inherently has great value in itself. True, there is an additional element, namely the final destination, and the ultimate objective of the whole exercise is to join the European institutional family.

The players themselves also deserve to be mentioned. Formally, the negotiations take place in the framework of the IGC, between the governments of the Member States and of the candidate country. In legal terms, the Commission is not a negotiator. Nevertheless, the role of the European Commission is enormous. It is the facilitator, the broker. Hungary's experience is that the Commission was, in fact, an *honest* broker. It knows very much—some times 'too much'—about the candidate, and is thus in position to suggest to the Member States a balanced draft common position. On the other hand, the Commission only has the power to recommend, and the decision is up to the Member States.

The Member States developed different approaches. Some of them relied fully on the Commission, accepting without comments the draft common positions. Others tried very intensely to influence both the Commission and the Council secretariat which finalized the DCPs, while other Member States had their own bilateral negotiating strategy towards the candidates. In issues such as labour, agricultural land, and cabotage we had intensive bilateral contacts with the most interested Member States.

The EU, as a negotiating partner, is the most complex and most complicated in the world, for a rather simple reason. Before reaching a common EU negotiating position, it is required to have a long bargaining process among the Member States and the EU institutions. The history of the WTO talks is another example for that. In the accession process, we had to learn that Member States are basically interested in negotiating a deal among themselves. If this agreement is achieved, the interest to negotiate with the candidate is rather limited. The candidates had to also realize that some Member States were ready to create internal linkages which have at the moment nothing to do directly with the accession process, but which could significantly influence its progress. One should remember the context in which the question of labour was linked to the future of the cohesion policy in spring 2001.

Finally, we should point out, eighteen months after the biggest ever enlargement, this was a great success for Europe; it was properly prepared, and hence proved to be a clear win-win exercise. Hungary is firmly convinced that the European Union should continue on the same basis, building upon the Copenhagen criteria. The new candidates have to see that the process is becoming more and more complex. The EU 10 had to realize that in order to facilitate their accession, they had to accept longer transitions that they would have wished, that there the room for opt-outs decreased continuously, and that the sense of solidarity could be injured in the process. This phenomenon continues to exist. Europe is changing and that does not make the life for the new candidates any easier. But we are convinced that enlargement had no alternatives.

12

The Accession of Latvia to the EU

Andris Ķesteris
Kristīne Plamše

1. POLITICAL BACKGROUND

The ten countries that joined the European Union on 1 May 2004 are seen today as a single group because they joined simultaneously—in the last wave of enlargement. This has not always been the case, although they all presented their candidacies to the EU almost simultaneously (around 1994–5), and free trade agreements, later replaced by association agreements, were concluded with one after the other. The division of the group occurred for the first time in July 1997 when the European Commission presented its opinions on the readiness of candidate countries to start accession negotiations. Six of them were deemed ready to start the negotiations the following year; the other six—among them Latvia—were left in what was later famously branded the Helsinki group (named after the Helsinki European Council in December 1999 that decided to also commence accession talks with Latvia, Lithuania, Slovakia, Bulgaria, Romania, and Malta).

Apart from the division of candidate countries according to their 'preparedness' in two groups that—as was proven later—was largely artificial, there are some other objective circumstances which explained the important differences that existed between the ten candidate countries. The three Baltic states, the Visegrad countries and Bulgaria and Romania, and finally the two Mediterranean islands presented three distinctly different historical backgrounds. Unlike the others, Latvia, Lithuania, and Estonia were states that regained their independence after fifty years of Soviet occupation (the Republic of Latvia regained its independence from the Soviet Union in 1991, the same year as Estonia and Lithuania). The particularity of this recent past entailed, apart from the necessary economic and political reforms, a complete reshuffling of their constitutional and legal systems, as well as substantial institutional changes. It also implied that a complete reorientation of their external trade was taking place, as in 1991 more than 90 per cent of trade was with the CIS. All these changes were nothing less than radical.

Therefore, the preparations for accession to the EU went hand in hand with the reinforcement of the newly regained statehood; this involved deep economic reforms to complete the transition from state-planned to the market economy, trade reorientation and new production standards, and the building of new state institutions and civil society. These aspects played an important substantive role in the accession negotiations of Latvia, as many of the solutions elaborated and offered to the other candidate countries did not automatically fit the Baltic states (for instance, that was largely the case with regard to agriculture.)

If one looks at the story of accession of the Baltic states from the perspective of the tremendous reform process in which these states were engaged before launching their EU membership applications, Latvia like Estonia and Lithuania succeeded in completing an enormous amount of work in a short period of time. Accompanied by a robust and sustained economic growth, this work resulted in their successful accession to the EU together with five other Central and Eastern European and two Mediterranean countries. Latvia became a full-fledged member of the EU exactly fourteen years after it declared independence from the Soviet Union.

2. ORGANIZATION OF THE NEGOTIATIONS

Coordination and negotiation team

The coordination and preparation of the accession negotiations in Latvia was carried out by several players. As for many other Central and Eastern European countries (CEECs) that sought to join the EU, the Ministry of Foreign Affairs assumed the overall preparation of the accession negotiations and also acted as the actual negotiator as talks were started. At the same time, inter-ministerial coordination of transposition and implementation of the *acquis communautaire* was reinforced by a specially created office—the 'European Integration Bureau'. Finally, the European Affairs Committee in Saeima (Parliament of Latvia) was placed in charge of coordinating the adoption of, and necessary modifications in, the legislation according to the schedule resulting from negotiation commitments. That was an important task because progress in the negotiations was conditioned upon the relevant progress in the transposition and implementation of the *acquis*.

During the summer of 1997—well before Latvia was actually invited to the accession negotiations—a Group of Negotiation Preparation was set up in the Ministry of Foreign Affairs of Latvia under the chairmanship of Eduards Stiprais and supervision of Undersecretary of European Affairs Andris Ķesteris (in October 1999 appointed as the chief negotiator). This group, along with the necessary representatives from line ministries, was involved in the screening process, preparing the overviews of each and every area of the *acquis communautaire*. It was also responsible for preparation of position papers for the negotiations. This work actually started as early as 1998. Regular reviews of legislation in the framework of the screening process helped Latvia in its legislative approximation.

As in most other countries, preparation for the accession negotiations required setting up a completely new inter-ministerial coordination mechanism. This was a new experience that required both awareness of available resources and know-how of the administrative and budgetary solutions. The uncompromising willingness of the various ministries to cooperate was vital for this to happen. In order to facilitate the work of the negotiation delegation, the Negotiation Preparation Group was transformed into the delegation's secretariat. Since this institution possessed the necessary knowledge of the screening, it could assist the various ministries in identifying the negotiation issues and preparing the draft positions. In this effort, Latvia, like other Baltic countries, received unprecedented support on the part of the Nordic friends, especially Denmark. A number of training activities were organized together with Denmark, Sweden, and even Norway (which conducted skilful negotiations, but failed in referendum); this allowed us to benefit from the Nordic experience from their negotiations and the internal coordination work in their public administration.

One of the advantages of Latvia was that it was a relatively small country with a small administration and a well-established direct contact amongst the ministry officials dealing with EU affairs. These circumstances substantially contributed to the effectiveness of coordination. It was also a fact that EU accession was an agreed political priority, supported by all political parties. This aspect is important to note, as this consensus helped the momentum for reform despite a frequently changing political environment.

In view of the negotiations, a number of new administrative structures were set up at the senior administrative level. A group of senior administrative officials consisting of EU experts from all ministries met on a regular basis to jointly prepare the draft negotiation position papers and discuss issues arising from the commitments in the negotiations. The negotiation delegation consisted mostly of undersecretaries of state for European affairs from various ministries. The horizontal institution—European Integration Bureau—also took part in this coordination effort, mostly focusing on the transposition of the *acquis*. In parallel, the Saeima (Parliament) European Affairs Committee was closely involved, since this committee was ultimately responsible for pushing through the adoption of all draft laws submitted by the government. The negotiation team and ministerial experts regularly assisted in the meetings of the European Affairs Committee to inform MPs of the negotiation position papers. The fact that the head of the European Affairs Committee from Parliament was part of the negotiation delegation was unique to Latvia (throughout most of the negotiations, MP Edvīns Inkens held this position). In the same vein, and in order to increase the transparency and credibility of the achieved deals, Latvia also asked and received permission for representatives of stakeholders from the agricultural sector to participate in the technical consultation meetings with the European Commission.

An important role in negotiations was also played by the team of Latvia's mission to the EU, headed by Ambassador Andris Piebalgs throughout the accession process. Their work proved crucial in contacts with the EC officials dealing with negotiations and representatives of Member States. They helped to anticipate early demands on behalf of the EU, and reactions to Latvia's requests, thus increasing preparedness in negotiations.

The President of Latvia, Mrs Vaira Vīķe-Freiberga, also deserves a special mention. With her vivid interest in the accession negotiations, a result of her awareness of the fundamental significance that EU accession had for Latvia, she followed some of the strategic issues in her meetings not only with Commission President Romano Prodi and Commissioner for Enlargement Günter Verheugen, but also with her interlocutors in the EU 15. Last but not least, her assessment of the negotiation results was crucial for the positive outcome in the accession referendum.

3. THE NEGOTIATIONS

From all the negotiation chapters, six were strategically particularly important for Latvia: agriculture, fisheries, regional policy, taxation, environment, and justice and home affairs. There were, of course, negotiation issues to be agreed with the EU in many other chapters. But since this is a short *compte rendu* of Latvia's negotiation effort, we can only afford to focus on the most interesting of the negotiation highlights.

Free movement of capital

Land acquisition by citizens of other EU Member States was the main bone of contention during the negotiations in this chapter. Unlike the Visegrad countries that linked the negotiations under this chapter with those under the chapter on free movement of people, Latvia was not demanding any transitional period for granting the EU citizens the right to freely purchase the agricultural land and real estate in Latvia. One has to note here a Latvian particularity. As a result of a long period of negligent practices because of collective farming, and, after restoration of independence, subsequent restitution of the land to its former owners or their relatives already mostly living in cities, large parts of agricultural land were not cultivated. In such circumstances, imposing restrictions would have been, at the least, counterproductive or even senseless. Such restrictions would also have been contrary to the agreements on investment protection that Latvia had already concluded with most EU Member States, except Ireland. From a less legal, more practical point of view, it was considered by many in Latvia that it would even be desirable that vast areas of agricultural land and run-down properties in the Latvian countryside would potentially find new owners (why not rich EU farmers!), as this would contribute to the revival of the countryside and would reduce the poverty in provincial areas of Latvia. Others, however, were somewhat more cautious—subconsciously, a fear of 'foreigners buying out Latvia' existed.

From the point of view of negotiation tactics, Latvia was also trying to keep the number of demands for transitional periods as limited as possible, in order to be better able to obtain derogations where they would matter the most. Therefore, the chapter was provisionally closed already in May 2001.

Nevertheless, the issue came back to the political discussion at the end of the negotiations as, in the final phase, it became possible to obtain transitional arrangements granted to others even though the chapter for Latvia was already closed. By that time, a growing number of parliamentarians in Latvia were starting to show bigger interest in protecting the local farmers from the forthcoming competition. It was also thought that this particular restriction would increase the votes in the affirmative in the referendum. Therefore, the EU horizontal offer to grant a transitional period until 2012 for imposing restrictions on agricultural land sale to foreigners was accepted with satisfaction and relief.

Free movement of services

Latvia accepted most of the *acquis* under this chapter upon accession with two exceptions in the area of financial services. One transition period, until 1 January 2008, was negotiated for introducing the savings guarantee schemes. The main consideration behind this demand was the comparatively small amount of savings held by the banks and the disproportionally high additional costs that financial institutions would have to undertake in order to increase the guaranteed amount of savings and to create the savings guarantee fund. In 2002, the guaranteed amount of savings was LVL3,000; by 2008 banks had to ensure that the guaranteed savings amount would reach LVL13,000.

Another transitional period—also until 1 January 2008—was negotiated on the introduction of an investment compensation system. This provision implied that banks had to be able to guarantee a compensation for lost savings—not less than €20,000—in case they were no longer able to meet their obligations.

Free movement of persons

This freedom was obviously the most attractive benefit of the EU accession and crucial for gaining support in public opinion. Therefore, restrictions—five years from accession—imposed by the EU Member States were obviously met with heavy criticism among the general population. From the government's point of view, however, the picture was slightly different. Unlike the case of Poland, which already had considerable experience and statistical data on emigrating and commuting labour, it was estimated that the Latvian population would not be very willing to go abroad for work in another EU Member State. This is because Latvia was the most remote from the old Member States and commuting—the most profitable form of labour mobility—was out of the question for Latvians. A reciprocity clause that was obtained during the negotiations meant that Latvia would maintain its right to take countermeasures if workers from other EU Member States increasingly snight work in Latvia. This morally facilitated the acceptance of the EU's request among Latvians.

The first two years after accession proved that both sides somewhat underestimated the trends in the labour market. The EU, where only three countries—the UK, Ireland, and Sweden—actually opened their labour markets to the citizens of new Member States, has not seen massive labour immigration. In the case of Latvia, estimations turned out to be wrong in another sense, as well. The government was taken by surprise by tens of thousands of Latvians who went to work in Ireland (23,000 officially registered, according to Irish estimates) and the UK.

Free movement of goods

This chapter actually proved that belonging to the so-called second group of accession countries was not a barrier to advancing fast in the negotiations, provided that one was well prepared. Latvia provisionally closed this chapter on the same day it officially opened it—30 March 2001. At the same time, it took two years for some of the first group countries, such as Poland and Hungary, to reach a provisional agreement on this chapter.

Out of the four freedoms, this chapter required the biggest workload in terms of legislation approximation and implementation, as well in the setting up of implementing institutions. The principal challenge was to ensure the adoption of EU standards. Producers of food, pharmaceuticals, and construction materials were, in the case of Latvia, the most affected sectors. In the area of food production and legislation on maximum allowed levels of certain substances in foodstuffs, the government had to dissipate a particularly high number of popular myths and horror stories related to the European food standards.

Another area which underwent considerable changes was the system for granting licences for entrepreneurship. Compared to the EU *acquis*, legislation in Latvia required licences for a much broader scale of business activities.

Company law

The negotiations under this chapter did not pose any principal problems. Reforms required in this area of legislation were without doubt regarded as beneficial for the improvement of the business environment and company legislation in Latvia. For the most part, the package of the EU company law directives was taken over through the adoption of the new 'commercial law' (the areas of accounting and auditing were an exception to this). With regard to ensuring the transparency of company shareholders, Latvia was already rather advanced. A modern European enterprise register was established and had been running since the mid-1990s, according to the law 'On the register of enterprises'. The register provided for any potential investor, business partner, or even the media the right to access the data on any registered enterprise, including its shareholders, annual turnover, etc.

Somewhat of a bigger challenge was the task of ensuring the implementation of legislation in the area of intellectual property rights. As in the case of other Eastern European countries with lower per capita income, the existence of a sizeable market for pirated music records and counterfeit goods was a well-known fact. National legislation was strengthened in this area.

Competition policy

With the adoption of two laws on competition and state aid, national legislation was already largely aligned with the *acquis* at the beginning of accession negotiations. Due to limited budgetary resources, national state aid programmes in Latvia were rather limited and there were no considerable industry sectors that would heavily rely on state aid (such as steel). Particular attention in the negotiations was devoted to the state aid schemes granted to the companies operating in the so-called special economic zones (SEZs) in Rēzekne (east Latvia) and Liepāja (west Latvia) and two free ports, Riga and Ventspils. These support schemes were designed to reinvigorate the economic development of some regions in Latvia that had come into severe economic difficulties. Explaining the support schemes to the European Commission took more time than had been originally anticipated. The Commission took a cautious position mainly because of the very notion of 'special economic zone'. In fact, the level of tax incentives provided under these schemes was compatible with the EU rules on regional aid, while the aid intensity in special economic zones was well below EU allowed thresholds in Objective 1 regions.

In the anti-trust sector the main issue was to convince the EU side about the strength of institutional capacity—Latvia's Competition Council.

Agriculture

The most difficult, time-consuming, and complex chapter for Latvia (much like most of the other candidate countries) was that of agriculture, where the task was to obtain a smooth entry into the EU for our farmers. Agriculture, although its share in our GDP was marginal—2 per cent (another 2 per cent for forestry and 2 per cent for fisheries)—was important because of its traditional role in the economy and society. It is also the most visible gain or loss that public opinion would associate with accession to the EU. Additionally, for most Latvians living in the countryside, not only farmers, the EU provided precious hope that they would soon be able to rise above the total destruction and economic decline that was left over after Soviet collectivization.

When it came to negotiations on this chapter, a substantial part of the Latvian population felt that any result would have a major impact on them, as a majority of people felt that they were—one way or another—affected by the future of the countryside and the environment. The pressure on the government was, unsurprisingly, very strong indeed. It was considered that Latvia's accession to the EU should not devastate rural communities and the physical environment, nor undermine the prospects for increased agricultural production. In this regard, the negotiations were put under thorough public scrutiny. The ensuing public assessment of whether a fair deal on accession conditions had been reached proved to be critical for the accession referendum.

Due to historical reasons, the majority of farms in Latvia (up to 70 per cent), as it was the case in the other two Baltic countries and Poland, were subsistence farms, a fact that explains why the contribution of agricultural production to the GDP was negligible. During the Soviet occupation, previously privately owned farms were denationalized and agricultural land and production was placed under collective farms. After the collapse of the Soviet Union, a complete restitution of private property was carried out. It led to the dismantling of collective farms, and the return of the land to its former owners or their families. Those who worked on collective farms, or who went back to the countryside in the early 1990s, had to start their farming business from scratch. Due to this, the levels of production fell significantly below even those of the Soviet period. In such a situation, the EU common agricultural market was logically perceived by many as a severe threat to the nascent and fragile agricultural sector.

These historical arguments, together with the constructive cooperation and the developed mutual trust that existed between the negotiation team and the Council of Agricultural organizations (LOSP united all associations of producers in the agricultural sector), were crucial for the success achieved in this chapter. As much as the negotiation team achieved at the level of technical consultations and meetings with Commission officials, the President and the Prime Minister of Latvia provided critical value added through their contacts with their European counterparts. To give the Commission a better historical picture and to explain the impact of the Russian economic crisis on the milk sector in Latvia, President Vīķe-Freiberga sent her famously dubbed 'milk letter' to Commission President Romano Prodi, pleading to take these historical externally imposed circumstances into account when carrying out the Commission's calculations for production quotas for individual countries. In the final phase of the negotiations, where agricultural matters were discussed among other issues, targeted, focused, and visible political messages played a crucial role.

The first part of the negotiations was devoted to the veterinary and phytosanitary standards in the food processing plants. Only a very limited number of recently established plants in Latvia were actually fit to meet the tough hygiene standards. Our national food safety agency (veterinary service until 2005) inspected all milk, meat, and fish processing facilities and every one of them had to provide a restructuring plan. On the basis of these plans and commitments of the food industry, transition periods were negotiated for meat, and fish producers and processors, as well as the milk production sector. The meat production industry was the least prepared, and seventy-seven plants and slaughterhouses were granted a transition period until January 2006. The milk sector was better prepared to meet the standards as it was traditionally better developed and bigger enterprises were already preparing for competition in the common market, partially exporting to the European Union. As for the milk suppliers (farmers), a transition period was negotiated until January 2006 to allow more time for improving the milk quality. This, however, created a discrepancy between the transitional periods for processing on the one hand, and production on the other. Because of new EU law, certified processing facilities did not have the right to work with lower than the highest-quality milk. The compromise solution was found in the *acquis* itself: the processing of milk into cheese with maturation time of more that thirty days was allowed.

On other issues, e.g. common market organization, all efforts were turned towards ensuring the maximum production quotas. Other support measures, such as the level of direct payments and support for rural development, were largely horizontal issues and were left for the very end of the negotiations. The reference yield and base area, as well as milk and sugar, were crucial for Latvia. These sectors had the biggest number of active farmers and producers, and substantial investments in these sectors had been made in recent years to modernize the production line. An EU-like quota system already existed in Latvia for sugar production. This explains why the initial position that the government presented to the EU was based on a maximalistic approach—the requested production quota was to cover the actual production levels and provide additional reserve for increased production (close to self-sufficiency) over the next few years. The first EU position paper in response to that demand was a shockingly disappointing one—the EU had slashed the milk and sugar quota by half. As to the reference yields for arable crops, the EU offer covered 60 per cent of Latvia's demands. The efforts to change the reference numbers in the meat production sector, notably for obtaining special and slaughter premiums on beef, suckler cows, and sheep, was also a very challenging one.

Political arguments, anchored on the exigencies created by Soviet collective farms and the impact of the Russian economic crisis in the mid-1990s, proved insufficient to convince the EU that Latvian farmers deserved more. Quota and production references required precise numbers on their evolution over at least five years. Unlike the well-organized farming sector of the EU countries, however, the small and medium-sized farmers in Latvia did not run precise accounting in their farms. This was particularly true in the case of the milk sector, as most of the production was consumed on the premises, and only part of it was given to the processing industry. The EU position nonetheless took into account only this fraction of the produced milk. Convincing the EU on the real production levels required a great deal of creativity on the part of the negotiation team.

As regards the meat sector, the situation was even more interesting. The traditional Latvian species of cows were typical milk cows and the population of meat breeds was rather limited. Given the overall EU production ceilings on milk, the EU was generally positive towards farmers switching from milk to meat production, a process that came under way in Latvia. Many of the milk cow farmers had recently started to reorient themselves towards meat production, as meeting the EU standards in the meat sector was easier than in milk production. The beef meat sector was fast evolving and EU production support was crucial for that. In the absence of historical reference data, Latvia, like the other two Baltic states and Poland, obtained a transitional arrangement during which additional breeds are entitled to receive the suckler cow premium. Together with other categories of EU support available for meat producers, this allowed for additional income to those farmers who had recently embarked on the change from milk into meat sector.

The overall achievement of production quotas was very satisfactory. On average, the EU's initial offer was increased by 40 per cent. Milk producers received a quota that was twice as big as the initial EU offer. In quantitative terms, none of the other countries managed to obtain such an increase on the original quota offered by the EU. Today one can say that the finally agreed quota ceiling largely corresponded to the actual amount of produced milk, plus a small reserve. In some of the other sectors, the finally agreed quota even offered a potential for a 30 per cent production increase. Together with single area payments and rural development money that all agricultural landowners were entitled to receive, farmers came out of the EU accession as the biggest direct winners.

Fisheries

The negotiations on fisheries were actually the first substantial negotiations of non-horizontal character in which Latvia engaged with the EU in order to defend vital national interests by obtaining important exceptions for the fishing in Gulf of Riga. They lasted more than a year, as this chapter was provisionally closed on 26 October 2001. The obtained result was generally regarded as a success and the negotiation team was well praised for that, especially amongst the fishermen.

Obtaining a special fishing access regime with restrictions on maximal allowed catches was regarded as fundamental to the national interest of Latvia. Even before accession, Latvia already applied, over a number of years, scientifically based restrictions on fishing activities in the Gulf of Riga in order to allow for the natural replenishment of the fish population. As a result, the only non-depleted herring resource in the Baltic Sea was precisely in the waters used by Latvian fishermen. After the EU enlargement, the Gulf of Riga would have entered in the category of common EU waters and the fishing fleet of other EU Member States would have the right to extend their activities to the waters formerly accessible only to the fishermen of Latvia and Estonia. Increased fishing capacity was scientifically regarded as undesirable and even as dangerous for the recovery of the limited fish population. Therefore, for the sake of continuing the conservation measures, Latvia requested that only historically allowed vessels with limited engine capacity (221 kW and applying limited fishing gear) be allowed to continue to fish in the Gulf of Riga. In reality this meant that fishing effort in the Gulf of Riga was possible only from the coastal villager-fishermen. Thus, an important side effect, namely, the protection of the traditional fishing and economic activity in coastal villages, was also ensured.

Another two issues were related to securing the extension of certain fish consumption habits that were different in Latvia and the EU. One of them regards the so-called *Sprattus sprattus*, a small-sized sprat that is used in Latvia for human consumption whereas in the EU 15, this fish was mostly used for producing fishmeal. Positive agreement was obtained on this matter, although intervention monies had to come from national sources and not the EU budget as was the case with other species like herring.

Another fish issue was related to the size differences of traditional herring. Whereas in the EU, herring smaller than 10 g in size were not foreseen in community *acquis* as available for human consumption (in order to uphold the price of herring), this was not the case in Latvia where fish of this size were generally available and widely consumed. This exception was also obtained.

Finally, a limited transition period—until 1 January 2005—was obtained for restructuring twenty-nine fish processing facilities which were required to refurbish the production units according to the community hygiene and food safety standards.

Transport

Similarly to the other accession states, negotiations under this chapter took place mainly on some of the sensitive parts of transportation *acquis*, such as access of non-resident hauliers to the national road transport market of other Member States. It was, in fact, in the interest of the EU to limit the access of the transport companies from new Member States to the national road transport markets of other Member States. Being far from EU 15 Member States (1,000 km separate Latvia from Germany), the interests of Latvian transport companies were not at stake. Therefore, none of them regarded the EU requested transitional period of two years (with a right for any existing EU Member State to prolong it up to five years) with concern. In return, we opted for reciprocal restrictions to the Latvian market, as some restrictions in this area were already in place.

Two other issues were related to installation of driving time recording equipment in heavyweight vehicles and requirements for financial standing for transport undertakings providing road haulage and passenger transport operations.

On tachographs, or road time recording equipment, Latvia agreed to the transition period until 2005 for vehicles registered before 2001 and engaged exclusively in domestic transport operations.

With regard to the directive on financial standing of transport undertakings, Latvia requested a transitional arrangement until the end of 2006 in order to allow our national companies longer time to reach the full level of financial standing for admission to the road haulage and passenger transport operations.

Taxation

Two issues were at stake in negotiations under this chapter: applicable minimal levels of excise tax for cigarettes, and VAT application exceptions on certain groups of products or services. Requests for transition periods for applying the new rates were based on the fact that the purchasing power of Latvian citizens was well below that of the citizens of EU Member States; therefore, sudden price hikes on a number of goods and services such as household heating and cigarettes would lead to severe social and economic problems. For instance, if immediately applied in full, the EU level of excise tax on cigarettes would increase their price in Latvia fourfold. Therefore, a transition period was requested until 2010 for reaching the minimal level of excise tax on cigarettes. This implied a gradual increase of minimal rates over a period of six years. Because several of the Central and Eastern European countries were asking for the same transition period in this regard, the EU side agreed to offer a horizontal solution to all of them.

Regarding the VAT exceptions, demands differed among the candidates and the EU approach was appropriately different. Latvia requested a short transition period—until 1 January 2005—for exempting private households from paying VAT on heating. This was seen as very important, especially in towns and villages where the district heating was run on biomass (forestry by-products). The VAT application to the final product would have meant a steep increase in price, because biomass itself (unlike gas and oil) was cheap. Arrangements for several other derogations were also made. For example, Latvia also obtained the right to continue the existing practice of exempting from VAT all international air and sea passenger services. Another permanent exemption that was gained was related to the yearly turnover limits from which a company has to register itself as VAT payer.

Energy

The main issue in the negotiations regarding energy was the requirement to establish the oil stocks at the level of ninety days of consumption. Establishment of this new system would have required investment of tens of thousands of euros. This would burden oil and fuel companies and the state, and could also have an impact on the final consumption price. Therefore, Latvia requested a transition period until 2009 to reach the total required reserve levels.

Latvia also committed itself to the liberalization of the electricity and gas market (the second internal market package required that Member States would liberalize their energy market by 1 July 2007). However, all legislative aspects of the preparations for the market opening had to be completed before accession. From the moment of accession, Latvia formally had a right to request derogation for opening of the gas market, as, according to the relevant directive, it could be treated as a newly established market. Apart from the infrastructure that would allow Latvia to be interconnected with the EU Member States, actual gas supplies did not exist either. Since Gazprom, the only possible supplier, was also the sole supplier of the neighbouring Estonian and Lithuanian markets, it would be hard to imagine the emergence of a 'third' player in the Baltic gas market.

Regional policy

Being the poorest of all the EU acceding states according to purchasing power parity statistics, Latvia had no difficulties in justifying the need for funding from EU Structural and Cohesion Funds. With the average income level standing at just 30 per cent of the EU average (at the moment of accession), Latvia qualified for Objective 1 Structural Funds regulations (average level of income below 75 per cent of EU average). What proved to be somewhat more difficult was establishing the institutional structure for planning and dealing with EU Structural Funds, and some time elapsed until the delegation of tasks was agreed upon between the various ministries. It was decided different departments of the Ministry of Finance would be both the planning and paying authority.

From the very beginning of various calculations on the distribution of monies among the new Member States, Latvia, like the other two Baltic states, were quite confident that we would obtain the highest per capita funding. The various tables with numbers that had circulated since mid-November 2002 were, with some minor corrections, acceptable to Latvia. At the last formal negotiation meeting before the Copenhagen Summit, when some of the countries announced their agreement on the whole negotiation package, we decided not to hurry to follow suit. Even though we were assured that any further offers would be horizontal, we chose to wait until Copenhagen to give our agreement.

The final deal for Latvia was a rather generous one. We obtained around 3.5 per cent or €574.8 million from the total envelope of Structural Funds and an indicative allocation of 5.07 to 7.08 per cent or around €455 million from the envelope of Cohesion Funds.

Environment

From all areas of EU *acquis*, environment legislation, for example, on phytosanitary and veterinary issues, is the most costly one to adopt. Adopting the higher standards in areas like drinking water, sewage systems, waste management, and fuel quality required enormous investments. According to the calculations of the Ministry of the Environment, in the case of Latvia the cost would have been at least LVL800 million (approx. €1.5 billion). Although EU money from the ISPA pre-accession fund was available for such projects, it could cover only a fraction of all investment needs. The rest of it would have to be shouldered by the state budget and private investment. The absence of funds, and thus of the possibility to achieve a speedy implementation of the *acquis*, was the reason why this was the area in which Latvia requested the highest number of transitional periods; all requests were granted. With eight transition periods, Latvia was second after Poland in the number of transition periods obtained under this chapter. It required lengthy and difficult (but worthwhile) technical consultations, as it gave us extra time to prepare for the implementation of the costly EU environment standards. For different areas of legislation, the length of those transition periods was between one and twelve years.

Water

As happened with all candidates, the longest transitional period (until the end of 2015 in the case of Latvia) was requested for reaching full compliance on drinking water standards. It was estimated that 60 per cent of the water supply network infrastructure had to be changed in order to improve the purification systems and replace old water pipelines with new ones. This burden would lie mostly on the budgets of local and regional governments.

A transition period of the same length was also requested for the modernization of sewage treatment systems in the largest cities because both pipelines—for sewage and drinking water—physically lie next to each other. For the three most populated cities, including the capital of Riga, the transition periods were the shortest ones (until 2008) as the health of more people would have been at stake. The less populated the area, the longer the transition period. Thus, approximately sixty-five towns accounting for only 15 per cent of the total population of Latvia were allowed until the end of 2015 to install new systems or otherwise bring their outdated sewage and water systems in order.

Waste

Another area involving huge investment needs was that of waste treatment. Waste storage and treatment in Latvia was improving compared to the situation in the beginning of the 1990s and the awareness on environmental issues was growing. However, the lack of effective waste collection and storage facilities meant not only that official storage areas failed to comply with EU standards, but also that plenty of illegal and hidden waste disposal areas could be found around the country. EU legislation requirements therefore served as a strong incentive for bringing waste collection, storage, and treatment systems into place. Bringing this system in order required time, however; therefore, the negotiation team had to realistically calculate the necessary time and investments needed for such changes. The EU agreed with the Latvian demand for a transition period until 2006 to cover 70 per cent of the households (population) by a centralized waste management system. All waste disposals had to comply with EU standards by the end of 2012. Half of the existing waste dumps had to undergo a clean-up by the end of 2008. The other half would be given until end of 2015. More than ten new waste storage sites had to be constructed.

Concerning dangerous waste, Latvia requested a short transition period—until the end of 2004—to construct a new waste collection and disposal station which also served for the disposal of infectious waste of medical origin. For packaging waste, Latvia required a transition period until the end of 2007 in order to improve the recycling system and to increase its capacity. A number of large industrial plants, after having submitted detailed reconstruction and investment plans, obtained transitional periods until the end of 2010 to comply with the directive on integrated pollution prevention and control.

Fuel quality

Fuel quality requirements were an additional issue that required rather lengthy technical consultations and negotiation. Latvia undertook a commitment to ensure that, as of 2004, only high-quality fuel will be on sale. This implied that in the future, fuel could be taken only from wholesalers that were selling high-quality fuel matching EU standards. Imports of cheaper Russian and Belarusian fuel would no longer be allowed, as the quality standards in those countries were lower than in the EU. The requirements concerning environmental standards on fuel distribution stations put an additional burden on the fuel retailing companies, especially the smaller ones. Therefore, it was expected that fuel prices would rise as a result of implementing the requested changes. This could have a rather painful effect on the market and would be very unpopular in public opinion, as the EU would be blamed for higher fuel prices. One should not forget that the minimal excise duty rates on energy products were also a source of concern and a potential cause of rising fuel prices. To this end, a transition period was requested both for complying with the environmental quality standards in fuel stations, and for applying the minimal excise duty rates (under the chapter on taxation).

Nature reserves and protected species

Latvia, with a territory of more than 64,000 km^2 and only 2.4 million inhabitants, is among the most sparsely populated countries in Europe. Almost the entire country, outside the larger cities, is covered with vast areas of forests (more than 40 per cent of all territory) and agricultural land. Therefore, Latvia has long been (and still is) home to hundreds of wild species of plants, birds, and animals, until recently enjoying an undisturbed habitat without any specific protection regimes. Because of their rather large populations, no severe hunting restrictions were imposed on wolves and beavers. Latvia was initially somewhat opposed to establishing additional protection sites for wild birds and animals, as that would impose restrictions on human activities in places which were so far open for modest agricultural activities and in some cases also on hunting. Additionally, in many cases, a number of species were widely present in dispersed areas, which made the task even more difficult. Latvia finally committed to submit lists of areas home to wild birds, and to protect those areas. We also committed to submit lists of protected areas for their inclusion in the NATURA 2000 network of nature reserves. As far as existing reserves were concerned, we did not have any particular difficulties. The NATURA 2000 network was already well known before accession, not the least because some of the reserves in Latvia had already benefited from EU financial support in this area.

Curiously, the hunting of lynxes remained one of the last unresolved issues in the negotiations, being treated in the same group of issues as milk quotas and financial provisions. Submitting scientific evidence on the numbers of the lynx population and their reproduction trends, Latvia and Estonia managed to prove to the EU that this was not an animal in danger of disappearing, even though neither I nor anyone else in our negotiation team, I think, had ever seen a live lynx in any of the Latvian forests (which is evidence that the lynx is an animal rather difficult to hunt). No ban on hunting wolves and beavers was imposed, either.

Justice and home affairs

Latvia, among the acceding states, belonged to that group which after accession would have to assume responsibilities for taking care of the EU external border. Our land border, and thus EU external border, with Russia, is 246 km long, and with Belarus it is 161 km long. After the restoration of independence in 1991, construction of new infrastructure and border control points took place gradually, requiring huge investments from public finances. That was not enough in view of EU accession. Implementing the Schengen agreement and requirements on the visa regime, as well as installing information and data exchange systems, required additional investments worth hundreds of millions of euros. Most of the investment needs were related to technical and IT equipment necessary for ensuring speedy data exchange and document checks at the external borders. This is where, at the final stage of negotiations, the EU decided to grant additional financial assistance to those new Member States that would have to assume responsibilities for external border controls. Latvia was one of those that qualified for this type of support, and received €71.1 million. As far as the other part of the Schengen *acquis* was concerned, namely that of lifting the border checks on the EU internal borders, it required additional investments and the meeting of a number of preconditions in order to gain access to the Schengen information system. None of the acceding states was ready to implement it upon accession; therefore, this part was left pending to be tackled at a later point. As in the previous enlargements, it was actually the EU, and more precisely, the Schengen area countries, that made it clear from the very beginning that Latvia's accession to Schengen would only take place some years after becoming a member of the EU.

In other areas of this chapter, no transition periods were requested. Latvia agreed to align its visa policy with that of the EU, which entailed also some changes in the visa regimes, mainly with third countries and in the border-crossing regime for inhabitants of bordering areas of Russia and Belarus.

As regards the legislation on migration and asylum issues, we accepted it without major problems, despite some sensitivities and fears on its impact on public opinion. It was thought that Latvia might have to accept asylum seekers from third countries and that was one of the arguments later taken over by Eurosceptics during the referendum campaign. Those claims have not been justified, because Latvia has neither been a target nor a transit point for considerable numbers of asylum seekers.

Financial and budgetary provisions

As this was a horizontal issue, and it was clear from the very beginning that Latvia would be a net recipient, our main efforts were focused on obtaining a delayed date for assuming our obligations to contribute to the 'own resources payments'. Another issue concerned the temporary budgetary situation after accession, where contributions to the EU budget had to be made, but the EU money would not have yet started to flow in. To this end, the EU finally agreed to grant all acceding states a temporary cash flow facility. Our share in the last-minute envelope was €26 million.

4. CONCLUSION

The negotiations for Latvia lasted, all in all, for three years, from the moment of their official opening in early 2000. They were preceded by two years of preparations (screening), and led to full accession of Latvia, and the other nine candidates, on 1 May 2004.

The main achievement of the negotiations was, of course, a smooth passage of the country into the EU. The economic growth of Latvia remained robust and even accelerated, currently being the highest in Europe (10.1 per cent in 2005). However, taken from a purely negotiation-focused point of view, Latvia's talks could be regarded as being among the most successful ones. Altogether, Latvia arranged for thirty-two derogations of different kinds from the *acquis*. Thus, the country shared the second place in this regard with Malta and was 'surpassed' only by Poland.

One could feel little tempted to come back to what I mentioned in the very beginning about being divided in two groups. Latvia was one of the 'second group' countries. This division, although largely artificial, has nonetheless left some traces of hidden jealousy and competition among the acceding states. The first group had their reason to feel more advanced and appreciated at the beginning of the talks. Latvia had its own reasons to feel left behind—at least in the beginning. But there were positive sides to that, as the speed and individual country performance in the negotiations proved later. The countries of the 'first group' commenced negotiations with the EU earlier, but, for both sides, it was a sort of common learning process that took its time to discover things and learn from some of the mistakes. In this learning process, Latvia was able to bide its time, and learned from the experience of the countries of the first group ('Luxembourg group') of candidates. It was well worthwhile. We started our bilateral negotiations later, but we moved on faster, working on the so-called catch-up principle. The end of the process and the data on the closed chapters, even called 'chapterology' (so much appreciated by media!), proved that the initial division between the countries was an artificial one, but not necessarily a negative one.

13

The Accession of Lithuania to the EU

Petras Auštrevičius

1. INTRODUCTION

Lithuania's twentieth-century history has been shaped by a complicated domestic political life, on the one hand, and the long-standing relations of the country with the West, on the other. During the last century, Lithuania has not spent more than thirty-three years as an independent state.

On 16 February 1918 Lithuania proclaimed its independence, thus re-establishing its state. The largest states of the world and Europe soon recognized the independence of Lithuania, and Lithuania established reciprocal diplomatic relations with many of them. Independence, however, did not last for more than twenty-two years, as the country came under Soviet occupation and subjugation in 1940.

If the country was completely subjugated, however, its desire for independence was not subdued by the fifty-year occupation that followed. Alongside the dissolution of the Soviet Union on 11 March 1990, Lithuania again proclaimed its independence. Diplomatic relations were soon renewed with many countries.

Lithuania, as a state with a European history and culture, immediately began implementing the necessary comprehensive policies to become once again an equal member of the western club. With the declaration of Lithuania's independence, the gradual reorientation of economic relations from the east to the west started taking place.

2. RELATIONS BETWEEN LITHUANIA AND THE EUROPEAN UNION

The beginning of the official relations between Lithuania and the European Communities dates back to 27 August 1991, when the EU countries recognized officially the re-establishment of Lithuania's independence. Thus was laid the foundation for further development of relations and the ensuing economic and political dialogue between the EU and Lithuania.

On 11 May 1992, Lithuania and the EC signed the Treaty on Trade and Commercial and Economic Cooperation that came into force on 1 February 1993. The declaration on the EC–Lithuanian political dialogue that formalized the political relations between the countries was also signed at the same time.

One of the decisive stages in the relations between Lithuania and the EC was the signing of a free trade agreement. The granting on 7 February 1994 of the mandate to carry out negotiations was the green light to the Commission to conclude the European association agreements with Lithuania and other Baltic countries, which would become an intermediate step towards the membership of the European Union.

The historical significance of this step lay in the fact that it granted a different status to the Baltic countries from other former Soviet Union republics, while also laying down the prerequisites for a more rapid integration into western structures and markets. A free trade agreement between Lithuania and the EU was signed on 18 July 1994, and the negotiations on associate membership were started at the end of the same year.

On 25 June 1995, Lithuania and the EC signed the European Association Agreement, which came in to force on 1 February 1998. Lithuania, after becoming an associated member of the EU together with other Baltic and Central and Eastern European states, embarked on a new stage in the relations with the EU. The agreement officially recognized the objective of Lithuania to become a member of the EU.

The Luxembourg Summit, in December 1997, split the EU enlargement process into two 'waves'. Lithuania, according to the Commission's conclusions and recommendations, together with Latvia, Bulgaria, Romania, Slovakia, and Malta, was part of the second group of candidate countries. This decision created an atmosphere of deep disappointment, which led us to seriously ponder the consequences for the country's future, while at the same time, public pressure to take the necessary steps towards harmonization declined.

On the other hand, the message from the EU that Lithuania was unready for membership mobilized the politicians and the administration to pursue more aggressive preparation for membership. This policy line later paid significant dividends.

At the Helsinki Summit in December 1999, it was agreed to start negotiations with all candidate countries, giving the possibility for Lithuania and other 'second-wave' countries to catch up with other candidates that had by that time advanced in the negotiations.

3. INSTITUTIONAL AND PROCEDURAL SETTING

Lithuania's preparation for EU membership was reflected in several institutional adaptations designed to ensure conformity to the main practices established by the EU. These institutional changes took place in the context of a 'Euro-institutions' plan. In principle, it marked the recognition that EU membership, apart from being a major priority in our foreign policy, also had a strong dimension in domestic policy as well. In May 1995, the Governmental European Integration Commission was established. The Governmental European Integration Commission, chaired by the Prime Minister, discussed and solved the main issues related to the preparation for membership.

To support and enhance the accession process, a European Integration Department at the Ministry of Foreign Affairs was created in 1995. European integration divisions in the line ministries were also established in parallel. At the end of 1996, the Ministry of European Affairs was also created, marking the transformation of the national accession policy from a foreign policy instrument, to an instrument of domestic policy as well. This development led to some tensions, however, as the division of responsibilities and competences between national actors became less obvious.

At the beginning of 1998, the uncertainty over competence and efficiency reached a climax. In May 1998 the Ministry of European Affairs was reorganized into the European Committee under the Government of the Republic of Lithuania, directly subordinated to the Prime Minister. The Committee was in charge of co-coordinating the overall process of the internal preparation for EU membership. This decision demonstrated the introduction of a centralized system for integration management, which proved to be a timely move.

Prime Minister Gediminas Vagnorius asked me to establish the institution and become its Director General. The main task of the European Committee was to participate in formulating the policy of integration into the European Union and to oversee the co-ordination of its implementation; to participate in the negotiations with the European Union and its Member States and to coordinate the drafting (preparation) of the Lithuanian Accession Treaty. The European Committee was a supervising body for inter-institutional programmes in preparation of EU membership, including the National Programme for the Adoption of the *Acquis*. The impartiality of the European Committee was instrumental in resolving institutional conflicts, while it also provided value added in expertise that was instrumental in solving the residual gaps of responsibility. One of the major tasks was to run a public information campaign during the accession process, leading up to the referendum on EU membership. It also performed the functions of the secretariat of the Governmental European Integration Commission.

The European Committee, as a dynamic institution staffed with young and motivated experts, was divided into three departments, based on eight projects. The Committee issued an annual appraisal based on performance results, in the National Progress Report of 1998. An extensive elaboration of NPAA followed in 1999, and a report on internal market reform was prepared in 2000. Impact assessments were prepared from 1999 onwards, as were reports on institution building plans for all sectors of *acquis*, on the negotiations in 2000–2, the drafting of the Accession Treaty 2002–3, and the referendum in 2003.

Table 11. Law approximation action plan, 2000–2003

	2000	2001	2002	2003
Laws	10	65	37	70
Resolutions of the government	6	53	33	38
Orders of the ministries and other institutions	81	202	190	233
Totally Lithuanian legal acts	97	320	260	341
Totally EU legal acts	481	747	569	715

Source: Database of the European committee, www.euro.lt

The European Law Department provided the necessary expertise in ensuring that the national legislation complied with the EU *acquis.* It oversaw Lithuania's law harmonization with EU law.

The legal harmonization constantly required good coordination, because of the large number of institutions involved, and the volume of legal acts that were acted upon (see Table 11).

The European Affairs Subcommittee of the Foreign Affairs Committee of the Seimas (Parliament), set up in 1995, was in September 1997 reorganized into a new committee called the Seimas European Affairs Committee, which, due to its composition, as well as its functions, was a 'super-committee' of sorts. The new Committee, comprised of twenty-four members, was granted special powers as compared to other Seimas committees.

As a response to the Commission's White Paper for integration into the internal market in 1996, the first special programme for preparing for membership (the National Programme for Law Approximation) was drafted. In 1998, the National Programme for the Adoption of the *Acquis* (NPAA) became the main tool in implementing the EU accession priorities identified in the accession partnerships. It provided detailed and concrete short-term and long-term tasks for preparing for membership—programmes for internal reforms, drafts of legal acts, and measures for strengthening institutions.

The European Committee worked scrupulously on the NPAA, improving it and adjusting it as the developments dictated. As a result, we were in a position to indicate that Lithuania would be fully prepared for membership in 2004, to the surprise of many. Being the overarching basis of the Lithuanian accession strategy, it became part of the government programme in the beginning of 2001. The programme was renewed annually with six versions during the period of 1998–2003. More than forty state institutions participated in the preparation and implementation of the NPAA.

Lithuania had no other option but to fully integrate into the single market of the Union. In March 1998, the first programme for Lithuania's accession into the common market of the European Union was prepared, and was soon approved by the government. The National Programme for the Adoption of the *Acquis* (NPAA), prepared in 1998, covered the transposition of the European Union 'law' regulating the single market.

The Strategic Trends for Stimulation of Lithuania's Economic Integration into the EU Single Market, prepared in 2001 by the European Committee under the Government, was addressed at the players of the market, who needed to learn how to work under new conditions—after the transposition and implementation of the European law requirements.

Organization and players of negotiations

As a result of the Helsinki European Council decisions, Lithuania's integration process moved from the pre-accession stage to the stage of accession negotiations.

During the meetings of the conference on accession to the EU, the Lithuanian delegation usually consisted of the representatives of the Foreign Ministry, the chief negotiator of Lithuania, representatives of the European Committee under the Government of the Republic of Lithuania, and the Mission of the Republic of Lithuania to the European Communities.

In Lithuania, the chief negotiator was appointed by decree of the President of the Republic on the proposal of the government. As a chief negotiator, I assumed my position from 5 January 2001 replacing Vygaudas Ušackas, while also maintaining the position of the Director General of the European Committee. This allowed me to maintain a continuous and coherent control of both the preparation for membership and of the accession negotiations.

The procedure for preparing the negotiation position of Lithuania followed the process of accession coordination. Specially established interdepartmental working groups, headed by deputy ministers, heads of the governmental institutions, or their deputies, started preparing the initial draft of the negotiation position for every negotiation chapter (see Fig. 3).

The negotiation delegation and the co-ordination group of the delegation played a very important role in the negotiation process. The Minister of Foreign Affairs headed the delegation. The chief negotiator held the duties of deputy head of the negotiation delegation and head of the co-ordination group of the delegation. The negotiation delegation coordinated the work related to the negotiations and the planning of actions to be taken; it also prepared the negotiation documents and discussed drafts of the decisions to be taken by government. The delegation included representatives of the Ministry of Foreign Affairs, the European Committee, the European Law Department under the Government of the Republic of Lithuania, the Lithuanian Mission to the European Communities, and the heads of thirty negotiation working groups.

The coordination group of the delegation, as the core team of negotiators, was, in fact, a real centre of everyday activities, where major negotiation activities took place, tactics and different proposals were discussed, meetings with socio-economic partners were held, and so on. All major integration institutions were represented in the co-ordination group.

The Seimas of the Republic also played a prominent role in the negotiations, by providing the necessary political support for EU membership. During the

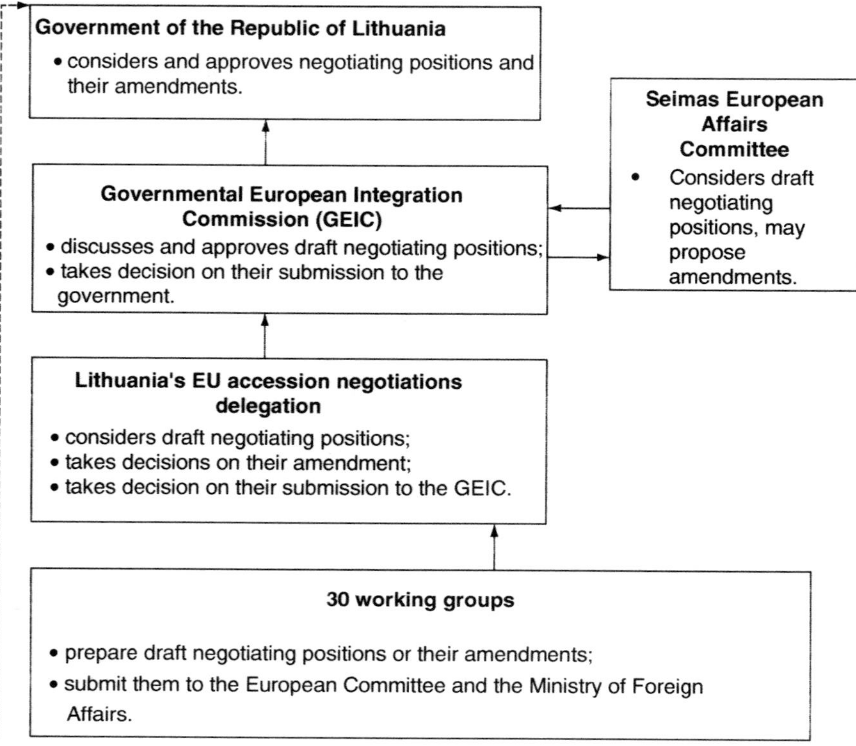

Figure 3. Organization of the preparation of the positions in Lithuania

Source: Lithuania's road to the European Union: unification of Europe and Lithuania's EU accession negotiations, Vilnius: Eugrimas, 2005).

negotiation process, I stayed in close touch with the heads of political parties as well as the leaders of the Parliament. The European Affairs Committee co-ordinated activities related to Lithuania's integration at a parliamentary level, providing the necessary political impetus for many unpopular but necessary decisions.

4. ACCESSION NEGOTIATIONS

The beginning and the first stage of the negotiations (2000)

Our negotiation strategy, presented at the first conference on accession, was based on following three principles: first, to conclude the negotiations in 2002 together with the first enlargement wave and become a member of the Union in 2004; second, the preparation for EU membership to act as a push factor for the internal reform programme; and third, that each candidate country should be treated equally to the others.

Portugal planned to start negotiations with Lithuania on eight (as a rule, relatively uncomplicated) negotiation chapters and, on 28 March 2000, Lithuania officially presented its first package of eight negotiation positions. The negotiations started officially on 25 May 2000. This, apart from being a significant milestone in Lithuanian history, also demonstrated that 'catch-up' was taking place.

The negotiations were concluded on five negotiation chapters: statistics, small and medium-sized enterprises (SMEs), science and research, education and training and the common foreign and security policy (CFSP). The chapters of external relations, competition, and culture and audio-visual policy remained under negotiation.

France's working programme for the second part of 2000 foresaw the opening of negotiations with Lithuania on eight chapters. During the first accession conference in October 2000, the negotiations in the chapters of external relations and industrial policy were concluded.

The provisional closure of the chapter on external relations necessitated an amendment of Lithuania's position on free trade agreements with Latvia, Estonia, and Ukraine, since even temporary exemptions with respect to the EU common trade policy were unacceptable because they could potentially distort the EU internal market.

In the course of 2000, Lithuania, being part of the Helsinki group, sought to come as close as possible to those in the Luxembourg group, in order to secure a place in the first enlargement wave. Indeed, by 2002, twenty-nine negotiation positions were presented to the EU. Submitted position papers contained thirty-four requests for transitional periods in twelve negotiation chapters, as well as several exemptions and reservations.

The negotiations gather momentum (2001)

In December 2000, the Nice European Council agreed on the road map (chapter-by-chapter timetable) of negotiations until the second half of 2002. The road map was a useful tool, foreseeing that nine chapters were to be negotiated in the first half of 2001, nine more in the second half of 2001, and five in the first half of 2002. In fact, the EU did not commit itself to the closure of the mentioned chapters, but rather proposed certain 'rules of the game' intended to 'produce' a fixed date of the end- game.

In 5 January 2001, I assumed the role of chief negotiator but the overall picture did not look good at all. Measured by the number of closed chapters, Lithuania stood at the eleventh position out of twelve candidates, with seven chapters provisionally closed (half those of Slovenia that was first). It was clear that something radical and immediate had to be done. I saw a necessity to improve considerably the negotiation planning process, to establish stronger links between the negotiation team and the line institutions responsible for real implementation and revive the political commitment of the major political parties.

In January 2001, following our proposition, the Governmental European Integration Commission approved the so-called Göteberg (named after the June summit) action plan. The plan indicated the negotiation chapters which Lithuania sought to close during the Swedish presidency and presented a plan for legal approximation and institutional development, and for the transitional periods which had to be reassessed. Accordingly, under Sweden's presidency we planned to conclude the negotiations on twelve chapters. Finally, the situation came to serve as a motive for internal mobilization and to symbolize our ambition.

On 30 March 2001 Lithuania concluded the negotiations on six chapters and made a real breakthrough.

With efficient planning of the negotiations, Lithuania and the EU agreed to close two more chapters (free movement of goods and company law) on 17 May 2001.

The closure of the chapter on the free movement of goods was closely related to the implementation of the EU requirements on good practice in the manufacture of medicinal products. Because of the fact that local manufacturers were not competitive, Lithuania initially asked for a transitional period until 1 January 2007. After extensive consultations with the economic partners, the European Commission, and other candidates, the transitional period was agreed upon for putting in order documentation dossiers for authorization of medicinal products in accordance with the EU requirements by 1 January 2007. An agreement provided the possibility for cost savings for pharmacy enterprises, while complying with single market regulations.

The negotiations on the chapter on company law revolved around the protection of the intellectual property of pharmaceutical products. An agreement was reached, foreseeing that the Supplementary Protection Certificate valid in the EU would also apply to pharmaceutical products that had a valid patent in Lithuania, provided that the patent had been issued prior to 1 February 1994 and that they were being marketed at the time.

On 11 June 2001, the negotiations on the chapter on the freedom to provide services and the chapter on fisheries were provisionally closed (fishing quotas were negotiated at the end of the negotiations).

The negotiations on the chapter of freedom to provide services required much harder efforts and more determination. Both sides agreed on two transitional periods lasting until 2008: one on the harmonization of the deposit insurance with the EU requirements, and one on the implementation of the system of compensation to investors in accordance with the EU requirements. An additional exemption was also given for the country's credit unions. The exemption concerns the minimum requirement for capital goods which does not apply to small-scale businesses.

Another particularly difficult issue was connected to an EU directive that required the compulsory civil liability insurance of users and owners of motor vehicles. Lithuania was the only country among the EU Member States and candidate countries that had no functioning compulsory insurance system in place, and was hence forced to ask for a transitional period until 2010 to implement this directive, arguing that without a transitional period, an additional financial burden would encumber the population of the country. The European Commission rejected the request for a transitional period. After prolonged consultations and discussions, Lithuania withdrew its request for a transitional period, and made the necessary arrangements to fully implement the requirements of the directive.

On 27 June 2001, after long and complicated negotiations the environment chapter was successfully closed. Because of technical complications and the high investments necessary at the initial stage of the negotiations, Lithuania asked for eight transitional periods.

After many contacts with responsible ministries, interest groups, and the EC some transitional periods were reconsidered or withdrawn (such as those related to directives regulating nitrates, landfills, and drinking water). Transition periods were finally agreed: until 2007 on the implementation of the directive on packaging and packaging waste, until 2010 on the directive on waste water treatment; and until 2008 on the directive on volatile organic compounds.

In autumn 2002, Lithuania reopened this chapter, linking it to the negotiations on the decommissioning of Ignalina nuclear power plant, and negotiated another transitional period until the beginning of 2016 with respect to emissions control from the combustion plants in Vilnius, Kaunas, and Mažeikiai electric power stations.

By the end of the Swedish presidency, Lithuania managed to conclude the negotiations on eleven chapters (no other candidate country had the luck to manage such a feat) and opened negotiations on all chapters, thus making considerable progress. In June 2001, Lithuania concluded the negotiations in eighteen chapters and caught up with the Luxembourg group countries (Cyprus and Hungary—twenty-two Chapters, Slovenia—twenty, the Czech Republic and Estonia—nineteen). It was at this time clear that the 'big bang' scenario was becoming increasingly likely.

By the beginning of the Belgian presidency, the accession negotiations had already reached the point where the more complicated chapters were beginning to be addressed. Among them was the chapter on the free movement of persons and the transport policy.

The chapter on the free movement of persons presented several political challenges because some EU Member States (Germany, Austria, and Finland) requested a derogation in order to restrict for a seven-year period the movement of workers from the new EU states. The initial position of the Commission to this request, based on a five-plus-two transitional period, was met with great disappointment from the candidate countries.

The Lithuanian position was that the 'four freedoms' were a vital principle of the Union, and that each country should be individually treated. Lithuania, with a comparatively small population, is not a threat to the EU labour market.

The EU common position was eventually based on the more flexible formula 2+3+2, allowing Member States to choose whether they were going to apply any transitional arrangement. Lithuania urged the Member States not to apply any transitional periods, or to conclude bilateral agreements with Lithuania allowing a more immediate opening of the labour market. The Prime Minister also wrote to the fifteen EU states urging them to open their labour markets.

Lithuania eventually agreed to the EU proposal on 28 November 2001, after Denmark, Sweden, the Netherlands, the United Kingdom, and Ireland declared they were ready to completely open their labour markets to Lithuanian workers, upon Lithuanian accession to the EU.

The negotiations on the transport policy chapter during the second half of 2001 were also important. After prolonged discussions, three transitional periods were granted to Lithuania. However, EU Member States requested a transitional period on cabotage (transport services within the boundaries of another Member State) based on a formula 2+2+1 formula. Since the EU request did not contradict the Carriers' Association of Lithuania interests, it was accepted.

Apart from the above-mentioned chapters, Lithuania also concluded the negotiations on the chapters on competition policy, customs union, and financial control in the second half of 2001.

Negotiations on competition policy did not present a big challenge to Lithuania, mainly because the EU recognized the considerable progress made in legal harmonization and administrative practice.

The chapter on customs union was provisionally closed after progress was made in the approximation of legal acts and the fight against smuggling. The closure of the chapter on financial control was conditioned upon the implementation of the financial internal audit system in state institutions. It particularly concerned the system of internal audit, which we introduced for the first time.

During the Belgian presidency we closed five more chapters, bringing the overall number to twenty-three, placing Lithuania amongst the front runner candidate countries.

The final and decisive stage of the negotiations (2002)

The Spanish presidency started at a moment when negotiations were about to be opened on some of the most complicated chapters, and as the preparations for the final stages of the accession process were being streamlined. Our negotiation tactics were represented by the 'Barcelona action plan'.

The starting point came with the European Commission's communication on 30 January 2002, discussing the 'financial negotiation package' which covered agriculture, the regional policy, the budget, and the issues of nuclear energy.

Lithuania's official position on the communication from the European Commission defined the following objectives:

1. On agriculture, to seek to receive as large as possible direct payments to farmers and to reduce the length of the transitional period for direct payments until 2006; to achieve a flexible use of 1990–2000 production data

for calculating production quotas taking into consideration the specificity of Lithuanian agriculture.

2. Concerning the Ignalina nuclear power plant, the dates of decommissioning to be directly related to reliable sources of financing the decommissioning costs, given that the EU financial assistance must be long term, provided in a separate EU budget line, and in addition to the EU structural assistance provided for Lithuania; obligations of both negotiating parties to become a part of the Accession Treaty.
3. The capping (4 per cent of the gross domestic product) rule applied to the EU structural assistance must be reviewed in 2007 and not applied to the assistance allocated by the EU to decommissioning of Ignalina nuclear power plant.
4. To seek a transitional period for Lithuania's payments into the EU budget.

On 21 March 2002, Lithuania provisionally closed the chapter on taxation. The main discussion was concentrated around the issue of the introduction of the minimum of the EU excise duty for tobacco products. Lithuania requested a transitional period until 1 October 2009 because of the huge difference between the minimal EU and the local rate (57 per cent against 30 per cent). The main arguments were related to the fact that a rapid increase in the excise duties would cause a price increase and lead to adverse socio-economic consequences, that it would lead to an intensification of smuggling from Russia and Belarus where prices are much lower, and to a possible fall in the revenues of the national budget. The European Commission's proposal for a three-year transitional period was rejected by Lithuania at an earlier stage in 2001.

Taking into account the new EU directive on the excise duty on tobacco products (with major increase), Lithuania presented its new position: a transitional period until 2012. After additional negotiations the transitional period until 2010 was agreed.

In this chapter Lithuania was also seeking a transitional period for the excise duty on diesel fuel until 1 January 2008. As a result of the constructive dialogue with the EU, Lithuania amended its position and abandoned the request for a transitional period. At the same time, it retained the right to compensate for the excise burden in such spheres as agriculture and railway transport provided that such compensation measures complied with the requirements for granting state aid.

During the 22 April 2002 accession conference, the negotiations on the chapter pertaining to justice and home affairs were concluded. The issues regarding the transit traffic to Kaliningrad were left for a later decision (see section on negotiations on Kaliningrad transit). The negotiations on the chapter pertaining to institutions were also concluded, as the provisions of the Nice Treaty were fully acceptable to Lithuania.

On 11 June 2002 Lithuania and the EU reached a principal agreement over the Ignalina nuclear power plant, making possible the closure of the energy chapter (see more in section on negotiations on Ignalina NPP).

The chapter on regional policy was also closed, apart from an agreement on the amount of the EU Structural Funds and the Cohesion Fund to be allocated to

Lithuania. In this chapter, Lithuania explicitly stated that financial assistance for the decommissioning of the Ignalina nuclear power plant must be regarded separately from the EU Structural Funds and the Cohesion Fund.

The negotiations on the agriculture chapter (veterinary and phytosanitary issues) were also concluded. Having in mind the special attention to the issues of veterinary and high food safety in the EU, Lithuania tried to find a balanced solution between the standards required and investments needed. Finally, the EU agreed with Lithuania's requests, granting transitional periods until the year 2007 for specified producers under concrete lists of undertakings and needed deadlines.

During the Spanish presidency, five more chapters were provisionally closed, although some of the most complicated aspects of these chapters (energy, regional policy, and agriculture) remained pending, as did issues relating to finance. These would be dealt with under the Danish presidency.

The final stage of the accession negotiations was concluded under the Danish presidency, culminating in Copenhagen, where the road to accession had started. Symbolically the period of negotiations was referred to as the time 'from Copenhagen to Copenhagen'.

For Lithuania, the Danish presidency marked more than the concluding phase of the accession process; this was a particularly decisive moment, because several residual (and difficult) issues like the decommissioning of the Ignalina nuclear power plant, the Kaliningrad transit traffic, and agriculture quotas were to be agreed on at this time. We had a clear understanding of the importance of timely and balanced solutions. Denmark has always been amongst the stronger supporters of the EU enlargement and we reasonably expected this to be once again confirmed during its presidency.

The final stage of negotiations, apart from those agreements that were reached among the EU Member States themselves, was organized in a rather informal way, based on a series of 'confessionals'. In fact, it was a good format for an informal, open, but necessary exchange of views between the delegations.

The Lithuanian delegation arrived for the first 'confessional' on 4 November 2002 with a very heavy negotiation package. Apart from the two horizontal issues of payments to the EU budget and agriculture (direct payments and quotas), we still had three 'sweets': the Ignalina nuclear power plant, Kaliningrad transit, and a transitional period for the sale of agricultural land to foreigners. The issue had been closed, and subsequently reopened as the new Lithuanian government decided to renegotiate a seven-year transitional period on the sale of agricultural land to foreigners.

The reaction of Denmark and the European Commission was that Lithuania should be realistic and reassess the requests submitted. After the first confessional, the positions of all sides remained evidently distant and it took several meetings, on 11 and 26 November and 2 December on a chief negotiator level and 9 December 2002 on a ministerial level, and many more contacts to settle these issues. The most significant questions were solved, however, and agreement was finally reached.

Lithuania had always maintained that that the payment contributions to the EU budget could result in considerable deficit in Lithuania's budget and the loss of macroeconomic stability, and that this issue was of vital importance, and should therefore be resolved by temporarily reducing payments into the EU budget. Lithuania's renewed position from 25 April 2002 stated the request for a seven-year transitional period for payments into the EU budget (the communication of the EC from January 2002 proposed no transitional periods at all) and an additional waiver on the United Kingdom rebate. We also requested that the direct EU assistance to cover the expenses of decommissioning the Ignalina nuclear power plant would not be included in the calculation of the net balance.

After the publication of the revised methodology for assessing the net balance by the European Commission, Lithuania argued that the Commission's methodology did not address the structural accession-related budgetary problems of the candidate countries.

From September 2002 Lithuania's position was based on three major principles: no contribution to the United Kingdom's rebate in 2004, a request to the EU to transfer direct payments in the year for which they are allocated in the EU budget and to improve the EU financial proposal. With these conditions satisfied, Lithuania was ready to abandon its requests for a transitional period on payments to the EU budget and would agree with budgetary compensations offered by the Commission.

The Lithuanian budgetary position improved after the EU offer to allocate additional funding for the protection of the new EU border on the east (through the Schengen programme) and to reduce contributions of the new Member States to the EU budget (by applying the *pro rata* principle). Furthermore, Lithuania and the EU reached an agreement on additional assistance of €75 million to finance expenses of decommissioning the Ignalina nuclear power plant (see Table 12).

A comparative assessment of the final financial positions of the candidate countries would show that Lithuania tops the list in terms of EU financial

Table 12. EU financial assistance to Lithuania, 2004–2006 (commitment appropriations)

	€m.	€/ca
1. Agriculture	724.8	209.1
Market measures	138.5	39.9
Direct payments	152.1	43.9
Rural development	434.2	125.2
2. Structural actions	1,366.0	394.0
Structural fund	822.5	237.2
Cohesion fund	543.5	156.8
3. Internal policies	538.6	155.4
Existing policies	92.2	26.6
Nuclear safety	285.0	82.2
Institution building	25.7	7.4
Schengen	135.7	39.1
4. Compensations	47.4	13.7
Total:	2,676.7	772.1

Source: The database of the European Committee, www.euro.lt

assistance per capita, if the Ignalina decommissioning assistance is included, and is second to Estonia if it is excluded.

On 13 December 2002, the Copenhagen European Council made no major corrections to the Lithuanian negotiation package. Lithuania, like the other candidate states, was given the right to use a part of the EU and national budgetary funds allocated to rural development to 'top up' direct payments to their farmers. A transitional period of five and a half years was agreed upon on Lithuanian payments into the European Investment Bank. Lithuania additionally received €12.6 million to its cash flow facility regulating the budgetary flows.

Leaving the Copenhagen Summit, the Lithuanian delegation returned home with a historic message: our country has managed to complete one of its most significant strategic goals, thanks to an attitude that sought solid results and enhanced confidence.

The negotiation agreements and settlements were scrupulously transposed into the Accession Treaty, which was signed in Athens on 16 April 2003.

5. SPECIFIC NEGOTIATION CHAPTERS

Negotiations on Agriculture

Two major issues—the amount of direct payments and the production quotas of some agriculture products—dominated the EU accession negotiations on agriculture.

Lithuania and the other nine candidate countries sought to receive 100 per cent of EU direct payments from the moment of accession, arguing that the contrary would mark an unacceptable discrimination and would likely lead to possible distortions of competition conditions in the EU market. Concerning production volumes, the candidates argued that they should be allowed to sustain and develop production in separate sectors, ensuring the agricultural sector's production capacity, rural development, and adequate employment.

Agriculture has played an important political, economic, and social role in modern Lithuanian history. In the pre-war period (1918–40), Lithuania was essentially an agrarian state, highly dependent on foodstuff exports to Europe. Later, under the Soviet regime, agricultural production accounted for a significant part of the economy (30 per cent of GDP and 18.5 per cent of total employment in 1990), acting as a secure supplier of foodstuff for the Soviet Union. Because of this role, the infrastructure of the agricultural production and processing industries was well developed.

In 1990, structural changes were initiated, but the loss of the traditional markets and shortage of financial means for development led to a considerable shrinkage of agricultural production and to considerable social decline in rural areas.

Like other candidates, in the negotiations Lithuania continuously tried to exploit the prospect of EU membership to the greatest degree possible.

The negotiation position paper on 'agriculture' stated these main objectives:

(*a*) Incorporation of Lithuania's agro-food sector into the common market;
(*b*) full incorporation of Lithuania's agro-food sector into the EU Common Agricultural Policy, ensuring the application of a uniform and sustainable form of support for agriculture and rural development;
(*c*) ensuring the demanded production output volumes, taking into account the historic production levels, the existing potential, and future production trends;
(*d*) transitional periods and technical adjustments as requested in the present position paper;
(*e*) technical assistance within the framework of the PHARE programme;
(*f*) financial support provided for in EU legislation;
(*g*) participation in the activities of the Standing, Scientific, and Advisory Committees.

The position paper requested that the production volumes for Lithuania be fixed 'ensuring the requested production output volumes, taking into account historic production, the existing potential and future production trends'.

Even while presenting our position paper, we were fully aware of the fact that our calculation method on quotas contradicted the EU definition. The EU chose as a reference period the years 1995–9.

On our side, we used criteria that were based on historic production levels coupled with estimates of the future potential, i.e. our methods were less statistical and more political and economic. The 1995–9 period was one of markedly decreased production levels, due to the ongoing reforms and the Russian crisis. Using the years 1995–9 as a reference period would lead to setting misleadingly low production volumes as a point of reference. Limited possibilities to develop agricultural production could have a very negative impact on the potential increase of farm income and rural welfare. Therefore, we felt obliged to insist on changing the EU methodology for quotas calculations.

In its initial position, Lithuania proposed determining the production quotas on the basis of 'potential' production volumes, taking heed of the trends of production growth rather than the real production volumes within a fixed period. The challenge was to prove that the proposed EU reference period did not reflect Lithuania's changing trends in agriculture, production, and consumption tendencies.

For example, Lithuania wished to establish that the basic yield should be at 3.5 t/ha even though between 1995 and 1999 the average yield was 2.3 t/ha. We justified this request by pointing out that production was expected to rise dramatically because of the ongoing process of concentration of the production of grain in specialized farms, the continuously improving financial position of farms, and the new technologies available for the production of cereals. Fortunately, the requests of the two other Baltic countries, Latvia (3.59 t/ha) and

Estonia (3.5 t/ha), were similar to ours. Similar justifications were made towards other quotas such as milk and sugar.

The most extensive and complicated stage of the negotiations for agriculture coincided with the mid-term review of the CAP reform scheduled for summer 2002, although formally the EU enlargement negotiations and the CAP reform were treated as separate issues. The financing of the enlargement had been agreed on during the Berlin European Council of 25 March 1999; thus the monies for the agriculture package were allocated before the real negotiations had started. Therefore, it was important for the Member States to ensure that the negotiated accession conditions for the application of the CAP reflected certain provisions: no significant increase of the EU agricultural budget; controlled agricultural production; reduction of the expenditures for market measures and an emphasis on rural development in order to continue reducing prices of certain products and bringing them down to world levels; the development of inefficient agricultural sectors of the new Member States to be directed towards the 'future' CAP, with the focus on organic farming, environmental issues, and diversification of business activities, rather than the increase of production volumes; and sustainability of prices.

The EU common position on agriculture for Lithuania was approved on 6 June 2001 and reflected the main principles applied to the Luxembourg group countries. Of course, the position paper made close reference to the general principles and the administrative readiness of Lithuania to implement the CAP. A section on the organization of the common markets (direct payments and quotas) and a section on veterinary and phytosanitary issues were also included. It did not include, however, the final EU provisions concerning direct payments and quotas, since the EU did not yet know when and how many of the candidate countries would be invited to accede to the EU.

On 11 June 2001 the Lithuanian conference on EU accession officially opened negotiations on agriculture.

The real negotiations (concerning direct payments and quotas) started after the European Commission issued the document *Enlargement and Agriculture: Successfully Integrating the New Member States into the CAP* on 30 January 2002. The document, acting as a proposal on behalf of the EU, carried enough weight to create the impetus for an honest discussion, even though it had no obligatory status as an official proposal of the European Union.

The proposal of the European Commission presented concrete suggestions concerning direct payments, quotas, and the financing of rural development. The European Commission proposed gradual introduction of direct payments to the new Member States.[1] The candidate countries were allowed to implement a simplified scheme on direct payments.

Concerning the quotas, the European Commission presented specific proposals, according to which the production volumes were to be determined by the data from the period between 1995 and 1999. The proposals, however,

1 This gradual introduction was based on the following formula: 25% in 2004, 30% in 2005, and 35% in 2006, and later an increase of 10% each year, reaching 100% in 2013.

allowed the candidate countries to select the most favourable years from the said period.

The Government felt that its reaction to this proposal should be measured and timid, as it marked an improvement from the previous position that the EU held, while also allowing Lithuania both to seek a better proposal, and to control the expectations of farmers and other interest groups.

The Lithuanian position on the application of direct payments was as follows: to seek to limit the transition periods for direct payments to the lifespan of this financial perspective; to seek the highest possible level of direct payments so as not to distort competition in agriculture between the existing and new Member States; to try to open the door to the possibility to redistribute the means between the structural assistance to rural development and direct payments; to be allowed to use special market safeguard measures in case of a crisis in the agricultural sector; to introduce milk production cessation schemes and negotiate for EU financial assistance in the application of common organization of the market.

Although the EU showed some understanding of our positions on the matter of direct payments (no doubt applying it horizontally towards all candidates), we at the same time started understanding that there would be little hope to achieve our goals on all issues.

With respect to production quotas, which were a priority issue, we focused our attention on the increase of the basic yield affecting milk and sugar quotas in view of the exceptional situation of the Lithuanian agricultural sector. Such priorities reflected the importance of the crop and dairy sectors for Lithuanian agriculture and the economy in general. Cereals and milk represented the largest agricultural sectors and thus they are economically and socially important.

Given that the arguments presented by other candidate countries proved to be either irrelevant or inadequate for us, we started looking for additional arguments. The only solution was to try to convince the EU to allow Lithuania to apply a flexible methodology for establishing the reference period, different from other candidate countries. After long discussions, and with the appreciated support from our Danish partners, we came with the proposal to apply a 'Baltic specificity' strategy. The main goal of the strategy was to present Lithuania (as well as the other Baltic states) as 'a unique case' and to create the basis for the EC to offer different solutions to Lithuania from other candidate countries. The arguments behind our strategy were the following:

1. Because of the Soviet legacy and the status of ownership rights (private farms did not exist), the structure of agricultural production in the Baltic states was different from other CEEC states. Because of the simultaneous processes of transition from the planned to the market economy and property restitution, the transformation of the Lithuanian agricultural sector was more radical and more profound than elsewhere, and was accompanied by a much more dramatic decline in agricultural production and consumption.
2. The early 1990s brought a disruption of traditional trade flows to the east, while relations with the west had not yet been established. As one of the

more serious consequences of Russia's economic crisis in 1998, trade in foodstuffs was further reduced.

3. During Lithuania's transition to a market economy, structural adjustments and rising unemployment reduced purchasing power and consequently led to lower consumption. The drop was especially pronounced in milk, sugar, and meat. At the time, the per capita food consumption in Lithuania was not more than two-thirds of the level in the EU.

As a reference period for setting the production volumes, Lithuania proposed using the more accurate and more fair years of 1990–2000, thus allowing for a more representative picture of the conditions in agriculture.

In preparation for employing this strategy, we approached our Baltic colleagues and successfully sold the arguments, which were supported and echoed by them. The Commission showed considerably more understanding, but the EC needed more support from the EU Member States and the candidates in order to sell the principle that the Baltic states presented 'an exceptional case' to which a more flexible position in fixing the quotas should be applied.

On 6 June 2002, the EU submitted its renewed common position to Lithuania and other candidate countries, in which it stressed that direct payments are part of the *acquis*, i.e. they have to be granted. With the exception of three cases, the EU position paper established the quotas for Lithuania on the basis of the proposal of the European Commission as of January 2002. It also acknowledged that the exceptional circumstances, such as particularly heavy weather and considerable distortions in the market, created such special conditions that they justified special treatment. The entire effort was corroborated by clear and persuasive evidence proving that such conditions existed in reality.

After the Brussels European Council on 24–5 October 2002, a compromise solution on direct payments and on the issue of quotas seemed to emerge.

At that time, our tactics consisted mainly of repetition and the spread of information in order to emphasize the exceptional situation in the agricultural sector of Lithuania. Additional information simply stated that the country's agriculture suffered 'serious disturbances' in the period from 1995 to 1999. For example, the basic yield in the period between 1990 and 1995 dropped from 3.06 t/ha to 1.86 t/ha. The data provided proved to be enough to convince the EU that the time period between 1995 and 1999 did not reflect 'business as usual' conditions in agriculture, and that, to the contrary, production had dropped to the lowest possible levels. Therefore, production quotas should be determined in view of the increasing production trends and consumption.

On 31 October 2002, the EU submitted one more position paper, which reflected the agreements reached in the Brussels European Council. The new Member States would gradually introduce EU agricultural direct payments between 2004 and 2013. Direct payments would start at 25 per cent in 2004, increase to 30 per cent in 2005 and 35 per cent in 2006, and to 40 per cent in 2007 of the present system. After that, they will increase by 10 percentage points to reach 100 per cent of the then applicable EU level in 2013. The position paper contained minor changes in the proposals on quotas for sugar.

After the position paper was issued, we entered a period of informal meetings, the so-called 'confessionals'. During the first meetings, we repeatedly stressed the argument that Lithuanian farmers should be given the opportunity to compete on equal terms with other producers in the Union. The argument applied to the basic yield, suckler cows, sugar, flax, potato starch, and dry fodder.

An accommodating attitude on behalf of the EC allowed noticeable progress, especially as the production levels of 2000–2001 were used for basic yield, milk, suckler cows, flax, and potato starch. The biggest disagreement was over the sugar quota because of the existence of differing statistics and data on consumption.

The EU proposal of 26 November 2002 represented the final and improved proposal on the basic yield (corresponding to the 2001 levels), milk quota (established milk quota, even excluding the given reserve, substantially exceeded the output of 2001) and the number of suckler cows (10 per cent of the total cattle). The milk quota fixed for Lithuania accounted for around 10 per cent of the total milk quota allocated for all ten new Member States (the local population accounts for 4.6 per cent of the total population of candidate countries).

With some incoming changes on use of the rural development fund for direct payments, the main negotiations were concluded, although some matters related to sugar and the basic yield were still pending.

In general, the outcome of the negotiations on agriculture were favourable for Lithuania. All agreed quotas (except sugar in terms of production, but not consumption) were higher than the recent production volume level of 2001 and 2002. Therefore, we reserved important leeway for a possible increase of production output and successful development of the agricultural and processing sectors. The financial assistance agreed for agriculture is the highest among the ten candidate countries.

Negotiations on Ignalina Nuclear Power Plant

The name of the city of Ignalina, located in the eastern part of Lithuania, became a central focus of the image of Lithuania in the minds of EU experts. The story had started well before Lithuania applied for EU membership, but it got to be a decisive point in the country's efforts to join the EU, and the final agreements on this issue became a focal point for the assessment of the success of our negotiation efforts.

Following the Chernobyl NP disaster, in July 1992 the G-7 declared that the so-called post-Soviet states were individually responsible for the safety of nuclear power plants located in their territory, and offered their assistance to them. For that purpose, a special International Nuclear Power Plants Decommissioning Fund, administered by the European Bank for Reconstruction and Development (EBRD), was established. Once this decision was taken, Lithuania, Bulgaria, and Russia signed separate nuclear safety account (NSA) agreements with the EBRD.

Lithuania signed the NSA agreement with the EBRD in 1994, agreeing to close down both units of INPP when gas gaps in the channels were reduced to the allowable limit. By the same agreement, Lithuania received assistance amounting to 32.8 million ecu to perform nuclear safety supervision and assessment works. Later, this agreement was defined by the EU as an unconditional obligation of Lithuania to close down Unit 1 in 2005 and, taking into account the difference in their age, to close down Unit 2 five years later. Ignalina NPP, using RBMK type reactors, came under the constant eye of the international nuclear safety institutions.

Although some of the potential candidates of the EU had nuclear power installations, the case of INPP was exceptional because it was the only one to employ the same type of reactors as those operating in Chernobyl. Additionally, the INPP supplied about 70–80 per cent of the electricity demand of the country, which significantly complicated the negotiations on its closure.

In the 1997 opinion of the European Commission on Lithuania's preparedness for EU membership, it was pointed out that Lithuania had to adhere to the nuclear safety account agreement and not change fuel channels, which meant that exploitation of Ignalina NPP could not be continued after the expiry of the term for use of the fuel channels. The regular report of 1998 and the accession partnership of 1998 demanded of Lithuania to approve a long-term energy strategy and the plan for decommissioning the Ignalina NPP devised in accordance with the obligations assumed according to the nuclear safety account agreement.

In the beginning of 1999, the European Commission proposed that groups of experts should be set up to consider the issues relating to the decommissioning of the Ignalina nuclear power plant, including possible financial assistance. Lithuania was also offered help in drafting its energy development strategy and assessing the consequences of decommissioning the Ignalina NPP. From Lithuania's point of view, participation in the group activities could not be interpreted to mean that a review of the nuclear safety account agreement was out of the question.

Numerous signals then came from the EU that if Lithuania failed to prepare a plan for decommissioning the Ignalina nuclear power plant by the middle of 1999, at the meeting of the heads of the European Council in Helsinki, the heads of the EU might express a negative opinion on Lithuania's invitation to start the EU accession negotiations.

Consequently, in the midst of 1999, the National Energy Strategy was renewed, thus avoiding short-circuiting any further talks on accession. On 9 September 1999, the initial agreement with the European Commission was announced. According to that agreement, Unit 1 would finally be closed before 2005 and, in line with its closure, Lithuania would receive substantial long-term financial assistance from the EU, the G-7, other states, and international financial institutions. The European Commission related the date for the decommissioning of Unit 2 to the difference in the age of the reactors (five years) and accordingly proposed that it should be finally closed in 2009. Additionally, a decision was made to hold a donor conference in Vilnius where the funds raised from separate institutions and states could be allocated to the preparation of decommissioning Ignalina nuclear power plant.

Accordingly, the Seimas (Parliament) of Lithuania approved on 5 October 1999 the renewed National Energy Strategy, which included the decommissioning of Unit 1 before the year 2005, and which took into consideration the long-term conditions and the substantial financial assistance offered internationally. Additionally, and since the age of Unit 1 and Unit 2 differed, decision on the conditions for closing Unit 2 and the precise date for its final closure were deferred to the renewed National Energy Strategy prepared for 2004, when more accurate information on the performance of Unit 2 would be available.

During the Helsinki European Council held in December 1999, the Member States of the European Union congratulated Lithuania for having adopted the decision on Unit 1 of Ignalina nuclear power plant, and invited Lithuania to start EU membership negotiations.

Following these arrangements, on 30 March 2000, an agreement on the establishment of the decommissioning fund was signed between the European Commission and the EBRD (as the institution responsible for administration of the monies allocated by foreign donors). On 20–1 June 2000, the government of the Republic of Lithuania, in cooperation with the European Commission and the EBRD, held the first donor conference to support closure of Unit 1 of Ignalina nuclear power plant. The result of the conference was €216 million to be spent for the closure of Unit 1 of Ignalina NPP (the largest part of this amount, €165 million, came through the PHARE programme).

The next developments came when the energy chapter was opened on 23 May 2001, in the context of the accession negotiations. Lithuania was duly reminded that it was necessary to take a decision on Unit 2 of the Ignalina NPP earlier than 2004 (in 2002), otherwise Lithuania would not be included in the first wave of EU enlargement. It was also stressed to us that Unit 2 of the Ignalina NPP had to be closed by 2009 at the latest.

At the same time, the EU sought to establish that issues of nuclear safety fall indirectly within the competence of the EU. On 1 July 2001, the Committee of Permanent Representatives (COREPER) approved the report of the EU Group for Atomic Issues and the Nuclear Safety Working Group (NSWG) and the related recommendations to Lithuania on the requirements for nuclear safety. The EU position that Lithuania had to close Unit 2 of Ignalina NPP by 2009 was also reaffirmed.

On 9 July 2001, and in an effort to keep up with the increasing speed of the negotiations, the renewed joint working group of Lithuania and the European Commission met to discuss the opening of energy markets, the dynamics of energy supply and demand, and the interconnection of networks. Additionally, the agenda included economic, environmental, and social costs of decommissioning the Ignalina NPP.

Technical work was followed by high-level meetings, which we treated as instrumental in establishing and maintaining the necessary trust and mutual understanding that existed between the two sides. Exchange of letters between the Prime Minister Algirdas Brazauskas and EU Enlargement Commissioner Günter Verheugen in November 2001 and January 2002 marked another significant point in the negotiations.

The EU Enlargement Commissioner stressed that RBMK type reactors were in essence unsafe due to specific design flaws and that, technically speaking, their safety, even after making certain improvements, could not equate with that of western-type reactors. The Commissioner also underlined the necessity to fix the exact closing date of Unit 2 because it would otherwise be difficult to begin the discussion on the consequences of decommissioning the nuclear power plant, or, for that matter, on arrangements for the financing of the closure of Unit 2. The fact that in his letter the EU Enlargement Commissioner agreed that the issue of Ignalina NPP was important to the entire EU and that it had to be supported by proper external assistance can be regarded as a strong political stimulus for the negotiations and as an important turning point in the position of the EU.

The Prime Minister agreed in January 2002 that the decision on the future of the Ignalina nuclear power plant had to be timed based on the schedule of Lithuania's accession to the EU. That's why the final date of decommissioning Ignalina NPP had to conform to the financing plan and the agreement on financing should be reflected in the EU Accession Treaty of Lithuania. Moreover, he mentioned that the long-term assistance of the Community to finance decommissioning of Ignalina NPP had to supplement the means of the future structural assistance and the funds which had been undertaken to be allocated through the PHARE programme.

On 21 February 2002, the EU adopted the position that Lithuania had to submit a clear and binding confirmation of its commitment regarding the final closure of Unit 1 before 2005, and a clear and binding commitment to close Unit 2 by 2009 at the latest. Fulfilment of these conditions became an official condition for the negotiations on closing the energy chapter, as well as a condition for the final conclusion of the negotiations on decommissioning Ignalina NPP by the autumn of 2002.

Respectively, Lithuania's position was determined by the already established positions on the scope of consequences of decommissioning the Ignalina NPP. Very broad scopes of consequences were considered in the chapters on energy, regional policy and coordination of structural instruments, financial and budgetary provisions, and even in the chapter on other issues. Three major arguments stood behind the position presented by Lithuania:

1. The Ignalina NPP was really unique, it was the only nuclear power plant among the candidate countries that had two RBMK reactors, and it was built in the years of Soviet power and not by Lithuania's own decision.
2. The Ignalina NPP provided about 80 per cent of the domestic needs for electric power.
3. Lithuania is not in a position to undertake the costs of the decommissioning activity and it will require considerable and long-term financial assistance from the EU.

We consistently emphasized that, due to the unique nature of the Ignalina NPP, both a separate and common decision for the entire European Union was necessary. To implement these provisions, Lithuania proposed that the decommissioning of the Ignalina NPP should be financed through a separate programme dedicated to this purpose from a separate line of the EU budget. This financing could not be placed into the 'common stock' of the Structural Funds, or count towards the 4 per cent cap on the gross domestic product (GDP). These considerations led to an exchange of declarations between the EU and Lithuania at the accession conference on 11 April 2002.

The EU Member States recognized that closure of the two 1,500 MW reactors of RBMK type inherited from the former Soviet Union would take Lithuania longer than the present financial perspective foresaw, and that it was an exceptionally heavy financial burden on Lithuania, especially given its size and economic capacity. The EU Member States also stated that they were ready to provide adequate additional assistance through the Community to decommission the Ignalina NPP even after Lithuanian accession to the EU.

Lithuania's declaration stated that it would close Unit 2 of the Ignalina NPP by 2009 with an understanding that the issues of organizing additional EU financial assistance to close Units 1 and 2 of Ignalina NPP after 2006 would have to be addressed at a later stage of the accession negotiations.

Given that the above-mentioned understanding was settled, the Seimas adopted, on 14 May 2002, a resolution proposing to the government to negotiate with the Member States of the EU and the European Commission on the dates for closing Unit 2 of the Ignalina NPP, taking into account the EU proposals on the date and financial conditions of the closure.

Having reached a political understanding, Lithuania presented to the conference on accession on 23 May 2002 additional information on the consequences of closing Units 1 and 2 of the Ignalina NPP and the issues related to their closure. Lithuania also underlined that the requested EU long-term financial assistance, which would help to resolve the problems of the consequences of decommissioning the NPP, should supplement rather than supplant the assistance provided to Lithuania through the Structural Funds and the Cohesion Fund.

The preliminary evaluation of the consequences of decommissioning the Ignalina station was officially presented for the first time during the negotiations as part of the annexe to the additional information, according to which the maximum costs were evaluated at about €800 million for 2004–6. According to Lithuania's evaluation, the total sum of investments from 2002 to 2020 amounted to €2.4 billion (almost half of the country's annual budget of 2002). Negotiations within Agenda 2000 led to an agreement on the indicative costs of decommissioning by 2007, but we insisted on the preferred option of decommissioning by 2020. This option, however, did not meet any support on the side of the EU. Lithuania repeated the main elements of this position during the negotiations on the chapter of financial and budgetary provisions. The consequences of decommissioning Ignalina NPP were broken down in five categories: technical works of decommissioning Ignalina NPP; socio-economic consequences; change of nuclear capacities (necessary renewal of power plants and construction of new co-generation power plants); environmental consequences; and impact on security of supply.

With the above-mentioned developments in the summer of 2002, the negotiations came much closer to a point of conclusion. On 10 July 2002 the government set up a special commission headed by the chief negotiator, charged with negotiating with the EU the programme for organizing additional EU financial assistance to overcome the consequences of closing Units 1 and 2 of the state enterprise Ignalina nuclear power plant. During the technical consultations with the European Commission, we considered and discussed the principles of financial assistance before and after 2006, the adjusted categories of consequences of decommissioning the Ignalina NPP, the instruments available for financial assistance, and other related issues.

During the technical consultations held on 4 November 2002 (i.e. following the meeting of the Prime Minister with the Enlargement Commissioner in the end of October 2002), it was agreed that the financial assistance for decommissioning the Ignalina NPP should continue after 2006. The EC informed Lithuania that on the basis of the agreements concluded in the negotiation chapter on energy, it would begin to prepare a protocol on the Ignalina NPP on the basis of the declarations adopted on 11 June 2002.

During the next meeting on 8 November 2002, in which the chapter on financial and budgetary provisions was discussed, the EU agreed that a special programme should be devised for Lithuania, and recalled the proposal of 30 January 2002 for financial assistance for decommissioning the Ignalina NPP and the declarations of June 2002. The EU negotiators noted that a final agreement would be reached under chapter 31 (other issues).

Keeping apace with developments, Lithuania presented on 13 November 2002 its renewed additional information in the chapters on financial and budgetary provisions and other issues. The new additional information concerned the consequences of decommissioning the Ignalina NPP, dividing them into five categories: the technical aspect of the decommissioning, including the personnel assistance measures relating to the safety of the plant, the investments necessary to change the capacities of the plant, the environmental investments, the security of supply investments, and the economic regeneration of the region. Accordingly, Lithuania requested as much as €376 million in investment funds for the period 2004–6, on the understanding that Lithuanian co-financing could be up to 30 per cent of the total expenses of eligible individual projects.

After the last meeting in late November, it became clear that additional assistance in the form of appropriations for commitments in 2004–6 would amount to €285 million instead of €210 million. The EU representatives also agreed to the proposals of the Lithuanian negotiators to specify the measures which would be financed through the Ignalina programme, and to plan complete financing from the EU budget for separate measures, provided that the offered assistance would be compatible with the rules governing the internal market as per the founding treaty of the European Communities.

The final text of Protocol No. 4 on the Ignalina nuclear power plant in Lithuania, which was part of the Accession Treaty, stated, *inter alia*:

Declaring the Union's willingness to continue to provide adequate additional Community assistance to Lithuania's decommissioning effort also after Lithuania's accession to the European Union for the period until 2006 and beyond, and noting that Lithuania, bearing in mind this expression of Union solidarity, has committed to close Unit 1 of the Ignalina Nuclear Power Plant before 2005 and Unit 2 by 2009,

Recognizing that the decommissioning of the Ignalina Nuclear Power Plant with two 1500 MW RBMK-type reactor units inherited from the former Soviet Union is of an unprecedented nature and represents for Lithuania an exceptional financial burden not commensurate with the size and economic strength of the country, and that this decommissioning will continue beyond the Community's current Financial Perspective,

The Ignalina Programme shall, inter alia, cover: measures in support of the decommissioning of the Ignalina Nuclear Power Plant; measures for the environmental upgrading in line with the acquis and modernization measures of conventional production capacity to replace the production capacity of the two Ignalina Nuclear Power Plant reactors; and other measures which are consequential to the decision to close and decommission this plant and which contribute to the necessary restructuring, environmental upgrading and modernization of the energy production, transmission and distribution sectors in Lithuania as well as to enhancing the security of energy supply and improving energy efficiency in Lithuania.

For the period 2004–2006 the Ignalina Programme shall amount to €285 million in commitment appropriations, to be committed in equal annual tranches.

Without any prejudice to the provisions of Article 1, the general safeguard clause referred to in Article 37 of the Act of Accession shall apply until 31 December 2012 if energy supply is disrupted in Lithuania.

The negotiations on the Ignalina NNP provided an excellent test case for Lithuania's negotiating and administrative ability and cooperation with socio-economic partners, while also acting as a test of the level of trust existing between Lithuania and the EU on sensitive issues.

Lithuania achieved these results by using a well-balanced strategy, and was able to resolve one of the most complicated issues of the negotiations, providing a solid ground for financing the decommissioning of the Ignalina NPP. At the same time, Lithuania avoided unnecessary politicization of the situation. The results of the negotiations on the Ignalina NPP were evidently successful, especially when compared with the outcomes of similar negotiations involving Slovakia and Bulgaria.

Negotiations on the Kaliningrad transit traffic

Negotiations on Kaliningrad transit represented another special case in Lithuania's accession talks with the European Union. The issues relating to this matter marked new ground in the history of the enlargement, as it touched upon relations with, and the territorial, political, and economic interests of, a third country.

Geographically, the Kaliningrad region (oblast), the former Königsberg, or East Prussia, today is a Russian enclave with about one million inhabitants located between Lithuania and Poland. Under Soviet rule, the Kaliningrad oblast was simply another part of the Soviet Union.

With Lithuanian independence, and later accession to the EU, regional geopolitics was radically altered, however. The accession negotiations sought to come to terms with a modus vivendi that would acknowledge the new situation and settle the practical issues that had arisen in relation to transit from mainland Russia to the Kaliningrad enclave.

Until 1 January 2003, the transit of citizens of the Russian Federation through the territory of Lithuania was regulated under the Provisional Agreement on the Travels of Citizens of both states, signed on 24 February 1995 in Moscow. Citizens of one state needed to acquire a visa in order to enter or leave the territory of the other state, to travel by transit through that territory, or to stay there on a temporary basis.

The Provisional Agreement provided for two essential exceptions: first, that no visas were required for the citizens of the Russian Federation residing in the Kaliningrad region on a permanent basis to enter Lithuania, travel through it by transit, and stay in its territory for a maximum of thirty days; second, no visas were required for the citizens of the Russian Federation travelling through the Lithuanian territory from the Russian Federation to the Kaliningrad region and back by direct trains. The agreement was reciprocal: no visas were required from Kaliningrad residents entering Lithuania or from Lithuanian citizens entering the Kaliningrad region. Lithuania was the only country that established a special border-crossing regime for residents of the Kaliningrad enclave: other neighbouring countries applied common visa regime facilitations to all citizens of the Russian Federation.

It should be noted that the special border-crossing regime applied for the Kaliningrad residents under the 1995 Lithuanian–Russian agreement was a demonstration of Kaliningrad importance in the Lithuanian regional foreign policy.

The issue of civil transit to and from the Kaliningrad region came as a spin-off effect of EU enlargement in respect of the third country—Russia; therefore, it involved Russia besides the traditional parties in the EU accession negotiations, a candidate country (Lithuania) and the EU. The unusual complexity of these negotiations can be seen in the stages that followed: during the first phase, Lithuania and the EU in accession negotiations aligned their positions on the justice and home affairs chapter; during the second phase (international negotiations), a political settlement between Russia and the EU was reached under the partnership and cooperation agreement between Russia and the EU; during the third phase (tripartite negotiations) Lithuania, Russia, and the EU agreed on the practical implementation of the agreement.

The negotiations on the justice and home affairs chapter (hereinafter the JHA chapter) were opened on 27 June 2001. The chapter itself involved a very broad range of issues and aspects, but, at the same time, involved relatively few legal acts in terms of transposing the *acquis*. The negotiations on this chapter concentrated more on the implementation of the legal acts and obligations undertaken, especially those related to administrative capacities and considerable financial expenditures.

Emphasizing its understanding of the importance of regional cooperation, Lithuania explicitly accepted its obligation to change (or cancel) provisional agreements between Lithuania and Belarus, Lithuania and the Ukraine, as well as Lithuania and Russia (concerning the Kaliningrad region) on the travel of citizens of both states and facilitated crossing of borders by border zone residents. This cancellation also involved the introduction of a visa regime. On its side, in the first common position, announced on 22 June 2001, the EU urged Lithuania to make every effort so that alignment of the visa policy with the *acquis* could be completed before the date of EU accession.

Lithuania maintained the position that the solution to the issue should retain a travel regime between Lithuania and Russia that would be as flexible as possible, rather than narrowly focusing on the particular issue of transit.

On 22 January 2001, Lithuania proposed to Russia to amend the provisional agreement on the travelling of citizens it had signed in the past with Russia, so that it could comply with the EU *acquis* requirements and to introduce in the meantime a facilitated visa-issuing procedure for residents of the Kaliningrad region (in addition to invitations, providing for 50 per cent cheaper multiple entry visas). In summer 2001, Lithuania's non-paper on the visa-free regime proposal for the Kaliningrad region was submitted to the European Commission.

For a while, increasing understanding on the overall complexity of Kaliningrad transit led to the approval of tactics suggesting that a closing of the JHA chapter would be possible, if the issue of the Kaliningrad region remained open for later discussions. Successful negotiations and the political determination of the EU Member States led to a provisional closing of the JHA chapter on 22 April 2002 without the transitional periods, exceptions, or changes in relation to Lithuania's commitment to harmonize its visa policy with the EU *acquis* until the end of 2003 (alongside the introduction of a visa regime with Belarus, Ukraine, and Russia (Kaliningrad region), in line with the Schengen requirements). A solution to the Kaliningrad conundrum was therefore postponed for a later stage.

Russian efforts to form a separate agreement for securing Kaliningrad interests in the context of the enlargement became visible even before the invitation to start accession talks was extended to Lithuania. The EU also interpreted the Kaliningrad issue as a part of its external policy towards Russia, although it avoided making a special case of it.

In October 2000, Russia submitted to the European Union a 'Letter of Concern' in reference to the implications that the enlargement of the EU would potentially have for the Kaliningrad region. In it, Russia emphasized the vital need to ensure free movement of persons, goods, and services between Kaliningrad and the rest of Russian territory by air, land, and water through Lithuania, Poland, Latvia, and 'possibly territories of other neighbouring EU countries' after the enlargement took place. The Russian government also requested adequate financial support for the region in order to avoid the opening of a socio-economic gap between

Kaliningrad and the neighbouring states and to compensate for the negative effects of EU expansion into the Baltic Sea region.

On 17 January 2001, the European Commission approved the communication 'The EU and Kaliningrad', accepting that due to the unique geographical location of Kaliningrad (also noting that Kaliningrad was an integral part of Russia) enlargement implications for the region might be more significant compared to other regions of Russia and other third countries. The Commission, however, underlined its position that there could be no exceptions from the *acquis* for Kaliningrad: Kaliningrad would have to be subject to the common visa and border control regime. The Commission proposed that problems arising from the movement of persons should be solved using technical facilitations allowed by the *acquis*, namely by issuing long-stay multiple entry visas, setting low prices for these visas, establishing new consular institutions, and streamlining the work of border-crossing posts. The European Commission also committed itself to analysing the likely effects of the *acquis* on the transit of persons to and from the Kaliningrad region and the possibilities to apply special mechanisms permitted by the *acquis*.

On 6 March 2001, Russia issued its amended position to the EU, stating that Russian citizens not residing in Kaliningrad had to be permitted to travel by rail, bus, or private vehicles through the territories of Lithuania, Poland, and Latvia (via highways agreed in advance) without visas (issuing free Schengen visas for the period of one year).

On 19 March 2001, Sergey Ivanov, the Russian Foreign Minister, presented to the European Commission the Russian official response to the Commission's proposals. The analysis stressed Moscow's concern not only over the border-crossing regime for Kaliningrad residents, but also over the travel of other Russian citizens to and from the Kaliningrad region. The document advocated the introduction of a simplified procedure for issuing national Lithuanian and Polish visas (and possibly Schengen visas) for permanent residents of the Kaliningrad region and reiterated the proposals of 6 March relating to the visa regime for Russian citizens travelling in transit through these countries.

In April 2001, further elaborating the existing proposals, the Russian government presented to the European Commission a memorandum on practical ways of realizing the idea of 'corridors' to ensure transit of goods and persons from and to the Kaliningrad region by highways and railways through the territories of Lithuania and Poland.

The European Commission's and the candidate countries' reaction to Russia's position was that it constituted an indication that the only possible way of reaching settlement was to improve border-crossing posts and apply a reasonable level of flexibility on the visa regime permitted by the *acquis*.

It took almost a year of exchanging interpretations and pressures until on 13 May 2002 the General Affairs Council approved a common line supposed to become the bottom line in the talks with Russia. The common position stated that residents of third countries (list provided by the Council Regulation EC 539/2001) must bear visas in their valid travel documents when crossing the borders of the EU Member States (also when travelling through such territories in transit). But until membership in the Schengen agreement, national visas will be issued by Lithuania (and other candidates) to residents of third countries; this meant that multiple entry and free or low-price visas could be provided, and specific exceptions could be established, in special cases, such as for the staff of diplomatic missions.

From this time on, the pressure that Russia exerted on the Member States and the European Commission was constantly on the increase. The Russian side strongly rejected any agreement that would regulate the travel arrangements of its citizens to another part of its territory, asking for a completely automatic issue of the travel permits at the border.

In the face of such Russian resistance the EU position started to waver. Various proposals started floating from different Member States, ranging from the idea of 'sealed' transit trains, to special transit documents issued at the border, and, finally, to creating a visa-free corridor. All these proposals were in clear contradiction to the existing Schengen *acquis*, and could lead to high costs of implementation. They were, therefore, politically unacceptable to Lithuania.

The situation became more clear after, on 18 September 2002, the European Commission announced a communication on 'Kaliningrad: Transit', proposing a three-stage strategy for solving the Kaliningrad transit issue:

1. The first stage foresaw cancellation of the visa policy privileges valid until then and the issuing of facilitated transit documents (FTD), corresponding to multiple entry transit visas, for travelling by highways and railways. The Russian authorities would provide a list of persons frequently travelling by transit, with the consulates of the candidate countries reserving the right to take the final decision.
2. During the second stage, the EU would be ready to reconsider the idea of fast non-stop visa-free trains after Lithuania's accession to the EU. Any decision on this issue could only be made after carrying out a comprehensive analysis and eliminating technical obstacles, and with legal guarantees that, after implementation of the above proposals, Lithuania would not be prevented from joining the Schengen agreement.
3. The third stage would begin with the possible abolishment of the visa regime between the EU and Russia (the EC made a positive assessment on Russia's appropriate proposal from August 2002), linking it to the progress achieved in cooperation in the fields of fighting illegal migrants and crime.

Our reaction to the EC communication concentrated on the requested set of guarantees that Lithuania would not be prevented from becoming a member of the Schengen zone as soon as possible and that the new regime would not result in an additional financial burden for the country. We also concentrated on the need for horizontal instruments proposed by the EU. Any studies related to the introduction of visa-free trains could only be conducted by Lithuania after accession. The first Russian reaction to the EU proposal was completely negative, calling it unacceptable, even though, in principle, the EC communication took aboard many of the initial proposals expressed earlier by Russia.

On 30 September 2002, the General Affairs and External Relations Council supported the European Commission's proposals and, under pressure from France, Spain, Italy, and Greece, there was a strong insistence that the feasibility study for visa-free transit by non-stop fast trains should be commenced immediately and that the preparation of this study should be concluded before enlargement took place. The decision had a direct connection to the possible changes of the Schengen agreement over the specific situation of Kaliningrad. At the same time, the necessity for granting political and legal guarantees to Lithuania, of avoiding a delay in the country's accession to the scheme agreement, was highlighted. In October 2002, the negotiations entered a final stage, even while the new Russian proposals, on visa-free transit by rail were still being prepared.

On 25 October, the European Council approved the decision of the General Affairs Council and agreed to include in Lithuania's accession treaty specific guarantees that stipulated that, first, the EU would provide financial support to Lithuania for covering any additional costs related to solution of the Kaliningrad transit and, that, secondly, a decision concerning visa-free transit by non-stop fast trains would be made only after Lithuania's accession to the EU materialized. The EU also committed itself to providing support to Lithuania during its preparation to join the Schengen zone and, thus, to ensure that Lithuania would be among the first new EU members to join the Schengen agreement.

The final agreement on the Kaliningrad transit was reached on 11 November 2002, when Russia and the EU signed the joint statement on transit between the Kaliningrad region and other parts of the Russian Federation. The agreement introduced two types of facilitated transit documents as of 1 July 2003: facilitated transit documents (FTDs), to be issued at Lithuanian consulates to the Russian citizens frequently travelling through the Lithuanian territory from and to the Kaliningrad region, and facilitated rail transit documents (FRTDs) to be issued to Russian citizens travelling through the Lithuanian territory to and from the Kaliningrad region by trains. These documents will be provided on the basis of the personal data submitted when acquiring train tickets and they will be issued by the Lithuanian institutions located at the borders. The EU also reiterated its intentions to approve a decision on commencing the feasibility study for visa-free transit by non-stop fast trains in 2003, after agreeing with Lithuania on the terms of reference for this study.

In its turn, Russia committed to conclude the readmission agreement with Lithuania, to commence negotiations on signing the readmission agreement with the EU, and to approve the development of Lithuanian consulates in Kaliningrad.

The official Lithuanian reaction towards the final agreement between Russia and the EU was reserved, focusing on further results to be reached after its implementation mechanism became agreed upon, as well as the entire package of legal and financial guarantees supporting the Accession Treaty. At the same time, we remained reserved in anticipation of the results of the implementation of Russia's obligations. Having had a good deal of experience in relations with Russia, Lithuania preferred to study the practical results before assessing the agreements reached.

An important aspect of implementation was related to financial requirements. According to Lithuania's estimates, in 2003 the expenses for implementation of the FTD/FRTD scheme could stand near €9.8 million, and close to €27 million in 2004–6. To this should be added an additional annual cost of €7.5 million for lost Lithuanian consular fees (the agreed EU support for implementing the Kaliningrad transit scheme during the period 2004–6 amounts to €40 million).

The EU commitments to cover any additional costs relating to the implementation of the Kaliningrad transit were verified in the European Council meeting of Copenhagen on 13 December 2002, when the EU accession negotiations were concluded, with the inclusion of the agreed draft protocol and a declaration as annexes to the Accession Treaty. Moreover, the agreement foresaw the adoption of the new *acquis* on the Kaliningrad transit (in consultation with Lithuania) before signing the Accession Treaty.

After additional consultations on 14 April 2003, the EU approved the regulations on facilitated transit and made the simplified procedure for transit between the two regions of the third country part of the Schengen *acquis*. In June 2003, the bilateral agreement between Lithuania and Russia on the procedure for issuing facilitated rail transit documents was signed. Later, in May–June 2003, Russia fulfilled its remaining obligations assumed under the joint statement.

The complicated and long negotiations on the Kaliningrad transit resulted in the new procedure for Kaliningrad transit for Russian citizens, which came into effect on 1 July 2003. In these unusual negotiations, Lithuania succeeded in achieving its major goals and received the maximum set of EU guarantees, along with support for further regional cooperation with the Kaliningrad region.

6. INFORMATION CAMPAIGN AND THE REFERENDUM

The campaign for the referendum on EU membership was planned and implemented as a more intensive effort to provide information to the public than had been the case in earlier stages of the accession process. The efforts to provide information about Euro-integration started in early 1999, when the foundation was laid for the system of cooperation between the governmental information sources, for more coherent relationships between governmental bodies and the mass media, and for the establishment of a network of European information centres in the various countries.

A second stage of the information campaign developed between 2000 and 2002, in parallel to the EU accession negotiations. During that period, a network of dissemination of information on Euro-integration was established (and subsequently further extended), the geography of cooperation with the mass media was expanded, and various projects on the provision of information were carried out in the regions. The referendum campaign coincided with a third stage in the efforts to provide accurate information to the public. During this final phase, the aim was to familiarize the public with the results of the accession negotiations, to maintain the current, sufficiently high, level of public support for Lithuania's EU membership, and, as was natural, to promote an affirmative result in the referendum itself.

The Law on Referendums establishes that mandatory referendums shall be held on the amendments of four articles of the constitution of the Republic of Lithuania and the Constitutional Act, as well as on the participation of the Republic of Lithuania in international organizations, provided that this participation is related to partial handing over of the competence of the Lithuanian state to the institutions of international organizations and their jurisdiction.

In trying to run a successful campaign that would take due notice of the realistic expectations that society had with regard to integration and membership in the EU, we widely used information acquired through sociological surveys, conducted by the European Committee on a monthly basis, starting in 1998.

The increasing trend in the public support for EU membership became particularly visible once the country was invited to start negotiations at the beginning of 2000. When the referendum campaign started, in February 2003, the opinion polls showed that 63.9 per cent of the respondents would vote in favour of Lithuania's membership in the European Union, 14.7 per cent would vote against it, and 21.4 per cent would abstain. As the campaign intensified, in March, the rates showed that 65.5 of the respondents supported EU membership, 13.3 per cent were against it, and 21.2 per cent would abstain. During the last month before the referendum, EU membership was supported by 66.3 per cent of the population of the country, with 13.3 against it and 20.4 per cent undecided.

With the information campaign gathering momentum, the number of people who were firmly determined to take part in the referendum increased. In February 2003, 52.5 per cent of the respondents really intended to participate in the referendum on EU membership. In April, that figure rose to 58.8 per cent.

There were two major objectives of the referendum campaign: to seek public approval of the country's membership of the EU and to raise the level of knowledge of the public about Lithuania's preparation for EU membership.

Those who supported our accession to the EU were mainly young people (in the age group of 18–29 years their number accounted for 61.2 per cent), people with higher education (64.2 per cent), those who earned higher income (70.5 per cent), and businessmen (69.2 per cent). The fact that the number of supporters of membership was so large showed that, in essence, what was necessary was to ensure their active participation in the referendum and to concentrate on the rural population.

The rural population, ethnic minorities, socially sensitive groups, the youth, managers, and employees of large undertakings were chosen as specific target groups, based on their particular interests and the influence they exert in the formation of opinions among the general public.

The referendum of schoolchildren, held on 29 April, in which pupils of the fifth to twelfth forms voted, generated great interest from the public. The referendum was conducted on the initiative of the schoolchildren's organization. More than 70 per cent of the schoolchildren participated in the referendum and it was held in more than 900 schools all over Lithuania. The results of the referendum were convincing: 83.31 per cent of the schoolchildren approved of Lithuania's membership of the EU, 14.82 per cent were against it.

In the run-up to the referendum, over 3 million copies of publications were prepared and disseminated. It can be stated that, having purposefully chosen main audiences and prepared specialized publications, we managed to reach a very large part of society, and particularly people residing in small towns and villages. A large part of the publications were disseminated during the 'Eurobus' action, in direct meetings with the public.

The 10–11 May 2003 referendum in Lithuania was conducted after the successful referendums in Malta, Slovenia, and Hungary, in which a range of 54 to 93 per cent of the population approved of EU membership, with a turnout that yielded a valid result.

When the voting results started came in, they painted a surprisingly good picture: with a turnout of 63.37 per cent, 91.07 per cent of the voters voted in the affirmative. This was the final victory of the campaign. After summing up both indicators, the voting activity and the amount of support, it became clear that Lithuania was the first among all the nine states which had conducted the referendum to approve the EU membership so strongly.

7. CONCLUSIONS AND LESSONS

The successful conclusion of the accession negotiations of Lithuania was made possible only because of a strong and unwavering internal political determination and a clear negotiation strategy during the most decisive times. The EU established the negotiating priorities, with the European Commission playing a major role. Also, we should admit that the EU negotiation strategy was also very helpful, yielding a positive outcome; the European Commission, in particular, played a very significant role.

For Lithuania, the end game at the Copenhagen Summit marked the validity of the 'catch-up' principle, and the meaningful implementation of a 'big bang' strategy. Lithuania caught up with the candidate countries that had started the negotiations two years earlier. This was neither easy, nor simple. This breakthrough became possible only because the long-term objective of fast EU membership overtook short-term interests.

The general dynamics of the negotiations depended on the EU political will and the negotiating strategy. Because of its late start, Lithuania preferred the high speed of the negotiations, which allowed it to become part of the core group of enlargement. Lithuania's negotiators saw the accession negotiations and the integration into the EU as a tool for necessary domestic reforms and modernization of the country, as well as for the establishment of best practices and a chance to push the country forward. The accession negotiations also became a good basis for establishing and expanding bilateral cooperation between Lithuania and the

Member States. We got to know each other; we created a network of contacts, which is extremely useful once you are a member of the club.

The Lithuanian strategy was based on focusing attention on the major issues of the negotiations; this proved to be both efficient and successful. The early agreement on the priorities of the negotiations made possible a flexible stance and a sense of autonomy among the members of the negotiating team.

It should be added that, in Lithuania, negotiating priorities were usually determined as a result of the interaction of the team of negotiators with the main political players of the country. The negotiating priorities were quite clearly defined at the beginning of the negotiations, and were often sustained during the negotiation process.

Thanks to dedicated and efficient work of many colleagues from the European Committee under the Government of Lithuania, other experts from different institutions, on one side, and our partners from the European Commission and the Council, on another, we were able to accomplish accession negotiations.

I wish as well to highlight the contribution of our long-term experts, whose efforts made it possible for us to stay on the right track: Walter Kittel, former state secretary of the Ministry of Economy (Germany); Henrik Shmiegelow, former head of the EC delegation in Lithuania; Alan Mayhew, Jean Monnet Professor and Professor Fellow; Dietrich von Kyaw, ambassador, former head of the permanent representation of Germany to the EU.

The accession negotiations became a real test for the system for coordinating the integration which had been created. Lithuania, having an advanced, dynamic, and well-structured centralized system, was able to keep a high speed in the negotiations while also sustaining a high quality of information and communication. Because of the overall complexity of the negotiations, the centralized system proved itself in many instances. Most importantly, we had been in a position to combine the outcomes of the negotiation with the management of the implementation process. After the negotiations, surely we all became more aware of the importance of administrative capacity.

The conditions under which Lithuania joined the EU can be regarded as favourable, and they provide a solid basis for the country's social and economic development. We received twenty-two transitional periods relating to the implementation of certain specific EU legal provisions; these require big investments, they are time-consuming, and they are characterized by complicated technical exigencies.

Additionally, it is important to stress the utmost significance of the provision of information to the public about the country's integration into the EU. We have successfully organized the accession referendum and achieved a positive result because of the continuous and intense information campaign that raised public support.

Finally, this chapter owes a debt to the material and valuable contributions presented by my colleagues in the recent book *Lithuania's Road to the European Union: Unification of Europe and Lithuania's EU Accession Negotiations* (Vilnius: Eugrimas, 2005).

14

The Accession of Malta to the EU

Richard Cachia Caruana

1. INTRODUCTION

Alone among the ten countries that acceded to the European Union on 1 May 2004, Malta faced major internal political controversy over the decision.

Since the Second World War the political landscape has been dominated by two large political groupings: the Partit Nazzjonalista (PN), founded in 1880 to work for Malta's independence from the United Kingdom, and the Malta Labour Party (MLP), which originated in Malta's naval dockyards in the 1920s.

Malta has used a proportional representation system known as the single transferable vote for all its general elections since 1921. Over the years the voters have used this electoral system to create a virtual two-party system. Every elected administration since self-government was reintroduced in 1947 has been led by one of these political groupings and since independence in 1964 administrations have been wholly formed by one of these parties. No third party candidate has, in fact, been elected to Parliament since 1962. Popular participation in elections has been extremely high with the difference in support between the two parties extremely small. In the forty-two years since independence, the government has been formed by the PN for twenty-four of these years (1964–71, 1987–96, and 1998 to date) and by the MLP for the remaining eighteen years (1971–87 and 1996–8).

This de facto two-party system has tended to bring with it a black and white approach to issues by both the electorate and the political parties. This necessarily impacted on attitudes to European Union membership which was a key policy issue before the electorate in the six general elections held following the PN's formal adoption of this policy in 1979. Showing remarkable consistency, the electorate gave the PN an absolute majority of the vote in five of these six elections.[1]

The political controversy over EU membership formed the backdrop of Malta's EU negotiations, affecting the internal processes followed by Malta as well as the positions adopted by it. It continued through the referendum held in March 2003

[1] The PN received over 50% of the vote in the 1981, 1987, 1992, 1998, and 2003 elections; a gerrymandering exercise had, however, prevented it from winning a parliamentary majority in the 1981 elections.

and the general election held five weeks later, as well as through Malta's accession process and first year of membership. The controversy only ended on 6 July 2005, when the Maltese Parliament unanimously voted in favour of the ratification of the treaty establishing a constitution for Europe. From this date, the anti-membership elements were relegated to the fringes of Maltese politics.

2. MALTA'S APPLICATION FOR MEMBERSHIP

A history in common

The Maltese islands are a group of small, barren rocks whose strategic location in the centre of the Mediterranean Sea has ensured them a place in Europe's history totally out of proportion to their size. A centre of religious worship 5,000 years ago, Malta eventually became a home to the great traders known as the Phoenicians and later the warring Carthaginians. Part of the Roman Empire from the third century BCE, it was witness to the rise of Christianity. Like other parts of the declining Roman Empire in the west, Malta became part of the new Germanic kingdoms in the fifth century CE. It was later incorporated into the eastern Roman Empire and captured by the Arabs in the ninth century CE. Malta was part of the southern Norman conquest[2] in the eleventh century CE, later forming part of the Hohenstaufen and Angevin domains until it became part of the Spanish succession in the thirteenth century. In 1530, Emperor Charles V ceded Malta to the Order of St John, a religious order of knights from the Catholic lands of Europe, to defend Europe's southern flank. Successful against the Ottomans in the Great Siege of 1565, the Knights of Malta[3] continued in their military and hospitaller role until being expelled by Napoleon in 1798. The Maltese revolted against French rule that same year and, following the Napoleonic wars, the Treaty of Paris recognized Malta as part of the British Empire in 1814.

Independence

Malta continued in its role as a military and naval fortress during the British period with its economy growing or shrinking in tune with world events. Population growth led to economic pressures and there was major emigration, first to North Africa[4] during the nineteenth and early twentieth centuries and later to North America and Australia with a major exodus to these two parts of the world in the 1950s and 1960s.

[2] One of Malta's national symbols, its flag, is claimed to date from the arrival of Count Roger the Norman in 1091.

[3] The eight-pointed cross, known as the Maltese Cross, came to Malta with the Order of St John.

[4] The large Maltese communities of Algeria, Tunisia, and Egypt moved to France, the United Kingdom, and Australia after the Second World War. Former Commissioner Edgard Pisani was one of such individuals.

Political developments tended to remain subject to military exigencies during the British period and, although the nineteenth century saw the introduction of elected representatives on the Council of Government, it was not until 1921 that full self-government was established. Self-government was, however, suspended at certain times of crisis including war. Malta survived relentless Nazi and Fascist bombardment during the Second World War[5] with extensive damage being caused to its buildings and other infrastructure. Self-government was restored in 1947. A major rebuilding exercise was started and, for the first time, serious consideration began to be given to the economic development of the islands.

While the PN continued to push for independence, in 1955 the MLP proposed integration with the United Kingdom as an alternative. This proposal failed to receive the required support in the 1956 referendum and both major parties prepared for independence. The independence negotiations with the United Kingdom were complicated given the need for economic viability and also considering the acceleration of the Cold War. At that stage, Malta hosted a NATO sub-headquarters in addition to the British naval, air force, and army facilities. Malta achieved independence on 21 September 1964. A ten-year defence and economic aid agreement was put in place with the UK government while the PN government immediately embarked on an industrialization drive and the development of Malta as a tourism destination. Both were necessary in the face of decreasing British military spending in Malta and were ultimately successful.

As part of this process, Malta requested an association agreement with the European Economic Community (EEC) in 1967. Negotiations were held in 1970 and the agreement was signed on 5 December 1970.[6] The ultimate aim of the Maltese government was EEC membership. While the main focus of the agreement was the gradual removal of barriers to trade and the establishment of a customs union, it also established the EEC–Malta Association Council made up of representatives of both sides at the highest political level as well as a Joint Parliamentary Committee. However, unlike the association agreement signed with Turkey seven years before—admittedly when the EEC was still working towards its internal customs union[7] and had not yet decided to move towards economic and monetary union or political union—the Malta association agreement did not include an explicit reference to accession to the Community at a later date.[8] Prime Minister Giorgio Borg Olivier had this to say during the signing ceremony in Valletta:

[5] The George Cross, which forms part of the Maltese flag, was awarded to the Maltese people in recognition of the fortitude shown by them during the Second World War.

[6] This was the third association agreement negotiated by the EEC and followed the 1961 agreement with Greece and the 1963 agreement with Turkey. Association agreements followed with Cyprus in 1972 and Spain and Portugal in 1985.

[7] The EEC's customs union was only completed on 1 July 1968.

[8] Article 28 of Turkey's association agreement: 'As soon as the operation of this Agreement has advanced far enough to justify envisaging full acceptance by Turkey of the obligations arising out of the Treaty establishing the Community, the Contracting Parties shall examine the possibility of the accession of Turkey to the Community.' There is also a preambular reference to accession in the same agreement.

The political significance of our association with the Community lies, for our part, mainly in the establishment of yet another strong link with the democracies of Europe. The association opens a new chapter in Malta's economic and political history during which the earlier bonds forged on common ideals and on shared experiences and sacrifices should, in our view, develop into a partnership of active cooperation and mutual assistance. We are also hopeful that in the course of time it could develop into fuller participation in a united Europe.[9]

The President of the European Commission, Franco Maria Malfatti, replied:

The Agreement is being signed at a very important moment in the construction of Europe. The Community, on its way to maturity, after having completed its customs union and having initiated its common policies, intends now to become an economic and monetary union and consequently a political union. Europe, now conscious of its unity and vocation, is historically well-timed in finding Malta once again at its side, confirming the cultural links and fidelity to one and the same civilization, which have permanently united Malta to Europe, thanks to the constancy and energy of its inhabitants, and at the cost of many sacrifices. ... An Association Agreement is not, of course, a simple trade agreement. It is much more complex and binding, since its aims go beyond the immediate scope of the Agreement. It creates common interests and is therefore a new and dynamic element of international life, since it opens short-term possibilities for a new and more stable organization of our Continent. This is the profound significance of the Agreement we are about to sign, as it will contribute to an economic structure which will enable Malta to realize her European vocation, while it gives the Community the occasion, once again, to be coherent as an integrated but nevertheless open entity. Ambitious in its long-term outlook, this Agreement is realistic in its options. It corresponds to the Community's present possibilities, which in the main still concern trade and takes into account Malta's competitive situation, permitting its adaptation through progressive actions which will have to be accomplished during a first stage, in full respect of the individuality and equality of the rights and obligations of the Contracting Parties. ... The will of Malta to be always more closely associated with the European Community may thus appear through progressive actions leading, when the moment comes, to options freely accepted.[10]

On behalf of the President in Office of the Council of the European Communities, Sigismund von Braun stated:

The Community is also aware of the fact, that, in seeking association with it, Malta has made a choice which goes beyond the mere settlement of economic matters—a choice with far-reaching implications for the future. The Maltese Government has in fact decided on the close participation of this country in the work of European integration. That is why the two Parties have chosen to place their relations within the framework of an Association Agreement, not merely a trade agreement, intending that this should be a sign of their common will to embark today on a course of particularly close, structured co-operation. In the same spirit, another significant feature of the Agreement is its dynamic nature: this Agreement is in fact only a starting point, not an achieved goal. It was undoubtedly wise at this juncture to define only the first stage of our relations, so that further arrangements for co-operation between us may be defined only in the light of experience. But at the same

[9] Government Department of Information, Malta, 1970.

[10] Government Department of Information, Malta, 1970.

time it was very important to outline prospects for our future relations which would be sufficiently precise to enable us to view with confidence the future course of our co-operation.[11]

During the same period, Malta was seeking to regularize its relationship with NATO given that it hosted a NATO sub-headquarters while not forming part of the alliance. Approaches were made to the Organization on membership of the alliance and later on observer status of the NATO Council. Both approaches were unsuccessful at the time of their being made mainly due to internal NATO issues, the withdrawal of France from the military command, and disagreements about NATO expansion. The failure of these approaches as well as the attitude of NATO countries to cost sharing where utilization of Maltese infrastructure was concerned were to have a profound effect on politics in Malta.

Socialism and Neutrality

The PN lost the 1971 elections in part due to the accusation that 'your own friends don't want you'. The new Prime Minister, Dom Mintoff, immediately ordered the NATO sub-headquarters closed and embarked on a renegotiation of the ten-year defence and economic aid agreement with the UK. As a result of these negotiations, this agreement was eventually extended to 1979 with major increases in the amounts of economic aid provided.

The EEC association agreement, which had come into effect on 1 April 1971, was reassessed internally and the technical arguments won over the 'ideological' misgivings held by elements within the new government. The association agreement remained in place although the government looked at it as an economic tool rather than a political one. The association agreement did, however, continue to be extended and expanded over the years. The most notable change was the introduction of a package of technical and financial assistance in the form of a financial protocol for the years 1978–83[12] with the 1976 enlargement amendments. The second stage of the association agreement leading to a customs union was, however, delayed.

The new government shifted Malta'sh traditional Euro-Mediterranean focus to an almost purely Mediterranean one. This was particularly noticeable in its attitude at CSCE discussions as well as in its relations with countries on the southern Mediterranean rim. Malta also joined the Non-Aligned Movement and the Group of 77. As the agreement governing the British military base drew to a close, the Maltese government adopted a neutrality declaration and sought

[11] Government Department of Information, Malta, 1970.

[12] In April 1976, the 1st Financial Protocol (1978–1983) was approved between Malta and the EEC worth 26 million ecu. This entered into force in November 1978. In 1983, the 2nd Financial Protocol (1983–8) entered into force, worth 29.5 million ecu. In December 1988, an Adaptation Protocol was signed leading to the 3rd Financial Protocol (1988–93) worth 38 million ecu. On 12 June 1995, Malta and the EU signed the 4th Financial Protocol (1995–8) worth 45 million ecu. This entered into force on 4 July 1996 to facilitate Malta's transition with a view to it being fully prepared for accession to the Union. A pre-accession package (2000–4) worth €38 million was put in place in March 2000.

guarantees of this policy from a number of countries including the USA and the USSR. Ultimately, Italy, Libya, and the USSR exchanged notes with Malta on the subject. The form of neutrality adopted was not the traditional form of international neutrality but one defined in terms of non-alignment, non-participation in military alliances, and the non-availability of Malta's shipyards to the two superpowers.

On its part, prior to the closure of the military base, the opposition PN[13] adopted a resolution on 16 February 1979[14] which, in making reference to the 1970 association agreement, recalled that:

> Malta cannot claim by right the advantages that can be derived from EEC institutions so long as it is not a full member of the Community. The European Community is gradually moving towards a political union increasingly guaranteeing peace and freedom for its member countries. The longer Malta takes to declare its intention to join the European Community the greater will be the difficulties for its full membership.

And resolved that:

> It is in the interest of Malta to start negotiations with the European Community with a view to obtaining the right conditions for Malta's full membership of the European Community and that the PN should, as from now, take initiatives to enable Malta to obtain suitable conditions which will render possible the Islands' accession to the European Community.[15]

The electorate were presented with two completely different futures for Malta: a centralized, socialist economy versus a liberalized, social market economy within the European Community. An absolute majority of the electorate in a 95 per cent poll chose the latter in December 1981 but a re-districting exercise held prior to the elections gave the MLP an absolute majority of the parliamentary seats.[16] The subsequent constitutional crisis was brought to an end by amendments to the electoral system which ensured a direct link between a party's share of the vote and its parliamentary seats. But this agreement came with an MLP price: the insertion of the neutrality declaration in the constitution.

The bitterness caused by the majority feeling doubly cheated—out of the government of their choice and Community membership—was exacerbated by the MLP's blackmail tactics. This was followed by a further period of increased state control of enterprise, education, and limits on individual freedoms.

[13] The PN had also consulted NATO in the years prior to the closure of the military base; the opinion was that Malta had a negative strategic value rather than a positive one and that the primary issue should be to not make its extensive facilities available to Warsaw Pact countries.

[14] The PN leader, Eddie Fenech Adami, announced this new policy at two press conferences: the first in Malta with the rest of the party leadership; and the second in Bonn at a joint press conference with the CDU Secretary General.

[15] Briefing Note No. 1, *The Nationalist Party Policy on Malta–EEC Relations*, PN, Malta, 27 May 1981.

[16] International concern at this undemocratic outcome was overshadowed by the declaration of martial law in Poland on the same day.

The EEC–Malta association agreement continued in force although the second stage leading to a customs union was again delayed.[17] A second financial protocol was agreed between the two sides for the years 1983–8.

The Long Wait

In 1987, the PN was finally able to enter government, ending sixteen years of socialist rule. This ushered in a major period of change for Malta. The country prepared for EU membership. Trade was liberalized, whilst telecommunications, banking, and financial services were deregulated and/or privatized. Malta's physical infrastructure was completely overhauled as were the legal and business structures. A third EU–Malta financial protocol (1988–93) came into force.

The Berlin Wall fell in November 1989. The Bush–Gorbachev Summit which buried the Cold War was held in Malta on 2–3 December 1989. Malta formally applied for European Community membership on 16 July 1990.[18] German reunification took place on 3 October 1990. The July 1990 applications of Cyprus and Malta were followed by those of Austria (August 1991), Sweden (July 1992), Finland (November 1992), and Norway (March 1993).

The Lisbon Summit in June 1992 decided that priority was to be given to the applications received from EFTA countries, and in the light of decisions taken at the Edinburgh Summit in December 1992, enlargement negotiations got under way in February 1993 with Austria, Finland, and Sweden, and in April 1993 with Norway. There had been the expectation in Malta that negotiations would also be opened with it at the same time. Indeed, press reports from the Lisbon Summit had initially included Malta in the European Council decision.

The June 1993 Copenhagen Summit 'welcomed the Commission's intention to present shortly its opinions on Malta and Cyprus. These opinions will be examined rapidly by the Council taking into consideration the particular situation of each of the two countries.' The Commission's opinions on the applications of Cyprus and Malta were in fact issued on 30 June 1993. Though positive, the opinion on Malta brought in questions such as neutrality, language, institutional development of the Community, and Malta's participation in the Community institutions, thus ensuring that the application would be delayed. The opinion on Cyprus linked progress to the intercommunal talks in that country proposing a reconsideration of the application in January 1995. The President of the European Parliament, Egon Klepsch, speaking at the Corfu Summit[19] in June 1994, stated, 'The European Parliament has long been urging the Council to decide to open negotiations with Cyprus and Malta. ... We must not disappoint these two

[17] The first stage had been extended on a regular basis since 1977, first by agreement between the EEC and Malta, and, since December 1991, automatically on an annual basis without notification. Given that the first stage was not completed, the second stage which was to lead to a customs union was never initiated.

[18] Malta and Cyprus had discussed coordinated dates for their EC membership applications. Cyprus applied on 3 July 1990.

[19] Held in a palace built in the 19th century by Maltese stonemasons utilizing Maltese limestone.

countries any longer.' The Corfu European Council concluded by welcoming 'the significant progress made regarding the application by Cyprus and Malta for accession to the European Union' and considered 'that an essential stage in the preparation process could be regarded as completed'. It noted that 'the next phase of enlargement of the Union will involve Cyprus and Malta'. The Essen Summit in December 1994 confirmed 'that the next phase of enlargement of the Union will involve Cyprus and Malta' and invited 'the Council to examine in early 1995 new reports to be presented by the Commission'.

The line drawn between the applications of Cyprus and Malta and the later EFTA applications caused a political backlash in Malta. The new leader of the opposition MLP, Alfred Sant, who had been elected in the aftermath of the PN's major victory over the MLP in the February 1992 elections, took a hard-line position on the EU application as a result of this.[20]

In early 1995, Malta and the EU negotiated a fourth financial protocol (1995–8) to facilitate Malta's transition with a view to it being fully prepared for accession to the Union. The Cannes Summit in June 1995 reaffirmed 'that negotiations on the accession of Malta and Cyprus to the Union will begin on the basis of Commission proposals, six months after the conclusion of the 1996 Intergovernmental Conference and taking the outcome of that Conference into account'. The Madrid Summit in December 1995 while reiterating its June 1995 conclusions added: 'It is pleased that structured dialogue with both countries began in July 1995 within the framework of the pre-accession strategy.' The Florence Summit in June 1996 reiterated the need for 'the Commission's opinions and reports on enlargement to be available as soon as possible after the completion of the Intergovernmental Conference so that the initial phase of negotiations with countries of Central and Eastern Europe can coincide with the beginning of negotiations with Cyprus and Malta six months after the end of the IGC, taking its results into account.'

An Interlude

Elections were held in Malta in October 1996 and were won by the MLP. The MLP opposition had successfully exploited popular resentment at the unpopular decision to introduce value added tax (VAT) which had coincided with the non-inclusion of Malta in the 1995 EU enlargement (almost a replay of the 1971 NATO issue). It promised to scrap VAT, withdraw Malta's EU membership application, and also withdraw Malta from NATO's Partnership for Peace (PfP) Programme. The PN government, and to some extent the electorate,[21] were taken by surprise by this MLP victory. The new Prime Minister, Alfred Sant,

[20] On his election to the leadership he had said the PN had a mandate to start negotiations for EC membership but he later declared that since the PN government had led people to believe that Malta would be included in the forthcoming enlargement and this was not the case, then they no longer had this mandate.

[21] Following the election, opinion polls registered 10% of the population as having regretted the way they voted.

immediately withdrew Malta from the PfP's Individual Partnership Programme and froze (but did not withdraw) the EU membership application. He held that it would be more beneficial for Malta to develop ties with the European Union in the form of a free trade zone and to cooperate in financial, political, security and other matters rather than for it to join the Union. His main objective was to transform Malta into what was termed 'a Switzerland[22] in the Mediterranean'. Against technical advice, instead of removing the negative aspects of the VAT regime, the new government began work on developing a new indirect tax system.

In November 1996, the government expressed its wish to seek 'as close a relationship with the Union as is compatible with Malta's particular economic and geo-political circumstances, while mindful of the Union's *acquis* and its framework of operations'. In response to a request of the Council, the Commission transmitted in February 1998 a communication to the Council[23] on 'future relations between the EU and Malta' based on the existing framework of agreements. It was clear from the outset that the European Union was not in a position to enter into any special partnership agreement other than those already enjoyed by countries such as Iceland and Norway whereby Malta would have had to adopt large elements of the EU *acquis* without reaping the full benefits of EU membership.

The feeling in the Commission and Member States at the time was that EU membership was in Malta's interests and they could not understand why the MLP was opting for a partnership option when something more beneficial was on offer. This affected the government's efforts to preserve those EU–Malta structures that it believed were still necessary.[24] After only twenty-two months, the MLP government collapsed[25] under the weight of a slowing economy, a new badly thought-out indirect tax system and its internal divisions on EU membership. With the decision of the Luxembourg Summit of December 1998 to open negotiations with five former communist countries and Cyprus, the so-called

[22] This was to a certain extent a return to a previous MLP policy of the 1950s, following the collapse of the MLP government in the wake of the 1958 integration debacle. Ironically, Switzerland joined the PfP at precisely the same time that Malta withdrew from the PfP Individual Partnership Programme.

[23] The substance of this communication was endorsed by the 10th EC–Malta Association Council in April 1998. In the margins of the Association Council, two joint declarations were adopted, one on political dialogue and the other on cooperation in the fields of justice and home affairs.

[24] Roderick Pace in a paper entitled 'The European Union's Next Mediterranean Enlargement: Challenges and Opportunities' includes the following: 'In another development a member of the COREPER in Brussels was reported to have said that there was no point in continuing the Structured Dialogue with Malta once it was no longer interested in membership. The government's position on relations with the EU is amply clear, though some confusion has been created in Brussels over what to do with the Structured Dialogue once Malta was making it abundantly clear that it was not interested in pursuing the membership option. To clarify this "confusion", the Government circulated an aide memoire to all EU member states, explaining its position and reiterating that Malta's foreign policy will remain oriented towards Europe while at the same time cultivating a complimentary Mediterranean policy to it.' Jean Monnet Working Papers in Comparative and International Politics, January 1997.

[25] Eventually, former Prime Minister Dom Mintoff brought the government down by voting against the government in Parliament on the issue of a yacht marina in his electoral district.

Luxembourg group, as well as a further five former communist countries in the future, the electorate realized that EU membership had been within their grasp and that Malta might now end up getting left behind.

Full Speed Ahead

The PN easily won the September 1998 elections. Prime Minister Eddie Fenech Adami immediately reactivated the island's application to join the European Union. VAT was also immediately reintroduced in a less rigid form than the 1995 version. The Vienna Summit in December 1998 welcomed 'Malta's decision to reactivate its application for European Union membership' and took 'note of the intention of the Commission to present at the beginning of next year an updating of its favourable opinion of 1993'. In February 1999, the Commission issued its updated opinion which was less equivocal than the 'positive' opinion of 1993. It recommended that screening should begin as soon as possible with a view to beginning accession negotiations at the end of that year. The Cologne Summit of June 1999 welcomed 'the fact that, on the basis of the Commission's updated opinion ... it has now been possible to make a start on analytical examination of the Union "acquis" with Malta'.

This initial phase of the EU accession process is known as the screening process. It is carried out between the EU and candidate countries on two levels; multilateral and bilateral. This process involves an actual screening of all EU rules, collectively known as the *acquis communautaire*, which is divided into thirty-one different chapters, ranging from external relations to fisheries. Multilateral screening involves more than one candidate country at a time whereas bilateral screening involves each candidate country in sessions where their national legislation and policies are compared with the *acquis*. In areas where the candidate country's legislation already complies with the *acquis*, the Commission needs to be satisfied that the necessary national structures and procedures are in place or would be set up for the effective implementation of the legislation involved. This is referred to as the 'capacity to implement' the *acquis*. In areas where the candidate state's laws do not comply fully with that of the *acquis*, but are expected to be harmonized by the date of accession, the Commission assesses the modalities and time frames in which compliance would be achieved and monitors developments until compliance. Where the Commission is not satisfied that complete compliance has been attained, or where the candidate country itself indicates that compliance would not be attained by the date of accession, the matter is deferred to the negotiation stage.

Malta started its screening process at the end of May 1999 directly on a bilateral basis and attended multilateral sessions only in few areas, such as agriculture. The extent of Malta's preparedness to start detailed negotiations on the *acquis* was made clear through the successful manner in which the whole screening exercise was completed in a relatively short period. This experience underlined the determination and commitment of the government to align with the Union's *acquis* in the shortest possible time-frame. It also confirmed the advanced stage, notwithstanding the unfortunate interlude of twenty-two months, of technical preparations in this regard.

The Helsinki Summit of December 1999 decided 'to convene bilateral intergovernmental conferences in February 2000 to begin negotiations' with Malta and five Central and Eastern European countries, Romania, Slovakia, Latvia, Lithuania, and Bulgaria, 'on the conditions for their entry into the Union and the ensuing Treaty adjustments'. Malta was finally in a position to start its negotiations and, although in the so-called Helsinki group, had the possibility of seeing those negotiations conclude within the current legislature. It was a priority for the government for Malta to be included in the first possible enlargement. This meant that it had to catch up with the Luxembourg group composed of Cyprus, Estonia, the Czech Republic, Slovenia, Hungary, and Poland.

A pre-accession financial package (2000–4) to assist Malta in its preparations for membership was agreed to in March 2000. This useful assistance, however, was not able to make up for Malta's lack of eligibility for assistance from the Instrument for Structural Policies for Pre-Accession (ISPA), aimed at the environmental *acquis*, and from the Special Access Programme for Agriculture and Rural Development (SAPARD), aimed at the agricultural *acquis*. This deficiency affected Malta's preparations for membership in these two areas.

3. STRUCTURE OF NEGOTIATIONS

Introduction

All governments engaged in an accession process of this type have to work to keep civil society and their citizens informed about the process itself as well as the implications of both the *acquis* and the positions being taken in the negotiations. In the case of Malta, this element had to be paramount. For the reasons outlined above, a consensus in Parliament was just not possible. Furthermore, the government was committed to holding a referendum at the end of the negotiations. The government accordingly decided to work towards a consensus in the country as a whole rather than in Parliament. This implied that all the sectors of the economy had to be involved in the negotiations, as did all non-governmental organizations with specific interests, and that by the time the negotiations were over they had to feel that they had also been *their* negotiations.

The efficient implementation of the *acquis* necessitated the transfer of all the *acquis* to national legislation together with the establishment of an appropriate administrative and legal set-up for its implementation. This was a complex process comprising numerous independent activities, which involved bodies of all the three branches of state authority: legislative, executive, and judicial. The transposition of the *acquis* in national legislation and its subsequent implementation was carried out by administrative bodies, namely ministries and their departments or other entities. This required maximum coordination at all levels of government and, given Malta's need to catch up, an effective decision-making process; issues had to be solved as soon as they arose.

At the point where Malta was entering into detailed technical and procedural aspects of the accession process, it was particularly important for it to identify the key players and create the required structures at the various levels that were to be actively involved in the process.

Government structures

In approving the negotiating structures that were to operate in Malta, Prime Minister Eddie Fenech Adami underlined his direct overall responsibility for the process, both internally in terms of decision-making and externally in terms of communicating with the general public. Ultimately, the 'buck' would stop with him. The Minister of Foreign Affairs, Joe Borg, had responsibility for the negotiations and for the interface with civil society and other stakeholders. At the Foreign Minister's request, the head of the Prime Minister's Secretariat, Richard Cachia Caruana, was made Chairman of the Core Negotiating Group (chief negotiator) with responsibility for the day-to-day management of the negotiations as well as the coordination of internal issues related to the adoption of the *acquis*.

The *Cabinet of Ministers* set the overall negotiations policy. It approved all negotiating position papers prior to their being forwarded to the European Commission. It was also responsible for the overall coordination of the adoption of the *acquis* and legislation. The cabinet included all ministers. Parliamentary secretaries (junior ministers) attended those sessions where their dossiers were discussed. The Chairman of the Core Negotiating Group attended cabinet as head of the Prime Minister's Secretariat.

The Prime Minister also set up a *Cabinet Committee on EU Affairs* under his chairmanship, with the Minister of Finance and Economic Services, John Dalli, the Foreign Minister, and the Chairman of the Core Negotiating Group as members. Since this Cabinet Committee cleared all negotiating position papers prior to their being adopted by the full Cabinet of Ministers, lead and secondary ministers were invited to attend meetings when dossiers falling under their responsibilities were being discussed.

In addition to its Chairman, the *Core Negotiating Group* included the permanent delegate of Malta to the EU, Victor Camilleri, the head of the Malta–EU Information Centre, Simon Busuttil, the head of the EU Directorate in the Foreign Ministry, Saviour Falzon, and the head of the Foreign Minister's Secretariat, Patrick Tabone. Additionally, officials were invited to attend when particular dossiers were discussed. The main tasks of the Group were to:

- ensure the timely and satisfactory preparation of the drafts of all negotiating papers including backing documentation;

- lead the individual negotiating teams into the negotiations at the operational level; and
- monitor and evaluate all action related to the adoption of the *acquis*.

The Core Negotiating Group was supported by the EU Negotiations Secretariat within the Office of the Prime Minister, the Permanent Delegation of Malta to the EU, as well as the EU Directorate within the Ministry of Foreign Affairs. The members of the Core Negotiating Group were also members of the core tier of the Malta–EU Steering Action Committee (MEUSAC), with the Chairman of the Core Negotiating Group also serving as Deputy Chairman of MEUSAC.

The *EU Negotiations Secretariat* within the Office of the Prime Minister, also headed by the Chairman of the Core Negotiating Group, was to:

- provide overall direction in the preparation of technical documentation including the adherence to deadlines and standard formats which had been rolled out to ministries;
- finalize the drafts of all documentation drawn up by the line ministries in liaison with the EU Directorate and the Permanent Delegation of Malta to the EU for the consideration of the Core Negotiating Group;
- ensure that the rest of the system is fully briefed on the action necessary as follow-up to the negotiations through the relevant permanent secretaries;
- oversee, in conjunction with the Permanent Delegation of Malta to the EU, all preparations connected with individual negotiations;
- liaise continuously with the Permanent Delegation of Malta to the EU, the EU Directorate, the line ministries, as well as the technical experts participating in the process; and
- troubleshoot practical problems that may arise at any stage of the pre-accession process for consideration by the Core Negotiating Group.

The administrative capacity of the *Permanent Delegation of Malta to the EU* was strengthened at the outset to ensure that it could carry out its main functions throughout the process. The main objective of the Permanent Delegation was to support the negotiations process. Its main tasks were to:

- carry out background technical work as input to Malta's positions with regard to the negotiations;
- support the negotiations process by forging contacts with the Commission including the Malta Team[26] in DG Enlargement, the Council Secretariat, the European Parliament, as well as with individual Member State delegations on a bilateral basis with a view to channelling these to the various supporting structures;
- follow the proceedings of the Council and the European Parliament; and
- liaise continuously with the EU Negotiations Secretariat, the EU Directorate, the line ministries, as well as the technical experts participating in the process.

[26] Ably led by Arhi Palosuo.

The main tasks of the *EU Directorate within the Ministry of Foreign Affairs* were to:

- assist in the formulation and projection of the government's European Union policy;
- monitor and evaluate Community directives, regulations, demarches, and opinions on all aspects pertaining to the *acquis* including, but not restricted to, the political, social, fiscal, economic, and monetary fields; and
- liaise continuously with the EU Negotiations Secretariat, the Permanent Delegation of Malta to the EU, line ministries, as well as consult with constituted bodies, trade unions, and sectorial interest groups.

The *line ministries* under the direction of their permanent secretaries were responsible for all the technical preparatory work within government. In view of its EU membership policy, the incoming government had commissioned a review of its administrative structures in 1988. The purpose of that review was to critically examine the role, organization, and operation of the entire machinery of government. The Public Service Reform Commission (PSRC) was directed to examine the public service and to recommend means by which the service can efficiently respond to the changing needs for effective government. The PSRC proposed restoring the institutional fabric of public service, building its administrative capacity and safeguarding employees' rights with an emphasis on staff development. Several initiatives were then put into effect with a view to improve the administrative capacity in the medium to long term; these continued to evolve over the years.

An important initiative undertaken to strengthen the administrative capacity of the public service was the setting up of an *Office of Review* within each ministry to lead the process of change and to implement identified initiatives. The Office of Review was tasked to develop and implement, along with senior management, action plans to address operational processes, systems, and the legal and organizational framework. The Office of Review reported directly to the ministry's permanent secretary who, in turn, was accountable to the Public Service Change Committee consisting of a minister, the head of the public service, and other change protagonists. The EU desk officers and the customer care desk officers in the ministries formed part of the review offices. The role of the Office of Review was to:

- plan, monitor, and evaluate the programme of change and project submissions of line departments to ensure that they are consistent with the overall vision and objectives of the ministry;
- monitor and control the implementation of the capital and recurrent programmes; and
- plan and evaluate the organizational and human resource development of the ministry.

Established in all ministries, Offices of Review became the ministry focal point for the accession process. These offices facilitated the coordination and communication of the negotiations throughout the process. They were the main point of call in the day-to-day operations of the EU Negotiations Secretariat and the EU Directorate.

The *Office of the Attorney General* within the Ministry for Justice and Local Government was a key player in the process of preparing domestic legislation in line with the *acquis*. This Office was also responsible for handling internal queries related to the alignment of legislative proposals as well as other regulations. The Office was also tasked with the responsibility to prepare the draft legislation as required and vet the legislation drafted by the respective line ministries.

Interface with the social partners and civil society

Given the need for a consensus in society, the government established the *Malta–EU Steering and Action Committee* (*MEUSAC*) to follow the overall accession process, thus rendering it a focal point of Malta's accession preparations. The main roles of MEUSAC were to:

- make recommendations to the Cabinet Committee on EU Affairs at both the screening and negotiation stages;
- monitor the processes at each stage of the negotiations;
- discuss the draft position papers drawn up by the line ministries in liaison with the EU Directorate, the Permanent Delegation of Malta to the EU, and the EU Negotiations Secretariat;
- ensure optimal coordination between the various government ministries and their counterparts within the MEUSAC structure; and
- work in line with the government's commitment to include all interested sectors in the process towards EU accession, thereby rendering the process more transparent.

MEUSAC had a two-tier structure. The first tier, or core tier, was made up of the Foreign Minister, the government's Core Negotiating Group, the head of the public service, other senior government officials, nominated technical members who were leading experts in their fields,[27] together with representatives from the three political parties namely the PN, the MLP,[28] and the Alternattiva Demokratika (AD). This core tier managed the MEUSAC process and was ultimately responsible also for the work of the Malta–EU Information Centre. The second tier met in configurations based on the chapters of the *acquis*. The members of the core tier attended all chapter configuration meetings together with the government officials responsible for the dossiers and the special interest members for the particular chapter configuration. Around 100 different organizations, ranging from trade unions to employers/business associations to environmental NGOs, attended the various chapter configuration meetings; naturally, certain organizations such as the main trade unions (General Workers' Union, Union

[27] One of these was a former MLP deputy leader attending in a personal capacity.

[28] The MLP never nominated its representative to sit on MEUSAC.

Haddiema Maghqudin, Confederation of Malta Trade Unions) and main employers/business associations (Federation of Industry, Chamber of Commerce and Enterprise, Malta Chamber for Small and Medium Enterprises) were members of a number of the chapter configurations.

MEUSAC's wider representation ensured that all concerned parties were afforded the equal opportunity to give their input to the process at all stages and that the final negotiated position for each chapter fairly reflected the best interests of Maltese society. It is, therefore, safe to state that MEUSAC was a national body which institutionalized transparency and consultation throughout the process. This was one of the key successes of Malta's negotiations, in that all key players felt that they were an integral part of the process. The social partners and civil society were fully engaged in the moulding of the new environment they would have to operate in once membership became a reality. Notwithstanding the political divisions in the country on the question of EU membership, with the exception of the MLP, there was full participation in the process. The success of the MEUSAC process could also be seen in the civility of the proceedings as well as the absolute respect for the confidentiality of discussions and documents, thereby avoiding having the Malta–EU negotiations being carried out via the media. Naturally, this also depended on ensuring that journalists had the information they needed for them to do their jobs properly.

The *Malta–EU Information Centre (MIC)* was set up to increase awareness and education on the European Union and on the accession process. In particular, it was tasked with disseminating information on the:

- European Union in general;
- ongoing accession process;
- impact of EU accession; and
- outcome of accession negotiations.

MIC provided the link between the ongoing process and the Maltese public. In order to ensure objectivity and transparency, the Centre was placed under the guidance and supervision of MEUSAC.

The *social partners* and *civil society* were an essential part of the negotiating process. In the main, their organizations established EU helpdesks for their membership. Two of the larger business organizations (the Federation of Industry and the Chamber of Commerce and Enterprise) also combined to establish an office in Brussels to look after their members' interests. The social partners and civil society organizations were also involved in the impact assessments that were commissioned in those sectors where the *acquis* required this. Government assistance was provided where required.

The more complicated sectors also saw specific technical committees, bringing together the responsible government officials on the one hand and the special interest members on the other, meeting under the auspices of the ministry concerned or the EU Negotiations Secretariat.

The processes

On the basis of other accession negotiations, priority elements were drawn up by the government's Core Negotiating Group for each chapter as well as for the negotiations as a whole. Where necessary, policy discussions were held within government as well as within MEUSAC. The strategy adopted included prioritizing every item first on a technical basis and then on a political basis to ensure that the 'battleground' both internally and externally was clearly defined. Given the political context of the negotiations in Malta, the list was obviously longer than those of other candidate states. A table was prepared for each chapter with the following information:

- the special arrangements necessary in that chapter;
- other special arrangements being considered in that chapter;
- matters in that chapter which have importance in Malta;
- pending *acquis* transposition in that chapter;
- pending *acquis* implementation in that chapter;
- matters requiring consultation with the Commission;
- special arrangements granted to other countries (all enlargements) in that chapter; and
- candidate countries' negotiations status for that chapter.

Within this defined 'battleground' scenario, Malta's negotiating position papers were then drafted by the line ministries on the basis of the screening exercise that preceded the negotiations and utilizing input provided by the sectoral non-governmental entities (see Fig. 4). The EU Directorate within the Ministry of

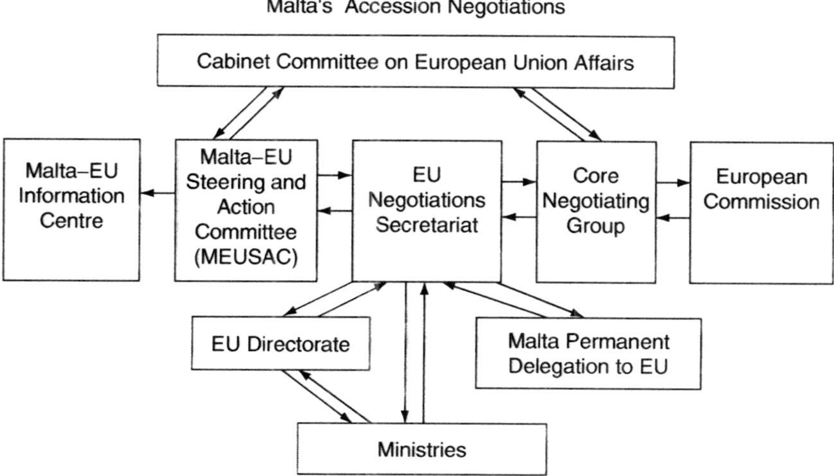

Figure 4. Malta's accession negotiations

Source: EU Secretariat, Office of the Prime Minister, Malta.

Foreign Affairs provided legal and policy advice on the related *acquis*. Where useful, specific impact assessments were commissioned from external consultants. Where necessary, these impact assessments had terms of reference agreed with the interested representative sectoral bodies to ensure that the position paper took specific non-governmental concerns on board. The EU Negotiations Secretariat within the Office of the Prime Minister ensured that the views of all ministries had been incorporated in each draft position paper. Differences of opinion which could not be settled at this stage were referred to the Chairman of the Core Negotiating Group and, on those rare occasions where they were not settled with permanent secretaries and ministers, they then moved up to the Prime Minister.

Once a draft negotiating position was cleared by the Core Negotiating Group, the Cabinet Committee on EU Affairs, and, where necessary, the full cabinet, it was then forwarded to MEUSAC for discussion. MEUSAC normally decided by consensus. In the few cases where this was not possible, a majority vote was taken with dissenting views recorded in the form of minority reports; these were then transmitted to the Cabinet Committee. It was up to the Cabinet Committee to adopt a final political decision on behalf of the Maltese government. The Cabinet Committee either approved the relevant negotiating positions as presented or made amendments; occasionally a dossier was sent back to MEUSAC for further discussion. Only following the approval of a particular dossier by the Cabinet Committee did a Malta negotiating position become official. The dossiers adopted by MEUSAC and approved by the Cabinet Committee were then referred to the Core Negotiating Group which coordinated the required negotiations on the basis of these dossiers. Any departure from these positions had to be approved by both MEUSAC and the Cabinet Committee.

The same decision-making process was adopted also at follow-up stages of the negotiations. The system was designed to ensure that all interested parties had direct input at all the stages of the process while still leaving the final decisions in the hands of the government. There were a number of in-built safeguards to ensure a single policy line across the board:

- all draft negotiating positions had to go through the EU Negotiations Secretariat in the Office of the Prime Minister and could not proceed to the next stage, internal or external, without the approval of the head of the Negotiations Secretariat who was also Chairman of the Core Negotiating Group;
- all discussions with the Commission services and Member States had to be coordinated through the EU Negotiations Secretariat; and
- all documents forwarded to the Commission services and Member States had to be cleared by the EU Negotiations Secretariat.

As soon as negotiations on a particular chapter were completed, the results were transmitted back to the Cabinet Committee and, in turn, to MEUSAC. The Minister of Foreign Affairs then reported to Parliament's Foreign Affairs Committee on the outcome of the negotiations on the chapter.

4. THE KEY ITEMS

Malta started its negotiations two years late. This necessitated very focused requests. Together with all the players in each sector, those areas where specific problems existed had to be identified as well as what was necessary to cater for these problems. This was important because it allowed real flexibility in defining solutions together with the Commission and the Member States. It also meant that although the list of requests might have been quite long, the list of successfully negotiated solutions was almost as long.

Although there was clear support for EU membership, the ultimate decision to go ahead would depend on a successful referendum and, almost certainly, a general election. This meant that, given the position of the MLP, some supporters of EU membership would have to vote against their party, which is particularly difficult in the Maltese political context. The possible final majority in a referendum and election could, therefore, be expected to be much smaller than those actually in favour of membership. Given the background political noise, it was essential that the general public felt that their negotiators did not believe in 'EU membership at all costs' and that they would be hard in their defence of the Maltese corner. Malta had, occasionally, to win things that were thought difficult if not impossible.

Fortunately, the MLP opposition helped in this process by repeatedly insisting that certain things would not be possible in the EU: a good financial package, the 25-mile fishing conservation zone, Maltese as an official language, hunting, neutrality, restructuring subsidies for the shipyards; while also insisting that the EU would force some unwelcome items on the country: a flood of foreign workers, major house purchases by EU nationals, abortion, increases in VAT. It was only late in the process that the MLP held back from declaring the possible, impossible. By then it was probably too late.

In chronological terms, the most successful closures were:

- common foreign and security policy, in May 2000, which, following on the Nice intergovernmental conference, laid to rest the neutrality issue;
- free movement of persons, in June 2001, which introduced the special arrangement allowing Malta to take unilateral action for the first seven years of membership if there was the danger of labour market distortion;
- free movement of capital, in December 2001, which gave Malta a permanent derogation related to the purchase of secondary residences;
- justice and home affairs, in March 2002, which laid to rest the myth that EU membership would undermine the agreement with the Holy See on Catholic marriages;
- institutions, in June 2002, which confirmed the Maltese language as an official language of the European Union;
- fisheries, later in June 2002, which established the 25-mile Malta conservation zone in EU law, thereby guaranteeing a future for Malta's artisanal fishing fleet;

- regional policy, in July 2002, which gave the island of Gozo regional status;
- environment, in October 2002, which made it clear that the birds directive did not ban hunting;
- competition policy, later in October 2002, which confirmed that the government's restructuring plan for the shipyards was acceptable to the Commission and also confirmed existing state aid assistance for small and medium-sized enterprises (SMEs); and
- in December 2002, at the European Council, agreement was reached on: budgetary and financial provisions, which gave Malta an extremely high aid package; taxation policy, which extended Malta's VAT zero rating on food and pharmaceuticals until 2010; agriculture, which introduced national aid measures for the first ten years of membership as well as extended the agricultural safeguard to the first five years of membership; and others, which included an unexpected protocol on abortion, a neutrality declaration, and a declaration on the island region of Gozo.

In numerical terms, Malta managed to secure no less than seventy-seven special arrangements in thirteen sectors, comprising:

- one permanent derogation on the acquisition of real estate by non-residents;
- forty-six transition periods on technical issues where time for adaptations was required;
- twenty-seven special arrangements which are specific to Malta's case (including those concerning fisheries, agriculture, and, of course, the financial package);
- a protocol on abortion; and
- two declarations: one on neutrality and one on Gozo.

While some of the issues negotiated may suggest that those who see the EU as a legislator for pure white milk are right, some were undoubtedly more far-reaching in their impact. Some areas called for very specific treatment touching on Malta's culture and identity. Those who were not familiar with Malta and its peculiarities, particularly the political climate, could not readily understand our particular issues on the various vulnerabilities which were both real and perceived in nature.

This section describes the more important of the items negotiated while Annex 14.1 contains a chronology of the Malta negotiations together with a full list of Malta's special arrangements.

Free movement of workers

While the government firmly believed that EU membership would bring about sufficient economic growth to cope with any possible, though unlikely labour influxes, there was particular concern among the population at large that Malta's small labour market could come under pressure. It was in this context that Malta sought to secure safeguards.

Under the agreement reached within the free movement of persons chapter, Maltese citizens were able to seek work in the EU and EEA countries from the first day of Malta's membership. On the other hand, for the first seven years of membership, Malta would be able to monitor the movement of workers—also by retaining its work permit system. Should the need arise, in urgent and exceptional circumstances, Malta would be able to suspend the application of the *acquis* and impose restrictions, generally or specifically, in one or more sectors of the labour market.

Malta was the only candidate country that sought and obtained an arrangement of this nature. Of course, these negotiations were made easier by the fact that some Member States, including the largest, faced the same concerns from their own citizens vis-à-vis the East European applicant countries. Once Member States had decided to impose restrictions on the movement of citizens of eight of the candidate countries (other than Malta and Cyprus) within their own countries, Malta's request for similar provisions for its small labour market vis-à-vis the fifteen Member States and other candidate countries appeared extremely reasonable.

Acquisition of secondary residences

The question of secondary residences under the free movement of capital chapter raised important political questions of particular concern to Malta which were not of a transitory nature, and the solution found needed to avoid adding to the already difficult situation regarding land use arising from the size of the country, the extreme density of the population, as well as the social effects that a substantial increase in demand for property would cause. Malta requested the retention, on a permanent basis, of remedial measures to address the situation.

Malta's conditions showed no similarity to that of any other candidate country or even of any Member State, although one Member State, Denmark, had earlier sought and achieved a special arrangement in this area. The validity of our case eventually permitted an agreement to be reached though it took some further detailed, and occasionally difficult, negotiations to translate this principle into a specific agreement due to the previous agreement among Member States that this enlargement would not include any permanent derogations.

The EU agreed that bearing in mind the very limited number of residences in Malta and the very limited land available for construction purposes, which can only cover the basic needs created by the demographic development of the present residents, Malta may maintain restrictions, on a non-discriminatory basis, on the right of EU citizens, who have not legally resided in Malta for at least five years, to acquire and hold secondary residences. This meant that for EU citizens to have full rights to purchase property in Malta, they would need to be resident in Malta for a period of at least five years. It also meant that even after membership, EU citizens seeking to buy a secondary residence in Malta would still require to apply for an authorization and satisfy conditions as was the case prior to membership and that no authorization would be given for the purchase of more than one property, unless that citizen had been resident in Malta for at least five years.

State aid

The competition policy chapter was one of the more complex chapters to negotiate, taking no less than twenty-three months to conclude. Negotiations on this chapter included the politically sensitive issue of subsidies paid to Malta's shipbuilding and ship-repair sector.

A Task Force for the Restructuring of the Maltese Shipyards, under the direct responsibility of Deputy Prime Minister Lawrence Gonzi, had been set up by the Prime Minister. The key objective of Task Force was to present a concrete and realistic plan aimed at achieving the yards' financial and economic viability by 2008. Consultations with the General Workers' Union (GWU), which represented the yards' workers, and between the management and workers were continuous and very intense. Government had to be cautious on the issue and had to show that it could do business even with those people who were completely intransigent on the issue of membership—the shipyards have long been an MLP stronghold. Eventually, the Task Force agreed on a programme to restructure the shipyards. The programme included reduced employment numbers, new work practices, capital investment, and operational aid until 2008. It demonstrated the government's resolve to implement, in a systematic, proportionate and realistic manner, those measures which were necessary to safeguard and enhance the future prospects of this important industry in Malta. Furthermore, the viability of the industry and the redeployment of excess public sector personnel into productive jobs were certainly aspects which the taxpayer appreciated.

The agreed plan was used as the basis for the intensification of consultations with the Commission. The EU negotiations in this area were focused on reaching a politically and socially acceptable solution on the lines developed in the restructuring plan. Ultimately, agreement was reached on a transition period allowing sufficient time for the implementation of the seven-year plan.

Negotiations in the competition chapter also included the existing incentives and other state aids that SMEs were eligible for. Transitional arrangements were agreed up to 2008 and, in some cases, up to 2011.

Agriculture

As explained earlier, during the negotiations the negotiating team approached the various chapters by first analysing where Malta was in comparison with the *acquis*, identifying those areas where harmonization could be achieved before accession, and then focusing on the exceptional items where a transitional or special arrangement was necessary. An exception to this was the vast agriculture chapter. This sector was in dire need of reform. Maltese agriculture was subsisting on protection and handouts which were, in themselves, preventing the further growth of the sector. The problem was further exacerbated by the fact that at the time the ministry responsible for the sector was undergoing considerable reform which had a direct impact on its day-to-day operations. As a result, negotiations on this chapter were only opened in December 2001. Also, apparently for reasons linked to its late start in its negotiations, Malta was not given access to SAPARD, the EU programme designed to get agriculture in the candidate countries closer to the Common Agricultural Policy.

Detailed studies on the sector showed that, on membership, Maltese agriculture would face a price shock, and in order to avoid this shock turning into a major drop in income for Maltese farmers, compensation had to be provided. The rationale for such compensation lay in the specific, very unfavourable conditions of Malta's agriculture. Furthermore, Maltese agriculture specialized in production for which the CAP did not provide significant support. Accordingly, the negotiations had two key objectives: that a suitable income would be guaranteed for farmers; and that the multifunctional role of agriculture would be encouraged and enhanced. Farmers had to feel that agriculture had a future in Malta. The proposed main instruments for the implementation of these measures were the Special Market Policy Programme and the Rural Development Programme.

It is important to understand the sector in order to appreciate the rationale of Malta's requests in the sector. Agriculture and fisheries accounted for only about 2.8 per cent of Malta's gross domestic product (GDP), a share which increases to a little more than 6 per cent if the whole agri-food chain is taken into account. It employs 1,800 full-time farmers and approximately 13,000 part-time farmers. The agricultural land area covers only 12,000 hectares of which 85 per cent is dry land. Approximately 42 per cent of the agricultural land is devoted to cereals, legumes, and forage crops, 29 per cent to vegetables, and the remaining 19 per cent to fruits, flowers, seeds, and minor crops.

The agriculture chapter is a striking example of the extensive discussions held with the private sector during the negotiations: three formal consultation sessions at ministerial level; six meetings of MEUSAC with a total of forty-seven special interest members from the sector; together with many informal and other technical meetings. The task of formulating and finalizing the negotiating position on agriculture also called for extensive consultations at the technical level, both internally in Malta and with the Commission services.

The arduous negotiations did pay off in the long run. Support was to be provided until 2014 to compensate those farmers who may incur a loss of income, allow them to restructure, as well as benefit from rural development measures. For items of particular importance to Maltese agriculture such as tomatoes and milk, quotas were also secured. So were special provisions for traditional products undergoing major reinvestment such as grapes for wine and olives for olive oil.

The agreed Special Market Policy Programme was to provide for the removal of import levies by accession and their replacement with direct income support and restructuring assistance. This financial assistance, which is co-funded by the EU, will allow local production to compete in the single market. In this context, Malta also negotiated an extended safeguard clause that will apply for the five years following accession. This is designed to permit measures to assist farmers in the event of serious difficulties, particularly where these difficulties are liable to persist.

The Rural Development Programme provided a framework to build, over the medium to long term, a new agricultural sector that is integrated with the rest of the economy. It will also include technical assistance and agri-environmental measures.

Twenty-five-mile fishing zone

The issue of major concern to Malta under the fisheries policy chapter was the 25-mile conservation zone that Malta had successfully managed for over thirty years. As an island, Malta's dependence on the sea and its many resources is an obvious feature. Less obvious, but equally determining, is the fact that as a small island, Malta developed a keen sense of the delicate balance between the exploitation and the conservation of marine resources.

Malta had traditionally attached high priority to the conservation of living resources within the 25-mile fishing zone established in 1971. Malta's fisheries are characterized by a fishing fleet exerting sustainable fishing effort, little by-catch, and practically no discards. Its fleet does not suffer from over-capacity. Catch rates have remained relatively stable as well as sustainable and the zone has served as an important *refugium* for several species within the heavily exploited central Mediterranean. The Maltese fishing industry is mainly artisanal in nature since the vast majority of its vessels are less than 8 metres in length and are engaged in coastal or small-scale fishing. Only forty-six vessels are over 15 metres and can therefore be considered to be industrial.

Malta recognized that the matter touched upon aspects of general principle which were of concern to the Union, and provided scientific and economic data with regard to its request. The Union recognized Malta's efforts to conserve fish stocks within its 25-mile management zone and accepted the principle that the accession of Malta should not lead to a decline in the protection of living resources within this zone. With this objective in mind, technical experts from Malta and from the Commission succeeded in identifying a number of non-discriminatory conservation measures to ensure that the fishing effort in the management zone will be maintained at a sustainable level and that the conservation of fishing stocks will be adequately guaranteed.

Value Added Tax

As was explained earlier, the introduction of VAT in 1995 had proved extremely unpopular and was one of the reasons for the Government's electoral defeat in 1996. Malta's main concern under the taxation policy chapter was its request to benefit from valued added tax (VAT) exemptions which were already permitted to some Member States. This issue was sensitive both in Member States as well as in Malta.

Taxation policy proved to be one of the more complex chapters of the negotiations. Two Member States in particular, France and Germany, with a measure of support from Sweden, opposed the granting of a transition period to Malta for zero rating food and pharmaceuticals similar to that already availed of by the UK and Ireland for food items and the UK, Ireland, and Sweden for pharmaceuticals. After months of discussions at technical and political levels, including specific bilateral discussions in Paris and Berlin, Malta was granted a transition period until 2010 for the maintenance of the VAT zero rate on foodstuffs and pharmaceuticals. In a declaration attached to the Accession Treaty, Malta stated that it had agreed to this date on the premiss that the equivalent exemptions currently enjoyed by three Member States will have expired on that date. It is relevant to note that an identical request by another candidate state was settled with a shorter transition period.

Although this was the item that got the most publicity in the taxation policy chapter, primarily because it dragged on until the last days of the negotiations, it was not the only taxation arrangement achieved. Special exemptions were negotiated for international passenger transport, inland passenger transport, inter-island sea transport, water, and new buildings and building land.

Environment

Although in most aspects of the negotiations the general population was of one mind, or willing to go along with things that were important for a particular minority such as farmers, there were a few areas where different Maltese groups held opposing views. Perhaps the best example of this concerns the hunting and trapping issue and the conflicting views of the hunters and environmentalists. It was clearly necessary for a solution to be found that was fair to both sides, as well as to the rest of the population.

The two aspects of the hunting and trapping issue were, however, very different. In the case of hunting a very strong hunting lobby exists in a number of Member States as well as Malta. We were also assured by the Commission that what was required for hunting could be provided through the derogations that were already permissible under the birds directive. In the case of trapping, a transition period was required to put a captive breeding programme in place. Agreement was reached but not before it became abundantly clear that this was a subject where emotion had as much of a role as rational thought. The directive ultimately aims to regulate these types of pastime with a view to protecting vulnerable species by ensuring sustainable practices; the agreements and understandings reached in this area underlined the government's commitment to bring Maltese practices fully in line with this objective.

The issue of waste was also a major item during the negotiations. Small islands the world over face issues related to the disposal of solid and liquid waste. Malta is no exception. A considerable amount of time was spent on this subject which included some EU positions which could be termed contradictory. Clearly, the final aim of the *acquis* in this area is to cut the amount of waste actually being generated. Malta had in place a reuse system for soft drinks containers, obliging all products to be sold in reusable glass, which naturally cut the number of containers entering the waste stream. Following Denmark's withdrawal of its European Court of Justice case on the same issue, the Commission insisted that Malta remove its ban on plastic and aluminium containers. Eventually, a transition period was agreed on to allow the ban to remain in place for a number of years while more complicated waste management systems were developed.

There were also difficulties related to recycling targets which were settled during the negotiations. Transition periods were also agreed to for landfills and the purification of liquid waste.

Gozo

The island of Gozo which lies a few kilometres north of Malta is home to 8 per cent of the country's population, living in slightly less crowded conditions than the rest of the population since Gozo has 20 per cent of the country's land area. Malta has always attached great importance to the need to address the permanent and specific disadvantages faced by the Gozitans. In 2000, Gozo's regional gross domestic product per capita stood at €6,160, which amounted to 71.7 per cent of the Maltese national average. The government's concern was that owing to its inherent handicaps, primarily as a result of its double insularity, there was the risk that while the economy of Malta and the Maltese islands as a whole would grow beyond the EU threshold for cohesion and structural funds, Gozo may remain below this level. It was vital to ensure that any assistance that may be available to Gozo would not be compromised because of such a situation. Accordingly, Malta proposed a separate arrangement to provide for measures that take into account the island's permanent and specific needs stemming from the structural handicaps linked to Gozo's status, in particular, double insularity, environmental fragility, small size of total population coupled with a high population density, and extremely limited resources. A declaration in this sense was drawn up in conjunction with the Commission and attached to the accession treaty.

Additionally, there was concern in Gozo over its regional status, caused by a proposed EU regulation which gave candidate countries less flexibility in determining regions under the Nomenclature of Territorial Units for Statistics (NUTS) classification system. Ultimately, an agreement was reached with the Commission for Gozo to be a NUTS 3 region.

Abortion

The EU has no laws on the legalization of abortion nor does it have any competence to make such laws. However, the fact that all EU countries except for Ireland had legalized abortion gave cause for concern that the EU might indeed call upon its members to legalize abortion at some point in time. This was an extremely sensitive issue which was made more so by declarations in favour of abortion made by the European Parliament. It was crucial for the EU to recognize Maltese sensitivities on this matter and to confirm that it had no competence whatsoever in the area. Unless there was a clear message in this regard, the Catholic Church, which retained an influential position on matters of this nature, could have opposed accession, even if not openly.

The protocol on abortion annexed to the Accession Treaty, similar in drafting to the Irish text, gave legal certainty that EU law, present or future, cannot change Maltese law on abortion. The wording of this protocol clearly ensured that in any case of possible conflict between EU law and Maltese law or jurisprudence on the issue, Maltese law will prevail.

It is also pertinent to note that the issue on abortion was discussed at large during the campaign on the referendum on EU membership. The PN assured the Maltese public that joining the EU would not affect Malta's stand on this issue at all, whereas the MLP claimed that Malta would eventually be pressured to adopt abortion if it joined the EU.

Neutrality

The whole issue of neutrality remains politically sensitive in Malta. For reasons of history there is no movement whatsoever, in either political party, in favour of joining NATO. Notwithstanding the fact that the EU can in no way be termed a military alliance, the MLP continued to express the opinion that EU membership would, in some way, be a threat to Malta's neutrality and non-alignment policy. As in the case of Ireland, this was primarily an issue of perception. Accordingly, Malta added a declaration to the Accession Treaty stating that its participation in the European Union's common foreign and security policy did not prejudice its neutrality since any decision of the Union to move to a common defence would have to be taken by unanimous decision of the European Council adopted by the Member States in accordance with their respective constitutional requirements.

Language

This matter was not technically part of the negotiations since it has always been the norm for the official languages of Member States to be official languages of the Union. The exceptions had been Gaelic, at the time of Ireland's accession very much a minority language, and Luxembourgish, which was not an official language of Luxembourg when it co-founded the Union. Nevertheless, the 1993 Commission opinion had indicated that it would be useful to explore not making

Maltese an official language of the Union. Furthermore, Commission preparations for Maltese as an official language of the Union were not put in place until late in the accession process. Apart from obviously putting Maltese nationals at a disadvantage in terms of employment with the EU's institutions, not giving Maltese official status would have been a political disaster.

In fact, the decision to add Maltese to the list of official languages of the Union was widely welcomed and was confirmation for the general population that the EU was not a threat to the identity of Member States, large or small.

Budget for the period 2004–2006

Malta started from the premiss that the funds available for post-enlargement financing up to 2006 were circumscribed by the agreements reached in Berlin on Agenda 2000. The negotiators also fully understood that the criteria to be applied for the sharing of funds among the new Member States would need to be based on criteria that already existed within the *acquis*.

Malta's main concern arose from the fact that in the sharing of available post-accession funds among the new Member States during the period 2004–6, it would be handicapped in a number of ways due to a very low population base, the very small size of its territory, a relatively high gross national product per capita compared to the other new Member States, as well as a very limited eligibility for EU agricultural funds.

It was extremely important politically that an agreement be secured giving Malta an adequate positive net beneficiary status. Ultimately, Malta achieved a financial envelope which was one of the highest per capita financing of all candidate countries, putting it on par with existing Member States of equivalent wealth over the period 2004–6. During its first three years of membership Malta was to receive the following approximate amounts:

- €29 million for the agricultural sector;
- €79 million for projects under the EU's cohesion policy;
- €30 million from various community programmes; and
- €233 million as budgetary compensation.

5. A REFERENDUM AND AN ELECTION

Negotiations end on 13 December 2002

The Copenhagen Summit opened on 12 December 2002. The only element left for discussion was the financial package. The figures that had been discussed in the previous weeks were beneath the government's expectations and it was not ready to accept anything below its established threshold. Nevertheless, the negotiators were confident that the Union would come up with an offer that was fair and equitable but that this would only be done at the eleventh hour. During the morning of 13 December 2002, the Maltese delegation led by Prime Minister Eddie Fenech Adami held its final meeting with the EU delegation led by Prime Minister Anders Fogh Rasmussen and Commission President Romano Prodi. The EU's new offers were acceptable and the deal was done.

The Referendum is called for 8 March 2003

In 1998, the Maltese government had undertaken to hold a referendum on the outcome of the accession negotiations. Prime Minister Eddie Fenech Adami announced the holding of the first referendum among the candidate countries on 29 January 2003. The vote was to be held on 8 March 2003 and the whole country immediately embarked on a fiercely fought campaign split between the YES campaign led by the Prime Minister and the NO campaign led by MLP opposition leader Alfred Sant. The YES campaign focussed on the advantages of EU membership, emphasizing that the fundamentals of life in Malta will, however, remain unchanged. The NO campaign expounded a 'doomsday' scenario where all that was held dear to the Maltese would be destroyed.[29]

The five weeks of the formal campaign were very intense and marked by high emotions on both sides. Large mass rallies were held up to the very eve of the referendum. Discussions on radio and television were incessant. Most major unions, employers/business organizations, and NGOs backed the YES vote, also turning up together with the Prime Minister during one of the main campaign press conferences. The voter turnout during the referendum was 91 per cent, about 5 per cent below the average for general elections, with the YES vote approximating 54 per cent of valid votes and the NO vote 46 per cent.

The decision to join Europe under the negotiated conditions had, therefore, been easily confirmed by the referendum but, in a surprise announcement, the MLP leader claimed that the YES campaign had actually lost the referendun since only 48 per cent of total eligible voters had voted in favour of membership. This thesis was not valid, either by political tradition or in legal terms,[30] and there was a major backlash across the media and among public opinion. Prime Minister Fenech Adami immediately called an election for 12 April 2003, four days before the scheduled signing date of the Accession Treaty in Athens.

[29] The working time directive also featured heavily here with MLP exponents insisting that the directive would prevent people from working the number of hours they wished to work, thereby undermining workers' incomes and Malta's competitiveness.

[30] The relevant legislation had been approved by both sides of Parliament six months prior to the referendum stating that the approved opinion will be the one receiving the majority of the valid votes cast in the referendum.

Election held on 12 April 2003

Following the announcement of the election on 10 March 2003, the two main parties plunged back into full-scale campaigning. As a general election rather than a referendum, the agenda was naturally wider and the risks higher. The government presented an electoral programme entitled. 'For Malta to Grow in Europe' and focused its campaigning on the economy, jobs, health, education and infrastructure, also giving these issues an EU dimension. The opposition presented its programme entitled 'A Better Future: You Come First' and accused the government of neglecting the country in its desperation to join the EU; it also declared that, if elected, it would exempt sectors of the economy, such as farmers and fishermen, from income tax.

In the face of the MLP threat to pull the plug on EU accession if it won the general election on 12 April 2003, the PN was returned to power with 52 per cent of the vote in a 96 per cent poll. The MLP conceded defeat and Malta joined the other nine acceding states in Athens on 16 April 2003. Prime Minister Eddie Fenech Adami, Foreign Minister Joe Borg, and chief negotiator Richard Cachia Caruana signed the Accession Treaty on behalf of Malta, putting an end to years of debate on this fundamental issue for the country's future.

Afterword

From 1987 onwards, Malta was engaged in an ambitious programme of administrative and legislative reform. We sought to ensure along the way that while this programme was closely geared to our own national development process it also met the commitments that would need to be undertaken during EU negotiations. Although our legislation was to a significant extent already moulded in the shape of the Union's own legislation, the sheer size of the *acquis* still seemed overwhelming at times. We were fortunately always able to look beyond the individual building blocks of the process to the expected longer-term political and economic returns emanating from accession to the EU.

No effort was spared in engaging the social partners fully in our internal deliberations. This created a feeling of ownership of the negotiations process which motivated an almost immediate urge to start reaping the benefits of membership. The results of the referendum and the election which ensued were proof of this.

The very useful and thorough investment in understanding the *acquis* during the screening and negotiations process is now paying dividends. The process, complicated as it is, helped us to fully understand the institutional and regulatory framework which has evolved in the Union; it also helped us to appreciate the complex procedural and technical apparatus with which the Union works.

The large team of people who embarked on the process were continuously on a roller-coaster the likes of which had not been faced before. Not only did we have to work to secure the best possible package for Malta but we also had to cope with the broadsides—often untrue and unfounded—flung at us by those who believed that the EU would not adjust to the specific needs of a country like Malta. The agreement brought back from Copenhagen was proof that the EU is not a one-size-fits-all entity as they had claimed.

Two years on from 1 May 2004, the Maltese people are still developing their understanding of the vast opportunities membership of the Union puts before the country as a whole. This learning process will undoubtedly continue for a few more years but it is not a one-way process. The Mediterranean ingredient of our European identity, moulded as it has been by our history, gives us something unique to add to the already immensely rich and varied European landscape. As a country, we are proud to be able to make our own contribution to the European process which continues to evolve.

Annex 14.1: The Chronology of the Negotiations

Portuguese Presidency: First Semester 2000

The first intergovernmental conference at ministerial level on the accession of Malta to the European Union was held on 15 February 2000. Foreign Minister Joe Borg headed the Maltese delegation while the presidency was represented by Portuguese Foreign Minister Jaime Gama. The Commission was represented by Enlargement Commissioner Günter Verheugen. Malta formally opened its accession negotiations.

The second session at chief negotiators' level was held on 25 May 2000. Chief negotiator Richard Cachia Caruana headed the Maltese delegation while the presidency was represented by the Portuguese permanent representative to the EU, Ambassador Jose Vasco Valente. The Commission was represented by Enlargement Director General Eneko Landaburu. The following chapters were opened for negotiation: industrial policy, small and medium-sized enterprises, science and research, education and training, telecommunications, culture and audio-visual policy, external relations, and common foreign and security policy. The following seven chapters were provisionally closed:

- *Industrial policy (chapter 15):*
  No special arrangements were requested.
- *Small and medium-sized enterprises (chapter 16):*
  No special arrangements were requested.
- *Education and training (chapter 18):*
  No special arrangements were requested.
- *Science and research (chapter 17):*
  No special arrangements were requested.

- *External relations (chapter 26):*
  No special arrangements were requested.
- *Common foreign and security policy (chapter 27):*
  No special arrangements were requested but Malta had come a long way since the first Commission opinion on Malta which made reference to Malta's neutrality and non-aligned status and 'the problem of their compatibility with Title V of the Maastricht Treaty'. Obviously, since that Commission opinion had been issued in 1993, Austria, Finland, and Sweden had joined Ireland in the European Union. Malta did, however, attach a declaration to its Accession Treaty on its neutrality.

French Presidency: Second Semester 2000

The third session at chief negotiators' level was held on 24 October 2000 with the presidency being represented by the French permanent representative to the EU, Ambassador Pierre Vimont. The following chapters were opened for negotiation: statistics, consumers and health protection, and fisheries. The following three chapters were provisionally closed:

- *Statistics (chapter 12):*
  No special arrangements were requested.
- *Consumers and health protection (chapter 23):*
  No special arrangements were requested.
- *Culture and audio-visual policy (chapter 20):*
  No special arrangements were requested.

The fourth session at chief negotiators' level was held on 16 November 2000. The following chapters were opened for negotiation: company law, economic and monetary union, free movement of capital, competition policy, and social policy and employment. The following two chapters were provisionally closed:

- *Company law (chapter 5):*
  No special arrangements were requested.
- *Economic and monetary union (chapter 11):*
  No special arrangements were requested.

Swedish Presidency: First Semester 2001

The fifth session at chief negotiators' level was held on 29 March 2001 with the presidency being represented by the Swedish permanent representative to the EU, Ambassador Gunnar Lund. The following chapters were opened for negotiation: financial control, free movement of services, transport policy, regional policy, and financial and budgetary provisions. The following chapter was provisionally closed:

- *Financial control (chapter 28):*
  No special arrangements were requested.

The sixth session at chief negotiators' level was held on 1 June 2001. The following chapters were opened for negotiation: free movement of goods, energy, environment, and customs union. The following three chapters were provisionally closed:

- *Free movement of goods (chapter 1):*
  1. Transitional period until the end of 2006 for the renewal of authorizations for the marketing of pharmaceuticals.
  2. Malta will retain current labelling on milk and chocolate products.
- *Free movement of services (chapter 3):*
  No special arrangements were requested.
- *Energy (chapter 14):*
  Transitional period of four years (till end of 2006) to allow the purchasing of fuel stocks and to increase fuel storage capacity.

The fourth session at ministerial level was held on 12 June 2001 with the presidency being represented by Swedish Foreign Minister Anna Lindh. The following chapters were opened for negotiation: free movement of persons and taxation.

The seventh session at chief negotiators' level was held on 27 June 2001. The following chapter was opened for negotiations: justice and home affairs. The following chapter was provisionally closed:

- *Free movement of persons (chapter 2):*
  1. For the first seven years after date of membership, Malta may impose restrictions unilaterally in urgent and exceptional cases where the influx of workers from the EU creates pressure on the local labour market or particular sectors.
  2. After the first seven years since the date of membership, in case of great influx of workers from the EU, Malta will seek a remedy with the EU institutions.

Belgian Presidency: Second Semester 2001

The eighth session at chief negotiators' level was held on 26 October 2001 with the presidency being represented by the Belgian permanent representative to the EU, Ambassador Frans van Daele. The following chapter was provisionally closed:

- *Transport policy (chapter 9):*
  1. Transitional period until the end of 2004 for the obligatory roadworthiness testing (VRT) of vehicle suspension and general conditions of the vehicle.
  2. Transitional period until the end of 2005 for the retrofitting of speed limitation devices in certain categories of vehicles.
  3. Transitional period until the end of 2004 for the introduced of minimum road taxes on Maltese registered heavy goods vehicles that operate internationally.
  4. Transitional period until the end of 2005 for the introduction of minimum road taxes on Maltese registered heavy goods vehicles operating nationally.

The ninth session at chief negotiators' level was held on 28 November 2001. The following chapter was provisionally closed:

- *Social policy and employment (chapter 13):*
  1. Transitional period until the end of 2003 to implement parts of an EU directive, particularly those dealing with hearing tests, reducing the risk of exposure to high levels of noise, and existing workplaces and apparatus.

2. Transitional period until the end of 2006 to implement the EU directive that covers the minimum requirements concerning the use of work equipment.
3. Transitional period until the end of 2004 to implement an EU directive that sets out minimum safety provisions at temporary and mobile construction sites.
4. Transitional period until July 2004 (end 2004 at the latest) for the adoption of EU legislation dealing with the minimum requirements covering certain aspects of working time.

The fifth meeting at ministerial level was held on 12 December 2001 with the presidency being represented by Belgian Foreign Minister Louis Michel. The following chapter was opened for negotiation: agriculture.

The tenth session at chief negotiators' level was held on 21 December 2001. The following chapter was provisionally closed:

- *Free movement of capital (chapter 4):*
  Malta may maintain restrictions, on a non-discriminatory basis, on the right of EU citizens, who have not legally resided in Malta for at least five years, to acquire and hold secondary residences.

First Semester 2002: Spanish Presidency

The eleventh session at chief negotiators' level was held on 21 March 2002 with the presidency being represented by the Spanish permanent representative to the EU, Ambassador Javier Conde de Saro. The following chapter was provisionally closed:

- *Justice and home affairs (chapter 24).*
  No special arrangements were requested or obtained in this chapter. However, on Malta's request, the EU accepted that in the area of jurisdiction, recognition, and enforcements of judgements in matrimonial matters and in matters of parental responsibility for children, the relevant EU Convention need not apply to Malta in cases of particular concordats with the Holy See.

The sixth meeting at ministerial level was held on 10 June 2002 with the presidency being represented by Foreign Minister Josep Pique. The following chapter was opened for negotiation: institutions. The following chapter was provisionally closed:

- *Institutions (chapter 30):*
  No special arrangements were requested or obtained in this chapter. However, during negotiations it was agreed that the Maltese language will be among the official languages of the European Union. Again, this had been identified as a difficulty in the 1993 Commission opinion.

The thirteenth session at chief negotiators' level was held on 28 June 2002. The following chapter was provisionally closed:

- *Fisheries (chapter 8):*
  1. A 25-mile fishing conservation zone around Malta was agreed.

2. The *Lampuka* to be included in the list of fish for common market organization.

Danish Presidency: Second Semester 2002

The fourteenth session at chief negotiators' level was held on 29 July 2002 with the presidency being represented by the Danish permanent representative to the EU, Ambassador Poul Skytte Christoffersen. The following chapter was provisionally closed:

- *Regional policy (chapter 21):*
  No special arrangements were requested or obtained in this chapter. However, during negotiations it was agreed that the island of Gozo will be classified at NUTS 3 level for statistical purposes; while the Maltese islands will be classified together at NUTS 1 and 2 levels.

The seventh meeting at ministerial level was held on 1 October 2002 with the presidency being represented by Danish Foreign Minister Per Stig Moller. The following chapter was provisionally closed:

- *Environment (chapter 22):*
  1. Transitional period until end of 2004 to adapt tanker fleet on VOC emissions.
  2. Transitional period until end of 2005 to bring the Delimara power station in line with EU standards.
  3. Methyl bromide will be phased out by end 2005.
  4. Nitrates and fluoride in water will be reduced by end 2005.
  5. Transitional period until March 2007 to allow industry to adapt to EU rules on dumping of dangerous substances into the sea.
  6. Transitional period until March 2007 to complete waste water infrastructure.
  7. Transitional period until end of 2005 to reach the overall recycling target.
  8. Transitional period until end of 2009 for the recycling of plastics.
  9. Transitional period until end of 2007 to keep ban of bottling of soft drinks in plastic bottles until a new environmentally friendly bottling regime is introduced.
  10. Malta will apply a derogation whereby Maltese hunters can continue hunting quail and turtledoves in spring.
  11. A derogation will also allow trappers to continue trapping seven songbirds using traditional methods. By end 2008, Malta will establish a full captive breeding system. A moratorium on new trapping licences was introduced in August 2002.

The fifteenth session at chief negotiators' level was held on 18 October 2002. The following chapter was provisionally closed:

Competition policy (chapter 6):

1. Transitional period until end of 2008 for Malta to implement its seven-year restructuring plan at the shipyards, starting in 2002.
2. Transitional period until end of 2011 for Maltese small firms to continue benefiting from incentive packages that were given under the old Industrial Development Act.

3. Transitional period until end of 2008 for Maltese small firms to continue benefiting from operating aid under the Business Promotion Act.
4. Transitional period until end of 2005 for the orderly and complete adjustment of the market in the importation, stocking, and wholesale marketing of petroleum products.

During the Copenhagen European Council on 12–13 December 2002 the chapters that had been provisionally closed during the previous nineteen months were formally closed. The Maltese delegation was headed by Prime Minister Eddie Fenech Adami and included Foreign Minister Joe Borg and chief negotiator Richard Cachia Caruana, the presidency delegation was headed by Danish Prime Minister Anders Fogh Rasmussen and included Foreign Minister Per Stig Moller and permanent representative to the EU Poul Skytte Christoffersen, while the Commission delegation was headed by Commission President Romano Prodi and included Commissioner Günter Verheugen and Director General Eneko Landaburu. The following chapter was opened for negotiation: other. The following five chapters were also closed:

- *Budgetary and financial provisions (chapter 29):*

  €233 million as budgetary compensation for 2004–6 which meant that Malta's net receipts on a per capita basis were similar to those of existing Member States of equivalent wealth.

- *Taxation policy (chapter 10):*

  1. Food will remain free from VAT until 1 January 2010. Malta accepted this arrangement on the premiss that by that time, no other EU country would still have an exemption.
  2. Medicines will remain free from VAT until 1 January 2010. Malta accepted this arrangement on the premiss that by that time, no other EU country would still have an exemption.
  3. International passenger transport will remain exempt from VAT.
  4. Regular inland passenger transport will remain exempt from VAT.
  5. Passenger transport between the Maltese islands will remain exempt from VAT.
  6. Water supplied by public authorities will remain exempt from VAT.
  7. New buildings and building land will remain exempt from VAT.
  8. SMEs will remain eligible for special VAT scheme.

- *Customs union (chapter 25):*
  For the first two years after membership no external tariff rate will be charged on woven fabrics of combed wool or of combed fine animal hair (CN Code 5112 11 10) up to a maximum of 20,000 square metres per year, denim (CN Code 5209 42 00) up to a maximum of 1.2 million square metres per year, woven fabrics of artificial filament yarn (CN Code 5408 22 10) up to a maximum of 110,000 square metres per year, and other made-up clothing accessories (CN Code 6217 10 00) up to a maximum of 5,000 kg per year. The tariff will be phased in from the third to the fifth year of membership.

- *Other (chapter 31):*

  1. Protocol on abortion.
  2. Declaration on neutrality.

3. Declaration on Gozo.

- *Agriculture (chapter 7):*
  Fruit and vegetables

1. Fruit and vegetables – €28.39 million in financial support until 2014.
2. Potatoes – €27.08 million in direct financial support until 2014.
3. Tomatoes – €31.16 million in financial support until 2014.
4. National threshold for production of tomatoes set at 27,000 tonnes.
5. Tomatoes used for *kunserva* eligible for EU aid.
6. Transitional period until the end of 2009 allowing Maltese tomato processors to sign a share of their contracts with individual producers who would not be participants of a producers' organization.
7. EU aid of €132.25 per 100 kilos of olive oil produced.

Wine industry

1. Vintners and farmers will get €18.29 million in financial support until 2014. Aid includes support for new plantings and additional aid per hectare.
2. New planting rights for a total planted wine area in Malta of 1,000 hectares.
3. Transitional period until the end of 2008 for the enrichment of wine from indigenous varieties.

Pigmeat

1. Pigmeat sector will get €34.08 million in financial support until 2010.
2. National quota of 135,200 slaughtered pigs every year.

Dairy sector

1. Dairy sector to be given direct financial support of €19.72 million until 2010.
2. Milk quota set at 48,698 tonnes.
3. Transitional period of five years on the stocking density requirements in farms for qualifying for the special premium and the suckler cow premium.
4. Transitional period of five years to keep current minimum of 2.5 per cent milk fat content.
5. Transitional period until the end of 2009 on EU hygiene and quality requirements in dairy farms.

Poultry and eggs

1. Eggs sector to get €14.46 million in financial support until 2010.
2. Poultry sector to get €10.91 million in financial support until 2010.
3. Transitional period until end 2006 on EU rules on the welfare of laying hens.
4. Malta will use laboratories in other EU Member States for tests of residues and substances in live animals and animal products.

Imported sugar and cereals

Upon membership, prices of imported sugar, cereals (wheat, barley, maize, rice, malt, and semolina), semi-processed tomato products, and some beef and dairy products (concentrated milk powder, butter, and cheese) will be subsidized until 2010. Subsidies must benefit consumers and will be paid to industry and recognized retailers on price difference between EU price and world market price.

Rural development
€4.64 million in EU funding (2004–6) for Rural Development Plan.

Special safeguard, status

1. Five-year safeguard to protect agricultural sector in case of difficulties.
2. Specific ad hoc measure for Maltese agriculture to assist full-time farmers in adapting to the new market environment.
3. Malta will be eligible for EU aid of €2.2 million per year as a Less Favoured Area. This aid is paid on a per hectare basis.
4. Transitional period of five years for the continuation of existing support for transport of agricultural goods from Gozo to Malta.

Pets

For cats and dogs to enter Malta they must first have an individual vaccination record.

Traditional products

Malta will still protect the traditional Maltese cheeses: *Gbejna* and *Rkotta.*

Plant health

1. Transitional period of five years during which Malta would postpone the application of EU rules on the marketing of seeds of those varieties listed in its official catalogues of agricultural plant species and vegetable plant species which have not as yet been accepted according to EU law.
2. Provisional protected zone status for Malta in respect of the Colorado beetle and *Citrus tristeza* plant health harmful organisms.

The final negotiations on the chapters on agriculture and the budgetary and financial provisions included a series of bilateral 'confessionals' at ministerial and chief negotiators' levels. At the ministerial meetings, the Maltese delegation was headed by Foreign Minister Joe Borg, the presidency delegation by Danish Foreign Minister Per Stig Moller, and the Commission delegation by Commissioner Günter Verheugen. At the chief negotiators' meetings, the Maltese delegation was headed by chief negotiator Richard Cachia Caruana, the presidency delegation by Danish permanent representative to the EU Poul Skytte Christoffersen, and the Commission delegation by Director General Eneko Landaburu.

15

The Accession of Poland to the EU

Jan Kułakowski
Leszek Jesień

The accession negotiations of Poland, as in the case of five other countries, started from a decision of the Luxembourg European Council in December 1997. As of March 1998 preparations in Poland were done: the story began.

Basically, we were negotiating the transition periods that were to allow Poland to adopt certain Community norms at a later date than the accession date. Hence, the subject of the negotiations was the means and eventual duration of the transition periods. In fact, transition periods were not only requested by Poland but also by the EU Member States. The European Union could also apply for this kind of exclusion from particular legal norms. The best example is a transition period during which the EU Member States decide upon the granting or not of access to their labour markets. The negotiations may be defined as 'do ut des' of rights and obligations of the Member States.

The first task of the chief negotiator, even before the negotiating team was created, was to explain to the public the essence of the negotiations. The public opinion had been misinformed by the opponents of the European Union claiming that the negotiations were to take place 'on the knees'; that it was 'known' that we would have to adopt all conditions given by the EU, without exception.

Public opinion, however, finally agreed with the negotiators on the following general reasoning: we applied for the membership in a certain club; the club has its own rules that we have to accept; we are able to negotiate only the way and the date of the adoption of those rules; we will, nevertheless, be able to modify those rules, once we become a member of the club.

The area of negotiations has been divided into thirty-one chapters. It has been suggested to the Prime Minister, Mr Jerzy Buzek, to propose candidates to the negotiating team. They were not, however, the representatives of the line ministries, but were given as *ad personam* nominations by the Prime Minister. Our aim was to create an independent team characterized by a team spirit of group decision-making. Henceforth, all members of the negotiating team were responsible for the decisions taken.

Once agreed by the negotiating team, the country positions were formally adopted—with necessary amendments—by the Committee for European Integration (a specialized committee of the government that handles EU-related issues) and finally by the Council of Ministers. The Committee, together with the Foreign Ministry, provided horizontal support to our work, while the line ministries were helpful in specific issues. In the course of the negotiations, the negotiating positions could be changed only by the Council of Ministers on the basis of a proposal from the negotiating team. This system proved to be good and effective, although the mechanism was indeed difficult. Certainly, the team as such was responsible for all negotiating positions as well as for the course of the negotiations.

Within the government structure there was an informal body created—a 'political management of negotiations'—and it was responsible for the process of negotiations in general. This body was composed of four persons: the Prime Minister, the Minister of Foreign Affairs, the head of the Committee for European Integration, and the chief negotiator.

The negotiations begun with the so-called screening: a review of the compatibility of the Polish legislation with the EU legislation. From the beginning, the negotiations faced three profound problems.

First, we had to deal with a sort of race between the candidate countries: who will lead in closing off negotiations in subsequent chapters? It was a temporary closure of the chapters, until complete termination of the negotiations, but it had a significant political impact on the public and the government.

Second, we had to decide whether the rhythm of the negotiations is more important than their content. In other words, whether the negotiations should be conducted as if a closing of each chapter would be definite. An alternative would be a kind of faster proceeding of the negotiations, more flexibility in closing of the chapters, while leaving some issues open until the very end of the process. We opted for the way of negotiations that some well-respected people defined as 'harsh', because—as a rule—we left no issues open when closing chapters. This, however, led to a somewhat anxious public mood, since sometimes we experienced delays as compared to other countries. Those delays, however, were made up by the quality of the negotiations, which ensured that we did not need to revisit the chapters that had been 'provisionally closed'. In this respect the strategy we followed was, in fact, very successful.

Third, we had to make a choice between the package deals (giving concessions in one field in return for concessions in another) and treating each domain separately, thus limiting the compromises within each domain. It turned out that it was possible to apply both methods; package deals were possible in less important fields, while compromise strategy had to be applied in the more important fields, such as agriculture.

Fourth, we faced an issue particular to our country, namely whether the political significance of Poland may in certain respects make up for some weaknesses or shortcomings in its preparedness. The EU claimed officially that there is no such possibility. However, informally, we had to decipher the meaning of declarations that noted that the EU enlargement without Poland would lose its political value. Therefore, we had a sort of political advantage that we could use, although we could only do so in a very subtle manner, lest we lose our substantial position.

Finally, an issue closely linked to the negotiations was the problem of informing public opinion about the development of negotiations. This was a rather sensitive subject. On one hand, the negotiating team was not allowed to publicize the country positions when the negotiations took place. On the other hand, it had to confront a popular feeling that there is a great deal going on behind closed diplomatic doors. It was important that public opinion supported the process of negotiations and the negotiators. Therefore, a special public opinion campaign programme 'Understanding the Negotiations' was created. It consisted of numerous publications, including brochures concerning the most important negotiating issues. The chief negotiator with his team travelled around the country and discussed the negotiating problems in public with the cooperation of the regional governments. Altogether, in the regional capitals, there were sixteen conferences that took place during the negotiation proceedings. Those were a great chance for the chief negotiator to inform the public about the integration and—on the other hand—to listen to the opinions and criticism as well as having conversations with various social circles.

The negotiators were, naturally, in constant contact with the lower chamber (the Sejm) and the Senate of the Polish Parliament, informing them on the state of play during the plenary sessions. They also remained involved in European Integration Committee proceedings. Additionally, other standing parliamentary committees were informed if the need arose.

The parliamentary elections of October 2001 effected a change of government. Although the negotiations were not the left's or right's business, but a common business of the country, Prime Minister Leszek Miller decided to change the chief negotiator. Mr Jan Kułakowski, who was the first chief negotiator for 3.5 years, was replaced by Mr Jan Truszczynski, previously the Polish ambassador to the EU, and subsequently a Deputy Minister of Foreign Affairs.

Luckily, it turned out that this change did not influence the process or strategy of the negotiations. Some claimed that more concessions had to be given than otherwise would be necessary. Yet, regardless of the quality of the government and the chief negotiator, certain concessions had to occur during the last phase of the negotiations. Of course, they had to be based on good compromises—and that is what actually happened.

The Copenhagen Council of December 2002 finally closed the talks. It was not only a formal procedure, but some crucial decisions had to be taken as well on matters relating to agriculture and budget. The previous chief negotiator and his team were briefed regularly. This allowed us to confirm the results of the summit and made him co-responsible for the overall result.

Was there any chance to gain more? Perhaps there was, but there was also a possibility of gaining less. This is like an old story about a bottle that for some is half-full, while for others half-empty. Nonetheless, the outcome of the Polish accession referendum in 2003 and the development of the first year of the country membership in the European Union have clearly proved that the metaphorical negotiation bottle was almost full.

Let us take a closer look in turn at the most interesting and particular problems of Poland during the years of accession negotiations with the European Union.

1. AGRICULTURE

Perhaps the most difficult negotiations concerned the Common Agricultural Policy, and, in this respect, particularities of Poland's membership conditions in the EU. It was in this chapter that the future membership conditions were negotiated in the most visible way. In other words, when the negotiations concerned, say, the Supplementary Protection Certificate and the patent policy in general, the problem being important for the Polish pharmaceutical industry and the consumers, it was never perceived by the general public as the biggest issue for the country.

It was important, and vested interests on both sides (Poland and the EU) pressed hard for their causes, but it was never a *vital* interest. Such was agriculture, however, and it was not surprising since the country still boasts a large agricultural sector, whose importance for Polish social and political life is comparable to that in France. As, in the past, France always treated its agricultural sector as crucial within the EEC, so today it was for the Polish negotiators.[1] This was clearly visible whenever any issue related to agriculture was touched upon by the negotiations: the press covered the problem extensively and all comments from the EU side, from the Commission as well as from the Member States, were reported carefully. Any delays in negotiations were considered as important stumbling blocks. In sum, we all knew that the agricultural negotiations were vitally important for the country, and thus for the rhythm of negotiations and the eventual judgement of their general outcome.

Those were also one of the longest: they started in June 2000 with presentation of the Polish initial position paper in the chapter and did not end until 13 December 2002, during the Copenhagen European Council when the final round of negotiations was concluded.

The single most difficult negotiating problem in agriculture, if not for all negotiations altogether, was that of direct payments for farmers. In its financial perspectives for 2000–6, known as the Agenda 2000, the European Union assumed that the new Member States' farmers would not be eligible for the direct payments from the EU budget.[2] The reasoning was simple: the direct payments

[1] While the Polish agricultural sector has been changing rapidly, for the purposes of the country negotiating position it was calculated that over a quarter of employment is in the sector (27%), while it produced only less then 5% of the GDP (4.8%). It was estimated that about 70% of the agricultural population is employed by the sector as part-time workers. It was not surprising then that only about half of the Polish farms were considered economically oriented as their products entered the markets. The others, however, were regarded as subsistence farming, their production being largely consumed locally.

[2] European Commission, 'Agenda 2000: For a Stronger and Wider Union' (COM(97) 2000 final), Brussels, July 1997.

were originally conceived as compensation payments for lowering of prices that the EU farmers received back in the beginning of the 1990s. Since, it was assumed in Agenda 2000, the newcomers' farmers would get higher prices for their production compared to those before membership, they would not need additional payments from the point of view of their competitiveness.

On the other hand, the Polish negotiators, backed largely by local public opinion, approached the issue from a completely different perspective. The direct payments made a part of the legal construction of the Common Agricultural Policy; they were thus a part of the *acquis communautaire.* Since the *acquis* was to be applied in full (an essential and fundamental rule of the accession negotiations), the payments were to be extended to the new farmers, regardless of whether they are considered necessary or not.[3]

On both sides, an important consideration was given to a perceived level of economic effectiveness of the respective farmers from both the EU and Poland. Both sides were afraid of the competitive advantages of the other side. The EU farmers were afraid of the Polish cheap labour productivity. The Polish farmers were afraid of the EU's subsidized cheap products that might push their own products off the shelves of Polish grocery shops. The situation was even more complicated by the fact that the EU was until October 2002 unable to reach an internal agreement on an overall financial package or the inclusion in it of the direct payments. The Franco-German deal on freezing agricultural expenditures until 2013 left room for the accession negotiations to enter their final stage on agriculture and finance.[4]

The final deal was only struck during the Copenhagen European Council Summit in December 2002. It consisted of three stages. The basis of it was the EU proposal—agreed among the fifteen Member States back in October at the summit in Brussels—to extend the direct subsidies to the new Member States' farmers starting from 25 per cent of the level actually offered to the EU 15 farmers. Those were to gradually grow by 5 per cent each year until 2007 and then to accelerate to 10 per cent yearly.[5] Hence, taking into account the direct payments extension to the new Member States, this was actually a transition period in favour of the EU allowing for a gradual extension of the direct payments until 2013, when those were to reach finally 100 per cent.

However, this was not enough to equalize the farming effectiveness between the EU with full direct subsidies and Poland. That is why Poland and the EU agreed in Copenhagen to increase part of the appropriations for the Polish rural areas in the form of direct payments. It was to be 15 per cent yearly until the end of 2006 (in other words, the remaining 85 per cent of rural development appropriations would indeed remain for rural development). This would allow a better use of the EU funds during the initial years of membership. Normally, the rural areas

[3] For all Poland's position papers and other accession negotiations related documents, see **www.negocjacje.gov.pl/neg.nsf/xml/stne2**

[4] Presidency conclusions, Brussels European Council, 24–5 October 2002, 14702/02, point 12.

[5] Ibid.

development funds, constituting the so-called second pillar of the Common Agricultural Policy, are used like any other structural instrument, and thus require an elaborated administrative system and detailed programming, the lack of which may actually hamper their effectiveness. Transferring a part of those funds to direct payments would certainly improve an overall financial benefit of the country from the very first day of accession.

The final deal struck on the direct payments for the Polish farmers included therefore a combination of both traditional direct payments starting at the 25 per cent level topped with a part of the rural areas appropriations and eventual support from the country's own budget. Hence, a total of direct payments from the Polish point of view was to be up to 55 per cent in 2004, then 60 per cent of the level observed in the old EU 15. Any eventual combination of the Structural Funds vis-à-vis direct payments after 2006 would require an agreement of the EU 25 within the framework of the new financial perspective for years 2007–013. This way, and this was also the case with previous enlargements, the deals on and around the accession moment do indeed influence parameters of future financial negotiations that are normally done inside the Union.

It is worth noting that the deal makes both sides generally happy. It does not undermine the general EU position that additional funds should not be offered to the new Member States beyond the amounts originally foreseen before Copenhagen. Yet, it allows the use of other available sources of money to overcome the reciprocal competitiveness problem as outlined above. That is why the deal was generally seen as fair on both sides and was claimed as a success by politicians of both sides.

Yet, the agricultural sector being the most elaborated one within the *acquis*, the final deal on agriculture also included other elements. The total amount of direct payments support is naturally linked with the question of how it was to be distributed. The normal way is to link the direct payments with the instrument of administrative control of agricultural production named IACS (Integrated Administration and Control System).

The specificity of the Polish sector, its sheer economic size, the existence of small farms, and the number of farmers to apply for EU support were all factors favouring a simplified system of support distribution. It was based not on actual level of production but on the size of farming areas, regardless of what is actually being produced there. The system is supposed to last for five years after accession. The low-production farms will be able to gain a special subsidy of €1,250 per year per farm. This is clearly a social benefit for those farmers that would not be able to compete on the Community markets for their products and will have to move their profession out of agricultural production. It is worth noting that the latest instrument of low-income farm subsidy is in fact the first step ever taken by the Union budget into the area of social benefits. Normally, the EU was rightly considered to be market-determined and social protection was left entirely in the hands of the Member States. Yet, in the latest case of enlargement, the low farming subsidy called for an exception in recognition of particular needs of the rural population in Poland. This contributed to the growing popularity of the idea of European integration among the poorest parts of the Polish society.

Table 13. Comparison of production quotas requested and agreed between Poland and the EU in some market organizations of the CAP

Production quotas negotiated	Initial request of Poland on 9 December 1999	Final agreement of 13 December 2002
Potato starch	260,000 tonnes	144,985 tonnes
Dried fodder	160,000 tonnes	13,538 tonnes
Sugar A	1,650,000 tonnes	1,580,210 tonnes
Sugar B	216,000 tonnes	91,926 tonnes
Isoglucose (A+B)	0 tonnes	26,781 tonnes
Tobacco	70,000 tonnes	37,933 tonnes
Milk (base production)	11,845,000 tonnes	9,380,000 tonnes
Slaughter premiums	3,038,000 heads total	2,654,948 heads total
Special beef premium	2,200,000 heads	926,000 heads
Ewe premiums	600,000 ewes	335,880 ewes
Suckler cows premium	1,500,000 heads	325,581 heads

Source: Own calculations based on the Polish position paper in chapter 7 on agriculture from 8 October 1999 and final results of the negotiations as presented in the Polish government communiqué of December 2002 'Raport na temat rezultatów negocjacji o członkostwo Rzeczypospolitej Polskiej w Unii Europejskiej', as well as the special edition of the Information Bulletin of the Polish Ministry of Agriculture and Rural Development, no. 1–2/2003 (74) of 10 January 2003.

Compared with the financial, economic, and political importance given to the final package and direct payments altogether, the other market elements of the CAP were perceived by the general public as items of minor importance. However, the farmers on both sides perceived them as equally important to the more savvy aspects of the CAP. The major contention was over the levels of production. Of course, the EU estimated these levels on a basis that was smaller than Warsaw would like. In detail, the total base area was raised from just over 9.2 million hectares to almost 9.5 million hectares, while the reference yields were slightly higher than 3 tonnes per hectare. These would have an effect on overall financial standing of the country in the EU in future, until there are direct payments applied in agriculture management. The production limits agreed concerned all market organizations within the CAP and they were generally similar to those requested initially by Poland. There were a couple of differences, however. The final package included a higher quota for milk production, in particular over 400 tonnes as restructuring reserve (see Table 13).

The milk quota issue was of course linked to the milk sector problems of the country. Generally speaking, there were those dairy production facilities that already conformed to the EU standards, and those that would have been ready to apply them by the date of accession. However, those that were not able to do so have been granted transition periods of two and four years (for various aspects of their standard conformity) in order to prepare for the Community market. During this period their production is treated as directed for the local markets, while the whole territory of Poland is considered as such a local market. A similar solution was found for those meat processing facilities that were not able to meet the EU standards by the accession date.

In both the case of milk and meat treatment facilities, the way to distinguish between the products for the local market versus those for the Community markets was based on the labelling. In order to give a taste of those negotiations, some figures need to be recalled in order to demonstrate how detailed and precise the negotiations were. So, for exactly 113 dairy processing facilities (out of 401 total), a transition period had been granted until the end of 2006, for 332 meat processing facilities (out of 4,123 total) their transition period would last until the end of 2007, while for 40 fish production facilities (out of 223 total) their transition period is to run until the end of 2006.

2. FISHERIES

In the case of fish processing facilities, the negotiations were automatically linked to those on veterinary questions normally treated within the Common Agricultural Policy chapter and those that were conducted under the label of the common fisheries policy. Here the label was not important, of course. However, the heading under which the negotiations were done dictated to a certain degree the abilities of both sides to link and/or disconnect separate issues. In essence, the negotiations on local dairy products that were intended to solve the issue of dairy facilities dictated the conditions under which similar problems of fish facilities would be treated: either there would be a single solution that would not result in keeping the border after accession, or the border would be maintained. The problem of the border was, of course, of crucial significance, as it was exactly this issue (the removal of the border after enlargement) that both sides treated as a gauge by which to measure their success in the negotiations.

While the solution was similar in fisheries to that in agriculture, in the beginning of the negotiations the two issues were treated as completely different and separate. The fisheries portfolio looked relatively easy as compared to the level of complication and political and financial importance of the agricultural sector. However, the negotiations on fisheries lasted longer then those on agriculture. The chapter was opened in May 1999 and the deal was closed only in June 2002; in total they lasted more than three years, clearly one of the chapters that remained open the longest.

What was so difficult in fisheries that comprise a few hundred thousand families across the EU 25? Well, as was always the case since the time the fisheries policy was born just before accession of the United Kingdom to the EEC in 1973, it was a difficult subject because it concerned a traditional profession in traditionally sea-oriented countries. Here, the EU policy touches the core of what is considered important and sometimes vital for a country.

As in previous enlargements, where disagreements arose between the UK and France (over the North Sea), and later on between Spain and France (over the Mediterranean), this time the problem was concentrated on the Baltic Sea.

The Polish fishermen were afraid that, once the maritime economic zone of the country became 'EU' territory rather than 'Polish', hence opening the sea to fishermen from the other EU Baltic Sea countries to explore, they would be pushed away from their business since their vessels are technically unable to compete with modern and powerful fishing fleets of Denmark and Germany.

Therefore, initially the Polish negotiators tried to keep some sort of administrative protection of the Polish shore after accession. The first mechanism attempting to protect Polish fishermen was the re-establishment of the so-called 'Hague preferences' that exist on the North Sea, which limit the access of fishing vessels in some areas. Yet, since the Hague preferences are an exception for the sake of protection of natural breeding zones in the areas concerned, the case for their re-establishment in the southern part of the Baltic Sea proved to be technically and scientifically untenable. Later on, the EU agreed to limit the access of the other EU Member States' fishing vessels to the Polish economic zone with a request of a transition period. This demand, however, was coupled with the possibility of limiting the Polish fishermen's access to the instrument allowing them to restructure their fleet: the FIFG (Financial Instrument for Fisheries Guidance). Given this prospect, Poland accepted the underlying principles of the Common Fisheries Policy, and Community competence in managing the total allowable catch (TAC) according to the general rules in the EU legislation. As a result, one of the longest-pending chapters was closed with one of the shortest formulations: the unconditional participation of Poland in this policy, expressed on less than half of a page of printed paper.

3. ACQUISITION OF REAL ESTATE BY FOREIGNERS

The real estate problem was among the three most difficult and politically charged issues during this negotiating period, apart from agriculture and free movement of workers. The problem was in fact very simple: due to historic and economic reasons, a large fraction of the Polish population was straightforwardly against opening the real estate market to foreigners. On the other side, the EU legislation, as a part of free movement of capital, requests that there may be no discrimination in favour of nationals against other citizens of the Union with respect to the 'four freedoms'. That is why Poland initially asked for rather a long transition period: eighteen years for agricultural land and forestry as well as eighteen years for secondary houses and five years for investment land. In order to understand the reasons for such demands, we need to address the local background of the issue.

The first observation that needs to be noted here is that the Polish law did not prohibit acquisition of real estate by foreigners but obliges any prospective foreign buyer to obtain a permit from the Ministry of Interior and Administration. In delivering one, the Ministry reviews the legality of the funding involved, agricultural structure of the local farming, environmental issues, as well as the local planning for the real estate to be purchased.

Second, Poland, as a part of the post-Second World War settlement of the Great Powers with the Soviet Union and Germany, was generally moved westwards, leaving traditionally Polish lands in the east and transferring to Poland some lands in the north and west. It was there that the populations that had left the eastern parts of pre-war Poland had to be settled. As a consequence, the local population living in those areas is generally more reluctant to consider liberalization of real estate acquisition, being afraid of possible pressure for rebuying of those territories by eventual buyers from Germany.

An additional reason that plays a role in combination with the above historic factor is the important difference in purchasing power between the relatively less affluent local (read Polish) population and the relatively richer potential buyer from Germany. An immediate opening of the real estate market would result in a hike of local prices that would distort the local market, which was considered to be particularly dangerous in the first years after accession when the bulk of farming restructuring was supposed to take place.

These two factors together created an important political consideration. The negotiating government ordered a public opinion poll on the issue. It revealed an obvious truth: out of the vast majority of up to 70 per cent Poles ready to vote in favour of Poland's membership in the EU in the future referendum, over 60 per cent of them were ready to turn 'no' if there would be an immediate liberalization of real estate acquisition. A further analysis of the issue showed that there is a threshold of almost twenty years of eventual transition period after the lapse of which this anxiety slowly disappears. In short, the opinion polls provided a further argument in favour of requesting a rather long transition period. While nobody among the EU negotiators was really surprised that Poland had requested a transition period in the area of real estate, the actual length of the demand (eighteen years) was perceived as rather long.

For quite a long time the EU tried in vain to apply to all the acceding countries a common solution worked out at a previous enlargement for Austria, Sweden, and Finland where a general transition period of five years had been agreed. While some of the candidate countries seemed ready to accept the offer, it was clearly far short of the Polish demands. That is why it took until March 2002 to agree a somewhat complicated solution.

First, the request for an investment land transition period was dropped by Poland. Second, the secondary houses transition period was agreed to be five years. Third, the agricultural land and forestry was to be protected by the Polish law as described above for the next twelve years after accession. In order to make this solution compatible with the right of establishment, a further sub-solution was devised: a farmer wanting to buy agricultural land for his own use needs to lease it first for three years before he can actually buy it, while in the northern and western regions of Poland the time for compulsory lease before purchase is seven years.

4. FREE MOVEMENT OF CAPITAL

The free movement of capital chapter also included a number of politically minor, but still technically important issues. Among them stood out an issue of proper definition and calculation of the state budget deficit. It was debated with the European Commission and the Eurostat for a long time before accession, and even after 1 May 2004. The question was whether the deficit derived from application of the pension scheme reform that moved a large share of pension expenditure into the hands of the private-run pension funds should nevertheless be regarded as 'public' money because the pensions are partially guaranteed by the state, or rather as 'private' money because it is in the hands of private funds. If it were private, it should not be calculated as part of the public deficit. The issue remained unresolved before accession and only the deal on the Stability Pact in early 2005 allowed for its closing: temporarily the Eurostat treats the pension funds money as private and thus outside of the state budget. For some years they will not count them as contributing to the state budget deficit. Yet before Poland's accession to the Eurozone this will change and any prospective government has to take into account that the state budget deficit needs to be lowered further by some 1.5 per cent of its GDP, that is roughly the amount of transfers into the pension funds' hands. Here we see a case where a minor and seemingly technical issue of statistics was touched upon during the negotiations but remained unsolved for some time after accession.

5. FREE MOVEMENT OF WORKERS

Free movement of workers being one of the cornerstones of the EU single market, it was the EU Member States that requested this transition period. In this famous case, the transition period negotiated by the EU mainly on behalf of Germany and Austria, applicable to all new Member States, and Poland in particular, follows the formula of 2+3+2. The formula was necessary due to the lack of agreement between fifteen members of the EU as to what extent this freedom should be limited to after accession. One extreme position was mostly favoured by Germany and Austria, who feared a sudden influx of workers from Poland[6] on their fragile labour markets. At the other extreme stood the UK and Ireland who in fact did want new labour force on their flexible labour markets which face a shortage in the workforce.

Hence the formula was agreed as follows: during the first two years after accession the EU legislation providing for free movement of workers is generally suspended on the whole territory of the old EU 15. This, of course, does not

[6] Unemployment rates in Poland were of the order of 18 per cent.

prohibit the Member States from concluding separate bilateral agreements liberalizing their labour markets for workers from new Member States. Poland had indeed entered into such agreements with Ireland, the United Kingdom, and Sweden. The effect was that three labour markets were opened for the Polish workers and the first year was carefully observed by all parties, including those countries that decided to keep their markets closed. In fact, only a handful of Polish job seekers travelled to those countries where they legally could look for new jobs. The overall effect on the British labour market remained limited with many positions still vacant there at the time of writing.

The first two years after accession having lapsed in May 2006, freedom of workers would be introduced, as defined in the EC legislation. At this stage, those countries that wished to do so could notify in time the European Commission and maintain their transition periods. Others, however, were free to open their labour markets on the basis of the EU legislation.

The second three-year tier of the scheme would lapse in May 2009, when the countries that still wished to maintain their transition period would need to apply to the Commission with a substantiated case favouring derogation, in order to win the Commission's approval of their extension. In other words, it would no longer be enough to just wish to continue the transition period, but the country in question would need to justify its case with concrete data showing that eventual opening of its labour market would be still risky. It is in the hands of the Commission to eventually grant the transition period extension.

Much as in the case of real estate acquisition, the issue of free movement of workers was a hot political case. For obvious reasons, it was an important issue in the countries that feared most an opening of their markets, like Germany and Austria. But it was also important in Poland for an entirely different set of reasons, namely that the Poles are in fact an eagerly travelling nation and any limit to that is perceived very badly, even if a particular person does not plan to travel herself. That is why the Estonian negotiators spared no effort in the negotiations to explain domestically why the EU, and Germany in particular, found the transition period to be politically necessary.

In fact, both cases (real estate acquisition and labour mobility) made an additional complication in the course of negotiations as they requested those involved to move their efforts beyond classical multilateral negotiations with the help of the Commission towards including a bilateral aspect of them, namely those between Poland and Germany only. It was in fact necessary, as both issues linked both countries almost by definition. Yet, we may conclude from our negotiating history that it was not a Polish–German deal that actually preceded the general one and allowed for conclusion of the negotiations between the other candidates and the EU in general. Rather, it was a dense network of exchange of ideas via government links, regional connections, and meetings between the non-governmental organizations that allowed for a better understanding of reciprocal positions. In other words, thanks to an intense effort on both sides, both public opinions, German and Polish, came to accept the other side's requests as a natural political reality. The Poles finally came to terms with the German need to have an extra protection buffer of their labour market, and the Germans bowed to the Polish need to extend the national protection of their real estate market after accession.

6. FINANCIAL PACKAGE

As was the case during other accession negotiations, the final financial package was discussed until the very end of the talks and was not finally settled until the Copenhagen European Council meeting itself in December 2002. On the one hand, the deal on finances covered all other aspects of the negotiations. On the other hand, its symbolic value of closing the negotiations as well as its consequences for the EU budget required participation of the top politicians from all Member States. Hence, only the European Council could decide on finances.

From the very beginning of negotiations it was clear to all Polish negotiators that there might be a problem because of the country's relative position with regard to the financial flows into (and out of) the EU budget.

The potential problem lay in the fact that, from the very moment of accession, the country has to pay its share to the EU budget, while it normally takes some time before a recipient country's administrative structures will get able to absorb funds from regional policy. In the case of Spain it took two years before the country turned net beneficiary of the EU budget.

Poland's situation was complicated further by one other condition: before accession the country was a net recipient of the so-called pre-accession aid that was intended to help Poland's preparation for implementing the *acquis communautaire*. In a sense, without contributing to the EU budget, Poland was receiving net almost €1 billion a year. For the Polish public opinion, very cautious about the future financial position of the country, it was almost unacceptable to reach a net financial position that would be worse than before accession. Hence, for the negotiators the task was not only to secure a beneficial net position vis-à-vis the budget, but also to set the post-accession financial benefits to a point higher than those before accession.

On the other hand, thanks to the pre-accession funds the country was supposed to get ready for a better, quicker, and more efficient use of the Structural Funds after accession. The beneficial effects of the pre-accession instruments were to be expected, however, only a couple of years after accession, since the moment of accession creates a hiatus between two flows: the pre-accession projects and therefore the pre-accession money on one hand, and the future projects and the structural money on the other.

That is why the original Polish position paper requested a solution to avoid this politically untenable situation for a country so much less affluent than the EU 15 average. Initially, the Polish side proposed a transition period of five years during which its contribution to the EU budget would accrue by 20 per cent yearly from 90 per cent discount in the first year, i.e. along the following scheme: 90, 70, 50,

30, and 10 per cent. Yet, since the EU did not want to complicate further the situation of budgetary contribution (already quite difficult due to the British rebate), it refused to agree to the budgetary transition period.

Therefore the issue remained open until the Copenhagen European Council and it needed an agreement between the heads of governments and states to solve the problem. The solution was found in agreeing an additional €1,443 million as a special instrument to solve the Polish budgetary flows problem. In order to get the money for Poland, while not breaching internal EU agreements on total ceilings for enlargement, it was decided to move 12 per cent of appropriations for Structural Funds for Poland for 2004–6 to this special instrument on the assumption that this would solve the problem of the net position of the country. On top of it, another special instrument for all new Member States was created in order to help them in preparing their external borders to the Schengen standards. Out of this, €280 million were appropriated for Poland alone in the same period of time covering the remaining part of Agenda 2000 financial perspectives.

7. ENVIRONMENT AND TRANSPORTATION (PROBLEMS OF ADMINISTRATION)

It may appear somehow unusual to deal with environment and transportation problems in accession negotiations together. Normally they are not perceived as similar. They were not linked during the talks either. While the greens point to some negative environmental effects of transportation, the issue is not really of EU relevance and was not discussed as such during accession negotiations. Clearly, both chapters in negotiations were considered to be similar for a rather obvious reason: in both environment and transportation (especially in road transport), the candidate countries of Central and Eastern Europe were rightly thought as needing the most costly investment. Their environmental and transportation infrastructures were either outdated or simply lacking and they obviously needed to update them to the standards required by the EU law. This was expected to cost money. A report by the World Bank put the total cost of updating the CEECs' environmental infrastructure at about €120 billion, of which a quarter, or up to €30 billion, was to be spent in and by Poland.[7]

On the one hand, this was clearly a heavy burden on the public budgets; on the other, however, it was an obvious indication of investment and business opportunities. Indeed, the legacy of a communist obsession with heavy industry and an attitude of neglect for environment had their effects, regardless of the amounts of money Poland had already spent after 1989 on upgrading the worst-polluting

[7] Gordon Hughes and Julia Bucknall, *Poland: Complying with EU Environmental Legislation* (Washington: World Bank, 2000); see also Tomasz Żylicz, 'Environmental Protection', in Cezary Banasinski et al., *Costs and Benefits of Poland's Membership in the European Union* (Warsaw: Natolin European Centre, 2003).

industries. In total, over the last fifteen years Poland has been spending on environment between 1.6 and 1.8 per cent of its GDP a year.

Yet, there is one more important reason to look at those negotiating chapters together. What made them similar over the time was a particularity of the problems they provoked. For Poland it proved to be difficult, it needs to be said, because of the particular historic experience of administration and the political elites. In both cases it was obvious from the very beginning of the negotiations that Poland would need a transition period that would allow it to be able to fulfil the EU standards in roads and environment. Yet, the most difficult problem that the negotiators on both sides faced was how to calculate a proper length of requested transition period. In other words, what would be the tools by which to judge which duration of a transition period obviously needed would serve both the country and the EU best.

Normally, evaluations of that kind are carried out by the central government (responsible for negotiations in general) in cooperation with the local governments (responsible for implementation of the relevant directives and in fact responsible for investment programmes) together with the local businesses that would make a reality out of the investment programmes.

However, it proved difficult to collect viable data and put it together into coherent planning. The main reason for that was the still fairly recent unpleasant experience of many people with the communist 'planned economy'. In the past approach, plans were used not only to direct the way economy should go, but more and more to distort the reality. In fact, life was divided between economic reality of permanent shortage and artificial reality of 'plans' where everything was basically all right.

The further away from centre the putting together of plans lay, the more resistant were the people in charge to putting together plans that they considered to be useless. Not surprisingly, then, the initial justifications of the transition periods requested by Poland were not satisfactory to the European Commission. They rather provoked numerous questions from the Commission than set the stage for proper negotiations. Negotiations of both chapters resulted in numerous rounds of field-specific exchanges between the EU and Poland: position papers, multiple questions and answers to them, a number of meetings of experts. The process of administrative rapprochement started from the screening and continued with the Commission officials as well as with the national experts delegated to Poland from the Member States within the twinning scheme.

On top of the problem described above, the Polish environmental administration traditionally understood environmental protection as nature protection only. Some time was needed to introduce it to a more EU-like approach where the environmental policy indeed means a bit of nature protection (i.e. the Birds Directive), but the bulk of it is concerned with limitation of damage an industry can make to the environment.

For both reasons, cooperation of the Polish environmental and transportation central and regional administrations with the European Commission proved extremely important to properly understand what the EU *acquis* in respective chapters is really about. Here, the Commission played very well its role as 'teacher' to the Member States' administrations. Further, the system of administrative twinning, establishing closer links between administrations of various Member States and those of the candidate countries, was very useful. Nevertheless, it took some time before the Polish administration accommodated itself to the way of thinking about the environment that is the case inside the EU.

Although the environment chapter proved to be a hard nut to crack, the negotiations resulted in agreeing a set of well-defined transition periods that never provoked any serious sign of criticism from either side. This seems to be proof that the negotiating effort was worth its pain and sweat. A total of ten transition periods were agreed out of seventeen requested by the Polish side in the environment chapter. The transition periods agreed do not affect the functioning of the single market and should not be seen as 'environmental dumping'. They rather reflect the inability of a relatively less affluent state to provide its citizens with the level of environmental protection normally seen in the EU. One classic example of this is the waste water directive (91/271) that is covered by a set of transition periods for various dwellings with different number of inhabitants that will last five to twelve years.

Environmental negotiations were also the stage of another interesting phenomenon: a chapter once closed had to be reopened because the EU adopted a new directive that was not covered initially by the screening or by the negotiations before closing the chapter. What makes the case even more interesting is that the new directive (large combustion plants directive, 2001/80) is intended to be applicable in 2008, well after the time when the negotiations were taking place. Hence, the transition periods agreed cover the years of 2008–15/17 and 2016–17 for various kinds of polluting agents. In other words, this is a clear example that the accession negotiations can be rightly regarded as a first practical step for an acceding country to 'practise' membership without yet being an EU member.

With respect to the transportation chapter, the key problem was again related to the country's administrative capacity. A transition period regarding Directive 96/53, namely the weight of allowable vehicles, was agreed. The directive requires that lorries weighting up to 115 kN per axle be allowed on the roads of a Member State country in order to maintain an efficient grid of transportation across the Union. Yet, in Poland, only a very limited number of roads were able to sustain this maximum weight. Again, as in the case of environment, it took a while before both sides were able to understand correctly the reciprocal needs and requirements. Finally, a transition period until the end of 2010 was agreed. With the help of the Structural and Cohesion Funds, the transition period will allow the country to build a sufficient network of roads to allow traffic of very heavy trucks.

One more interesting case also concerned transportation and it showed how sensitive the sector can be for the countries trying the ways of integrating their respective economic sectors. In this case it was about cabotage, namely the legal possibility of a carrier to transport persons within the other countries. In other words it was about the Polish transport companies being allowed to offer services in—for example—Germany. And vice versa: whether the French transportation companies would be allowed to operate within the borders of—say—Slovakia. Reciprocal uneasiness of companies from the EU 15 against companies from Poland and vice versa resulted in a transition period agreed for the sake of the EU 15 and Poland in a mirror-like way: both sides would not be allowed to offer cabotage for three years with a possibility of a further extension that would not exceed five years in total. In other words, the final integration of cabotage was postponed—as a result of transportation sector operators—for three to five years. So were postponed all benefits of integration in this sector. The case of transportation integration between EU 15 and CEECs 8 is no different from the case of transportation integration between the original founding six and later on the EEC 9, or EU 12. Transportation has always been a sector that was very reluctantly integrated. This is still the case today.

8. ENERGY AND TELECOMMUNICATIONS (CASES OF STATE-OWNED COMPANIES)

On the side of the negotiations in transportation it needs to be noted that those were largely helped very much by the decision of the Polish government to privatize the key companies in respective fields. The same is true with respect to the chapters on telecommunications and information technologies. Hence, before the start of the accession negotiations, and irrespectively of the acquis requirements, it was decided that the Polish airline Lot, as well as the Polish telecommunications company TP SA, would be privatized -and indeed this happened. In the course of the accession negotiations the government did not have to deal with the position and future of those public companies. To the contrary, in the chapter on energy (no. 14) the negotiators had to take into consideration the position of the state-owned natural gas transmission and distribution company, PGNiG SA. Its inability to open the natural gas market for competition, as required by the third party access (TPA) principle enshrined in the gas directive (98/30), resulted in an initial demand for a transition period on behalf of this company. Later on, as a result of extensive cooperation with the company, it was dropped. Nevertheless, it was one of the major problems in closing the chapter.

The treatment of companies based on their ownership status (either private or state owned) is not due to any ideological obsession of the negotiators or the negotiating government in question. It comes from a simple fact that in the past those companies were not only state owned, but also monopolies. Obviously, the EU legislation does not prohibit state ownership, while it does forbid monopolies regardless of their ownership status. In fact, privatization in those cases meant not only change of owners, but also—and more importantly—liberalization of the respective markets.

There was yet another important problem in the energy area: the EU requests its Member States to maintain a stock of oil and/or petroleum products that correspond to ninety days of average consumption (Directives 68/414 and 72/425). Poland, independently of the *acquis* requirement, started to build its own reserves back in 1996. Its key mechanism provided for a build-up of stocks by a small 2 per cent a year, in order to avoid putting too much pressure on private companies that are supposed to carry on the stocks, and protecting the state budget from excessive strain. By accession, the mechanism would not, of course, provide for the stocks that satisfy ninety days' requirement. That is why a transition period was requested and agreed to last until the end of 2008.

Yet another story comes from cooperation with companies in the telecommunications sector. The country telecommunication company (TP SA) having been privatized, the negotiators did not expect any major difficulty there. However, during the screening it came out that some parts of radio frequencies that are supposed to be freed for the mobile phone operators of the GSM system only (Directive 87/372) were still used by old parts of military equipment functioning according to the old Soviet technical system. Of course, the changeover to the new frequencies that would free them for public use by the mobile phone operators would cost additional money, so initially the negotiators requested a transition period.

Luckily enough, after closer scrutiny and having asked the Commission to give its legal assessment, the transition period was transformed into a schedule of gradual liberation of those frequencies. This was domestically possible thanks to a very close cooperation of three ministries (Telecommunications, Finance, and Defence) together with mobile phone operators. The solution worked out not only allowed for closing the chapter in the framework of the EU accession negotiations, but—as a side issue for the negotiations, although very important for real life—it also made room for more users of those frequencies. Hence, a range of the frequencies newly opened to public use allowed an extra mobile phone operator to enter the market. That introduced more competition and was thus beneficial for customers. The case shows how accession negotiations can contribute to solving of domestic problems in a country.

9. PHARMACEUTICALS (A BRIDGE BETWEEN CHAPTERS)

Although there is no such negotiating chapter as 'pharmaceuticals' per se, they need to be discussed separately. It is so because there had been two separate problems that concerned pharmaceuticals in the course of negotiations. One concerned patent protection and it appeared in the chapter on company law (chapter 5). The other concerned re-registration of pharmaceutical products and was dealt with under the chapter on free movement of goods (chapter 1). Both, however, clearly concerned pharmaceuticals and their industry.

The patent protection problem was fairly complicated and reflected the fact that there is no single European patent in the EU and—on the other side—the candidate countries introduced their domestic patent law in accordance with the EU legislation (twenty years of protection of inventor's rights) at different moments. Hence, the situation is that there is no equal patent protection across the EU territory. On the other hand, one of the core fundamentals of the single market is the principle of free movement of goods. These two situations remain in conflict since a patented good (which advanced pharmaceutical products are) cannot be without restrictions, as non-patented products can be.

Some of the elements of the situation cannot be easily improved. We cannot, for example, change the fact that the Polish law on patent protection was introduced in full conformity with the EU requirements as early as in 1999. As a consequence of this, Poland tried in its position paper to introduce the supplementary protection certificate (SPC) that extends patent protection by up to five years as of the date of accession. Initially the intention of the negotiators was for the SPC to be applicable only to the patents granted after this date. It would mean that actual SPC could have been granted only after expiry of the normal patent protection starting at the accession date, that is, twenty years after accession. The other consequence was that those patents that were to be granted before the date of accession could not get an SPC. Of course, any earlier granting of the SPCs would result in longer patent protection and with that in higher prices of pharmaceuticals for consumers who would not be able to get generic products during that time.

This proposition was not acceptable to the EU, especially to those countries with a large pharmaceutical industry which was in a position to exert influence over government policy. That is why a number of friendly conversations with the governments of Great Britain and Italy, for example, could not change their positions.

As a result, a compromise had to be reached: the SPC can be granted to the products already patented at the date of Poland's accession, but only to those that were first marketed since the beginning of 2000. The parallel imports are to be prohibited.

There is a strong link between the above-mentioned issue and the problem of registration of pharmaceuticals in Poland. Normally, registered medicines stay in the market for five years and they need to be re-registered. The procedure is determined by law. The law has been changed during the negotiations in order to be in line with the EU legislation. Hence, the problem: after accession, there will exist certain products will have been registered under previous legislation. It is really impossible to re-register all the pharmaceutical products on the market in a short period of time. That is why a solution was found to allow those products that are registered already to be accepted on the market, and the procedure of re-registration would last until the end of 2008.

10. SPECIAL ECONOMIC ZONES AND THE PROBLEM OF COMPETITION

The special economic zones were created in Poland as a way of attracting foreign direct investment (FDI). They started to be set up in 1997 in regions particularly affected by unemployment, normally with a twenty-year period of various forms of state aid available for the investors that decided to settle their businesses there. A large part of this aid was in breach of EU rules on competition as defined in chapter 6 on competition policy. The forms that gave a reason for intensive negotiations that lasted as late as November 2002 were: export aids, the right to accumulate various forms of state aid, ceilings of aid received, and subsidies for the motor vehicles industry.

From the Polish perspective, while these forms of aid were in breach of the EU competition rules, they were used in the least developed regions, where unemployment was particularly high. At the same time, the country was at the end of negotiations on the regional policy chapter (chapter 21), which covered the whole of Polish territory under Objective 1 of the Structural Funds (i.e. its average GDP per capita was lower than 75 per cent of the EU average).

The negotiations on state aid in the special economic zones were in fact done on two different aspects. The first considered the ways of solving the issue of non-compatibility of the forms and levels of aid granted with the EU rules. The second was about how to respect the acquired rights of investors who came to the special economic zones before accession and invested there in their goodwill, according to the rules legally applicable at the time. Those should be respected and, if changed, they should only be altered with the full consent of the investors in question.

Hence, the final agreement was in fact a compromise, this time not really between the EU and Poland, but between two competing realities: one of the investors' acquired rights, the other of the needs of the EU competition policy. The agreement is in fact a list of certain agreed forms of transition periods, precisely describing forms of aid used on the territory of the Polish special economic zones that will be temporarily allowed until expiry of the terms agreed within the compromise. To be precise, those rules agreed are: a general transition period for the small and medium-sized companies (SMEs) until 2011 and 2010 respectively; a higher level of aids allowed that may reach 75 per cent of investment in the case of large companies that started their operation in the special economic zones in 1999 and up to 50 per cent for those companies that begun their activity there in 2000; total aid granted for the car industry cannot exceed 30 per cent of total investment.

As a separate, but fully linked issue, the agreement was reached on the total aid that may be granted to the Polish steel industry and the aid allowed was linked to a restructuring programme for the sector. The total aid was agreed at over €800 million, while the total reduction in steel mill production capacity was to reach over 1.2 million tonnes until 2006.

11. A WAY OF CONCLUSION

As a way of conclusion, we will offer an anecdote from the negotiating table. It concerns domestic problems, as they indeed pre-define the outcome of the negotiations with external actors. In this case, the administrative machinery of the country was unable to take a decision. There truly was a deadlock: no other level of the negotiating structure (neither line ministries involved, nor the negotiating team and the Committee for European Integration) was able to take the decision and the issue was left open for the Council of Ministers to decide. Yet, the Council sitting was still split over the issue and then it was only the Prime Minister himself that cut the discussions short and tilted the balance in favour of one of the options on the table.

The matter discussed concerned two transition periods considered by Poland in the social policy and employment chapter (chapter 13). A transition period of three years was requested with respect to the Council Directives 89/655 and 89/656 that concerned the minimum standards of working conditions in regard to machines in operation in small and medium-sized businesses. On the other hand, a transition period with respect to the personal protective equipment (also within the scope of the mentioned directives) was dropped.

Clearly, all through the process of formulating the position paper in chapter 13, the administration and politics of the country have been split into two camps. One was concerned more with protection of jobs and thus tried to avoid unnecessary burdens for businesses, especially in the small and medium-sized sector that was considered to be the most dynamic one. The other camp, however, was more concerned with protection of workers in their workplace and was thus more inclined to use legal tools to enforce their concerns. Both camps proved irreconcilable over the duration of the transition period, and it needed the political and personal authority of the Prime Minister himself to solve the issue. Here is how a proper bureaucracy and a political authority complemented each other. Without either of them, any positive outcome of the negotiations would not have been possible.

Those negotiations were to bring the two sides together. Those were the EU 15 and the ten applicant countries. Yet, they were also about bridging two differently developed groups of countries: advanced western ones and the post-communist eastern ones (the cases of Cyprus and Malta showed their particular while different facets). They were also about clashing interests that needed to be cushioned in any given sector. Still, they were also about turning our history: the Cold War division of Europe imposed in Yalta had to be overcome.

The finesse of the negotiations lay in three aspects: great attention to the smallest details in the directives, intermixed with the larger general trends of European economies, while all the time maintaining a clear understanding of the historical opportunity we create. All were present in our work. We think those helped us to understand each other better. It was a clear exercise of European integration in practice: a detail, a trend, the history.

16

The Accession of the Slovak Republic to the EU

Ján Figel'
Miroslav Adamiš

1. INTRODUCTION

The European Union is the institutional expression of the integration of its Member States into a community, the primary aim of which has been to secure peaceful cooperation. By the same token, its 2004 enlargement symbolized the fact that the Continent had definitively overcome its Cold War divisions.

However, the process of integration goes beyond the mere needs of economic cooperation. It is based on common values and principles. Their implementation is of inherent interest to every free society. At the end of the 1990s, after decades of totalitarianism, democracy prevailed again in the countries of Central and Eastern Europe, including Slovakia. Slovakia set out to strengthen its international position as a sovereign country in 1993 and, through intensive participation in the process of European integration, has become a full-fledged member of the community.

The accession negotiations took the form of an intergovernmental conference. This process differed from regular international negotiations not only in terms of its scope, contents, and duration, but also in terms of the number of participants involved. Slovakia, seated on one side of the table, negotiated with fifteen EU Member States seated on the other side of the table under the helm of the presidency and the European Commission, which acted as the organizer and moderator of preparations for individual rounds of negotiations. At the same time, Slovakia was part of a larger group of twelve candidate countries, ten of which acceded to the European Union in May 2004. Although each of the candidates negotiated individually, many issues were dealt with horizontally.

The negotiations between the Slovak Republic and European Union were based on a constructive and realistic approach. Our underlying assumption was that being a participant of the European integration process is in the country's primary interest. The integration was, to a large extent, a response to the necessary economic and social reforms, increased security, regional development, and environmental protection. We understood that entry into the Union would mean the transposition and, in some areas, specific adaptation of the *acquis communautaire*. The negotiating strategy of the Slovak Republic was based on the need to secure beneficial and acceptable conditions for membership in the Union, including an appropriate share in the decision-making and administrative structures of the common European affairs.

During the Helsinki Summit, we set 2004 as the reference date for accession. At the same time, other candidates planned their accession for 2002 or 2003. Our interest was to join the Union, if possible, along with our neighbours from the region—the Czech Republic, Hungary, and Poland—for a number of reasons. Apart from the geopolitical interest in improving and strengthening its position on the Continent and in the world, Slovakia wanted to maintain the benefits of its customs union with the Czech Republic up until the point of accession, to progressively align its border regime to the Schengen criteria together with its neighbours, and to strengthen the cross-border cooperation between regions.

Rather than demanding as much as possible under various negotiating chapters, our tactic during the negotiations was to focus on priorities and sensitivities and, based on clear justification, objective arguments, and mutual trust, put them through. After thirty-four months, Slovakia successfully completed its negotiating road from Helsinki to Copenhagen. The results of these negotiations reflect the priorities and requirements for transitional periods and are, both as a package and in their particulars, comparable with the results achieved by other countries. It is the results, rather than gestures and rhetoric, which count. Trust is equally important, albeit difficult to measure, as it builds consensus and makes easier the complicated negotiations which, in turn, build up trust, thus completing a virtuous cycle.

The accession negotiations and various technicalities represented only a part of the comprehensive and long-term endeavour of the country and its representatives to join the European Union. Upon signature of the Accession Treaty and its ratification by referendum, Slovakia effectively avowed its EU membership. It is, however, necessary to ensure that all important stakeholders continue to be engaged in the preparations for the country's proper functioning in the new legal and economic environment. The success of integration will largely depend on the ability of the institutions, public administration, economy, and the civil society as a whole, to make use of this new environment to the benefit of Slovakia's overall development.

Slovakia submitted its application for EU membership on 27 June 1995 at the Cannes European Council in France. On the basis of the applications presented by several candidate countries, the Madrid European Council in December 1995 asked the European Commission to draw up its opinion (*avis*) on the applications of the association countries for EU membership. Further to that request, the Commission prepared (in July 1997) its *avis* on Slovakia's application for EU membership, alongside with opinions on applications submitted by the other nine applicant countries.

The purpose of the opinion was to assess the progress achieved by Slovakia in fulfilling the Copenhagen criteria.[1] The Copenhagen European Council in June

[1] Article (6)1 of the consolidated Treaty on European Union reads: 'The Union is founded on the principles of liberty, democracy, respect for human rights and fundamental freedoms, and the rule of

1993 concluded that an associated country which has applied for EU membership may become a member only if it complies with the political and economic criteria:

- to ensure the stability of institutions guaranteeing democracy, the rule of law, human rights, and respect for and protection of minorities;
- to ensure the existence of a functioning market economy as well as the capacity to cope with competitive pressure and market forces within the Union; and
- to demonstrate the ability to take on the obligations of membership, including adherence to the aims of political, economic, and monetary unions.

In order to create conditions for gradual and harmonious integration of the candidate countries, the Madrid European Council in December 1995 broadened the Copenhagen criteria, emphasizing that candidate countries must also put in place the necessary administrative capacities to implement the *acquis*.

In its 1997 opinion on Slovakia's application for EU membership, the Commission stated that Slovakia failed to comply with the political criteria set by the Copenhagen European Council, citing instability of constitutional institutions and deficient functioning of democracy. On the basis of this assessment, the Luxembourg European Council in 1997 did not recommend opening negotiations on accession with Slovakia. The failure to comply with the Copenhagen political criteria effectively excluded Slovakia from the integration process.

The Luxembourg European Council furthermore decided that, from the end of 1998, the Commission would submit regular reports[2] to the Council, together with any necessary recommendations for opening bilateral intergovernmental conferences, reviewing the progress of each Central and Eastern European applicant state towards accession in the light of the Copenhagen criteria.

2. YEAR 1998: POLITICAL CHANGES

Further to the decision adopted by the Luxembourg European Council, in March 1998 the Commission opened accession negotiations with six countries which complied with the Copenhagen criteria: Cyprus, the Czech Republic, Estonia, Hungary, Poland, and Slovenia.

Parliamentary elections in Slovakia took place on 25 and 26 September 1998. After the formation of the new government, Commissioner Hans van den Broek

law.' In compliance with this, Article 49 of the consolidated treaty provides that 'Any European State which respects the principles set out in Article 6(1) may apply to become a member of the Union.' These principles were reiterated by the Charter of Fundamental Rights of the European Union proclaimed by the European Council in Nice in December 2000 and the treaty establishing a constitution in Europe signed in Rome in October 2004.

[2] On this basis, the European Commission presented the first series of regular reports in November 1998 before the Vienna European Council; the second series of reports was adopted in October 1999 before the Helsinki European Council, the third in November 2000 before the Nice European Council, the fourth in November 2001 before the Laeken European Council, and the last one, i.e. the fifth, in October 2002 before the Brussels European Council.

offered Prime Minister Mikuláš Dzurinda, during the latter's visit to Brussels, an invitation for the creation of a high-level working group. The proposal was accepted. The objective of the group was to underpin Slovakia's endeavours and give the process of preparations for EU membership a new momentum. The working group focused its activity on the adoption and monitoring of the fulfilment of the key measures which Slovakia had to adopt in order to comply with the Copenhagen criteria and short-term priorities for accession.[3]

The European Union showed its appreciation of the post-1998 political changes in Slovakia at the Vienna summit of heads of states and governments in December 1998, where it stated that the democratic election had given Slovakia the possibility to solve its political issues and adopt steps towards meeting the political criteria. Nevertheless, neither Slovakia nor any other candidate country was invited to accession negotiations at the time.

3. YEAR 1999: BACK AMONGST THE FRONT RUNNERS

The period following the 1998 parliamentary election meant the beginning of a new quality in relationships and intense political dialogue between Slovakia and the European Union, during which the atmosphere of mutual contacts progressively changed. A clear priority of the Slovak government and the Parliament in 1999 was to ensure that the European Council adopted a decision that would allow the opening of accession negotiations, based on a positive recommendation by the Commission.

This objective was met, and the integration priorities were set, partly thanks to the activities of the High-Level Working Group. During its ten-month existence, the Working Group met five times. It was led by Deputy Director General François Lamoureux for the European Commission and, on the Slovak side, by Ján Figel', the state secretary at the Foreign Affairs Ministry and chief negotiator for Slovakia's accession to the EU.

As regards the political criteria for EU membership, Slovakia aligned its Election Act with the Constitutional Court ruling and, in December 1998, held municipal elections. The first-ever direct presidential elections in May 1999 ended a fifteen-month vacancy in the office of president. The Act on the Use of Minority Languages in Official Communication was also adopted in July 1999. Slovakia aligned its legislation in this area with the Constitution, as well as with international standards and the majority of specific recommendations issued by the OSCE, Council of Europe, and European Commission in this respect.

In the field of economic criteria, the Working Group dealt mostly with measures designed to ensure macroeconomic stability and restore both the internal and external macroeconomic balance. The country adopted important

[3] Partnership for Accession was a programme of objectives and priority tasks adopted by the respective candidate country to improve its preparedness for the process of accession and future membership, supported by the European Commission and EU members.

decisions concerning the efficient restructuring and privatization of the banking sector and tighter tax discipline in the business sector. In the area of the internal market, Slovakia adopted the State Aid Act, the Act on Technical Requirements and Conformity Assessment of Products, and the Act on Public Procurement. These measures helped to increase the transparency of economic decisions.

In June 1999, the Working Group set up a joint sub-group for nuclear energy, the objective of which was to define the overall nuclear strategy and set up a plan to create conditions enabling the early closure of two units of the V-1 nuclear power plant in Jaslovské Bohunice. The EU considered these two units impossible to upgrade at reasonable cost and thus postulated the setting of an acceptable deadline for their earlier decommissioning as a precondition for the commencement of accession negotiations. In September 1999, the Slovak government adopted a decision to decommission the two units in 2006 and 2008 respectively. Acting on behalf of the Union, the Commission pledged to contribute towards the cost incurred until the point of decommissioning.

After the 1998 parliamentary elections, Slovakia made profound political changes, stabilized its political system, and strengthened democracy. Thanks to persistent effort, the political criteria for EU membership were thus met. In the field of economic criteria, the government adopted measures designed to improve the overall economic situation and allow sustainable economic growth. Based on this evident progress, the Helsinki European Council in December 1999 stated that Slovakia complied with the political criteria and invited Slovakia to accession negotiations.

We were aware that the success of negotiations in Brussels would be determined by thorough preparations and diligent work at home. On the other hand, the success of the negotiating process generated new stimuli and momentum to intensify preparations for integration. Slovakia created various bodies at the governmental level and individual ministries, to coordinate, in consultation with non-governmental organizations, the process of negotiations and preparation for accession. The coordination of the integration process was the responsibility of the Ministry of Foreign Affairs where the chief negotiator held the post of state secretary. The negotiating positions were assessed by the Ministerial Council for European Integration and, subsequently, approved by the cabinet. The Parliament was also involved in the process of negotiations through regular briefings which took place before each negotiating round.

4. YEAR 2000: BEGINNING OF NEGOTIATIONS

Portuguese presidency (first half of 2000)

Further to the decision of the Helsinki European Council in December 1999, Slovakia and five other candidate countries (Lithuania, Latvia, Malta, Bulgaria, and Romania) opened accession negotiations at the opening of the conference on accession on 15 February 2000. Slovakia declared its general negotiating position on accession negotiations in which it presented an ambitious yet realistic plan. Slovakia committed itself to aligning its legislation with the *acquis* and building the corresponding administrative capacities by the end of 2002. The government set 1 January 2004 as a reference date for accession to the Union. This enlargement scenario, which later became pan-European, was for the first time confirmed by the conclusions of the Göteborg European Council in June 2001.

At the time, Hungary had its reference date for accession set for 1 January 2002, while the Czech Republic and Poland had their dates set for 1 January 2003. Slovakia assumed that following the ratification of the Treaty of Nice, the Union would be prepared to welcome new members from the end of 2002. That was the time by which Slovakia intended to complete accession negotiations and, subsequently, launch the process of ratification of the Treaty of Accession and complete the process within a year.

In order to assist Slovakia and other candidate countries of the so-called 'Helsinki group' in following this strategy, the principle of differentiation in the opening of individual negotiating chapters and conducting negotiations was applied. Our ambition was to open as many chapters as possible: half of them by the end of 2000 and the rest gradually by the end of 2001. We did not perceive these negotiations as a race or beauty contest among candidate countries. Our goal was to catch up—within a reasonable time and subject to thorough advanced preparations—with the countries of the so-called 'Luxembourg group'. At the same time, this meant the acceptance of the open offer of the EU 15 from Helsinki.

Slovakia entered the negotiations convinced that their outcome, i.e. accession to the European Union, would be mutually beneficial to both sides. European integration is a unique project not only of our times, but also in the development of modern civilization. The accession process had a positive influence on the stability of the domestic political environment and relationships in the region. Slovakia viewed the accession process as a complex of mutually interdependent elements. That is why the country strived for membership in OECD and NATO[4] in parallel.

At the onset of negotiations, Slovakia confirmed that it fully accepted the goals of the Amsterdam Treaty as defined in Article 2 of the Treaty of European Union and that, by the time of accession, it would be prepared to accept the *acquis* in the applicable scope. Slovakia expressed interest in becoming integrated into the single market of the Union and the policies of the Community, including accession to the economic and monetary union (subject to meeting the convergence criteria) and adoption of the euro (first pillar). Slovakia supported the objective of the common foreign and security policy and expressed interest to participate in the defining and forming of the European security and defence policy (second pillar). In the area of justice and home affairs, Slovakia had already

[4] Slovakia became the thirtieth member of the Organization for Economic Cooperation and Development in December 2000 and a member of NATO in April 2004.

expressed interest in deepening cooperation in the fields of border control, asylum law, and migration, as well as in combating organized crime, terrorism, and drug smuggling, during preparations for membership (third pillar).

During negotiations, Slovakia did not plan to apply for derogations from the implementation of *acquis communautaire.* It did, however, request transitional periods in those areas where their granting was justified by a need to enhance competitiveness of the Slovak economy or ensure major capital investments. These requests were not only substantiated, but also supported by a realistic plan of steps to be taken to ensure harmonization with the *acquis.* This also included a calculation of the costs necessary in order to achieve compatibility and specification of the resources needed to finance such costs. The rules of negotiation included the possibility of modifying the requests for transitional periods during negotiations to better reflect changes in the legislation and/or the actual situation.

In terms of their scope and contents, the negotiations were particularly complex in the areas of internal market, taxation, transport, environment, energy, agriculture, regional policies, and coordination of structural instruments.

During the Portuguese presidency in the first half of 2000, the EU had already opened the first eight negotiating chapters of the *acquis* with Slovakia and provisionally closed six of them. Chapters such as small and medium-sized enterprises (SMEs), education and training, science and research, common foreign and security policy (CFSP), statistics and external relations, did not require substantial modifications in the Slovak legislation because the degree of integration in these areas within the Union was not as high as in the chapters that followed later on. The course and the results of negotiations under the Portuguese presidency can be viewed positively because the negotiations were dynamic and, from Slovakia's perspective, successfully set the process in motion in an encouraging way.

Chapters opened under the Portuguese presidency

6. Competition
12. Statistics
16. Small and medium-sized enterprises
17. Science and research
18. Education and training
20. Culture and audio-visual policy
26. External relations
27. CFSP

Chapters provisionally closed under the Portuguese presidency

12. Statistics
16. Small and medium-sized enterprises
17. Science and research
18. Education and training
26. External relations
27. CFSP

French presidency (second half of 2000)

EU Member States decided to open eight more negotiating chapters during the French presidency. Slovakia closed four chapters of *acquis communautaire*—fisheries, consumer protection, industrial policy, and culture and audio-visual policy. Expecting further progress in the negotiations, Slovakia submitted to the Union its negotiating positions on all remaining chapters by December 2000. The agenda set for the French presidency was met, despite delays on the part of the EU that occurred mainly in the early stages of the period.

Chapters closed under the French presidency

3. Freedom to provide services
4. Free movement of capital
8. Fisheries
9. Transport
15. Industrial policy
19. Telecommunications and IT
23. Consumer and health protection
25. Customs union

Chapters opened under the French presidency

8. Fisheries
15. Industrial policy
20. Culture and audio-visual policy
23. Consumer and health protection

Status of negotiations in the year 2000

In the first year of negotiations Slovakia, opened sixteen chapters in total, and thus met its internal objective—to open at least half of the negotiating chapters during the first year. Ten chapters were provisionally closed and six remained on the table either for the Slovak side to furnish supplementary information or for both sides to look for modified solutions. Measured by the number of provisionally closed chapters, Slovakia ranked second to Malta within the Helsinki group of countries.

5. YEAR 2001: A STEP CLOSER TO THE EU DOOR

Swedish presidency (1st half of 2001)

The Nice Summit in 2000 endorsed an important strategic document of the Commission concerning enlargement: the so-called 'road map', which set out the EU priorities for negotiations with candidate countries during the three forthcoming presidencies—Swedish, Belgian, and Spanish. Given its ambition to join the Union along with the other Visegrad four countries, Slovakia focused mainly on the priority areas of the Swedish presidency, i.e. the internal market-related chapters (freedom of movement of goods, freedom of movement of persons, freedom to provide services, free movement of capital), as well as the chapters on company law, environment and social policy, and employment.

The goals set for the first half of 2001 were accomplished. By the end of the Swedish presidency, Slovakia had opened all twenty-nine chapters of the *acquis*, with negotiations provisionally closed in nineteen of them. Slovakia closed all the chapters related to the internal market, including some chapters wherein it requested transitional periods (freedom to provide services, free movement of capital).

Chapters opened under the Swedish presidency

1. Free movement of goods
2. Free movement of persons
5. Company law
7. Agriculture
10. Taxation
11. Economic and monetary union
13. Social policy and employment
14. Energy
21. Regional policy
22. Environment
24. Justice and home affairs
28. Financial control
29. Budgetary provisions

Chapters provisionally closed under the Swedish presidency

1. Free movement of goods
2. Free movement of persons
3. Freedom to provide services
4. Free movement of capital
5. Company law
11. Economic and monetary union
13. Social policy and employment
19. Telecommunications and IT
25. Customs union

Environment was the only chapter where the schedule for the Swedish presidency was not adhered to. This was due to the need to draft detailed financial and implementation plans for twenty-one directives with a particular focus on those where Slovakia requested transitional periods. As envisaged by the catch-up principle, after seventeen months of negotiations, Slovakia, with nineteen chapters provisionally closed, caught up with countries which had already been engaged in the negotiation process for more than two years. The extraordinary commitment of the Swedish presidency and the positive atmosphere in favour of the enlargement agenda helped Slovakia a great deal in meeting its negotiation objectives.

Description of transitional periods agreed under the Swedish presidency

Free movement of persons

The common position of the EU represented a compromise on the part of the Member States and its proposal included a request by Austria and Germany for a seven-year transitional period in the '2+3+2' structure. The proposed model is flexible. It enables those countries that so wish to liberalize access to their labour markets immediately after enlargement (this position was at that time officially declared by Sweden, the Netherlands, Denmark, Ireland, and the UK). At the same time, it enables Slovakia to apply reciprocal measures vis-à-vis Germany and Austria in the field of service provision in border regions.

At the accession conference on 26 October 2001, the EU offered Slovakia an extension of the compromise with regard to the movement of persons, agreed in June 2001. Based on the adopted negotiation amendment, Slovakia may apply a mechanism of so-called safeguard measures against a new Member State even if no Member States apply restrictions against such a new Member State.

Free movement of capital

After accession, Slovakia will apply a seven-year transitional period for the acquisition of agricultural and forest land by foreign nationals. Should a serious disturbance on the agricultural land market occur upon expiry of the transitional period, the Commission shall, upon Slovakia's request, rule on its extension by a maximum of three additional years. This amendment, agreed in the final stages of the negotiations, will allow Slovakia to apply, if necessary, a ten-year transitional period for the acquisition of agricultural land by non-nationals. This transitional period does not apply to private farmers, who may acquire agricultural and forest land in Slovakia provided that they are resident in Slovakia and perform agricultural activity for three years without interruption.

Freedom to provide services

Slovakia has been granted a three-year transitional period until the end of 2006 for the application of Article 4 of Directive No. 97/9/EC which lays down investor compensation schemes and sets the minimum level of cover for investors to €20,000.

This article will be implemented in three stages. In the initial stage, after the introduction of compensation schemes, the level of cover in respect to money and securities entrusted to an investment firm is envisaged to be around €5,000–6,000 and shall apply only to investors who are natural persons. Depending on the development of the capital market, the number of providers of financial services, and the amount of the administered funds, the amount of compensation for the unrecoverable monies and securities will be gradually adjusted to up to €20,000.

Belgian presidency (second half of 2001)

As the overall negotiation agenda advanced, the negotiations became more difficult in the second half of 2001. They concerned chapters that were more complex in terms of both the volume of the related *acquis* and Slovakia's negotiation requirements. Maximum emphasis was laid in particular on the chapters scheduled for the Belgian presidency, as well as on the environment chapter, which was left opened from the Swedish presidency.

Under the Belgian presidency, Slovakia closed three more chapters (energy, environment, financial control), bringing the total number of provisionally closed chapters to twenty-two. Slovakia's intention was to close two more chapters scheduled for the Belgian presidency—transport and taxation. These plans were not met, partly due to objective reasons: the short duration of the Belgian presidency and the events of 9/11, which caused the attention and human resources to be primarily focused on the fight against international terrorism and related activities. At the same time, the negotiations entered a difficult stage, in terms of both the volume of the *acquis* involved, and the negotiation requirements put forward by the candidate countries and the Union. With a view to eliminating delays in the negotiating agenda, the EU organized an additional accession conference at a ministerial level in the end of December, which partly eliminated the deficit in accomplishing the priorities of the Belgian presidency.

In comparison with other candidate countries, Slovakia confirmed its negotiating potential and the realism of its plan to join the EU in the first wave of enlargement in 2004. This fact was also acknowledged by the EU summit in Laeken, which included Slovakia among the ten candidate countries (Cyprus, Czech Republic, Estonia, Lithuania, Latvia, Hungary, Malta, Poland, Slovakia, and Slovenia) expected to join the EU in 2004, provided that they keep their negotiating momentum.

Chapters provisionally closed under the Belgian presidency

14. Energy
22. Environment
28. Financial control

Description of transitional periods agreed under the Belgian presidency

Energy

Slovakia negotiated a five-year transitional period (until 31 December 2008) for the building of the necessary oil storage facilities, after which it will be able to hold the obligatory minimum stock of oil and petroleum products (Directive

No. 68/414/EC as amended by Directive No. 98/93/EC). It is the longest transitional period negotiated with the EU under this chapter (the same applies to Poland).

In 1999, Slovakia undertook to decommission two units of the V-1 nuclear power plant in Jaslovské Bohunice (in 2006 and 2008, respectively). The Commission earmarked €150 million for the years 1999–2006 towards the cost of decommissioning. Because the sum increased by €30 million during negotiations, Slovakia will receive funds whose total worth is €180 million. Moreover, the EU also undertook to co-finance the decommissioning of the two units even after 2006. The decommissioning funds will be provided via the Bohunice International Decommissioning Support Fund (BIDSF), which was set up for this purpose by the European Commission at the European Bank for Reconstruction and Development (EBRD). The list of donors also includes several EU Member States (Austria, the Netherlands, United Kingdom, Denmark, Spain, and Ireland).

Environment

Environment was a difficult chapter of the *acquis* in terms of both size and negotiating requirements. Slovakia managed to put through seven transitional periods; those requests and goals for transitional periods that were officially withdrawn will be dealt with using the existing conditions and possibilities of the applicable *acquis,* i.e. by way of derogations:

- Slovakia obtained a four-year transitional period (until 31 December 2007) for three operators of new large combustion plants;
- where hazardous waste incineration is concerned, the EU agreed to a three-year transitional period (until 31 December 2006) for eleven hospital waste incineration plants and seven industrial waste incinerators;
- for the existing petrol storage facilities, a one- or four-year transitional period (until 31 December 2004 or 31 December 2007) has been agreed depending on the type of the facility;
- for the directive on urban waste water treatment, a seven-year transitional period (until 2010) was agreed for agglomerations with more than 10,000 inhabitants and an eleven-year transitional period (until 2015) for those between 2,000 and 10,000 inhabitants.
- with respect to three existing facilities, a three-year transitional period from the application of the directive on water pollution caused by discharges of certain dangerous substances has been agreed;
- with respect to ten existing facilities, an up to eight-year transitional period (until the end of 2011) has been agreed from the application of the directive on integrated pollution prevention and control; and
- Slovakia negotiated a transitional period until the end of 2007 from the directive on packaging and packaging waste.

In three cases, Slovakia applied the provisions of the existing directives without requesting transitional periods:

- Slovakia applied the provision of the directive on the protection of water against pollution caused by nitrates from agricultural sources, which allows for the drafting of action programmes for the gradual reduction of nitrate-polluted waters by the year of accession. The implementation of these action programmes is envisaged to be completed in the next four years, i.e. by the end of 2007.
- Slovakia used the opportunity offered for the existing installations by the directive on limitation of emissions of volatile organic compounds. They should be harmonized with the *acquis* by 30 October 2007 and the new installations regulated by the directive will be in compliance with the directive by the date of Slovakia's accession into the EU.
- Where the directive on drinking water is concerned, Slovakia was granted a derogation to allow compliance to be achieved regarding the individual quality indicators of drinking water and the relevant water sources for public drinking water distribution within the period of three years as of the date of EU accession. In properly justified cases, Slovakia may request extension of that period upon its expiry.

Overall status of negotiations in 2001

The European Union opened negotiations with Slovakia in thirteen chapters, twelve of which were later provisionally closed. Before the last year of negotiations, two chapters remained on the table and a total of ten chapters remained to be closed. Slovakia proved that the catch-up system worked and indeed caught up with the V 4 countries in terms of the number of chapters closed. On the whole, the 'regatta' principle proved successful, which in practice meant that instead of the Luxembourg and Helsinki groups, a new, the so-called 'Laeken group' of candidate countries was formed.

6. YEAR 2002: COMPLETION OF NEGOTIATIONS

Spanish presidency (first half of 2002)

Slovakia's priority goal for the Spanish presidency was to complete negotiations on all outstanding chapters from the previous period and achieve as much progress as possible in the chapters defined in a schedule for the Spanish presidency, i.e. agriculture, regional policy, and budget. Save for the competition chapter, the above goal was successfully accomplished.

During the Spanish presidency, Slovakia provisionally closed negotiations on four chapters—taxation, transport policy, justice and home affairs, and institutions.

At the same time, a part of the agriculture chapter concerning veterinary and phytosanitary *acquis* was closed. Having provisionally closed a total of twenty-six chapters, Slovakia joined the ranks of the most advanced candidates for EU accession. This fact was also confirmed by the Member States at the Seville Summit. Preparations for the drafting of the Treaty of Accession were also launched under the Spanish presidency.

Opened chapters

7. Phytosanitary and veterinary part
30. Institutions

Closed chapters

9. Transport policy
10. Taxation
24. Justice and home affairs
30. Institutions

Description of transitional periods agreed under the Spanish presidency

Taxation

The taxation chapter constituted a priority chapter as Slovakia requested several transitional periods and derogations in the field of value added tax and excise duties.

Slovakia requested a one-year technical transitional period in compliance with Article 12(3)(b) of the existing sixth directive on value-added tax. This technical transitional period will enable Slovakia, based on situation assessment carried out by the Commission, to apply a reduced VAT rate on electricity and gas after accession to the EU.

Slovakia managed to negotiate the possibility of preserving a reduced VAT rate on heat energy until the end of 2008. The grounds for the above request included mainly the social impacts on the population which would have occurred had the VAT rate been increased by applying a unified base rate immediately after accession.

Slovakia negotiated the possibility to apply a reduced VAT rate on buildings and construction works for residential housing for a period of four years, i.e. until the end of 2007. No agreement was achieved with regard to the possibility of applying a reduced VAT rate on buildings and construction works funded by the state and public budgets, since the introduction of an increased tax rate would not have any social impact on the population but only on the state budget expenditure, and the application of the basic VAT rate would be neutral in relation to the state budget.

Slovakia, however, did not actually apply the aforementioned transitional period on the reduced VAT rate after the accession since it introduced a flat 19 per cent value added tax as part of its tax reform applicable from 1 January

2004 with no exemptions. Therefore, since 2004, Slovakia has applied only a base rate of value added tax.

Slovakia requested a permanent derogation on the application of a set mandatory registration limit for VAT payers (€5,000) with annual turnover lower than €35,000. The above implies that undertakings with an annual turnover not exceeding €35,000 are not required to register as VAT payers.

The most complex and lengthy negotiations in the field of taxation concerned the enforcement of a transitional period for attaining a minimum tax burden on cigarettes. The Slovak Republic requested a five-year transitional period. The EU conditioned the award of its consent upon the submission of a binding schedule for increasing the excise duty rates on cigarettes in the course of the agreed five-year transitional period starting in 2002, in order to harmonize them with the EU legislation. In addition to the minimum excise duty of 57 per cent of the retail price of cigarettes in the price category most in demand, a new fixed rate in an amount of €64/1,000 cigarettes is being introduced across the EU pursuant to Directive No. 2002/10/EC. The Slovak Republic has submitted its binding schedule for adjusting the minimum tax burden and fixed tax rate on cigarettes, which also respects the amended directive.

Slovakia also negotiated a permanent derogation in the field of small fruit growers' distillation, under which producers of fruit spirits are allowed to annually produce, in compliance with the directive, a maximum of 50 litres, with up to 50 per cent of the standard excise duty rate applicable to ethyl alcohol. The above derogation basically retains the current level of non-taxed volume of alcohol exempt from excise duty produced in distilleries for small fruit growers' distillation for the personal needs of a single fruit grower.

Transport policy

The chapter was closed with a single 2+2+1 year transitional period pertaining to cabotage. It has been agreed that the operation of national road haulage services in the territory of another Member State will not be mutually permitted for a transitional period of two years. Before the end of the second year after Slovakia's accession to the EU, both the 'old' and the 'new' Member States may notify the prolongation of the transitional period by two more years and, subsequently, by one additional year, if such prolongation is necessary in order to avert serious disturbances in their national road haulage market. If a Member State fails to notify the Commission of the prolongation of the transitional period, it is assumed that the respective Member State will fully apply *acquis* and open up its domestic market for cabotage operation by carriers from another Member State which will then open up its domestic market in the same manner.

Agriculture: phytosanitary and veterinary legislation

The veterinary and phytosanitary sections of the agriculture chapter focused mainly on the legislative and technical aspects. The issue of food safety represented the most sensitive area of negotiations. Slovakia submitted a complete list of food establishments describing the state of their readiness to comply with the EU requirements concerning food production and processing. All food producers provided written commitments that their establishments would fully comply with the respective *acquis* by the date of Slovakia's accession to the EU. In the case of two establishments, the EU accepted a request for a three-year transitional period in order to achieve the required hygienic standards. Slovakia, however, changed its requirement upon the conclusion of negotiations to apply only to one establishment—a slaughterhouse and cutting plant.

Danish presidency (second half of 2002)

From Slovakia's point of view, the strategic goal was to implement the conclusions drawn up at the Laeken and Seville summits, i.e. to complete the accession negotiations with the EU before the end of 2002. The regional policy chapter was closed at the end of July, right at the offset of the Danish presidency. The competition chapter was closed during the accession conference in October, thus marking the accomplishment of the common Slovak–EU goal to complete negotiations on all non-financial chapters prior to the October meeting of the European Council.

The priority for the Danish presidency was to successfully complete negotiations on sensitive chapters that had financial implications, namely, the horizontal part of the agriculture chapter and the budget chapter. The aim of the Slovak Republic in these chapters was to ensure a balance between the rights and obligations arising from EU membership, ensure a positive budgetary balance during the first years of EU membership, i.e. a better budgetary balance compared to the year preceding accession, and achieve a starting position that would ensure the competitiveness of Slovak agriculture and food industry undertakings, hence having an acceptable impact on consumers and on the country's macroeconomic position.

An important area was also represented by negotiations under the last chapter (the so-called 'others' chapter) which included issues forming part of the EU legislation but not placed under any of the previous chapters (contributions to EU funds, conditions and criteria for accession to the European Central Bank and the European Investment Bank, safeguard measures for the fulfilment of obligations arising from EU membership).

In October 2002, the Commission published its regular report assessing the progress of candidate countries in their preparations for EU membership. The Commission's overall assessment of Slovakia's progress in meeting the accession criteria was rather positive. The Commission recommended that the accession negotiations with Slovakia be closed before the end of 2002. The above position of the European Commission was later also confirmed by EU Member States at the 24–5 October 2002 European Council meeting in Brussels.

The October EU summit in Brussels represented an important turning point in the negotiations, as it laid the ground for defining the EU's substantive position on various financial and agricultural issues. Granting the new Member States an entitlement to draw direct payments, the specification of their amount and the modalities of their application, as well as an overall so-called financial package, may be described as the main outcome of the European Council meeting. Under the financial package, the funds earmarked for structural actions were reduced by €2.5 billion to a total of €23 billion for all ten candidate countries.

One of the important moments in the negotiations was also the Member States' decision, adopted by the Council for General Affairs on 18 November 2002, which scheduled the date of the new members' accession on 1 May 2004. A decisive fact from the perspective of the acceding countries was that their payments to the EU budget were to be due only as of May 2004 (i.e. after accession) while their revenues from the EU budget would not be reduced. Hence, the new Member States would receive funds (with the exception of market instruments in agriculture) for the whole of 2004, while only being charged for the EU budget from May onwards.

A new round of negotiations was launched at a meeting of the Prime Ministers of the Laeken group of candidate countries with the Danish presidency in Copenhagen at the end of October. The whole of November saw intensive negotiations, facilitated by a negotiation package presented by the Danish presidency. The negotiations with the presidency and the EC were dominated by questions pertaining to the regime of direct payments and, with regard to curtailing the Berlin ceiling for the financing of enlargement, also the issue of utilizing the reserve created to cater for individual needs of the acceding countries. In the case of the Slovak Republic, this mainly included rural development, compensation payments, and strengthening of the future Schengen border.

The final decision was adopted at the closing meeting of the heads of governments at the EU summit in Copenhagen (12–13 December 2002) where Slovakia attained the following results in the area of direct payments, increase in non-allocated funds from the Berlin ceiling reserve, and a payment schedule for contributions to the European Investment Bank (EIB):

- an increase in the possibility to apply national top-up payments to farmers by a further 10 per cent; i.e. up to the maximum amount of 55–60–65 percent of the EU direct payment level during the period from 2004 to 2006;
- in 2007–13, additional payments provided exclusively from domestic funds can be up to 30 per cent higher than originally set in the schedule for increases in direct payments;
- an increase in one-off compensation payment by €22.7 million from non-allocated funds from the Berlin ceiling reserve; and
- extension of the payment schedule for Slovakia's contributions to the European Investment Bank. The Slovak Republic will make a total payment of

€20,424,475 in eight instalments (always payable by 30 September in years 2004–6, by 31 March and 30 September in years 2007–8, and by 31 March in 2009).

The heads of governments approved the final form of the accession conditions for new Member States, thus opening up a road to finalization of the Accession Treaty. All in all, the Slovak Republic accomplished its goals: a positive budgetary position in 2004–6, balance of rights and obligations, as well as an acceptable amount of direct payments and agricultural quotas.

Chapters opened under the Danish presidency
31. Other

Chapters provisionally closed under the Danish presidency
6. Competition
7. Agriculture
21. Regional policy
29. Budgetary provisions
31. Other

Description of transitional periods agreed under the Danish presidency

Competition

The Slovak Republic managed to negotiate two transitional periods. The first one, lasting until the end of 2008, covers the provision of state aid to a company operating in the automotive industry (VW Bratislava) in an amount of 30 per cent of eligible capital expenditures. If the set limit on state aid is achieved before the end of this period, the state aid will be terminated. The second transitional period, pertaining to the provision of state aid until the end of 2009, was negotiated for a company operating in the steel industry (US Steel, Košice) provided that the total amount of state aid does not exceed $500 million, that the company upholds its employment, that it does not scale up its product portfolio, and that it observes the set limits on the production and sale of certain products. Since US Steel failed to meet one of the conditions stipulated for the provision of state aid (it exceeded production volume in 2003), the total amount of state aid was reduced to $430 million and, in addition to this, US Steel was required to pay additional taxes in the amount of $32 million in two instalments in 2004 and 2005.

In order to attract foreign direct investments (FDI) to Slovakia, which represent an important instrument for economic revitalization, the government and Parliament passed measures offering investors a more attractive business environment in the form of tax holidays.

Under the applicable EU legislation, the tax holidays constitute a regional investment aid and must therefore be granted in compliance with the rules for the provision of state aid. In this context it was necessary to amend specific laws so as to ensure that each potential state aid and its volume are notified to the State

Aid Office in advance. Tax holidays in the territory of the Slovak Republic are currently granted under the laws that are in compliance with the EU state aid rules.

Agriculture: horizontal part

Slovakia negotiated a three-year transitional period (until 31 December 2006) for the use of the warehouse receipt system.

Slovakia accepted a ten-year transitional period (until 2013) for direct payments to farmers. In the period of 2004–6, these will be paid in the amount of 25–30–35 per cent with a possibility to increase them to 40 per cent from the funds earmarked for rural development (in the event of funding from the national budget, according to the formula 80 per cent from EU funds and 20 per cent from the national budget). If need be, additional so-called top-up payments from the national budget may be provided in addition to the direct payments, to attain the cap of 55–60–65 per cent (in the period of 2004–6) of the EU direct payment levels. Direct payments provided from EU funds will increase by 10 per cent annually from 40 per cent in 2007 to reach 100 per cent in 2013. The top-up during this period (paid solely from the national budget) may reach the maximum of 30 per cent. The total level of direct payments may not exceed 100 per cent of the EU level.

Financial and budgetary provisions

After accession, Slovakia will have to contribute to the common EU budget in the form of 'own resources' (see Table 14). Payments of the Slovak Republic to the common EC budget will consist of the traditional own resources, a resource based on value added tax (VAT), and a resource based on the gross national product (GNP). According to the current EU legislation governing the system of the Community's own resources, Member States contribute to the financing of the so-called budgetary correction mechanism afforded to the United Kingdom.

In the shortened financial period of 2004–6, the overall EU commitment appropriations towards the Slovak Republic represent €2,603 million (see Table 15),

Table 14. Contributions of the Slovak Republic to the EU budget (at 1999 prices; €m.)

	2004[a]	2005	2006	2004–6
Traditional own resources	33	54	54	141
VAT resource	26	40	41	107
GNP resource	146	226	232	604
UK rebate	20	30	32	82
Contributions to the EU budget	225	350	359	934

[a] New Member States pay contributions to the EU budget as of their accession date, i.e. 1 May 2004.

Table 15. Overview of EU commitment appropriations in accordance with conclusions of the Copenhagen Summit (at 1999 prices; €m.)

	2004	2005	2006	2004–6
A. Agriculture	125	239	263	627
Market measures	17	48	49	114
Direct payments	0	73	88	161
Rural development	108	118	126	352
B. Structural actions	436	495	629	1,560
Structural funds	262	351	437	1,050
Cohesion fund	174	144	192	510
C. Domestic policies	112	110	108	330
Existing policies	53	56	58	167
Jaslovské Bohunice	30	30	30	90
Institution building	13	8	4	25
Schengen	16	16	16	48
D. One-off compensation	63	11.5	11.5	86
Contributions from the EU budget	736	855.5	1,011.5	2,603

while, according to the Council and Commission's methodology, the ceiling on payment appropriations (real income) has been set at €1,756 million. The difference is due to the fact that a portion of the allocated funds will be disbursed gradually in the next period.

The income from the general EC budget will consist of the following:

A. Income in the fields of agriculture and rural development paid from the EAGGF guarantee section: €627 million.

The annual commitment appropriations for Slovakia in the area of agriculture and rural development will gradually increase to reach €125 million in 2004, approximately €239 million in 2005, and €263 million in 2006. The allocations to agriculture and rural development paid from the Guarantee Section of the European Agricultural Guidance and Guarantee Fund (EAGGF) will cover the following areas:

- market-oriented expenditure €114 million
- direct payments €161 million
- rural development €352 million

The funds in the area of agriculture provided from the EAGFF Guarantee Section are, in essence, subsidies designed to maintain agricultural production, support the use of agricultural land in various areas under different conditions, and stimulate exports of agricultural products outside of the EU. These funds should largely replace subsidies paid from the national budget to maintain agricultural production.

B. Structural operations: €1,560 million

During the shortened programming period, the annual commitment appropriations for Slovakia to support structural operations will gradually increase to reach €436 million in 2004, approximately €495 million in 2005, and €629 million in 2006. Structural operations are aimed at supporting development activities and consist of the Structural Funds and the Cohesion Fund.

- Cohesion Fund €510 million
- Structural Funds €1,050 million

C. EC internal policies: €330 million

Commitment appropriations for Slovakia over the shortened budgetary period of 2004–6 represent €330 million in total: they will reach €112 million in 2004, about €110 million in 2005, and €108 million in 2006.

The EC internal policies are designed to support development activities which cannot be supported from the Structural Funds or the Cohesion Fund. Slovakia will be able to draw funds in the following areas:

- Internal measures €167 million
- Decommissioning of two units of the V-1 NPP €90 million
- Institution building €25 million
- Building of Schengen borders €48 million

Following EU accession, Slovakia will attain a positive net position and, in the period of 2004–6, will receive payments from the EU exceeding those paid to the EU budget by €831 million, which represents €154 per capita (see Table 16).

Table 16. The Slovak Republic's estimated net position after accession in accordance with the Copenhagen Summit conclusions (at 1999 prices; €m.)

	2004	2005	2006	2004–6
Pre-accession aid	120	102	64	286
Agriculture	57	205	260	522
Structural actions	118	244	289	651
Internal policies	19	33	45	97
Additional income	21	52	52	125
One-off compensation	63	11	11	85
Total revenues	398	647	720	1,765
Traditional own resources	−33	−54	−54	−141
VAT resource	−26	−40	−41	−107
GDP resource	−146	−226	−232	−604
UK rebate	−20	−30	−32	−82
Total expenditures	−225	−350	−359	−934
Net budgetary position	173	297	361	831

Table 17. Chapters opened and closed, Slovakia

Year	Opened chapters	Closed chapters
2000	16	10
2001	13	12
2002	2	9
Total	31	31

Overall status of negotiations in the year 2002

Along with the nine other candidate countries, Slovakia concluded the accession negotiations at the European Council meeting in Copenhagen. The Union opened the remaining two chapters with Slovakia and nine chapters were closed (Table 17). Slovakia thus made the full use of the catch-up principle and confirmed its preparedness to join the EU on 1 May 2004.

7. 2003 AND 2004: SIGNING OF THE ACCESSION TREATY, REFERENDUM, AND ACCESSION TO THE EU

Greek presidency (first half of 2003)

Preparatory works on the draft of the EU constitutional treaty culminated during the Greek presidency.

The signing of the Accession Treaty itself took place on 16 April 2003 in Athens. The signatories on behalf of the Slovak Republic were: Rudolf Schuster, President of the Slovak Republic, Mikuláš Dzurinda, Prime Minister of the Slovak Republic, Eduard Kukan, Minister of Foreign Affairs of the Slovak Republic, and Ján Figel', chief negotiator for Slovakia's accession to the EU. On 19 February 2003, the European Commission had adopted a favourable opinion on the applications of the candidate countries, recommending the accession of all ten countries into the European Union. The signing of the treaty was also preceded by a vote of the European Parliament of 9 April 2003, which approved the accession of all candidate countries to the EU through clear support of the majority of MEPs (521 MEPs voted for Slovakia's accession, 21 were against and 25 abstained). The Council of EU Ministers for Foreign Affairs endorsed the accession of new members on 14 April 2003. All EU 15 states ratified the Accession Treaty within the given deadline enabling the new Member States to enter the EU on 1 May 2004.

The President of the Slovak Republic called a referendum on Slovakia's accession to the EU for 16–17 May 2003 with the following question: 'Do you agree with the Slovak Republic becoming a Member State of the European Union?' A total of 2,176,990 citizens voted in the referendum, representing 52.15 per cent of all registered voters; 92.46 per cent voted for EU accession, while 6.20 per cent were against. The National Council of the Slovak Republic approved the EU Accession Treaty on 1 July 2003. Of the 140 MPs present, 129 voted in favour, 10 voted against, and one abstained. The President of the Slovak Republic signed the ratification instrument to the EU Accession Treaty on 26 August 2003, completing the ratification process in the Slovak Republic. On 9 October 2003, the ratification instruments were handed over to the Italian government, the depository of the Treaties of Rome.

At the Thessaloniki Summit in June, the European Union concluded that the results of the European Convention in the form of a draft of the constitutional treaty represented a good basis for negotiations at the intergovernmental conference. In July 2003, the Convention on the Future of Europe completed its work by submitting the draft of the treaty establishing the constitution for Europe.

Italian presidency (second half of 2003)

The intergovernmental conference on institutional reform to adopt the EU constitutional treaty was opened in October. However, negotiations were not completed during the Italian presidency and continued in 2004.

Referendums were successful in all acceding countries (except Cyprus), and the ratification process came to a close. In November, the European Commission submitted the final monitoring reports on the state of preparations for EU membership of the future Member States, concluding that all candidate countries were prepared for entry as of 1 May 2004, providing that certain specified conditions were met.

Irish presidency (first half of 2004)

As expected, all ten countries became members of the European Union as of 1 May 2004, bringing the period of several decades of division in Europe to an end. On 10–13 June 2004, the European Parliament elections were held in individual Member States—the historical first MEP election in the new Member States. On 18 June, the Irish presidency succeeded in concluding an agreement on the final wording of the constitutional treaty within EU 25.

8. CONCLUSION: THE WAY FORWARD

Entry into the European Union was the culmination of Slovakia's long-term endeavour to become a part of the community of free and democratic countries. The beginning was not easy because Slovakia was initially excluded from the integration process, and it was only after the 1998 parliamentary elections that integration into the EU became a real priority of the Slovak government and, perhaps, the most consensual social and political theme in the country. Slovakia adopted a strategy which was ambitious and yet realistic at the same time. The realism of our strategy was confirmed by the fact that the Slovak timetable set in 1999 to complete the process of negotiations by the end of 2004 and enter the Union in 2004 became effectively a common European timetable for the accession of ten countries. Slovakia overcame its initial two-year handicap through a focused and concerted effort at home and abroad. This had a particularly positive impact on domestic reforms, harmonization of the legislation, legal framework, and business environment, and on the preparation of institutions necessary for entry into the Union. Significantly, these achievements underpinned the credibility of Slovakia abroad and improved our neighbourly relations.

Slovakia has always wished to enter the Union alongside the other countries of the Visegrad group, with whom it feels culturally, politically, and economically close. Any other scenario would have been a worse option for Slovakia and the CEE region as a whole.

Accession to the European Union will partly change the way in which our country functions. In selected areas, EU legislation overrides Slovak law and is, either directly or indirectly, enforceable in the territory of Slovakia. It is, therefore, critical for Slovakia to prepare itself for these changes in the most consistent fashion. This applies to all levels and the entire fabric of the society. In practical terms, Slovakia will have to train a sufficient number of experts who will be able to discuss and negotiate with their counterparts in the working languages of the Union. At the same time, the country and its representatives must open and maintain precise communication channels and coordinate the procedures and decisions adopted not only in Slovakia, but also in Brussels, Luxembourg, and Strasbourg.

Not only financial institutions, corporations, and economic operators, but also local administrations, trade unions, churches, and NGOs will progressively develop structured and active communication channels and links with their partners across Europe. This 'new' dimension in the development of our society, together with the participation of the country in the European decision-making process in the fundamental issues of European politics, are gradually changing the currently prevailing perceptions of European affairs from something that is remote, or even foreign, to something that is 'European', ergo (also) 'ours'.

The unity and diversity within the Union are, and will remain, compatible as long as unity stems from common values and diversity is respected as enrichment. Slovakia wants to contribute to the European Union, which should be shaped into a community of states and their citizens rather than into the 'state of states' or 'super state'. The biggest and the most important yet immeasurable fruit of the 1950 Schuman Plan was peace, close cooperation, and subsequent prosperity of the countries which, only a decade before, were in a state of total war.

Today's Europe needs to rely on what has proven its worth over time. Robert Schuman, Konrad Adenauer, Alcide De Gasperi, the Christianity-inspired founding fathers of the EC, were all successful. Successful founders should not be questioned, but rather be viewed as a torch of inspiration and encouragement.

Slovakia expects that its membership in the Union will foster further economic growth, that it will support its social and regional development, and that it will accelerate its economic modernization and restructuring. On the other hand, Slovakia wants to contribute to and enrich the Union with its political, security-related, and economic potential, as well as with its culture, history, identity, living values, and traditions.

When Jean Monnet, the first President of what is now the European Commission, was asked whether he was optimistic about the future of the first Community, he replied: 'I am not an optimist, nor am I a pessimist, but I am determined!' A determined and internally coherent Slovakia within the community of free European states will be the best guarantee for a bright European future.

17

The Accession of Slovenia to the EU

Janez Potočnik
Fedor Černe
Emil Erjavec and Mojmir Mrak

1. INTRODUCTION

The main objective of this chapter is to provide an overview and analysis of Slovenia's accession process to the European Union (EU). In addition to the introduction, the chapter consists of five main sections. First, the chapter discusses the relationship between newly independent Slovenia and the EU before the accession negotiations (section 2), and continues with the presentation of the institutional structure for effective carrying out of the negotiations (section 3). Further on, the chapter provides a brief overview of the negotiating process throughout the 1998–2002 period (section 4), and a more detailed analysis of selected issues of negotiations (section 5). These issues were chosen because they were of particular importance for Slovenia and required particular attention in negotiations. The final part of the text summarizes the lessons learnt by Slovenia in its process of accession to the EU (section 6).

2. SLOVENIA AND THE EU BEFORE THE START OF THE ACCESSION NEGOTIATIONS

Clear political orientation for accession to the EU

In the late 1980s, Europe was already free from the division which had characterized the post-Second World War period. It was the time defined by the fall of the Berlin Wall, German reunification, and also profound changes in the Soviet Union. The atmosphere in Europe was positive and future oriented, and the idea of a united Europe, liberated from its historical problems, seemed very realistic. In contrast to Europe, SFR Yugoslavia was confronted with a growing political and economic crisis. This crisis belatedly triggered the historical process of the formation of national states, a process that had been held back by the existence of a common Yugoslav state even though the nations of the SFR Yugoslavia never gave up their sovereignty. The federal structure of the state enabled and guaranteed this in the Constitution of 1974.

Under the conditions of violent infringement of the principles of equality and sovereignty of nations, Slovenia decided to exercise its right to self-determination. It is important to underline that becoming an independent state was at that time seen as the only realistic option which would enable the Slovenian nation to join the historical process of European integration. The institutional framework of the SFR Yugoslavia was backward oriented, relying on the instruments of ideology, the communist party and the army. The country was simply not capable of adjusting itself to the platform of democracy, human rights, and free market that would allow its participation in the European trends and clear the path towards European integration.

The Slovenes' desire to quickly join the western community, thus becoming an integral part of the Euro-Atlantic integration processes (i.e. becoming a member of the European Community and NATO), was contained in all documents today known as 'Slovenia's independence documents': the Statement of Good Intention which led to the Slovenian plebiscite in December 1990, the Fundamental Constitutional Charter and the Declaration of Independence of 25 June 1991.

Slovenia–EU relations from independence to 1997

The political recognition of Slovenia by the members of the European Community at the end of 1991 and in the first months of 1992 was a precondition for the institutionalization of relations between Slovenia and the European Community. They rendered Slovenia eligible for PHARE funds, and a total volume of 69 million ecu was allocated for its national programmes over the 1992–5 period. In April 1993, the institutional cooperation was entrenched with the signing of the following three basic agreements: (i) Cooperation Agreement between the Republic of Slovenia and the European Economic Community; (ii) Agreement between the European Economic Community and the Republic of Slovenia in the Field of Transport; and (iii) Protocol on Financial Cooperation between the European Economic Community and the Republic of Slovenia. The latter provided some 150 million ecu for road and railway projects over the three-year period.

The European agreement negotiations with Slovenia started in 1994 and were completed in June 1996. In the preamble to this agreement—Europe Agreement establishing an Association between the Republic of Slovenia and the European Communities—it is clearly stated that full membership of the EU is its ultimate objective. The document is based on a mutual understanding and shared values and is designed to prepare the country for its political, economic, and social convergence with the EU. It extensively covers trade issues and provides a framework within which Slovenia prepared its legislation and administrative structures for membership. An interim agreement implementing the trade provisions of the Europe agreement entered into force in January 1997. The Europe agreement entered into force in February 1999.

Slovenia was by far the last among the Central and Eastern European countries (CEECs) aspiring for EU accession to sign the Europe agreement. Other countries from the region signed similar contracts in the first half of the 1990s. There are several reasons that help explain this situation. First, Slovenia became an independent sovereign state only in mid-1991 and was not politically recognized by the EU Member States until a year later. Second, as one of the successors of the SFR Yugoslavia, Slovenia inherited problems with all the three groups of its foreign creditors, i.e. multilateral financial institutions, commercial banks, and governments, of which many were EU Member States. Third, late signing of the Europe agreement was partly also due to the de facto veto position of neighbouring Italy. Italy claimed that the issue of property of the territory that is now Slovenia that had been owned by Italian citizens before they opted for Italy after the second World War had not been finally resolved, which postponed signing of the Europe agreement for more than a year. The problem was resolved on the basis of the 'Spanish compromise'. Under this compromise, Slovenia agreed that citizens of the EU living in Slovenia for more than three years would have a right to buy property in the country.

On the very same day that the Europe agreement was signed, i.e. 10 June 1996, Slovenia applied for membership of the EU. It is interesting to note that for the above-mentioned reasons, Slovenia had filed its application for the EU membership even before the Europe agreement was ratified by its own Parliament. The ratification only took place on 15 July 1997, after Slovenia had amended its national constitution so as to incorporate the provisions of the agreed 'Spanish compromise'. With the inclusion of this compromise in the Europe agreement and the amendment of the constitution, Slovenia managed to deal with this problem even before starting the EU accession process and thus avoided one of the most controversial problems in the negotiations of many other candidate countries.

Strategic documents establishing the framework of EU accession negotiations

In the period between 1991 and 1998, i.e. between the independence and the beginning of the EU accession negotiations, Slovenia made substantial progress in stabilizing the economy and advancing the systemic transformation from a planned to fully-fledged market economy. In Slovenia, the process of EU accession has always been considered as an extremely important vehicle necessary for accelerating the reform agenda and implementing the needed structural changes aimed at strengthening Slovenia's economic growth prospects as well as its ability to compete on the enlarged EU market once it became a Member State.

As early as 1995, the first strategic document—Strategy for Economic Development of Slovenia—clearly outlined the EU framework of Slovenia's economic and social development. The document's central objectives were defined as follows: (i) to achieve higher growth rates than that in the EU in order to bridge the income gap with this group of countries; (ii) to enhance international competitiveness of the Slovenian economy; (iii) to integrate the country into European institutions; and (iv) to promote long-term economic growth that is environmentally, regionally, socially, and ethnically sustainable.

Although the 1995 Strategy defined its objectives rather clearly, it fell short in designing either the policy measures required to reach these objectives or their timing and sequencing. Both these issues then represented the core of the Strategy for the Accession of the Republic of Slovenia to the EU adopted in January 1998. This policy document defined and outlined a consistent set of medium-term economic and social policy measures required to complete the economic transformation of the country into a market economy and to prepare its economy for accession to the EU. As shown in Table 18, the strategy covered the period from 1997 to 2001 and took the end of 2001 as a target date for completion of the EU accession negotiations. The Strategy was presented publicly in Brussels in December 1997. As revealed later, its methodological approach was practically the same one as the approach of the Commission in designing the methodology for National Programmes for the Adoption of the Acquis to be prepared by all the candidate countries.

Based on the Europe agreement provisions, three main instruments were adopted for implementation of this strategy: (i) the Accession Partnership (AP); (ii) the National Programme for the Adoption of the *Acquis* (NPAA); and (iii) the PHARE financial instrument. The AP for Slovenia was approved by the European Council together with APs for the other five countries of the 'Luxembourg group'. It identified short and medium-term objectives and contained the provisions for cooperation between the EU and Slovenia designed to facilitate its pre-accession preparation. The AP called upon Slovenia to prepare its NPAA and submit it to the Commission. In the document submitted later that year—as already mentioned, it was conceptually largely based on the Strategy for the Accession of the Republic of Slovenia to the EU—Slovenia provided a detailed plan and timetable for implementation of objectives set out in the AP. The NPAA outlined the economic reforms to be implemented over the next medium-term period and envisaged the process of legal approximation. It also quantified the administrative adjustments and financial resources that were needed to implement the *acquis*. With the launch of the EU accession negotiations, the emphasis of the PHARE assistance shifted to preparation for membership. Consequently, it became focused on the areas identified in the AP/NPAA documents.

When comparing Slovenia's transition policy objectives and measures as outlined in the Strategy for Accession of the Republic of Slovenia to the EU with the requirements of the Commission embodied in the AP for Slovenia, one could easily conclude that the EU accession process had largely coincided with the requirements of the transition process. The two processes had by and large been two sides of the same coin.

Table 18. Major components of main reforms and their schedule

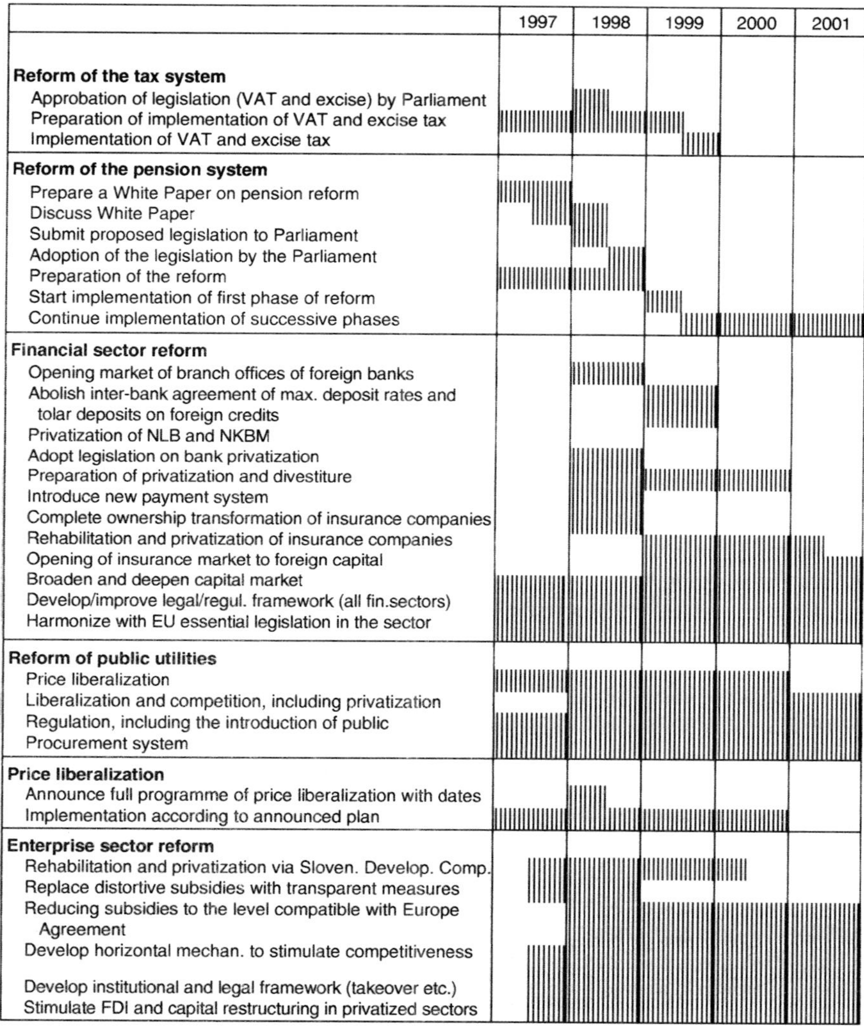

	1997	1998	1999	2000	2001
Reform of the tax system					
Approbation of legislation (VAT and excise) by Parliament					
Preparation of implementation of VAT and excise tax					
Implementation of VAT and excise tax					
Reform of the pension system					
Prepare a White Paper on pension reform					
Discuss White Paper					
Submit proposed legislation to Parliament					
Adoption of the legislation by the Parliament					
Preparation of the reform					
Start implementation of first phase of reform					
Continue implementation of successive phases					
Financial sector reform					
Opening market of branch offices of foreign banks					
Abolish inter-bank agreement of max. deposit rates and tolar deposits on foreign credits					
Privatization of NLB and NKBM					
Adopt legislation on bank privatization					
Preparation of privatization and divestiture					
Introduce new payment system					
Complete ownership transformation of insurance companies					
Rehabilitation and privatization of insurance companies					
Opening of insurance market to foreign capital					
Broaden and deepen capital market					
Develop/improve legal/regul. framework (all fin.sectors)					
Harmonize with EU essential legislation in the sector					
Reform of public utilities					
Price liberalization					
Liberalization and competition, including privatization					
Regulation, including the introduction of public Procurement system					
Price liberalization					
Announce full programme of price liberalization with dates					
Implementation according to announced plan					
Enterprise sector reform					
Rehabilitation and privatization via Sloven. Develop. Comp.					
Replace distortive subsidies with transparent measures					
Reducing subsidies to the level compatible with Europe Agreement					
Develop horizontal mechan. to stimulate competitiveness					
Develop institutional and legal framework (takeover etc.)					
Stimulate FDI and capital restructuring in privatized sectors					

Source: Strategy for the Accession of the Republic of Slovenia to the EU (IMAD, 1998).

3. INSTITUTIONAL SETTING OF THE EU ACCESSION PROCESS

Like all the candidate countries, Slovenia had to adapt itself to the general patterns of the EU accession process. Each of the candidate countries nevertheless designed its own institutional structure for the effective management of the accession negotiations. The final institutional structure was, on the one hand, a reflection of the objective requirements associated with the accession negotiations and, on the other hand, determined by political, economic, and social particularities of the country. Slovenia, for example, was the only one among the ten candidate countries where the Parliament was operationally involved in the negotiating process. Its Committee for International Relations had to approve each negotiating position before the government submitted it to the EU.

Figure 5 provides a schematic overview of institutions in Slovenia that had been involved in the preparation of the negotiating positions. On 2 April 1998,

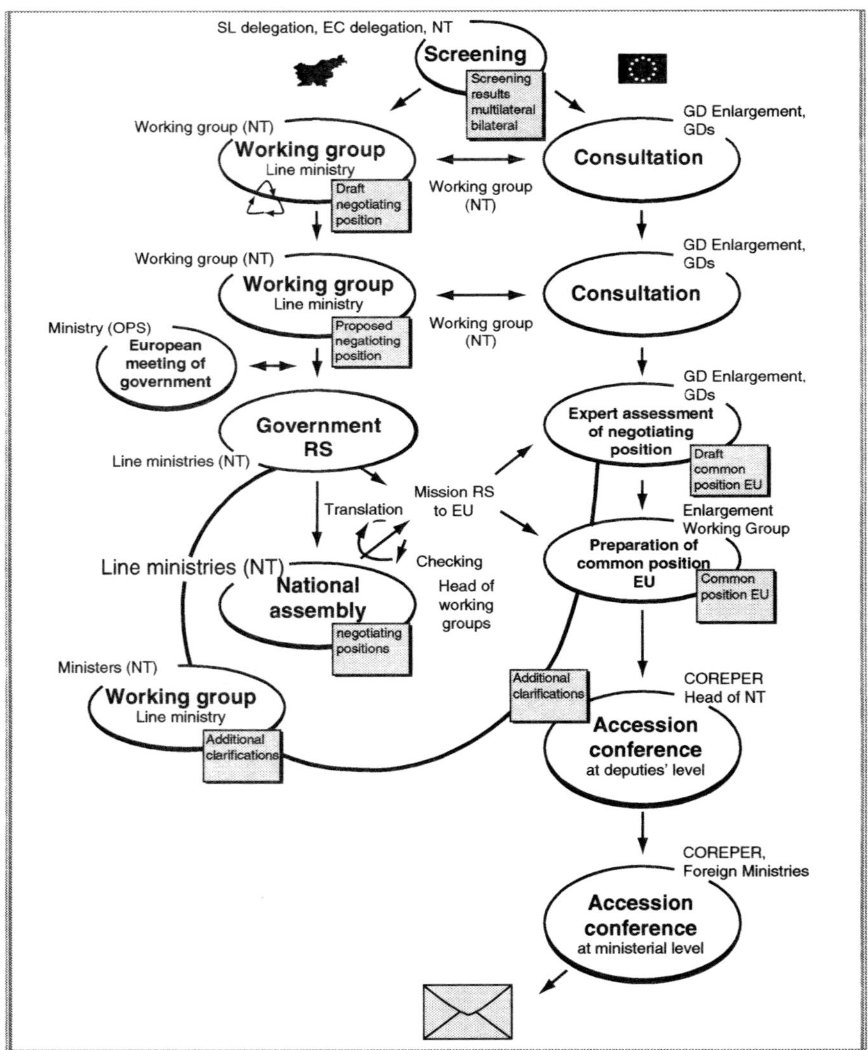

Figure 5. Organization of the negotiating process in Slovenia
Source: Negotiating Team (NT) Presentation Booklet.

the government appointed the negotiating team for accession to the EU, later on called the 'negotiating team' (NT), comprising a ten-member group of experts, including senior civil servants, a representative of the Chamber of Industry and Commerce, the Central Bank, and even a university professor. Each member of the NT was responsible for negotiations on one or more negotiating chapters. They took part in all phases of the preparation of the negotiating positions: screening of the legislation, drafting the position papers, coordinating the submission of the documents for approval to the government and the Parliament, and finally submitting the documents to the relevant EU institutions.

Of course, the NT did not work in a vacuum. The government also appointed thirty-one working groups, each of them responsible for one negotiating chapter. A working group consisted of officials from different ministries—thus dealing with the issue of inter-ministry coordination—as well as representatives of workers and employers. It was headed by a senior official of the so-called leading ministry, i.e. the ministry that was responsible for the largest proportion of the *acquis* to be dealt with by this working group. Each working group had a final responsibility for preparation of negotiating positions and other platforms for negotiations for its negotiating chapter. They had, however, to get the consent of the NT for submission of the document to the government procedure.

The work of both the NT and the working groups was closely related to the work of the Government Office for European Affairs (GOEA). This office was responsible for the management and coordination of the whole process of Slovenia's accession to the EU. More specifically, GOEA had the following responsibilities in the EU accession process: (i) to organize and coordinate the preparation and submission of negotiating positions, positions for conferences on accession, additional clarifications, and other documentation as well as EU accession-related meetings and visits in Slovenia and abroad; (ii) to keep the public informed about the process and progress of negotiations; (iii) to organize and implement the translation of the *acquis*; (iv) to monitor how Slovenia fulfils the commitments laid down in the negotiating positions, report on them, and signal where potential backlogs might occur; (v) to design and programme the pre-accession funds; and (vi) to provide logistic and legal support to the negotiating team. Experience shows that GOEA headed by a competent Minister for European Affairs having a permanent link with the Prime Minister was a key element of effective coordination in the EU accession process in Slovenia.

Negotiation positions and all other documents prepared in the context of the EU accession—they were prepared in close collaboration of all three structures (negotiating team, working groups, and GOEA)—were regularly discussed at weekly government sessions. At each of these sessions, EU issues were discussed as the first topic on the agenda, while in urgent cases, the cabinet ministers even gathered in special sessions dedicated exclusively to the EU issues.

As already mentioned, the Parliament had a very specific role in Slovenia's negotiations with the EU. Before being submitted to the EU, each negotiating position adopted by the government had to be confirmed by the respective parliamentary bodies. Typically, this process involved at least three parliamentary bodies: the committee that was in substantive terms responsible for the subject under consideration, and two horizontal bodies, namely the Commission for European Affairs and the Committee for International Relations. According to the law, the latter had to provide a mandate to the government for any negotiations that might result in an international agreement with Slovenia as one of the partners. As negotiations on individual chapters concerned an international agreement to be concluded between Slovenia and the EU, namely the Accession Treaty, it is logical that the mandate of this Committee was required.

After endorsement in the Parliament, the negotiating position was ready to be submitted to the EU. As an example, Table 19 provides the actual timetable for preparation of Slovenian negotiating positions for two chapters, those on the free movement of goods (chapter 1) and the environment (chapter 22). The table, of course, provides only a timetable for the starting negotiating positions, which have in many cases been amended in the course of negotiations. For technical explanations and amendments to the negotiating positions, the parliamentary procedure was much simpler: the government simply informed the respective bodies of the Parliament about the developments in the negotiations.

Table 19. Timetable of screening and preparation of the negotiating positions for free movement of goods (chapter 1) and environment (chapter 22)

Activity	Free movement of goods	Environment
Screening		
Multilateral screening	10–18 June 1998	7–8 Jan. 1999 27–28 Jan. 1999 26 Feb. 1999
Bilateral screening	30 June–8 July 1998	2–22 Jan. 1999 8–9 Feb. 1999 18 Feb. 1999
Governmental procedure for preparation of the negotiating position		
Introductory meeting for preparation of the negotiating position	2 Sept. 1998	22 Mar. 1999
Preparation of draft negotiating position	26 Nov. 1998	6 May 1999
Discussion of the draft negotiating position at the working group		23 June 1999
Discussion of the draft negotiating position with NGOs with the framework of GOEA and negotiating team	25 Jan. 1999	1 July 1999
Committees of the government	19 Jan. 1999	29 June 1999 13 July 1999
Government	21 Jan. 1999	1 July 1999 15 July 1999
Parliamentary procedure for preparation of the negotiating position		
Commission for European Affairs	27 Jan. 1999	14 July 1999
Committee for Economy	27 Jan. 1999	
Committee for International Relations	28 Jan. 1999	15 July 1999
Submission of the negotiating position	1 Feb. 1999	26 July 1999

Source: Negotiating Positions of the Republic of Slovenia for Negotiations on Accession to the EU (GOEA, January 2000).

4. THE EVOLUTION OF THE NEGOTIATIONS

Introductory stage: relatively 'easy' chapters

From April to the end of October 1998, the screening of sixteen out of the total of thirty-one negotiating chapters was completed by Slovenia and the other five members of the so-called 'Luxembourg group'.[1] The first session of substantive bilateral talks between Slovenia and the EU on the seven chapters screened—science and research, telecommunications and information technology, education and training, culture and audio-visual policy, industrial policy, small and medium-sized enterprises (SMEs), and common foreign and security policy (CFSP)—started in October 1998. For all but one chapter, Slovenia indicated that it could accept the *acquis* and would be in a position to implement it fully by the date of accession. The negotiating positions of Slovenia were based on the working hypothesis that Slovenia would be internally ready for joining the EU by 1 January 2002.

In the introductory stage, the negotiating process involved only the 'easy chapters', i.e. the chapters in which the EU and the applicant countries expected no problems. This also explains why at this stage of the negotiations there was only an insignificant differentiation among the countries with respect to the speed of their accession processes.

The differentiation, however, became more visible in 1999. That year, the screening was completed for all the remaining chapters, except for agriculture, for all six countries of the Luxembourg group. In the first semester of 1999, the EU Member States also decided to open negotiations with these countries on the following eight additional chapters: company law, statistics, consumer and health protection, fisheries, competition policy, free movement of goods, customs union, and external relations.

Although the same number of chapters was opened for all the six candidates, the number of chapters provisionally closed at the end of September 1999 varied between countries, ranging from seven to ten. Of the fifteen negotiating chapters which had been opened by that time, Slovenia had provisionally closed eight (statistics, telecommunications, industrial policy, consumer protection, research and development, SMEs, education and training, and fisheries).

[1] At the end of 1997, the chief negotiators of the 'Luxemburg group' countries met for the first time. Since then, and throughout the whole period of the accession negotiations, the members of this forum had regular meetings. The meeting took place in a different one of the six countries each time, on a rotational basis. The meetings had been particularly helpful in the first stages of the process—screening and preparation of negotiating positions; here, all the candidate countries were faced with more or less similar problems. Later on, however, when negotiations entered a more advanced stage and the problems to be addressed became more country specific, there was objectively less interest for coordination of the negotiation-related activities.

Central stage: 'more difficult' chapters exposed the candidates to important policy decisions

Differentiation among the candidate countries with respect to the number of chapters that were provisionally closed had intensified as negotiations progressed and moved into more difficult areas. Though the EU Member States were opening the negotiations for the remaining chapters simultaneously for all the 'Luxembourg group' countries—by the end of the year 2000, the negotiations were opened for all but the financial package chapters—the provisional closing of individual chapters depended very much on the specific situation of that issue in each individual country, including their requests for the transitional periods and even derogations from the *acquis*. For instance, by October 2001, the countries of this group provisionally closed between eighteen and twenty-three chapters, with Slovenia being in the middle with twenty-one closed chapters.

This was a period when the most difficult chapters (i.e. agriculture, environment, free movement of goods, and some others) were put on the table. For some of these chapters, Slovenia's negotiations proceeded very smoothly and without any major problems. Our country was, for example, the first to close the chapter on environment, during the Swedish presidency in the first half of 2001.

This is not to say, however, that this stage of negotiations was without problems. Some of these problems were caused by requests of either Slovenia or the EU for transitional periods. Slovenia, for example, requested a ten-year transitional period for the free trade agreements with some of the countries on the territory of the SFR Yugoslavia. The request for the transitional period was opposed by the EU on the grounds that it was in contradiction with the *acquis* on the internal market and trade policies. On the other hand, Slovenia considered completely unjustified the EU request for certain labour movement restrictions.

Another important source of problems was a possibility that a Member State, typically a neighbouring state, would use the EU accession process as a platform for addressing unresolved bilateral issues. Slovenia saw a glimpse of this problem in the pre-accession phase when Italy vetoed the beginning of Slovenia's EU accession negotiations because it wanted Slovenia to open its real estate market. At this stage of the negotiations, Austria—another neighbouring Member State—also applied a similar strategy. The issues of the Krško nuclear power station, the AVNOJ decrees, and duty-free shops were the most noticeable examples. Thanks to intensive collaboration with the Commission, the presidencies, and all the Member States, solutions were finally found for these and many other pending issues.

The major breakthrough in Slovenia's negotiations was actually made in 2001. By the end of that year the country provisionally closed all negotiating chapters except those related to the financial aspects of accession. Slovenia was therefore the only candidate country to fully meet the EU's negotiating timetable set out at the Nice Council in December 2000. It was at this Council that the year 2004 was set as a target date for membership of the most advanced candidate countries. In order to create the conditions conducive to meeting this target, the Council also endorsed the 'road map' for the negotiations over the next eighteen months.

Final stage: the financial package

Slovenia entered this stage of the negotiations with no issues pending. This means that it was internally ready to complete the negotiations in early 2002. Due to the 'convoy' character of the negotiations, Slovenia as the first ship in this convoy had no other choice but to wait for the group as a whole.

The negotiations on the financial package actually started in January 2002 with the Commission publishing the document 'Common Financial Framework 2004–2006 for Accession Negotiations', whereby it defined the basic framework for discussion of the financial aspects of accession, that is, agriculture, Structural Funds and regional policy, and the contributions to the EU budget. As a result of its horizontal nature, the document was not favourable for Slovenia as it failed to sufficiently take into account the specific features of our country as the most developed of all candidate countries from Central and Eastern Europe. The subject is discussed in more detail in section 5.

5. SELECTED EU ACCESSION NEGOTIATING ISSUES OF PARTICULAR IMPORTANCE FOR SLOVENIA

In contrast to the previous section, which discussed the general evolution of Slovenia's accession negotiations in the 1998–2002 period, this section provides a more detailed discussion of the negotiations on some specific issues that were of particular importance to Slovenia. One of them is agriculture, which deserves a more thorough approach for at least two reasons. First, this subject covers around one-third of the *acquis*, and second, Slovenia differed significantly from the other candidates with respect to their agricultural sectors. The second area selected for a detailed analysis is the environment. This is not only another area with particularly demanding *acquis* requirements but also an area where implementation of the *acquis* is associated with extremely high costs. Finally, the last section will provide a detailed assessment of Slovenia's financial package for the period 2004–6. This horizontal issue has been particularly difficult for Slovenia as the general framework for EU accession negotiations did not provide sufficient flexibility to address the specific needs of a country that was, on the one hand, highly developed compared to other candidate countries, but, on the other hand, still among the less developed countries of the enlarged EU.

Agriculture

Specific features of Slovenian agriculture

Slovenian agriculture is characterized by unfavourable natural and structural conditions, which also explains its status as a net importer of food and a relatively protectionist agricultural policy before the accession. The level of supports to agriculture was comparable to the level of supports in the EU, which placed Slovenia in a unique position in comparison with other acceding CEECs. In the preparations for EU membership, the agricultural policy in Slovenia had to undergo a comprehensive transformation. Whilst preserving the level of supports, their nature had to change. Gradually, Slovenian agricultural policy transposed the goals and mechanisms of CAP and had to a large extent put in place a comparable agricultural policy well before the accession. Simulating CAP was a clearly defined goal of the Slovenian agricultural policy, as it wanted to assure a 'soft landing' of agriculture on the common market and the timely establishment of comparable institutions as well as the necessary change of mentality of farmers and public institutions. Through the European integration process and in line with MacSharry's CAP reform, the agricultural policy in Slovenia lowered the level of price supports and compensated for the loss of incomes by direct payments.

Subject of the negotiations and their evolution

The negotiations in the chapter on agriculture were particularly politically sensitive, as their results would have serious financial consequences and would affect the future Common Agricultural Policy (CAP). Moreover, the *acquis* in this area was the most extensive. It can be divided into two basic areas: (i) CAP with common market organizations and rural development policy; and (ii) broad area of veterinary and phytosanitary issues.

Like overall negotiations (see Chapter 4), the negotiations in the area of agriculture could be divided into three stages: (i) 1998–9: drafting of negotiating positions by the Luxembourg group of candidate countries; (ii) 2000–1: negotiations on the implementation of the *acquis* and 'catching-up' process for the Helsinki group of candidate countries; and (iii) 2002: negotiations on financial issues.

Stage 1: screening (1998–1999)

For Slovene agriculture the first period was a period of intensive learning about CAP ('screenings') and drafting of the negotiating positions. The EU did not raise any financial issues on a technical level. Equal treatment was one of the requests made by the Slovenian government. Slovenia put the issues of the quotas and reference quantities off to later stages (2001) and focused largely on the implementation of the *acquis*. The government decided to carry out a radical reform of agricultural policy with the introduction of instruments that were comparable to the CAP and the establishment of harmonized institutions. Formulating implementation solutions was a demanding part of negotiations and it mostly involved the European Commission and the Slovene Agriculture Ministry. The commitments made to Brussels did contribute to faster integration and easier understanding and transposing of the *acquis*.

Stage 2: negotiations on non-financial issues (2000–2001)

The second stage (2000–1) brought a slowdown in the progress of negotiations for relatively advanced Slovenia. The negotiations proceeded mainly in the form of the exchange of common positions and additional clarifications and the number of technical meetings was down to only a few a year. The EU formulated clear questions about the implementation of the *acquis* and thereby forced Slovenia and other candidates to reveal their plans for harmonizing with the *acquis* and setting up the necessary institutions. This process was particularly intensive in the veterinary and phytosanitary area. As a leading candidate, Slovenia managed to close the majority of issues in the area of implementation and derogations from the *acquis* by December 2001 and was thus prepared to focus on the financial issues.

Before moving to financial matters, some comments should be made on the transitional periods and derogations from the *acquis* in the area of agriculture. Because of a high degree of regulation, the deviations from the *acquis* played only a minor role in the final agreement, although Slovenia, like other candidate countries, submitted a large number of requests. Most requests were turned down by the European Commission, whose attitude to the levels and types of deviations was rather conservative. Eventually, all the accepted deviations were largely of a technical nature, limited in scope and time and without any significant impact on the economic or political interests of Member States.

In the non-financial part, the only really important issue for Slovenia concerned the classification of wine zones. The first opinion of the European Commission was surprisingly very unfavourable for Slovenia, as it ranked all wine-growing regions to be Zone CII, which is typical for the Mediterranean area. If this zone had been adopted, it would have required a change in the technology and wine varieties and the allowed content of sugar and wine acid in the grape significantly, and would seriously worsen the economic position of wine production in the continental part of Slovenia. After turbulent discussion with the Commission and some Member States, the final solution was typically European—pragmatic. A continental part remained classified as Zone B, and the western part of Slovenia became wine-growing Zone CII, but with some provisions.

Stage 3: financial package negotiations (2002)

On 30 January 2002 the Commission published its enlargement strategy with a reference period for quotas and reference quantities, based on the statistical data in the reference period, gradual rising of the level of direct payments, and a possibility of topping up the direct payments from the national budgets (reference year 2001). This proposal triggered fierce reactions in all candidate countries and was rather unfavourable for Slovenia. The European Commission's proposal, which applied equal criteria to all candidate countries (horizontal approach), lowered the expectations of the candidate countries but also failed to take into account the opinion of some Member States which supported the reform of CAP. Besides, the quotas and reference quantities were lower than aspired to by the Slovene farmers' representative.

This introductory part of the financial package negotiations was followed by an intensive period of closing up the technical part of the agriculture negotiations and by preparations for the final phase of negotiations. This was the period between April and October 2002. It was also marked by the preparation of the final common position of the EU. In several versions of the draft common position, the politically sensitive issue of direct payments was excluded, whilst in the meantime an intensive debate took place between the Commission and the candidate countries on this issue. Slovenia used the opportunity provided by the numerous technical meetings, which contributed importantly to clarification of some issues. Very intensive discussions took place, especially with DG Agriculture, on all possible levels (from Commissioner to the technical experts). Therefore, before the final stage only a few politically sensitive issues for Slovenia remained on the table, i.e. the level of topping up, some important quotas, and reference quantities (like milk, suckler cows, rural development funds, and the wine zoning issue).

In the area of agriculture, the final stage of negotiations ended before the final negotiating round in December 2002. Denmark, the presiding Member State, prepared a final offer containing solutions for all the remaining pending issues in the agriculture chapter. By increasing the possible level of topping up for Slovenia, the presidency effectively addressed the specific request of the country. It also proposed some horizontal solutions in the area of quotas and reference quantities, based largely on the incorporation of more up-to-date reference data and some reserves. Last but not least, some additional funds for rural development were allocated to Slovenia at this stage of the negotiations. The proposed solutions in these three segments had largely met Slovenia's expectations, so one could say that the agricultural issue for Slovenia was in fact closed before the last round of the negotiations in December 2002.

Assessment of the agreement

The final outcome of financial negotiations issues for Slovenia in the area of agriculture can be assessed as favourable.

- *'Top-up' payments.* The direct payments were an important political issue for Slovenia. Although its prices, protection, and budgetary measures were comparable with those in the Member States, Slovenia decided to look for additional possibilities to preserve the economic position of its farmers after accession. Early in the negotiations (spring 2001) it informally proposed to complement—to 'top up'—direct payments from the national budget.

There is some evidence that Slovenia was the one to open the issue of topping up as a negotiation issue. Eventually, the Commission offered this possibility to all candidate countries; however, the level of these 'top-up' payments was intensively negotiated.

Underpinned by the results of a specific impact study showing that the economic position of Slovenian agriculture would deteriorate considerably in the event of lower top-up payments, a compromise solution was reached. Slovenia was thus given the possibility to start topping up payments above the level of payments reached in 2003, which stood at 75 per cent of the level applied in the present Member States. In 2004, Slovenia was allowed to raise this level by 10 per cent and in the following three years by another 5 per cent each year. Thus in 2007 a 100 per cent level of direct payments can be reached. Compared to other candidate countries (except Cyprus), Slovenia was granted the highest level of possible complementing of direct payments, even in the first period after accession. This is no doubt a favourable negotiating outcome for Slovenian agriculture.

- *Quotas and reference quantities.* Expectations on quotas and reference quantities—the amount of funds for individual direct payments—were very high and attracted a lot of publicity in Slovenia. The quotas and reference quantities got a symbolic meaning as an attempt by the EU to limit production and discriminate against the agricultural sectors of candidate countries. In its first proposal, the Commission—using the reference period 1995 to 1999—put forward levels that were much lower than both those stated in Slovenia's negotiating positions and the actual production levels. Slovenia's requests for quotas and reference quantities were based on production potentials rather than the existing statistical data, as was the rule when these measures were introduced into the CAP. Hopes were also raised by the farmers' representatives claiming that these 'justified requests' could be fulfilled in the negotiations if the negotiators were 'good'. The EU first succeeded in lowering the expectations and then opened a wide technical discussion about the data, reference years, and definitions, which altogether led to the results that were eventually much more favourable than the original offer. Slovenia tried, and partially succeeded in convincing the European Commission to change its original proposals. To do this, Slovenia used updated statistical data and new calculation methods (e.g. direct sale of milk at farms, number of suckler cows, and topping up direct payments). Thanks to the careful handling of the technical part of the negotiations, the final levels were in no case lower than the actual production levels at that time, while some additional development reserves have also been constituted. The levels finally agreed are even more important in view of the fact that they serve as a basis for calculation of the total value of decoupled area payments as per the CAP reform. Also, in the area of quotas and reference quantities, one cannot speak of any negotiations in the real sense of the word. This was an area where the role and the power of sectoral experts was of crucial importance on both the side of the EU and that of the national ministries.

- *Rural development.* Most candidate countries had no tradition in the type of rural development policy found in the EU, or any similar measures. Therefore, its political importance was smaller in comparison to other agricultural financial issues. Slovenia used this opportunity and—in line with the domestic sector reforms—strategically based its negotiation positions on the rural development policy. The European Commission distributed the proposed funds on the basis of objective criteria (economic development and the role of agriculture). This was of course very unfavourable in relation to Slovenia's demands. The protests of Slovenian representatives were so strong that eventually DG Agriculture set apart some funds as a special reserve for solving critical cases. These reserve funds were of particular interest to Slovenia, the Czech Republic, and Slovakia, the three countries which in the end got them.

  The negotiating outcome in the area of rural development funds for the period 2004–6 can be assessed as favourable. Slovenia was entitled to funds amounting to around €249.8 billion (in 1999 prices, paid out over a longer period of time), which is comparable with total funds earmarked for structural and regional policy. This amount makes up the largest share in the distribution of funds from the EU budget to Slovenia. Whilst other candidate countries focused their negotiating efforts on direct payments, Slovenian negotiators succeeded in convincing the EU side that Slovenia's primary interest lies in encouraging sustainable development of agriculture and that it intended to overcome its development problems in this area by means of rural development funds. This is a more modern form of protectionism, which uses those income and development supports to agriculture which are socially more acceptable and can also improve Slovenia's position in the negotiations on the next financial perspective. The agreed funds will, however, contribute to solving the structural disparities of Slovenian agriculture only to a small degree. They are tied exclusively to the supports for the less favoured areas and various forms of environmental supports. The classical agricultural structural measures of development nature, such as investment supports, will only be limited to the regional structural policy.

Final assessment of the agriculture chapter negotiations

The accession negotiations supported the transition process in the area of agriculture for which membership often meant a formal ultimate goal and the transposition of CAP elements to the essence of the national agricultural policy. Slovenia had to drastically change its agricultural legislation, reform its policy, and establish the institutions capable of functioning in line with the requirements of CAP. After the accession, the agriculture-oriented budgetary funds in Slovenia were expected to more than double and thus exceed the average level per inhabitant in the EU. Nevertheless, the average budgetary inflows per agricultural holding were expected to be significantly lower than in most present (and future) Member States. Slovenian farms are small in size, and this will crucially affect the competitiveness and economic position of Slovenian agriculture in the future. Despite higher budgetary inflows, Slovenian agriculture cannot become much more competitive. A favourable negotiating outcome could be seriously threatened by inefficiently utilized programmes and funds. The great debates about supports, which in the end all have a very simple goal (that is, to improve the income position of farmers), should not neglect the fact that agriculture is in the first place an economic activity. And the degree of competitiveness of the whole agro-food sector will eventually decide whether the accession was a success or a failure. It is evident that the outcome of the negotiations has opened the possibilities for further development of this sector and rural areas in general.

Environment

Introduction

Slovenia was the first among the candidate countries to provisionally conclude negotiations in the field of environmental protection. At the time, this fact received much attention as this chapter covered the first of the main themes of the negotiations. It was actually the second largest chapter in terms of the scope of the *acquis*. In political and psychological terms, however, a successful transposition and implementation of requirements in the area of environmental protection in EU 15 provided the guarantee that the market would not be affected by ecological dumping as a result of unmet environmental requirements.

In Slovenia, the significance of the area of the environment stemmed from the traditionally high awareness of the impact of changes on the environment and nature and from the long-standing tradition of nature protection. Four themes will be briefly outlined below: the state of the environment at the start of the negotiations, the main issues of the negotiating process, an overview of results of negotiations, and, finally, the challenges which were not covered by the negotiations, but were given special attention by the EU.

Start of the negotiations

Slovenia has a long-standing tradition in environmental protection. In 1973, a year after the international environmental conference in Stockholm, the Green Paper on the Environment was published. The publication of this paper is considered to be an important milestone in organized environmental protection. Slovenia is among the countries with the greatest tradition in setting up functioning institutions in the area of environmental protection among the CEECs. The *acquis* in the field of environmental protection was, however, more recent. The umbrella act on environmental protection was adopted as late as 1993. The process of negotiating and minimizing the differences in the area of environmental protection was instrumental in the adoption of the National Environmental Action Programme in 1999. The programme was comparable to similar EU programmes and covered all the tasks necessary for a successful adoption of the *acquis.*

When Slovenia started negotiations, it had no urgent environmental issues. Slovenia also has an exceptional biodiversity and is the third largest country in Europe in terms of the size of its closed forest areas. Slovenia introduced into the EU a multitude of plant and animal species from the Dinaric area, making them a new natural and geographic unit of the EU. However, it was not immune to the environmental issues.

One should mention a weakness in managing certain standard issues, such as water pollution and waste management. According to some estimates, approximately 80 per cent of all funds had to be earmarked for the implementation of the *acquis* in the field of environmental protection.

A specific problem of the negotiations was of a political/psychological nature. Slovenia was trying to enter the cradle of the industrial revolution, an effort that inevitably led to severe environmental degradation. The European industrial society had been rapidly developing for an entire century (1860–1960), without seriously considering the ecological consequences of its growth until as late as the 1960s, when environmental conditions became severe and required urgent measures. On the basis of the conclusions reached at the meeting of the heads of state and government in Paris in 1972, the European Commission submitted to the Council the programme for environmental protection measures adopted in 1973. Even though the EU made considerable progress in terms of its programmes and concrete action, public fear of environmental hazards relating to the entry into the EU was clearly manifest.

Main challenges in the negotiations

The process of negotiation and association carried four main challenges, which had to be managed:

- *Institutional challenge.* At the time of the negotiations, Slovenia already had in place certain institutions required from the point of view of the EU legislation. However, a comprehensive reorganization at all levels was inevitable in order to ensure functional compatibility with the EU. A lack of staff in certain areas was a specific problem, in particular in the area of inspection supervision. There was a lack of certain profiles of experts, which had not been necessary in the past for a number of reasons—there was a particularly severe lack of environmental economists and jurists.
- *Legislative challenge.* A comprehensive and detailed overview of the environmental legislation revealed a need for thorough modifications to regulations in the areas of water, preservation, nuclear safety, genetically modified organisms (GMOs), waste, and other. Throughout the negotiating process, the emphasis did not only fall on the importance of the

technical transposition of the regulations; it also concentrated with particular rigour on their implementation. There was a break with the past, when a gap between the normative requirements and practice was the rule rather than the exception.

- *The challenge of resolving environmental problems.* Slovenia defined its priorities on the basis of an autonomous analysis of issues and substantive classification of objectives. The comparison showed that, surprisingly, the negotiating process had not produced new goals. On the contrary, analyses showed a high degree of comparability between the goals expressed in the National Environmental Action Programme and those expressed in the *acquis*.
- *Financial challenge.* The cost of the adoption of the *acquis* in the area of environmental protection was estimated at €2.7 billion or 1.5 per cent of GDP,[2] of which the most important is in the area of water protection (approximately 43 per cent), waste management (approximately 41 per cent), air quality (approximately 9 per cent), nature protection (approximately 4 per cent), and other. Also significant were costs related to the reduction of emissions of greenhouse gases (Kyoto Protocol), which were not included in the estimate by the National Environmental Action Programme.

Transitional periods

Throughout the process of negotiations, Slovenia tried to find an optimal balance between the requests for transitional periods and internal efforts towards achieving a rapid implementation of the same level of environmental protection as that in the EU. The following transitional periods were agreed in the negotiations on this chapter.

- In the field of packaging and waste packaging, a transitional period of five years from the day of the envisaged entry into the EU (31 December 2002) for provisions applying to the prescribed percentage of material recycling and reuse.
- In the field of urban waste waters, in the part relating to the deadlines for the construction of the collection systems and sewage plants, a transitional period of ten years from the deadlines set in the directive (thus meeting the requirements of the directive by 2015).
- In the field of a comprehensive prevention and supervision of industrial waste (the field of the IPPC directive), in the part relating to the existing facilities, a transitional period until 30 September 2011—a four-year transitional period from the date of the implementation, 30 September 2007, applicable to the existing EU facilities. A transitional period of the duration of one to four years was approved for fifteen industrial facilities.

[2] See National Environmental Action Programme.

During the course of the negotiations, Slovenia also withdrew a number of requirements:

- In the field of the quality of liquid fuels, the requirement for a transitional period for the production of fuels with a high sulphur, lead, and benzene content in the existing refinery of Nafta Lendava until 31 December 2004, due to a modified national legislation (rules on the sales of fuels harmonized with the requirements of the *acquis*).
- In the field of waste management, the requirement for a transitional period in the part relating to the content of heavy metals in the packaging. In view of the fact that Slovenia imports the major part of packaging, a rigorous supervision of imports would suffice.
- Slovenian practice of balancing the population of the brown bear, lynx, and wolf has been estimated to be in compliance with the already implemented exemption from the *acquis.*

Challenges of EU membership

Negotiations for the entry into the EU were limited to the agreement on the method of transposition and implementation of the *acquis.* The issues directly linked to the negotiations, however, also opened a number of other issues relevant to environmental protection. In particular, it was important to understand and manage the negative and positive effects of membership on the environment. According to the estimates at the time of the negotiations, Slovenia's entry into the EU would provide a new impetus for the economy, increase the tourist and traffic currents, agriculture would approximate EU agriculture, and similar. These developments were expected to have both positive and negative effects on the environment. Nevertheless, adverse environmental effects are not an inextricable part of development. It was necessary to ask how to ensure appropriate responses to the challenges of development, while dealing with the requirements for the transposition of the *acquis* and the acute institutional deficit. In political terms, it was imperative to persuade the interested public and responsible political circles that the negative effects are not a reflection of Slovenia's entrance into the EU, but rather of its inability to identify the threat in time and respond to it. It was important to expand public awareness that any failure to face these issues might cause a loss of one of the most precious assets we were bringing to the family of the EU Member States—a relatively well-preserved nature, a high degree of biodiversity, the privilege that most of Slovenia's inhabitants can drink tap water, and so on.

Financial package

Similarly to previous EU enlargement negotiations, the negotiations about the financial package (i.e. about the amounts Slovenia would draw for agriculture, structural actions, and other common policies of the EU from the EU budget), and the amounts Slovenia would contribute to the EU budget were postponed until the very final phase of negotiations. The negotiations undertaken in the strict form of a package deal for all the ten candidate countries were limited for the period until the end of 2006, when the current medium-term financial perspective of the EU expires.

Objectives of this stage of the negotiations

Being by far the most developed of the all candidate countries—apart from Cyprus—Slovenia had an extremely unfavourable starting position for the negotiations on the financial package. Being aware of this problem, the country clearly defined the following two strategic objectives for this segment of the accession negotiations. First, the final agreement with the EU should allow Slovenia to continue the process of real convergence, that is, the process of further reducing Slovenia's development lag behind the EU average. Second, the agreement should not lead to the deterioration of Slovenia's public finance position and in no way cause any additional difficulties to achieving the fiscal part of the Maastricht criteria.

The results of the financial package negotiations in terms of meeting the development and public finance goals may be assessed from two points of view. First, in the short-term perspective, that is the period from the time when Slovenia became an EU Member State (in May 2004) to the end of the present financial perspective (the end of 2006). Second, in the long-term perspective, that is the period of the next seven-year financial perspective.

The course of negotiations

The negotiations on the financial package in fact began in January 2002 with the European Commission publishing the document 'Common Financial Framework 2004–2006 for Accession Negotiations', whereby it defined the basic framework for discussion about the financial aspects of agriculture, Structural Funds, and regional policy, and the contributions to the EU budget. As a result of its horizontal nature, the document was not favourable for Slovenia as it failed to sufficiently take into account the specific features of our country being the most developed of all candidate countries from Central and Eastern Europe.

The negotiations on the financial package proceeded through three phases:

- *Phase 1: from the issue of the above Commission's document in January 2002 to the Brussels European Council at the end of October 2002.* In this period, Slovenia's activities were oriented, first, to explaining our position on the basic approach to the financial part of negotiations, and, second, to the formation and well-justified presentation of Slovenian proposals to the Commission and Member States that would in an adequate manner respond to Slovenia's specific problems in the financial part of negotiations. At the Brussels European Council, the EU Member States adopted their official positions on the financial part of negotiations. The final outcome of this phase of the negotiations was favourable for Slovenia, as the amount of lump-sum payments that Slovenia was to receive from the EU budget in the period 2004–2006 was increased to a total of €33 million.[3]

- *Phase 2: from end October and end November 2002, i.e. in the period from the Brussels European Council to the first proposal of the Danish presidency of 26 November 2002.* This proposal contained some very positive and some less positive elements for Slovenia. Its most important positive characteristic was that those figures of the financial package that were increased (or introduced anew) were important from Slovenia's long-term development perspective which meant a good starting point for the negotiations about the next financial perspective. Among them, a considerably increased amount of funds for Slovenia from the EU budget in the area of agriculture should be mentioned (up by €191 million in the period 2004–6) as should be the funds from the new financial scheme called 'Schengen facility' (€107 million in the period 2004–6). In addition, a conclusion on the question of putting off the date of accession to the EU to 1 May 2004 also had a financially positive effect for Slovenia, as the foreseen amount of Slovenia's payments to the EU budget was reduced for that year by one-third, i.e. by €82 million. On the other hand, the first proposal of the Danish presidency was less favourable for Slovenia with respect to the attainment of short-term public finance goals in negotiations (i.e. the goals for the period 2004–6). The proposal assured that Slovenia would be in a positive net budgetary position—which was one of Slovenia's strategic goals in the financial part of negotiations. However, the increased amount of the foreseen receipts from the EU budget and a reduced amount of the foreseen payments to the EU budget did not result in an adequate improvement of its net budgetary position as was the case for other acceding countries that found themselves at a lower level of economic development. In turn, this meant that the amount of lump-sum payments which Slovenia was to receive in the period 2004–2006 was in fact reduced accordingly by €373 million.
- *Phase 3: the period from the first Danish presidency proposal to the European Council in Copenhagen.* As the long-term structural goals of the financial part of the negotiations were achieved in the previous phase, all the efforts in this last phase were focused on attaining the public finance goals in the period 2004–6. In concrete terms, this meant that the basic goal to be achieved in this phase was to improve the positive net budgetary position of Slovenia by increasing the amount of lump-sum payments, and in this manner to limit to the greatest possible extent the potential public finance risks related to Slovenia's accession to the European Union. Slovenia

[3] All the values in this statement are expressed in 1999 prices and are around 10% lower than the values expressed in current prices.

achieved the following results in this phase: first, more favourable assumptions on the basis on which Slovenia's payments to the EU budget are determined, leading to a net positive effect of €34 million in the period 2004–6. Second, the amount of lump-sum payments increased considerably. In the period before the Copenhagen Summit, they increased by €94 million for the whole period 2004–6, and during the summit by an additional €49 million. Third, the net budgetary position of Slovenia improved by €114 million for the period 2004–6. Altogether, Slovenia's net budgetary position thus improved from plus €135 million to plus €200 million in the run-up to Copenhagen, and to plus €249 million at the Copenhagen Summit.

Segment by segment analysis of results achieved

The following paragraphs provide a brief presentation of results of the negotiations in the areas of agriculture, funds for structural actions, Schengen border, lump-sum payments, and contributions of Slovenia to the EU budget:

- *Agriculture.* In this area, four strategic goals were set forth in the financial package negotiations: (i) full and equal participation in the Community policies; (ii) the economic position of Slovenian farmers should not deteriorate because of the EU accession; (iii) the levels of quotas and reference quantities that are subject to negotiations must not be lower than the present production levels in Slovenia; and (iv) the solutions should be adapted to the specific structural and development problems of Slovenian agriculture and should take into account the foreseen changes of the Common Agricultural Policy. These goals were fully met and the package of solutions was altogether favourable for Slovenia as presented in details in section 4.
- *Funds for structural actions.* In this area, Slovenia endeavoured to meet two major goals: (i) to increase the amount of funds the EU earmarked for Slovenia in the period 2004–6; and (ii) to reach an agreement according to which the less developed part of the Slovenian territory would maintain its status as an Objective 1 region (region with the widest possible access to EU Structural Funds) in the next financial perspective. Slovenia agreed in the negotiations to receive, in the period 2004–6 (this period is a kind of transitional period to full drawing of structural funds), a total of €404 million from EU structural instruments, of which €236 million from Structural Funds and €168 million from the Cohesion Fund. The final decision concerning regionalization of Slovenia for the needs of the cohesion policy (regionalization at NUTS 2 level) will be taken by the end of 2006. This in fact means that Slovenia gained an additional three to four years to reach an agreement on the number of regions at NUTS 2 level. In relation to the regulation on the EU criteria for regionalization—which was at that time passing through the last legislative phase—this agreement allows for a realistic chance that a large part of Slovenia's territory will continue to be

eligible for drawing funds from the EU Structural Funds in the period 2007–13. Those Slovenian regions that will preserve the status of Objective 1 region in the next financial perspective will at that time have full access to the Structural Funds assistance, which means, of course, a considerably greater amount of funds than in the period 2004–6.

- *Schengen border.* In addition to the possibility of topping up direct payments to farmers from the national budget and forming a special financial reserve for rural development, the solutions regarding the Schengen border were the third conceptual novelty introduced by Slovenia to the financial part of negotiations between the EU and the candidate countries. The EU accepted Slovenia's proposal to take over part of the costs of establishing and maintaining the Schengen border in the new Member States. Slovenia will thus, in the period 2004–6, receive a sum of €107 million for this purpose. This is 45 per cent of the total costs which Slovenia is estimated to incur under this project for this period.
- *Contributions to the EU budget and the net budgetary position of a country in relation to the EU budget.* In this area, Slovenia set forth the following goals in negotiations: (i) in the period 2004–6 to achieve a better positive net budgetary position than recorded in the year before the accession and (ii) in the period 2007–13 to ensure such a level of funds and structure of inflows from the EU budget that Slovenia will not be a net payer to the EU budget. The agreed solutions are in line with both goals. The Brussels European Council in October eliminated the dilemma on whether Slovenia could be a net payer to the EU budget in the 2004–6 period. This was due to the decision of the EU that no new member should find itself in a worse net budgetary position after accession that in the year before accession. Slovenia achieved this by an agreement whereby lump-sum payments amounting to €234 million were approved to it for the period 2004–6. By this move, Slovenia's net budgetary position improved from €45 million, foreseen for 2003, to around €80 million foreseen for each of the three years in the period 2004–6.

Final assessment of the financial package

The agreed financial package solutions, as presented in Table 20, can be assessed as balanced for Slovenia, both in the short and the long term. The agreements made in the area of agriculture, funds for co-financing the Schengen border, as well as the agreement on Slovenia's possibility for regionalization at NUTS 2 level are all the elements of the financial package which clearly indicate its long-term orientation. These elements will not only have important effects on Slovenia's development but will provide a solid basis for our country to remain a net recipient of the funds from the EU budget in the period of the next financial perspective, i.e. from 2007 to 2013. Undoubtedly, this would be an adequate solution for Slovenia, given its level of development in comparison with other Member States of the enlarged EU, and would, additionally, contribute to long-term public finance stability of our country.

Table 20. Financial package for Slovenia, 2004–2006 (€m.)

	2004	2005	2006	Total
A. Calculated inflows from EU budget into Slovenian budget	224	285	324	833
Pre-accession aid	51	43	27	121
Agriculture	43	124	157	324
Structural actions	27	59	73	159
'Schengen facility' and other	38	38	38	114
internal actions	12	21	28	61
Cashflow lump-sum compensations	52	—	—	52
B. Calculated outflow from Slovenian budget into EU budget	−187	−288	−296	−771
Traditional own resources	−18	−29	−29	−76
VAT resource	−22	−35	−36	−93
GNP resource	−129	−198	−203	−530
UK rebate	−17	−27	−28	−72
C. Calculated net balance before budgetary lump-sum compensation	37	−3	28	62
D. Budgetary compensation	43	85	54	182
E. Calculated net balance after budgetary lump-sum compensation	80	82	82	244
F. Calculated net balance after budgetary lump-sum compensation (% of GDP)	0.4	0.4	0.4	

Note: Calculated pre-accession aid 2003: €45 million.
Source: EU Commission, 17 December 2002.

6. CONCLUSIONS

EU accession as a tool for speeding up the process of transition

The transition to a well-performing market economy has been carried out in Slovenia simultaneously with two other processes, both of which had significant influence not only on the design of reforms and their implementation but also on their sequencing. In the period following independence (first half of the 1990s), a significant proportion of Slovenian efforts were devoted to reforms and policy measures with one common denominator—to establish Slovenia as an independent state in the areas of politics, economy, and finance. In the period from the mid-1990s on, the process of structural reforms coincided with the country's accession to the EU. The process of accession has, in fact, proved to be an extremely useful tool for speeding up the transition process. Clearly determined commitments, accompanied with a precise timetable of the course of the EU accession negotiations, mobilized the policy-makers and the public at large to implement the necessary tasks effectively. A large majority of these tasks would have to have be done irrespective of the country's accession to the EU.

However, without a clear and near perspective of EU membership, the risk of implementation of these tasks would increase substantially. For Central and Eastern European Countries (CEECs), including Slovenia, the EU accession process was a de facto insurance policy for effective completion of the overall transition process in most areas of their political, economic, and social life.

Adjustment to the EU 'rules of the game' was the groundwork of the EU accession process

The EU accession is in fact a matter of adjustment. It was clear from the very beginning that the initiative to join the EU came from the candidate countries and not from the EU. Therefore, a large part of the process called 'negotiations' should more appropriately be called 'adjustment' of the candidate countries to the *acquis*. This is logical, if one takes into account the fact that the candidate country joins the club with the established rules of the game resulting from the compromises achieved in the past among the existing members of the club. The subject of negotiations is essentially little more than the exemptions from the rules of the game in the form of transitional periods or, exceptionally, in the form of derogations. As for the real negotiations, experience shows that only a small proportion of them in fact take place between the EU Member States and the candidate country. They are largely conducted *within* a candidate country, in particular when preparing the negotiating positions for the submission to the EU.

The multidimensional character of the EU accession process

The EU accession process is multidimensional in its character. It involves at least two dimensions, a political one and a technical one. The political dimension of the negotiations can be clearly seen from the following: a majority of the countries from the 'Helsinki group' of the candidate countries, which only started negotiations two years after the 'Luxembourg group' on the grounds of their relative unreadiness, finished negotiations at the same time as the first group, in December 2002. It is simply not tenable to argue that less prepared countries required less time to successfully complete the negotiations than the countries from the better-prepared group. The process also has a clear technical dimension, as it requires a lot of expertise on the side of the candidate country both in the preparation of the negotiating positions and for the effective presentation and argumentation of these positions in negotiations with the EU Member States.

Another indication of the fact that EU accession process has a strong political aspect is the issue of sponsorship. In contrast to some other candidate countries, Slovenia never had a Member State—which is usually a neighbouring country (countries)—that would play the role of 'sponsor' in its EU accession negotiations. Slovenia had, indeed, good and working relations with all the Member States, but none of them can be considered to have played a role similar to that that, for example, the Nordic Member States played for the Baltic candidate countries. Being a non-problematic accession country, in fact, sometimes proved to be a problem for Slovenia: without a sponsor (or sponsors) it is much more difficult for a candidate country to forcefully present its case to the Member States.

Problems associated with the 'convoy' type of the negotiations

Another key feature of the last EU accession negotiations was the simultaneous carrying out of the negotiations of the Member States with a large number—twelve—of candidate countries. This hindered any faster negotiating process, as it put an enormous logistical pressure on both the Commission and the Member States. It should not be forgotten that negotiations with a candidate country mean also negotiations *among* the Member States. Although individual treatment of each of the candidate countries was proclaimed as an important principle of negotiations, it has not always been respected in practice. The larger the number of candidate countries, the smaller the flexibility in addressing specific concerns of individual countries. This horizontal treatment could be particularly harmful for small applicant countries. In the case of Slovenia, the negative consequences of the horizontal approach—where the country's specific concerns have not been addressed appropriately in spite of clear arguments—were clearly reflected in two areas of the negotiations. One was the free movement of persons, where statistical data clearly confirmed that there was no economic justification for the transitional period for free movement of people requested by the EU Member States. The second case was the negotiations on the volume of funds for structural actions to be received by Slovenia in the 2004–6 period. By applying the same methodology for all the ten candidate countries, Slovenia was, due to its relatively high level of development, among the candidate countries which were treated less favourably than other countries of this group.

Factors that are typically mentioned as crucial for successful EU accession negotiations of Slovenia

The main factor was a *strong political consensus* in the country on the EU subject. Ever since gaining its independence (and even before that), membership of the EU was considered to be the key national priority not only by practically all political parties but by the population at large. With the exception of one rather small parliamentary party, all the parties—both government and opposition—included early accession to the EU in their programmes. Strong political consensus on EU-related issues was constantly reflected in the day-to-day activities of the Parliament. In its working bodies, which had a clearly defined role in the negotiating process, the negotiating positions prepared by the government had in most cases been consensually accepted. Political consensus and support allowed the process of negotiations to proceed efficiently and in a quite undisturbed manner.

Strong involvement of the Parliament in the EU accession process combined with a *creative public awareness campaign* were also instrumental in ensuring that the population in Slovenia would be quite well informed on the key points of the negotiations. This conclusion is empirically supported by the results of the Eurobarometer surveys, whereby Slovenia was persistently the only candidate country where the proportion of the population claiming to be well informed or informed about the EU accession process was larger than the proportion of the population claiming to be badly informed or not informed at all about this process. Timely provision of information and its 'user-friendly' form were essential for high and stable public support for the EU cause also in more 'rough periods' of the negotiations.

Another important factor of success for Slovenia was its favourable starting position, reflected largely in its rather high level of economic development compared to other candidate countries, as well as its small size, which allowed it adequate flexibility. Effective internal coordination of the EU accession process performed by the Government Office for European Affairs and continuity in the negotiating team have proved to be important factors assuring the success of the negotiating process. Slovenia is one of a very few candidate countries where—in spite of the changes of government—the negotiation team remained unchanged throughout the five-year period of the negotiations.

Last, but not least, being aware of its small size and of the lack of support from 'sponsors', Slovenia always tried to work correctly, depending on expertise as much as possible. By using this approach, it tried to pursue its national interests but also to take due account of the interests of other Member States and the EU as whole. In this manner it was also establishing its image as a future EU Member State.

Index to The Accession Story